Leaders and Their Followers in a Dangerous World

OTHER BOOKS BY JERROLD M. POST

When Illness Strikes the Leader: The Dilemma of the Captive King
(coauthored with Robert S. Robins)

Political Paranoia: The Psychopolitics of Hatred
(coauthored with Robert S. Robins)

Know Thy Enemy: Profiles of Adversary Leaders and Their Strategic Cultures
(co-edited with Barry R. Schneider)

The Psychological Assessment of Political Leaders: With Profiles of Saddam Hussein and Bill Clinton (editor)

Leaders and Their Followers in a Dangerous World

THE PSYCHOLOGY OF POLITICAL BEHAVIOR

Jerrold M. Post

With a Foreword by ALEXANDER L. GEORGE

Cornell University Press

ITHACA AND LONDON

A book in the series Psychoanalysis and Social Theory,
edited by C. Fred Alford and James M. Glass.

First published 2004 by Cornell University Press

Printed in the United States of America

Library of Congress Cataloging-in-Publication Data
Post, Jerrold M.
    Leaders and their followers in a dangerous world : the psychology of
political behavior / Jerrold M. Post ; with a foreword by Alexander
George.— 1st ed.
        p. ; cm. — (Psychoanalysis and social theory)
Includes bibliographical references and index.
    ISBN-13: 978-0-8014-4169-1 (cloth : alk. paper)
    ISBN-10: 0-8014-4169-2 (cloth : alk. paper)
    1. Political leadership—Psychological aspects.   2.
Politicians—Psychology.   3. Heads of state—Psychology—Case studies.
I. George, Alexander. II. Title. III. Series.
JC330.3.P68 2004
320'.01'9—dc22   2003021237

Cloth printing   10   9   8   7

To Carolyn, the lodestar in my constellation,
without whom I could not navigate

Contents

Foreword

Policy specialists and academic scholars have long agreed that for U.S. leaders to deal effectively with other actors in the international arena, they need images of their adversaries. Leaders must try to see events, and, indeed, their own behavior, from the perspective of opponents. Only by doing so can they accurately diagnose a developing situation and select appropriate ways of influencing the adversary. Faulty images are a source of misperceptions and miscalculations that have often led to major errors in policy, avoidable catastrophes, and missed opportunities. History supplies all too many examples.

Prior to Germany's attack on the Soviet Union in 1941, Stalin had ample high-quality intelligence on Hitler's military dispositions. But the Soviet leader did not believe that Hitler would launch a surprise attack, for Stalin's image of Hitler encouraged him to expect demands and hard bargaining. Stalin misperceived the purpose of the German military buildup on the Soviet border and the frequent overflights of Soviet territory, believing it was all intended to set the stage for serious negotiations and coercive diplomacy.

An incorrect image of the adversary also played an important role in autumn 1950 in the Truman administration's mishandling of China's threat to intervene in the Korean War should U.S. forces cross into North Korea and attempt to eliminate the Communist regime. Washington believed that because the United States did not harbor aggressive intentions against mainland China, Chinese leaders should see that their perception of menace was unjustified. Instead of resorting to deterrence or entering into negotiations, the Truman administration chose to offer reassurances of its nonhostility, invoking the historical friendship between the Chinese and American peoples.

In the Cuban Missile Crisis the image of the opponent played an important role both in the onset of the crisis and in its resolution. On one hand, Khrushchev's defective image of Kennedy—whom he viewed as a young, inexperienced, weak leader, one who could be pushed around and, at the same time, a rational person who would not risk war to get the Soviet missiles out of Cuba—is widely believed to have played a role in Khrushchev's underestimation of the risks of his missile deployment. On the other hand, Kennedy's *correct* image of the Soviet leader—as one who was capable of realizing his mistakes and withdrawing the missiles if made to do so—played a role in the president's choice of strategy: coercive persuasion rather than a resort to military force. Critical in Kennedy's choice was the question whether Khrushchev was capable of a diplomatic retreat. Had the deployment of missiles into Cuba proceeded so far, were Soviet leaders already so committed to the daring venture that there could be no turning back? Knowledge of an important aspect of the Soviet political style, derived from studies of past Soviet behavior and political doctrine, suggested an answer. Readiness to retreat in order to extricate oneself from overwhelming danger was a cardinal maxim of Bolshevik doctrine. A good Bolshevik had to recognize when the time came for retreat and not let false considerations of pride or emotion get in the way. At numerous other points during the missile crisis, knowledge of the opponent that Llewellyn Thompson (the State Department specialist on the Soviet Union and member of Kennedy's advisory group) provided was of considerable help in interpreting Soviet actions and in gauging how Khrushchev was likely to react to possible U.S. moves.

There are many strategies for influencing other actors in the international arena: deterrence, coercive diplomacy, reassurance, conciliation, conditional reciprocity, and so on. Each strategy is much more likely to be effective and all diplomacy is better served if informed by a sound model of the adversary's behavioral style and patterns of action. A correct image of other leaders requires understanding of their personal and political development and early life experiences that shaped their self-image, values, and motivations. Special attention is needed to grasp the effects of mentors and role models. Personality analysis must be integrated with how a leader and leadership group have been shaped by historical events and memories and specific cultural influences in their political socialization.

We need to replace the common assumption that an adversary is both a rational and a unitary actor. Both components of this familiar assumption seriously oversimplify the task of understanding and influencing adversaries. Consider first the assumption that an opponent is rational. Not all actors in international politics calculate utility in the same way. Differences in political culture, attitudes toward risk taking, and so on vary greatly. There is no substitute for knowledge of an individual adversary's values, ideologies, culture, mind-set, and behavioral style. Attributing irrationality to an opponent when he or she acts at odds with one's expectation can lead to serious error as well as danger. Consider as well the limitation of assuming that the adversary is a unitary actor, that is, a single homogeneous entity—that there are no significant differences among the members of the ruling elite to influence the state's behavior. The unitary assumption also incorrectly implies that the top leader has effective control over all associates and subordinate officials.

Faulty assumptions that the adversary is a rational, unitary actor often occur in interstate conflict. Such assumptions are particularly damaging when one is dealing with *nonstate actors*, such as local warlords, terrorists, or rivals in intrastate conflicts and civil wars. It is critical, as Jerrold Post demonstrates in several chapters in this book, to distinguish different types of terrorists. Several general characteristics of nonstate actors and their implications for counterterrorist policy have been identified:

- Nonstate actors may lack identifiable or valuable assets that can be targeted in efforts to deter or coerce them.
- The mindsets, goals, motivations and behavioral patterns of nonstate actors may be very difficult to ascertain; as a result, efforts to formulate coercive strategies directed toward them are likely to lack understanding of how nonstate actors make cost-benefit calculations. When reliable information on terrorist motivations is lacking, the coercing power may develop simplified stereotypes that emphasize fanaticism and irrationality, particularly when their acts of terrorism are highly destructive.
- Nonstate actors generally lack well-developed decision-making structures, well-defined and reliable lines of authority, and command and control. In some cases, there may be competing power centers within the nonstate apparatus. As a result, leaders may have imperfect control over operational units, and, therefore, efforts to employ coercion against nonstate leaders may not lead to desired changes in the behavior of their subordinates.
- Coercive efforts against a multiheaded adversary in which subactors have divergent interests may have the unexpected result of strengthening the most radical elements. Coercion may lack credibility and efficacy insofar as the terrorists do not regard force as punishment but believe it enhances their legitimacy.
- Nonstate actors and terrorists often have stronger motivation than does the coercing state. Asymmetrical motivation may also favor some state supporters of terrorism, although they may have other interests that limit such support and make them more susceptible to

pressure to terminate or significantly limit their support for terrorists. To be sure, nonstate actors may be largely autonomous, with ambiguous or complicated relations with states that provide support. This possibility can be taken into account in devising coercive strategies. But it may be difficult to tailor such efforts where there is considerable uncertainty as to relations between sponsors and terrorists.

- Efforts to coerce a nonstate indirectly, by persuading states friendly to the nonstate actor to exert pressure, may work sometimes, but such efforts of indirect coercion are often difficult and may be counterproductive.
- Nonstate actors and terrorists are often adept at finding ways of exploiting constraints under which coercing states must labor. They can manipulate international opinion, exploit domestic constraints in coercing states, use "human shields" to deter actions against them, and counter efforts to coerce them by engaging in unpredictable ways such as detaining peacekeeping or humanitarian actors.

Faulty assumptions about opponents are not easily replaced by sophisticated actor-specific behavioral models. Even imperfect models can be useful, however, if only to make policymakers aware of relevant uncertainties about opponents and the need for care in trying to influence them.

These observations about the critical need for actor-specific behavioral models highlight the important, indeed unique, contributions Jerrold Post has made over the years in developing precisely such profiles of various adversaries and friendly leaders. Thirty years ago, he founded and directed the Center for the Analysis of Personality and Political Behavior for the CIA. Post played the lead role in developing profiles of Menachem Begin and Anwar Sadat for President Jimmy Carter's use at the Camp David talks. At the Center, Post pioneered in developing theory and methods for analyzing the political personality profiles of leaders. For his role in founding and leading the Center for the Analysis of Personality and Political Behavior, he was awarded the Intelligence Medal of Merit in 1979. He moved to George Washington University in 1987, where he is now professor of psychiatry, political psychology and international affairs and director of the political psychology program. He has continued to make significant contributions to theory and practice.

In his work, Post draws on a variety of relevant psychological and personality theories to develop incisive analyses. He utilizes all types of available data and supplements them with interviews with persons who have interacted with a particular leader and, on occasion, with individual terrorists who have been apprehended. He employs a broad and inclusive methodology that takes full account of relevant historical events, a particular leader's personal and political development, the impact of cultural forces, the role of mentors and role models, the development of a leader's self-image, his or her ways of compensating for damaged self-esteem, the sense of mission and dreams of glory that motivate some leaders and shape their ambitions and goals, and the situational constraints and opportunities that influence their behavior.

Post has made a pioneering contribution to the development of actor-specific behavioral models. Drawing together his publications over many years, this book is an exemplary, landmark work. His book should convince even the skeptics of the utility of diagnoses of leaders with whom U.S. policymakers have had to deal and with whom they will be forced to deal in the foreseeable future.

ALEXANDER L. GEORGE

Preface

A funny thing happened on the way to my career in academic psychiatry. In my final year as a clinical associate at the National Institute of Mental Health, planning to return to Boston where I had been offered an appointment in the Department of Psychiatry at Harvard Medical School, I received a cryptic phone call from a medical school acquaintance who wanted to discuss "a most unusual job opportunity." I was intrigued, and we met over lunch.

To my astonishment, I was offered an opportunity to start a pilot program for the United States government developing indirect assessments of the personality and political behavior of foreign leaders. The unit would be based at the Central Intelligence Agency but would serve as an analytic unit of common concern, providing in-depth personality studies of world leaders to assist the president, secretary of state, secretary of defense, and other senior government officials in conducting summit meetings and other high-level negotiations, as well as in dealing with crises. I thought that would be an interesting divertissement for several years, and then I would return to the groves of academe.

The planned two-year diversion ended up lasting twenty-one years, from 1965 to 1986, in what became a remarkable intellectual odyssey. It quickly became apparent that the field of psychodynamic psychiatry would be insufficient to the task at hand. Accurately locating the political actor in his historical, cultural, and political context would require substantial expertise to complement that of the psychiatrists in the unit. Accordingly, I proposed and received support to develop an interdisciplinary unit, the Center for the Analysis of Personality and Political Behavior, with specialists at the doctoral level in cultural anthropology, with a focus on culture and personality; political sociology; political science, with a focus on leadership; clinical psychology; social psychology;

and history, complemented by area studies experts. Typically, in approaching a major study of a world leader of concern, we used a team approach—for example, a psychiatrist working with an anthropologist or a clinical psychologist teamed with a political sociologist.

The studies were of great interest to senior policy makers. An event of singular importance to the program's acceptance at the highest levels was the preparation of the Camp David profiles of Prime Minister Menachem Begin of Israel and President Anwar al-Sadat of Egypt, developed for President Carter at his request in 1978. He later said these studies were of the highest importance in guiding his negotiating strategy and tactics at the Camp David talks; after meeting the participants, Carter said he "wouldn't change a word" of the profiles we had prepared. (A detailed description of the role of the Camp David profiles is found in the appendix.)

When an epidemic of international terrorism, ushered in by the seizure of Israeli athletes by Palestinian terrorists at the Munich Olympics in 1972, increasingly threatened U.S. interests, we were asked to apply similar indirect behavioral assessment techniques to the mind of the terrorist. We initiated the government's research program on the psychology of political terrorism.

When I left the government, I joined the faculty of George Washington University, where I was appointed professor of psychiatry, political psychology, and international affairs and was asked to develop an applied political psychology program. The program trains graduate students in international affairs in the psychology of leadership and decision making and the psychology of political violence and terrorism and conducts research in these areas.

In the first chapter I discuss the events of September 11, 2001, an event that in many ways encapsulates the powerful effects of psychological forces on politics. This chapter profiles Osama bin Laden and also considers the social-psychological climate associated with individuals willing to kill in the name of God. The book then addresses when personality affects political behavior in two senses of the word *when*: In what political circumstances does personality matter? In the life course of political leaders, when is personal psychology particularly apt to be determinative? A chapter about the psychopolitics of physical and mental illness in high office is followed by a chapter on terminal leadership, which addresses the impact of mortal illness on the conduct of leadership. One circumstance that regularly brings leader personality into play is crisis decision making, the subject of the next chapter.

The preoccupying issue of today is assuredly the epidemic of terrorism, and in chapter 6 I consider the psychology of terrorism, or, more accurately, the psychologies of terrorisms. The psychological themes addressed in this chapter are closely related to the psychology of ethnic-nationalist hatred, which dramatically increased in Eastern Europe with the disintegration of the Soviet empire. The need for enemies and the psychopolitics of hatred set the stage for the hate-mongering leadership of two Serbian leaders, Dr. Radovan Karadzic and Slobodan Milosevic, who exploited political instability to consolidate their political leadership, with the dreadful consequence of ethnic cleansing. One of the most dramatic examples of the powerful psychology between leaders and followers is then addressed—the charismatic leader–follower relationship. I consider an aging charismatic leader, Fidel Castro, in an aging revolution. I follow with an updated political personality profile of Saddam Hussein, originally presented in testimony to hearings conducted during the Gulf crisis of 1990 by the House Armed Services Committee and the House Foreign Affairs Committee, and a political personality profile of his fellow resident of the "axis of evil," Kim Jong Il of North Korea. The profiles are presented in the context in which they were developed, and then a brief postscript is added to recount subsequent developments.

J. M. P.

Bethesda, Maryland

1

9/11

The Explosive Force of Personality
and Political Behavior

On September 11, 2001, the world as we know it changed. It was a seismic shift. The coordinated attacks by al Qaeda suicidal hijackers on targets in New York City and Washington, D.C., were designed to strike at the core symbols of American power—the World Trade Center, the symbol of American economic might; and the Pentagon, the symbol of American military might. Had the fourth plane succeeded in attacking the White House or the U.S. Capitol, symbols of American political might, the effects on the national psyche would have been even more devastating. As it was, the successful attack by radical Islamic terrorists forever shattered American feelings of invulnerability and insular complacency that "it can't happen here." A week after the attacks, in a speech to Congress, President Bush gave voice to a question that has perplexed many American citizens, "Why do they hate us?"

How could this small group of terrorists bring the most powerful nation on earth, the sole remaining superpower, to its knees? How could it be that there was so much hatred targeted at the United States that these "true believers" were willing to sacrifice their lives as they took thousands of casualties, "killing in the name of God?" What kind of a man was Osama bin Laden that he could so inflame and inspire his followers? How can we understand the powerful wave of patriotism, exemplified by a profusion of American flags, that so united the American public? How would our leadership react to this unprecedented attack on our own soil?

These questions reflect central concerns of the discipline of political psychology, which deals with such issues as: What causes leaders to lead and followers to follow? What is the powerful tie between leader and follower? What are the perceptions and misperceptions that lead to international conflict? What are the psychological foundations of man's inhumanity to man associated with ethnic cleansing and genocidal conflict?

Without understanding the psychological foundations of leader personality and political behavior, these questions cannot be understood. Answering these and associated questions is the central concern of this volume.

Because the events of 9/11 so well illustrate the powerful psychological forces that underlie human conflict and violence, in the balance of this chapter I review the event from the perspective of political psychology. With tragic timeliness, I had a number of unusual opportunities that permitted me to contribute a measure of understanding to the U.S. government and to public/media audiences in the wake of this most spectacular terrorist event of all time. During the spring and summer of 2001, I served as an expert witness in the trial of the al Qaeda terrorists responsible for the bombing of the U.S. embassies in Kenya and Tanzania in 1998, during which I interviewed two al Qaeda terrorists, one for sixteen hours; with foundation support, I have been leading an effort for the past several years interviewing thirty-five Middle Eastern terrorists incarcerated in Israeli and Palestinian prisons, the last transcripts of which were received just a week before 9/11; and, as an inveterate profiler, for the past three years I had been developing profiling material on Osama bin Laden. In this review, emphasizing personality and political behavior, I will emphasize the social psychology of suicidal terrorism, contrasting the Israeli suicide bombers with the suicidal hijackers of 9/11, characterizing the latter as "true believers," who have subordinated their individuality to the destructive charismatic leadership of Osama bin Laden, and then provide a brief profile of bin Laden.

Killing in the Name of God: Osama Bin Laden and Radical Islam

What manner of men are these, living in American society, for years in some cases, aiming to kill thousands while dying in the process? Surely, one would think, they must be crazed psychotics; no normal person could do such a thing. But in fact, the al Qaeda terrorists were psychologically "normal." By no means were they psychologically disturbed. Indeed, terrorist groups expel emotionally disturbed individuals—they represent a security risk.

In many ways, these new terrorists shatter the profile of the suicidal terrorists of Hamas, Islamic Jihad, and Hezbollah developed in Israel. Seventeen to twenty-two years in age, uneducated, unemployed, unmarried, the Israeli suicide bombers were dispirited unformed youth, looking forward to a bleak future when they were recruited, sometimes only hours before the bombing. The group members psychologically manipulated the new recruits, persuading them, "brainwashing" them to believe that, by carrying out a suicide bombing, their lives would be meaningful and they would find an honored place in the corridor of martyrs; moreover, their parents would win status and would be financially rewarded. From the time they were recruited, the group members never left their sides, leaving them no opportunity to back down from their fatal choice.

The values communicated to the recruits by the commanders are revealed in the answers to questions posed in a series of interviews of thirty-five incarcerated Middle Eastern terrorists, who agreed to be interviewed in Israeli and Palestinian prisons. Twenty of the terrorists belonged to radical Islamic terrorist groups—Hamas, Hezbollah, and Islamic Jihad. The psychologically oriented interviews attempted to understand their life history, socialization, and recruitment. They were asked to explain their attitudes toward suicide, which the Koran proscribes, and whether they had any moral redlines in terms of numbers of casualties and extent of destruction. Their answers are revealing.

One terrorist took umbrage at the term "suicide." "This is not suicide. Suicide is weak, selfish, and reflects mental weakness. This is *istishad*" (martyrdom or self-sacrifice in the service of Allah.)

One of the commanders interviewed was Hassan Salame, commander of the suicide bombers who carried out the wave of bombings in 1996 that precipitated the defeat of Prime Minister Shimon Peres and the election of Prime Minister Benjamin Netanyahu. Forty-six Israelis died in the bombings. Salame was sentenced to forty-six consecutive life sentences. Concerning suicidal terrorism, he said: "A suicide bombing is the highest level of jihad, and highlights the depth of our faith. The bombers are holy fighters who carry out one of the more important articles of faith." Another commander asserted: "It is suicide attacks which earn the most respect and elevate the bombers to the highest possible level of martyrdom."

Asked how they could justify murdering innocent victims, another interview subject bridled: "I am not a murderer. A murderer is someone with a psychological problem; armed actions have a goal. Even if civilians are killed, it not because we like it or are bloodthirsty. It is a fact of life in a people's struggle—the group doesn't do it because it wants to kill civilians but because the jihad must go on."

Asked whether there were any moral redlines, another leader responded: "The more an attack hurts the enemy, the more important it is. That is the measure. The mass killings, especially the suicide bombings, were the biggest threat to the Israeli public, and so most effort was devoted to these. The extent of the damage and the number of casualties are of primary importance. In a jihad, there are no redlines."

The attitudes reflected in these statements characterize radical Islamic terrorists in general. But there is a striking contrast between the Israel suicide bombers and the nineteen terrorists who carried out the attacks of September 11, an unprecedented act of mass casualty terrorism. They had lived in Western society, in some cases for many years, and were exposed to its freedom and opportunities. Many were older, in their mid-thirties or late twenties. Several had received higher education. The ringleader, Mohammed Atta, for example, had received a master's degree from the technological university in Hamburg, where he lived and studied with two of the other terrorists. Several came from financially comfortable middle-class families in Saudi Arabia and Egypt. They blended in with society, eschewing the dress, customs, and personal grooming of traditional Muslims. And yet, on the appointed day, like the Manchurian candidate, they carried out their mission to hijack four airliners and give their lives while killing 3,173 people.

During my service as an expert witness in the trial of the al Qaeda terrorists convicted for the bombings of the U.S. embassies in Kenya and Tanzania, I obtained a copy of a Department of Justice exhibit, the al Qaeda terrorism manual, "Declaration of Jihad." It is a remarkable document that goes a long way toward explaining how the 9/11 terrorists were able to maintain their cover in the United States, "the land of the enemies." In lesson eight, "Measures that Should Be Taken by the Undercover Member," members are instructed to

1. Have a general appearance that does not indicate Islamic orientation (beard, toothpick, book, [long] shirt, small Koran).
2. Be careful not to mention the brother's common expressions or show their behaviors (special praying appearance, "may Allah reward you," "peace be on you," while arriving and departing, etc.).
3. Avoid visiting famous Islamic places (mosques, libraries, Islamic fairs, etc.).

The explanation offered to "An Important Question: How can a Muslim spy live among enemies if he maintains his Islamic characteristics? How can he perform his duties to Allah and not want to appear Muslim?" is compelling.

Concerning the issue of clothing and appearance (of true religion), Ibn Taimia—may Allah have mercy on him—said, "If a Muslim is in a combat or godless area, he is not obligated to have a different appearance from (those around him). The (Muslim) man may prefer or even be obligated to look like them, provided his actions bring a religious benefit. . . . Resembling the polytheist in religious appearance is a kind of 'necessity permits the forbidden' even though they (forbidden acts) are basically prohibited." (parenthetical comments added in Dept. of Justice translation)

Citing verses from the Koran, the instruction in effect says that Allah will forgive you for not living the prescribed life of a good Muslim, for it is in the service of Allah, it is in the service of jihad.

As I have come to understand them, these terrorists differ strikingly from the suicide bombers in Israel. Fully formed adults, they have internalized their values; they are true believers who have subordinated their individuality to the group. They have uncritically accepted the direction of the destructive charismatic leader of the organization, Osama bin Laden, and what he declares is moral is, for them, moral; indeed, it is a sacred obligation.

What matter of man can inspire such acts? How could the son of a multibillionaire construction magnate in Saudi Arabia become the world's number-one terrorist, the founder and leader of this powerful radical Islamic terrorist organization, al Qaeda?

Osama bin Laden was born in Jeddah, Saudi Arabia, in 1957, the seventeenth of twenty to twenty-five sons of Mohammed bin Laden, who had fifty-two to fifty-four children altogether. Originally an immigrant from Yemen, Mohammed bin Laden, by befriending the royal family, had established a major construction company and had amassed a fortune of some two to three billion dollars by the time of his death in 1967 in a plane crash. Although estimates range from $18 million to as high as $200 million, it is most commonly agreed that Osama bin Laden inherited approximately $57 million at age sixteen from his father's estate.

Osama's mother, Hamida, a Syrian woman of Palestinian descent, was the least favorite of Mohammed's ten wives, and Osama was the only child of this marriage. This may have been the basis for Osama bin Laden's later estrangement from his family. Hamida was reportedly a beautiful woman with a free and independent spirit who, as a result, often found herself in conflict with her husband. Reportedly, by the time Osama was born, Hamida had been ostracized by the family and had been nicknamed "Al Abeda" (the slave). As her only child, Osama was referred to as "Ibn Al Abeda" (son of the slave). Hamida did not live in the compound with her son and the larger bin Laden family and was virtually nonexistent in her son's early life. When Mohammed bin Laden died, Osama, at the age of ten, for all intents and purposes, did not know his mother.

Osama bin Laden attended King Abdul Aziz University in Jeddah. He is a certified civil engineer and was taking courses in business management, preparing him to play a leadership role in the family's far-flung business interests. These two skill areas would later serve him in good stead in Afghanistan.

An important influence on bin Laden's political ideology was Abdullah Azzam, a radical Palestinian professor at the university who became an important intellectual mentor. It was Azzam, a noted Islamist, who provided the vision to bin Laden of what should be done in response to the invasion of Afghanistan by the Soviet Union, and what role bin Laden could play. In particular, he conveyed to bin Laden the importance of bringing together Muslims from around the world to defend the Islamic nation of Afghanistan against the godless Soviet Union. Demonstrating his already blossoming management skills, Osama bin Laden assisted Azzam, who founded the international recruitment network Maktab al-Khidamat (MAK—Services Office). MAK advertised all over the Arab world for young Muslims to fight the Afghanistan jihad. This massive international recruitment effort brought in Muslims from around the world who were to become known as the "Afghan Arabs," the nucleus of bin Laden's loyal followers—five thousand were recruited from Saudi Arabia, three thousand from Algeria, and two thousand from Egypt. Recruitment booths were set up in the United States and Europe.

A leader is not formed until he encounters his followers, and bin Laden's leadership experience during the struggle in Afghanistan against the Soviet invasion was crucial in his psychological development and his transformation into a leader. He came to Afghanistan unformed and naïve. Generously using his own funds, he built clinics and hospitals. Eschewing an opulent lifestyle, he lived an ascetic life in the caves of Afghanistan with his followers. Regularly preaching about their holy mission, bin Laden inspired his followers, who came to adulate him. That they were able—with substantial American aid, to be sure—to triumph over the Soviet Union, in what was to become their Vietnam, surely confirmed the correctness of bin Laden's vision for himself and his followers. Allah favored the weak and the underdog, and surely they could not have triumphed over the Soviet superpower unless God was on their side. This was the template of the destructive charismatic relationship between bin Laden and his religiously inspired warriors, the mujahideen.

Bin Laden had not yet broken with the Saudi government, which, after all, was the main foundation for his family's wealth. But he had vanquished one of the three major enemies identified in *The Neglected Duty* by Muhammad Abdel Salam Faraj (an Egyptian political activist who was later executed for taking part in the assassination of Egyptian President Anwar al-Sadat). The three enemies were the existing Arab states, the Western-Zionist nexus, and the Communists. Throughout the 1960s and 1970s, the critical enemy among this triad was the "enemy who was near," that is, the Arab states, according to leading Islamic fundamentalists. In

Faraj's manifesto, he argued, "We must begin with our Islamic country by establishing the rule of God in our nation . . . the first battle for jihad is the uprooting of these infidel leaders and replacing them with an Islamic system from which we can build."

Bin Laden had come to see the Soviet superpower as a "paper tiger" that could be defeated, but he also had already set his sights on the remaining superpower, the United States, as the next target. This represented a fundamental departure from the strategy of Faraj, replacing "the enemy that is near" with "the enemy that is afar," the superpowers.

With the victory in Afghanistan, bin Laden, the warrior-king, and his loyal Afghan Arab fighters were eager to continue to pursue the jihad. Bin Laden broadened his vision and determined to pursue the jihad on a worldwide basis, seeking to reconstruct the nation of Islam throughout the world, assisting Muslims who were under attack, in Algeria, Bosnia, Chechnya, Eritrea, Somalia, Sudan, and so forth.

Although bin Laden was committed to the international struggle, Abdullah Azzam believed in focusing all efforts on building Afghanistan into a model Islamic state. Following a split with Abdullah Azzam in 1988, with the nucleus of his loyal followers, bin Laden and Ayman al-Zawahiri, a founding father of the Islamic Jihad of Egypt, established al Qaeda (The Base) as a direct outgrowth of MAK. The following year Abdullah Azzam died in a mysterious car bomb explosion. Although there has been suspicion of involvement by bin Laden, there has never been any proof linking him to the death of his one-time mentor.

But with the 1989 departure of the Soviet Union from Afghanistan, the warrior-king bin Laden and his loyal warriors had lost their enemy. As Eric Hoffer (the longshoreman philosopher who wrote *The True Believer*) has observed, the power of a charismatic leader derives from his capacity to focus hatred against a single enemy, as Hitler did in the 1930s, unifying the German people in their hatred of the Jews. Bin Laden traveled to Sudan in 1993 and was incensed to learn that the United States maintained a military base on Saudi soil in the wake of the Gulf War, defiling the sacred Islamic land "of the two cities" (Mecca and Medina). Decrying this desecration of holy Saudi soil by the infidel Americans, bin Laden seamlessly transferred his enmity from the first defeated superpower, the Soviet Union, to the remaining superpower, the United States, despite U.S. aid in the struggle against the Soviet Union, which he dismissed as irrelevant.

Initially, he sought only to expel the American military from Arab lands, but later, in the 1998 fatwa (religious directive), he expanded the enemy to include all Americans, whether civilian or military, throughout the world. (Bin Laden does not have religious credentials and accordingly cannot issue fatwas, but he has a group of compliant imams who dutifully put their official imprimatur on fatwas bin Laden has drafted.)

In the 1998 fatwa, "Jihad against Jews and Crusaders," bin Laden declared:

> In compliance with God's order, we issue the following fatwa to all Muslims: The ruling to kill the Americans and their allies—civilians and military—is an individual duty for every Muslim who can do it in any country in which it is possible to do it, in order to liberate the al-Aqsa Mosque and the holy mosque [Mecca] from their grip, and in order for their armies to move out of all the lands of Islam, defeated and unable to threaten any Muslim. This is in accordance with the words of Almighty God [in the Koran], "and fight the pagans all together as they fight you all together," and "fight them until there is no more tumult or oppression, and there prevail justice and faith in God." We—with God's help—call on every Muslim who believes in God and wishes to be rewarded to comply with God's order to kill the Americans and plunder their money wherever and whenever they find it.

Note that it is not bin Laden but God who has ordered religious Muslims to kill all the Americans, God for whom bin Laden speaks with authority. There is not an action that bin Laden orders that is not couched and justified in language from the Koran.

Moreover, he criticized the Saudi royal family for their apostasy, decrying the way they had defiled their stewardship of "the land of the two cities," Mecca and Medina. The vigor of his criticism led Saudi Arabia to revoke his citizenship in 1994, and his family, which depended on the Saudi leadership for their wealth, turned against him.

At this time bin Laden was righteously attacking the other two enemies in the triad of enemies, the Western-Israeli nexus, and one of the newly designated apostate Arab nations, Saudi Arabia. But he maintained the primary focus on the external enemy, the United States. Yes, the leadership of the apostate nations had to be replaced, but it was the United States that was the prime enemy, for it was responsible for propping up the corrupt leadership of these countries. Thus he continued the strategy born in Afghanistan of focusing on the enemy who is afar, the American "Zionist-Crusaders," rather than the enemy who is near, the *targhut* (oppressive domestic rulers.)

Bin Laden had a series of triumphs—the first World Trade Center bombing (1993); Khobar Towers, the U.S. military barracks in Saudi Arabia (1996); the bombings of the U.S. embassies in Kenya and Tanzania (1998); the attack on the U.S.S. *Cole* in Yemen (2000); and now, the most spectacular terrorist act in history, the events of September 11, 2001, an act of mass casualty or superterrorism. Each of these successes further confirmed for bin Laden and his followers that he was a man with a mission, a preeminent leader of radical Islam. Osama bin Laden seems to be on an expansive roll, with messianic grandiosity, ever expanding his vision.

The conflict initially was highly personalized, focusing on Osama bin Laden, who, in President Bush's words, was "Wanted Dead or Alive," with a $25 million bounty on his head. Each personalized threat against bin Laden only served to magnify his stature for his followers.

Moreover, there was an implication that the capture or death of bin Laden would mean the end of the threat. This assuredly is not the case, for al Qaeda differs significantly from other terrorist groups and organizations, perhaps reflecting bin Laden's training in business management. Al Qaeda is a loose umbrella organization of semiautonomous terrorist groups and organizations. In effect, bin Laden is chairman of the board of Radical Islam, Inc., a holding company that provides guidance, coordination, and financial and logistical facilitation and that he grew through mergers and acquisitions. Unlike other charismatically led terrorist organizations, such as Abimael Guzman's Sendero Luminoso (Shining Path) of Peru, or Abdullah Ocalan's Kurdistan Workers' Party (PKK) of Turkey, both of which were mortally wounded when their respective leaders were captured, bin Laden designated Ayman al-Zawahiri as his successor and number two and has delegated significant authority and responsibility to other members of his organization. Should bin Laden be killed or captured, the reins of the organization would pass seamlessly to Zawahiri. Should the entire leadership echelon be eliminated, the threat, although diminished, would still remain, for it is estimated that al Qaeda is operating in sixty-eight nations, and the semiautonomous organizations under the umbrella of al Qaeda would devolve and continue to pursue their terrorist mission.

President Bush and British Prime Minister Tony Blair have taken pains to clarify that this is not a war against Muslims, but a war against terrorism; but bin Laden, seeking to frame this as a religious war, has now laid claim, one could say, to the title of commander-in-chief of the Islamic world, opposing the commander-in-chief of the corrupt secular modernizing Western world, President George W. Bush, in a religious war. Alienated Arab youth find resonance in his statements and see him as a hero.

And this is the real challenge. Osama bin Laden may be eliminated and the al Qaeda network rolled up, but the path of anti-Western radical Islamist extremism is increasingly attractive to alienated Islamic youth.

Terrorism at heart is a vicious species of psychological warfare; it is violence as communication. Smart bombs and missiles will not win this war. The only way to counter psychological warfare is with psychological warfare, countering the distorted extremist rhetoric of Osama bin Laden and radical Islamist clerics, which rationalizes violence with verses from the Koran. This will be a long struggle. And key goals in this struggle are to inhibit alienated Muslim youth from joining the ranks of extremism, to not see violence as the only pathway. Most important, support for this dangerous movement must be reduced, so that radical Islamic extremism is marginalized, its leaders delegitimated.

The events of 9/11 were in many ways a "perfect storm." A destructive charismatic leader manipulated, in Eric Hoffer's words, "the slime of discontented souls" to focus the hatred and violence of his "true believers" against the identified enemy, the United States.

Each of the themes that contributed to this "perfect storm" will be elaborated in the balance of this book. In the next chapter, the relationship between personality and politics will be explored, with an emphasis on the particular circumstances under which political personality is likely to be an especially powerful influence.

2

When Personality Affects
Political Behavior

When in the course of human events the leader affects the march of history has been the subject of fierce debate among historians and political scientists. Early historians tended to depict history as an unfolding of events, with the king, prime minister, or president as steward of their nation. When political events occurred, it was a consequence of historical forces. If the role of a leader was described, he tended to be portrayed as being present during these events. This was particularly true of Middle Eastern histories, with their strong cultural emphasis on fate or destiny.[1]

In his classic 1895 analysis of social behavior and social systems, the French sociologist Emile Durkheim emphasized the role of what he termed "social facts," by which he meant factors external to the individual leader. Similarly, Max Weber, in developing his classic theory of bureaucracy, emphasized the importance of conformity to an organized and uniform system. Such personality factors as motivations and emotions, in contrast to impersonal rationality, were considered hindrances to smooth bureaucratic functioning that needed to be eliminated. As the political psychologist Gordon DiRenzo notes, in commenting on the contributions of these early theorists, "little concern is shown for the social agents as status-role occupants operating within the social systems."

Later, a shift from this impersonal view of historical systems occurred, to focus on the role of the leader as a causative agent in changing history, the so-called great man theory of history. In his book *The Hero in History* (1943), Sidney Hook distinguishes between two classes of heroes: eventful and event making. The eventful leader stands astride a crossroads in history. When he is confronted by major events, his manner of leadership will affect the march of history. Hook cites Thomas Jefferson as one who exemplified both eventful and event-making leadership. Jefferson's drafting of the Declaration of Independence (for which he is inscribed in every schoolchild's memory), was an eventful act that occurred when the forces of history, the fork in the road, required an inspiring document. Jefferson was selected by his peers to be the principal drafter of the declaration, but any of his peers could have drafted it. This was eventful leadership. In contrast, Jefferson's event-making act—which shaped the destiny of the United States through proactive leadership that reflected remarkable vision and perseverance—was the Louisiana Purchase.

Consider President George Bush's response when Iraq invaded Kuwait in the summer of 1990. Making use of the unique network of world leaders he had established during his service as ambassador to the United Nations and later as director of the Central Intelligence Agency, a network he had maintained and strengthened during his eight years as vice president, using personal persuasion that was often quite forceful, President Bush brought together a remarkable assemblage of Western and Middle Eastern leaders; working through the United Nations, he directed the political-military strategy that ultimately led to the expulsion of Saddam Hussein's forces from Kuwait. This was an exemplar of eventful leadership: President Bush was reacting to the crisis and did so in a remarkable fashion.

But, if George Bush confronted the fork in the road, it was Saddam Hussein who created it. Saddam Hussein was an event-making leader. In contrast to George Bush, who was reactive, he was proactive. He created the very fork in the historical road to which George Bush reacted. It is difficult to imagine a history of the crisis in the Gulf that did not refer to the singular leadership of Saddam Hussein and George Bush.

The early literature in political science was dominated by the study of power relationships. When a political event occurred, it was a consequence of political forces. If the role of a leader was described, he was the personification of those forces, a "black box" computer summing up inputs and producing outputs. Indeed, as Barbara Kellerman has observed, before Glen Paige's *The Scientific Study of Leadership* in 1977, the word *leadership* was not to be found in the index of any political science text. In a computerized keyword index of 2,614 articles that appeared from 1906 to 1963, the words "leader" or "leadership" appeared in such titles only seventeen times!

But since Paige focused attention on the crucial role of leadership, scholars have regularly addressed its role in shaping political events. In the 1980 Paul Anthony Brick Lectures, published as *Politics as Leadership* (Tucker 1981), Robert Tucker portrays leadership as the core element of politics. Observing that Plato in his focus on the philosopher-king had emphasized man's role in shaping history—in contrast to Socrates, who focused more on power—Tucker sees leadership as the very essence of politics. He identified the importance of nonconstituted leaders, who, even though they did not have a constituted leadership role as president or prime minister, through leadership actions took an issue that was being ignored by the duly constituted leadership and brought it to national attention. Examples include Rachel Carson, whose *Silent Spring* gave birth to the environmental movement, and Martin Luther King Jr., whose leadership of the civil rights movement transformed the nation, but, all the more remarkably, did so without an official constituted position.

As the leadership acts described above make clear, the historical, cultural, and political context in which the leader is acting is of central importance. The pendulum that overswung from the view of history as a consequence of power, ignoring the role of leadership, to the "great man" theory of history, which emphasized the centrality of leadership, has come to rest with the current working model, the leader in context.

As depicted in figure 1, M. Brewster-Smith has provided an extremely useful guide to the intimate interrelationship between the leader and his political context, a context that at once influences the leader's attitudes and is shaped and influenced by the leader. As conceptualized by Brewster-Smith, the most distal antecedents of the leader in context are the "historical milieu" (Panel 1), the historical, economic, political, and societal determinants. These in turn shape the societal context, the "social environment" (Panel 2) in which the person (Panel 3) was socialized. Comprising the family, social class, peers, and teachers, the social environment plays a crucial role in shaping the attitudes of political leaders and their followers.

Drawing on Kurt Lewin's field theory, Stone and Schaffner conceptual-

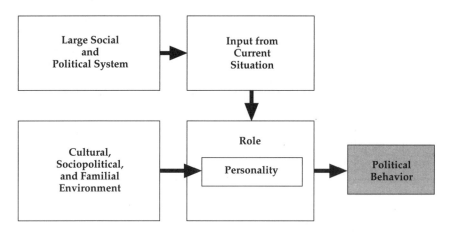

Figure 2.1. Variables Relevant to the Study of Personality and Politics

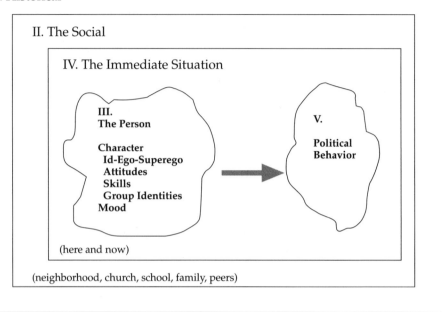

I. Historical

II. The Social

IV. The Immediate Situation

III.
The Person

Character
Id-Ego-Superego
Attitudes
Skills
Group Identities
Mood

V.

Political
Behavior

(here and now)

(neighborhood, church, school, family, peers)

Figure 2.2. Stone and Schaffner: Field Model

ize this as a cluster of fields, nesting one within the other, and the political life space (fig. 2). This can be envisaged as a Russian nesting doll, in which the smallest doll at the center, the person, is encapsulated within the next larger doll, the immediate situation, which in turn is embedded within the social environment, which is encapsulated within the historical context.

Each of the fields is highly subjective. It is history as related, history as perceived. In my studies of the Arab-Israeli conflict and of Palestinian nationalist/separatist terrorism, I have regularly been impressed with the alternate histories both sides to the dispute carry within them. Each side carries a history that emphasizes its minority status and its victimization. It is a competition of victimhoods.

Just as earlier studies of politics ignored the role of leadership, as the importance of leadership in shaping historical events came into focus, the role of a leader's personality was initially ignored. Rather, the leader was depicted as a rational decision maker, devoid of personality, with little attention being paid to affects, drives, and unresolved conflicts.

In *The Essence of Decision* (1971), Graham Allison subjects decision making during the Cuban Missile Crisis to searching analysis, distinguishing four levels of analysis. When senior U.S. policy makers grappled with the question "Why would the Soviet Union place offensive missiles in Cuba?" they were treating the Soviet Union as a rational national actor. In response to the initially ambiguous U-2 spy plane photographs, U.S. senior policy officials reasoned, "If the Soviet Union wanted to gain political-military advantage by placing offensive missiles in Cuba, surely it would have sought to accomplish this as a fait accompli and would have camouflaged the work in progress. But since there was no camouflage, that can't have been the motivation, so these must be defensive missiles," which led to a dangerous delay in grasping the danger facing the United States. When a foreign policy analyst begins a piece, "In response to economic pressures, Beijing will likely . . . ," he is employing the shorthand of rational national actor analysis, using the capitol city of the People's Republic of China to represent the nation as a whole making decisions.

But this perspective, all too often adopted in the analysis of foreign affairs, limits the analytic perspective. In effect, the analyst is asking, "If I were the People's Republic of China, what would I do?" As Allison emphasizes, the People's Republic of China or the Soviet Union did not make decisions any more than the United States makes decisions. Rather, the decisions are the consequence of the interplay between bureaucracies, with often competing bureaucratic interests, that is, the bureaucratic politics level of analysis. Soviet and American participants in the Cuban Missile Crisis have met and exchanged information, and we now know that the Soviet Politburo wanted to redress the strategic imbalance by placing offensive missiles just off the shores of the United States, just as the Soviet Union and the Warsaw Pact nations were ringed by Western missiles. But the Soviet Strategic Rocket forces used the same standard operating procedures in Cuba that they employed in constructing missile bases in the Soviet Union or Eastern Europe, did not employ camouflage, and, lo and behold, from the U-2, the missile bases under construction had the same configuration in overhead photography as those in the Warsaw Pact. Asking the question from the perspective of the Soviet Union as a rational national actor could not have provided the explanation that a bureaucratic politics perspective provided.

But in fact, bureaucratic organizations do not make decisions—policymaking groups do. Allison's depiction of the decision making within ExCom, the small group of senior U.S. foreign policy and military decision makers that were sequestered during the thirteen-day crisis, convincingly demonstrates that the interplay among the participants in the decision-making group—the group-process level of analysis—was critical. The group debated three political-military options: a surgical air strike on the missile base, an invasion of Cuba, or a blockade. Attorney General Robert (Bobby) Kennedy framed the air strike on the missile bases as analogous to the Japanese attack on Pearl Harbor and suggested to his brother, the president, that he would go down in history as the Tojo of the Western world if he carried it out. That was enough to remove this alternative from consideration by JFK, who already had his eyes on the pages of history. The group had narrowed the alternatives down to either an invasion or a blockade, and it was rapidly approaching consensus on initiating a naval blockade to prevent Soviet missiles from reaching Cuba when Adlai Stevenson, the U.S. ambassador to the United Nations, introduced a new idea. He argued against forcing the leadership of the Soviet Union into a humiliating corner, insisting that it would be important to give the USSR a way out. Since—as a consequence of bureaucratic inefficiency—the U.S. had not yet dismantled its outmoded missiles in Turkey, why not offer the Soviet Union a face-saving way out, Stevenson asked? If they would remove their offensive missiles from Cuba, the United States would remove its offensive missiles from Turkey. When he was out of the room, Stevenson was ridiculed as a weak and cowardly old man by one of the senior generals present, and Stevenson's creative suggestion was not considered. Indeed, it was inconsiderable, for to even discuss his idea was to risk being labeled as weak and cowardly. In his study *Groupthink*, Irving Janis characterizes this as an example of the mind-guard phenomenon, in which the group that is approaching consensus rejects a new idea with an ad hominem attack on the messenger.

But groups don't make decisions; individuals do. In his retrospective analysis of the failure of intelligence during the Cuban Missile Crisis, Sherman Kent, the father of U.S. estimative intelligence, concluded that insufficient consideration had been given to the decisive role of two key individuals, Nikita Khrushchev and Fidel Castro. This, in Allison's terms, is the individual actor level of analysis.

But in portraying the central importance of Khrushchev and Castro, Allison focuses on them as cognitive, wholly rational decision makers and neglects the emotional or irrational forces that might be driving them. In my discussions with Allison, he has acknowledged that a further level of analysis, a personality-driven one, might well be usefully added. Indeed, Kent concluded that the primary reason for the intelligence failure was too much emphasis on rationally analyzing the motives of the Soviets and the Cubans, with insufficient attention paid to the psychology of the two key actors, Khrushchev and Castro.

When in the course of human events leader personality affects political behavior is the subject of this volume. Most foreign policy analysis is conducted at levels one and two, the analysis of the rational national actor and of bureaucratic politics. This book addresses levels of analysis three and four, group process and the individual actor, with the major emphasis being on the fifth level of analysis, personality and political behavior.

Harold Lasswell, who can be considered the father of political psychology, played a singular role in emphasizing the centrality of leader personality in determining political action. His classic equation p}d}r}=P defines homo politicus, the power seeker, P, in which p displaces his personal needs, d, onto a public object and rationalizes it, r, as being in the public good (Lasswell 1930, 75). In particular, the power seeker uses the political arena to compensate for feelings of low self-esteem, unimportance, moral inferiority, weakness, mediocrity, and intellectual inferiority.

In their classic psychobiography of Woodrow Wilson, Alexander and Juliette George rigorously apply this theory to Wilson in seeking to explain the problematic nature of his leadership (George and George 1956). They hypothesized that if Wilson were driven to seek power to compensate for feelings of low self-esteem, he would be unwilling to let others share in the field of power, to take advice, to delegate, to consult, or to inform others and would demonstrate a desire to impose orderly systems on others. Their examination of his key decisions as president of Princeton University and as president of the United States confirmed that he did fit the profile of the power seeker.

An extreme example of the power wielder using his power to compensate for feelings of inadequacy, especially intellectual inferiority, is Idi Amin of Uganda (Post and Robins 1995, 57–61). His self-proclaimed title as His Excellency President for Life Field Marshal Al Hadj Dr. Idi Amin Dada, VC, DSO, MC, Lord of the Beasts of the Earth and Fishes of the Sea and Conqueror of the British Empire in Africa in General and Uganda in Particular could scarcely have been more grandiose. Idi Amin attended missionary school intermittently, leaving after the sixth grade, and had a reputation for limited intelligence. He seized the reins of power in Uganda in a 1977 military coup at age forty-five. His first public words on taking power show his discomfiture with his lack of education and the intellectual challenges of becoming chief of state: "Sometimes people mistake the way I talk for what I am thinking. I never had any formal education—not even a nursery school certificate. But sometimes I know more than Ph.D.s because as a military man I know how to act. I am a man of action" (*Idi Amin Dada*, 167). Amin tried to establish relationships with the educated elite, whose expertise he needed, but found himself unable to communicate with them. In a brutally direct manner for dealing with threats to his fragile self-esteem, he conducted a purge of the intelligentsia, in the process killing between 100,000 and 600,000 people during his six-year rule.

Like his contemporary Idi Amin, Francisco Macias, president of Equatorial Guinea, had a limited education and was extremely insecure intellectually. Early in his career it was remarked that he suffered from an "inferiority complex" in front of educated persons. He systematically eliminated the cause of his discomfiture by executing prominent intellectuals. The very word "intellectual" was prohibited, and he fired the minister of education for using it. In 1977, as he hunted down the remaining intellectuals in Equatorial Guinea, he identified the intelligentsia as Africa's most serious threat (Post and Robins 1995, 55–57). Both Amin and Macias were totalitarian rulers, who had no societal constraints on their giving full play to their psychopathology as they shaped society to fit their own distorted psychological needs.

In his epistemological analysis of personality and politics, Fred Greenstein systematically addresses the question of when personality affects politics (Greenstein 1987). He makes a useful distinction between what he terms action dispensability and actor dispensability. Action dispensability refers to those situations in which the actions of the leader affect events. What are the circumstances, Greenstein asks, under which the actions of individuals are likely to have a greater or lesser effect on the course of events? He separates this question from actor dispensability, that is, whether the action is best understood in terms of the actor's personal characteristics (Greenstein 1987, 41–46).

Greenstein has distilled much of the burgeoning literature on this topic and identified three propositions concerning when the actions of an individual actor are likely to affect events. The likelihood of personal impact varies with the degree to which the political environment is amenable to influence, the location of the actor in the system, and the strengths or weaknesses of the actor:

1. *The likelihood of personal impact increases to the degree that the environment admits of restructuring.* How many presidents have run for office vowing to "reinvent" government, to make it more responsive to the people, only to find to their frustration, after an altogether too short honeymoon, how difficult it is to move the entrenched bureaucracy?
2. *The likelihood of personal impact varies with the actor's location in the environment.* The secretary of defense and chairman of the Joint Chiefs of Staff will have a much greater influence on military policy than will the enlisted man—the level of his role permits this greater influence. But the role can be constraining as well—a reflection of the need, emphasized by Brewster-Smith's map, to distinguish be-

tween role and person. In some circumstances, the most liberal Democratic president and the most conservative Republican president would behave almost identically—the role would require them to do so.

3. *The likelihood of personal impact varies with the personal strengths or weaknesses of the actor.*

Concerning actor dispensability, Greenstein (1987, 50–57) proposes the following circumstances when personal variability, or variability in the actor's personal characteristics, affects behavior:

1. *Ambiguous situations leave room for personal variability to manifest itself.* This subsumes new or unique situations that have insufficient or contradictory information and situations where there is "information overload."
2. *The opportunities for personal variation are increased to the degree that political actors lack socially standardized mental sets that lead them to structure their perceptions and resolve ambiguities.*
3. *The impact of personal differences on behavior is increased to the degree that sanctions are not attached to certain of the alternative possible courses of behavior.* A totalitarian dictator with near total control over his political environment has a much greater sway of action than a democratically elected president or prime minister in a situation with built-in checks and balances.
4. *Intense dispositions in a contrary direction to the prevailing sanctions increase the likelihood that personal characteristics will affect behavior.*
5. *To the degree that individuals are placed in a group context in which their decisions or attitudes are visible to others, personal variation is reduced.*
6. *Intense needs to take one's cues from others will tend to reduce the effects of variation.*
7. *The greater a political actor's affective involvement in politics, the greater the likelihood that his psychological characteristics will be exhibited in his behavior.*
8. *The more demanding the political act—the more it is one that calls for an active investment of effort—the greater the likelihood that it will be influenced by the personal characteristics of the actor.*
9. *Certain kinds of spontaneous behavior—notably actions that proceed from personal impulse without effort or premeditation.*
10. *Even when there is little room for personal variability in the instrumental aspects of actions, there is likely to be variations in their expressive aspects.*

11. *Personal variations will be more evident to the degree that the individual occupies a position free from elaborate expectations of fixed content.* This applies, of course, particularly to autocratic leaders in closed societies with few constraints from the populace.

Insofar as individuals seek leadership roles in order to solve or resolve their personal conflicts in the public domain—that is, to the degree the leader resembles the power seeker described by Lasswell—certain issues will be particularly salient for their political psychology. Thus, a particular leader may be entirely objective in considering his country's economy, but issues of war and peace may engage his inner psychological needs.

Greenstein elaborates three conditions under which deeper psychodynamic forces will be at work and ego-defensive needs activated, relating them to environment, predispositions, and response:

1. *Certain types of environmental stimuli have a greater resonance with the deep layers of the personality than do others.*
2. *The likelihood that ego-defensive needs will affect political behavior is also related to the degree to which actors "have" ego-defensive needs.*
3. *Finally, certain types of response undoubtedly provide greater occasion for deep personality needs to find outlet than do others.*

Related to Greenstein's propositions, Margaret Hermann (1976) has identified a number of key circumstances where leader characteristics are likely to affect foreign policy behavior:

1. *In proportion to the general interest of the head of state in foreign policy.* Some leaders whose central interest is in domestic policy will delegate foreign policy to other officials and do not become involved in its management.
2. *When the means of assuming power are dramatic.* Consider how all attention focused on Vice President Lyndon Johnson when President Kennedy was assassinated. He played an important stabilizing role, conveying a sense of calm leadership and promising continuity and a steady hand at the tiller, which was reassuring to a traumatized nation. Similarly, when a leader assumes power in a coup, all attention will be focused on him.
3. *When the head of state is charismatic.*
4. *When the head of state has great authority over foreign policy.*

5. *When the foreign policy organization of the nation is less developed and differentiated.* (For both numbers 4 and 5, Saddam Hussein is an important exemplar. He liked to say "Saddam is Iraq; Iraq is Saddam," and what he declared to be policy was Iraq's policy.)

6. *In a crisis:* This is a preeminent occasion for leader personality to come to the fore; how a leader acts in a crisis will often be the measure of his leadership.

7. *When the external national situation is perceived to be ambiguous, the information-processing systems of the head of state play a key role.*

8. *The cognitive styles and beliefs of the head of state will affect foreign policy in relation to the degree of training in foreign affairs.*

For the most part, scholars exploring the question of when a leader's personality is most likely to affect political behavior are using "when" in the sense of "under what political circumstances," referring to the context in which the leader is operating, with only minimal attention to personal variability. But no matter what the political circumstances, no matter what the political constraints, idiosyncratic personality features can play a determinant role.

It is useful at this juncture to borrow a leaf from ego psychology. Heinz Hartmann (1958) conceptualized the very useful concept of the conflict-free ego sphere, the parts of the personality mediating between the environment and internal drives that are not involved in psychological conflict. The more psychologically healthy the individual is, the larger the conflict-free ego sphere. Similarly, we may consider a conflict-free leadership sphere: the more psychologically healthy the individual leader is, the greater the scope of political decisions that he can make that are free from personality distortion. For some executive problems, such as coping with the economy, a particular leader may be highly objective and able in a conflict-free way to bring all of his intellectual resources to bear on the problem-solving task. But for other issues that involve his personality, that engage his conflicts, highly subjective factors may come into play. Thus, a leader with a particularly strong need for control may feel impelled to be particularly repressive at a time of social unrest, even though the unrest may be an inevitable accompaniment of the social progress that he intellectually values.

In considering intrinsic personality factors, it is important to emphasize that personality needs and drives are not static but dynamic; they ebb and flow during an individual's psychological development, a process that continues throughout life. Let us now consider when in the course of a leader's life psychological forces are especially apt to be influential.

The Seasons of a Leader's Life: Reflections on the Life Course of Political Leaders

Erik Erikson called attention to the course of personality development throughout life in a chapter called "The Eight Ages of Man" in his classic first book, *Childhood and Society* (Erikson 1950).[2] He delineated eight phases of the life cycle, each one having its own developmental crisis to master. Although other students of personality development have focused on the vicissitudes of personality during adulthood and later life, it is only in the last several years that the implications of this area of inquiry have come prominently into our collective awareness through such popular books as Gail Sheehy's *Passages* (Sheehy 1976). No man in his late thirties or early forties can change careers or become divorced without being glibly diagnosed as "going through a midlife crisis." In *Adulthood* (1978), Erikson brought together articles by authors from varying disciplines and cultures that often were the fruits of the seeds he sowed four decades ago, calling attention to this increasing focus on psychological changes during maturity.

Building on Erikson, in *The Seasons of a Man's Life*, Dan Levinson (1978) made a seminal contribution to our understanding of the personality changes that can occur during adulthood. On the basis of a longitudinal study of forty American males from four socioeconomic groups, Levinson delineated four eras of the life cycle: childhood and adolescence (birth–22); early adulthood (17–45); middle adulthood (40–65); and late adulthood (60–?).

These four eras overlap, producing three transitional periods. In these transitions, the work of one era is being brought to a close while the succeeding era is getting underway. Thus preadulthood, which includes childhood and adolescence, ends at twenty-two, while the work of young adulthood is beginning by age seventeen or eighteen. These transitions are times of psychological stress when personality organization may be especially fluid, with a consequent potential for significant change and growth: (1) the "young adult transition," the transition between adolescence and young adulthood, roughly ages 17–22, the period of the "identity crisis"; (2) the "midlife transition," the transition between young adulthood and middle adulthood, roughly ages 40–45; and (3) the "late-adult transition," the transition between middle adulthood and late adulthood, roughly ages 60–65. The overlapping four eras and the three transition periods are illustrated in figure 3.

A note of caution: Levinson's study was based on a sample of forty American men between age thirty-five and forty-five, consisting of ten men each from four occupational and professional categories. In her com-

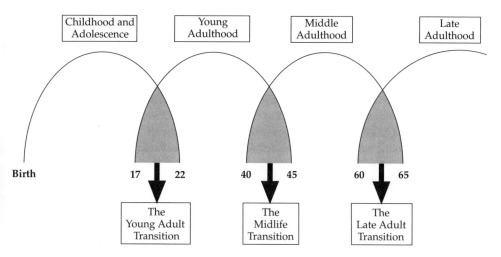

Figure 2.3. Transitions of the Life Cycle

prehensive review, "Time, Age, and the Life Cycle," Bernice Neugarten (1979) observed the variable timing of life events and suggested a trend toward a fluid life cycle rather than one characterized by discrete age-related stages. Vaillant (1977) too has called attention to a continuum of change, rather than a stage-related progression. Particularly as we consider the cross-cultural implications of studies in aging, the variability and timing of key life events become especially relevant. There is an increasing trend toward fluidity, with the timing of these transitions and challenges varying from culture to culture and in relation to both personal and historical events.

We are persuaded, however, that there is a regular progression through which individuals pass from youth through young adulthood through middle adulthood to old age in all societies. However, the age by which a man must "make it" varies considerably from society to society, and indeed from occupation to occupation. In more primitive societies, the pathway to achievement is often well delineated in early adolescence; in Western technocratic societies, the transition psychologically from youth to maturity may be delayed into the late twenties and even early thirties. Accordingly, the age of political socialization and consolidation of political identification will also be extended. This is particularly apt to be the case for youth during a period of profound social stress, such as the United States faced during the Vietnam War years.

The psychological pressures of the midlife transition may occur significantly earlier in some cultures where career success is identified at an earlier age. Moreover, in contrast to youth-oriented Western societies, in some Asian societies where age is revered it has traditionally been almost unthinkable to consider a man for an important leadership position before he has attained the wisdom and maturity of men in their sixties.

And, the psychological issues of the later years may be hastened by major illness or a life-threatening event either in the individual or in a close family member. Thus, an individual who suffers a heart attack in his early fifties may demonstrate an increased urgency to accomplish his or her goals in response to the internal perception that remaining time is short.

Accordingly, we do not want to fixate on the precise ages specified by Levinson but rather on the psychological timetable he describes. It is the internal clock, rather than the external calendar, that counts, and this is strongly influenced by cultural determinants. It is the internal psychological program that is crucial. Bearing these caveats in mind, whatever the timetable there are psychological issues and fluctuations that affect most of us as we progress through life. With the understanding that the timetable may vary, it is nonetheless instructive to consider the implications of the three phases delineated by Levinson for the study of political psychology.

The Young Adult Transition

The young adult transition is of particular importance to the field of political psychology, for it is during this youthful transition that psychological identification consolidates, including political identification. When an individual comes to maturity—that is, the political circumstances in his country during his adolescence and young adulthood—has lasting consequences for his political behavior. The relationship between the political moment and the personal moment, between political history and psychosocial development, is especially important for the late adolescent. What is occurring in the political world at that moment of individual personality development can be critical, fixing key attitudes and perceptions irrevocably within the personality structure.

What would be the impact on future leadership of the Vietnam generation's experiences? What did it mean to an adolescent in the Soviet Union needing psychologically to overthrow authority to hear Khrushchev's famous de-Stalinization speech? Many revolutionary leaders experienced social upheaval during their adolescence. They found social sanction for their own age-related drive to be independent of authority, often crystallizing hyperindependence and resistance to authority as permanent character features.

A vivid example of the relationship between the political moment and adolescent psychological development is found in Gamal Abdel Nasser's life. When Nasser was a youth, Egypt was in political ferment. On summer vacation in Alexandria when he was thirteen years old, Nasser experienced the world of politics for the first time: "One day on the way to school, I ran into a crowd that was demonstrating. What for or against I had not the faintest idea. But it looked like a good fight, so I joined" (Berindranath 1966).

Arrested and jailed overnight, Nasser was too excited to sleep, and spent the evening questioning the other prisoners about the demonstration. He had found a new life, where he immediately felt he belonged. He was liberated from his aimless apathy; he had at last found an outlet for the anger built up during his embittered childhood and also a cause that for the first time gave his life meaning.

The Development of the Dream during Childhood and Adolescence

What happens to a dream deferred? Although Langston Hughes, the black American poet, asked this poignant question about the black experience in the United States, it could as well be asked about the dreams that propel some to the heights of greatness, others to the heights of folly (depending on the outcome). To understand the influence of the life cycle on the political behavior of leaders, one must understand their unfulfilled ambitions, their goals, and their dreams of glory. Here we will focus on a particular class of political leaders who are consumed by dreams of glory—leaders with significant narcissistic features in their personality structures.

With the explosion of interest in the psychology of the self stimulated by the pathbreaking work of Heinz Kohut (1971, 1977) and Otto Kernberg (1975, 1985), the term *narcissism* has come to be much abused and rather glibly and carelessly applied. Many biographers and students of leadership have been seized by the concept of narcissism, relying on the description of the narcissistic character disorder in the American Psychiatric Association's Diagnostic and Statistical Manual of Mental Disorders IV (1994). As the features are recapitulated, it would be well for the reader to reflect on how often these features are characteristic of political leaders. The essential features described are:

> a pervasive pattern of grandiosity, need for admiration, and lack of empathy that begins by early adulthood and is present in a variety of contexts, as indicted by five (or more) of the following:

1. Has a grandiose sense of self-importance (e.g., exaggerates achievements and talents, expects to be recognized as superior without commensurate achievements)
2. Is preoccupied with fantasies of unlimited success, power, brilliance, beauty, or ideal love
3. Believes that he or she is "special" and unique and can only be understood by, should associate with, other special or high status people (or institutions)
4. Requires excessive admiration
5. Has a sense of entitlement, i.e., unreasonable expectations of favorable treatment or automatic compliance with his or her expectations
6. Is interpersonally exploitative, i.e., takes advantage of others to achieve his or her expectations
7. Lacks empathy: is unwilling to recognize or identify with the feelings and needs of others
8. Is often envious of others or believes that others are envious of him or her.
9. Shows arrogant, haughty behaviors or attitudes.

Individuals with this disorder have a grandiose sense of self-importance. They routinely overestimate their abilities and inflate their accomplishments, often appearing boastful and pretentious. They may blithely assume that others attribute the same value to their efforts and may be surprised when the praise they expect and feel they deserve is not forthcoming. Often implicit in their inflated judgments of their own accomplishments is an underestimation (devaluation) of the contributions of others. They are often preoccupied with fantasies of unlimited success, power, brilliance, beauty, or ideal love. They may ruminate about "long overdue" admiration and privilege and compare themselves favorably with famous or privileged people. . . .

Individuals with this disorder generally require excessive admiration. Their self-esteem is almost invariably very fragile. They may be preoccupied with how well they are doing and how favorably they are regarded by others. This often takes the form of a need for constant attention and admiration.

A sense of entitlement is evident in these individuals' unreasonable expectation of especially favorable treatment. They expect to be catered to and are puzzled or furious when this does not happen. This sense of entitlement combined with a lack of sensitivity to the wants and needs of others may result in the conscious or unwitting exploitation of others. They tend to form friendships or relationships only if the other person seems likely to advance their purposes or otherwise enhance their self-esteem. They generally have a lack of empathy and have difficulty recognizing the desires, subjective experiences, and feelings of others. . . .

These individuals are often envious of others or believe that others are envious of them. They may harshly devalue the contributions of others, especially when those individuals have received acknowledgment or praise for their accomplishments. Arrogant, haughty behaviors characterize these individuals.

Vulnerability in self-esteem makes these individuals very "sensitive to injury" from criticism or defeat. Although they may not show it outwardly, criticism may haunt these individuals and may leave them feeling humiliated, degraded, hollow, and empty. They may react with disdain, rage, or defiant counterattack.

Interpersonal relationships are typically impaired due to problems derived from entitlement, the need for admiration, and the relative disregard to the sensitivity of others. Though overweening ambition and confidence may lead to high achievement, performance may be disrupted due to intolerance of criticism or defeat. (American Psychiatric Association 1994, 658–70)

But to be "narcissistic" is not necessarily to be ill. Indeed, Kohut (1971, 1977) makes a particular point of emphasizing a distinct and separate narcissistic course of personality development that can lead to psychologically healthy narcissistic individuals. Vamik Volkan (1980), who has made major contributions to the psychoanalytic literature on narcissism, has been a pioneer in applying psychoanalytic concepts of narcissism to the study of leadership. He describes the individual with a narcissistic personality organization as

regarding himself as endowed with great power, physical appeal, and the right to assert his will. He gives the impression of ambitiously striving for brilliance in all he does. He seems to regard others—especially those not among his worshipers—as beneath notice. Although he views his supporters as adjuncts to himself, he is quick to deny their existence if they withdraw their awestruck allegiance. Behaving as though self-sufficient in a superior way, he feels that he exists for others to admire. Nevertheless, close scrutiny of the behavior of such a person will reveal that, although he lives a glorious albeit lonely life in such isolation that he could be said to dwell within a "plastic or glass bubble," he is, paradoxically, constantly engaged with others on another level because he is object-hungry. He actually has feelings of inferiority and thus is over-dependent on the approving attention of other people. (Volkan 1980, 132)

What is the childhood and adolescence like of individuals who go on to develop narcissistic personalities? Typically, the development of the sense of self has been damaged early in life by inadequate parenting, especially by the mother, who is at once rejecting (of the child's autonomy and individuality) and intrusive. Some mothers are cold and rejecting of their children, subjecting them to ridicule and scorn, so that they emerge from these early years with profound underlying insecurity and self-doubt. Although overprotection at first glance may seem to be the opposite sort of behavior, it is also rejecting. The mother who adopts this pattern sees the child as an overvalued extension of herself, and communicates in a continuing fashion from the earliest years not only that he or she is special in her eyes but also that her love is contingent on that specialness. This excessive and overinflated praise leads to an unconscious awareness that "the lady doth protest too much," producing an insatiable appetite for praise lest the underlying inadequacy be revealed.

Thus, in the narcissistic individual there comes to be an idealized self-concept, or "good self," and an inadequate, devalued "bad self." In healthy psychological development, the individual integrates into a realistic self-concept the "good" and "bad" aspects of the self, but in narcissistic individuals the devalued self is "split" off and denied (Kohut 1971, 1977; Kernberg 1975, 1979; Volkan, 1980)—hence, the sensitivity to criticism. Moreover, it is often projected onto significant others in the environment. This "splitting" is a critical aspect of the narcissistic individual that has special relevance for the narcissistic political leader (Volkan 1980).

In considering these aspects of the personality development of narcissistic individuals, it is important to emphasize that we are talking of a continuum. After all, it is the mother's pride, praise, and love which, when communicated in the context of reality with an appreciation of the child's individuality and limitations, leads to a healthy self-concept and self-confidence. The more unrealistic the expectations, the more likely we will find a narcissistic individual driven by dreams of glory.

The child may become the vehicle for the parent's unfulfilled dreams very early indeed. In my clinical work in family therapy, the mother of a troubled adolescent revealed that at the moment of conception she knew something very special had occurred. The mother of Robert J. Hawke, the Labor Party prime minister of Australia, said that she looked into the crib and knew that someday her son would be prime minister (d'Alpuget 1983). Some thirty years before he became chief of state, the mother of a future president of France remarked in a matter-of-fact fashion to her son's college friend, whom she had just met: "I'm so glad to meet you. I suppose you know that someday my son will be president" (personal communication, George Carver, 1975). Were these mothers merely prescient? No, rather they were revealing their special expectations of their offspring, the special manner in which they raised them, a self-fulfilling prophecy.

The letters of Woodrow Wilson's mother to her son, the future president, are a remarkable record of the origins of dreams of glory (Post 1983). Consider the following example:

My darling Boy, I am so anxious about that cold of yours—How did you take it? Surely you have not laid aside your winter clothing? Another danger is in sitting without fire these cool nights. Do be careful, my dear boy, for my sake. You seem depressed, but that is because you are not well. You need not imagine you are not a favorite. Everybody here likes and admires you. I could not begin to tell you the kind and flattering things that are said about you, by everybody that knows you. Yes, you will have no lack of friends in Wilmington—of the warmest sort. There seem to be an unusual number of young people about your age there—and of a superior kind—and they are prepared to take an unusual interest in you particularly. Why, my darling boy, nobody could help loving you, if they were to try. I have a bad headache this morning, dear—won't attempt to write you a letter. My chief object in writing is to tell you that I love my absent boy—oh so dearly . . . (Link 1966, 50)

In this brief missive, Mrs. Wilson communicates to her son (who is away, not at summer camp for the first time, as the tone of the letter suggests, but at college) that she and he are one and inseparable, that her well-being depends on him, and that among superior people he is especially admired. The perceptions and urgings of such mothers are not designed to produce sons of modest ambitions. Indeed, these early perceptions and the continuing psychological shaping undoubtedly played a major role in leading their "beneficiaries" to reach for—and achieve—the stars.

The concept of the Dream is particularly important to understanding the psychological development of future leaders. The Dream often arises earlier, in childhood or adolescence, but it is in the twenties that it is given adult form, and childhood fantasies are transformed into potentially achievable goals. The degree to which this transformation occurs depends in large part on the shaping influences of parents and other significant adults.

The influence of King Abdullah, the grandfather of King Hussein of Jordan, on the development of Hussein as a leader was profound. A charismatic man of towering political stature, Abdullah was ashamed of his son Talal, who suffered from chronic paranoid schizophrenia. He early selected his grandson to play a special role in the history of Jordan, and started shaping him to the role of future king. The boy was fifteen and at his grandfather's side on the steps of the Al Aqsa Mosque in Jerusalem when his grandfather was struck down by an assassin's bullet. Young Hussein too was struck by a bullet but was reportedly saved from death by the medal on his chest that his grandfather had given him earlier that day—probably a powerful determinant of Hussein's sense of destiny.

The more the grandiose dreams of childhood are left intact and adolescent narcissism is unmodified by reality, the greater the likelihood of persistent unrealistic fantasies and dreams. Persistent grandiose fantasies and difficulties in adapting to reality are attributes found in a number of left-wing terrorists who have been clinically interviewed (Bollinger 1981). Investigations of the psychology of terrorist behavior (Post 1984) suggest that narcissistic personality structures, although not universal, are frequently found in terrorists, particularly those who I term the "anarchic ideologues," such as the Red Army Faction of West Germany and the Red Brigades of Italy. Moreover, the analysis of the life course of West German terrorists (Jaeger, Schmidtchen, and Suellwold 1981) indicates a pattern consistent with the background of individuals who develop narcissistic personalities. Inadequate parenting was regularly reported, and a pattern of occupational, educational, and social failure was revealed. The terrorists maintained an exalted view of their own capabilities, blaming the government for their failures. They had "split off" the devalued, aggressive aspect of themselves, projected it onto the authority structure, and then justified their own aggressive antiauthority acts of political violence as being required to destroy the source of society's (and their) problems. Thus, some of the young people who choose the path of terrorism have not been able to reconcile grandiose and unachievable dreams with their realistic limitations.

Of particular help in making the transition to achievable dreams is the mentor. In Levinson's study, the mentor was usually eight to fifteen years older than the protégé. Biographies and autobiographies of military and political leaders regularly stress the shaping influence of an older role model. The relationship in its healthiest form is mutually beneficial, with the mentor taking pride in his protégé's achievements and having his own work benefit from the protégé's energies and talents. The protégé grows and learns from his model's experience and is assisted to ever higher levels of responsibility as his mentor opens doors for him.

The life of Stalin provides a fascinating example of the importance of the mentor relationship, and of the impact of the life cycle on the course of this relationship (Tucker 1973; Post 1980). As a young man in a very repressive seminary in Tbilisi, Georgia, that prohibited outside books, Stalin's adolescent rebelliousness to repressive authority was expressed by smuggling in the works of Marx and Lenin. Stalin became fascinated with the writings of Lenin and came to idolize him at a distance. He left the seminary at age twenty, and by age twenty-six was corresponding with Lenin, who, impressed by his young admirer, helped bring Stalin along the revolutionary path. The two had a close relationship, fighting together in the revolutionary cause.

But, however healthy the relationship, there comes a time when the man tires of being a promising bright young man and wants to achieve recognition in his own right. The degree of his urgency will in part be a reflection of his psychological maturity, and also of the willingness of the mentor to permit his protégé greater responsibility and autonomy.

These feelings are particularly apt to peak during the "age-thirty transition," the transition between the novice phase of early adulthood and what Levinson has dubbed the phase of "settling down." The age-thirty transition is often accompanied by feelings of "wanting to get on with it." It's time to get serious, time to settle down. In the years surrounding this transition (roughly age 28–33), the man feels, in Levinson's (1978) words, "If I want to change my life, if there are things in it that I don't like or things missing that I would like to have, this is the time to make a start for soon it will be too late" (85).

Art illuminates life, and in his fine novel *The Coup*, John Updike (1978) helps us understand the ambivalence of the protagonist, Colonel Eliellou, who has seized power from his aged mentor, the king of the fictional African kingdom of Kush. The king had given everything to Eliellou, had treated him like his own son, had taken him from obscurity and raised him to the heights. Yet, the colonel could not contain his impatience, even though one day the kingdom would be his. His dreams of glory had to be realized now, and he rationalized his own needs in terms of the needs of the people, which required that he remove his mentor from the seat of power.

In reviewing the biographies of a number of military leaders who assumed political control by means of coups, it is significant to note how frequently are encountered such phrases as "the twenty-eight-year-old major" and the "thirty-year-old colonel." Although I have not conducted a formal statistical analysis, it is my distinct impression that the period of the age-thirty transition is one of the peak periods for military takeovers.

Gamal Abdel Nasser is a case in point. He was a teenager when he became inflamed by the fires of nationalism that were sweeping through Egypt (Berindranath 1966). Caught up in the politics of protest, Nasser joined the Young Egypt Party at age sixteen. But it was not until he was in his age-thirty transition, at the age of thirty-two, that he led the free officers in the coup d'etat that overthrew King Farouk, profoundly altering the history of the Arab world. His fellow free officer and age peer Anwar Sadat, who succeeded Nasser as president of Egypt, was at his side.

During the period of settling down that is ushered in by the age-thirty transition, the predominant developmental goal is to consolidate the life structure. Levinson (1978) delineates two predominant tasks: to establish one's niche in society, and to work at advancement. But as the thirties wind down and the midlife transition approaches, an added urgency is imparted, especially if the goals have not been accomplished, if the dream has not been realized. This late settling-out period Levinson dubs "Becoming One's Own Man," or "BOOM."

But what is the psychological cost of being programmed for greatness? Can individuals who are designated in this fashion early in life ever achieve enough, ever be fulfilled, ever be truly satisfied? Scholars who have focused on the psychology of the life cycle (Erikson 1975; Vaillant 1977; Levinson 1978; Neugarten 1979) have found that, for the most part, individuals who are fulfilled in their personal relationships and are professionally successful accomplish the transitions of the life cycle with relative ease. As they go through the intense self-examination so characteristic of these transitions, they ask, "What have I accomplished? Am I a success?" If they are able to respond positively, these transitions are times of psychological consolidation and further growth.

But the criteria for success need to be carefully evaluated. Whose criteria? It is not success as measured by external standards but rather where the individual is in relation to his own internal goals. To be a cabinet minister at an early age may be perceived as failure by the narcissistic leader, if, programmed for the highest glory, only the prime ministership will do. Thus, it is the gap between reality and the Dream that is the measure of the stress of these transitions. And it is this gap that can propel leaders whose appetites for glory are as yet unsatisfied to acts of extreme assertion and major changes of political direction (Post 1980).

The Midlife Transition

Psychological seeds planted during the youthful period may only blossom later in life. In particular, the unsatisfied youthful aspirations may become particularly intense during the midlife transition, when, as Levinson points out, there is often an intensified need for self-actualization, for assertive action. The impulse to change careers in the business world, described by Levinson, may have parallels in the political world, with an increased push toward dramatic action.

The growing personal restlessness characteristic of the midlife transition may have contributed to dramatic changes of government through coups d'etat in a number of transitional societies. A personal need for self-actualization may have been congruent with the needs of the political moment in the officers who felt impelled to seize the reins of power.

Students of the life cycle find that the period leading up to the profound personal reassessment that occurs at midlife is frequently associated with major life-course decisions and actions. Political leaders are not immune to these psychological pressures; driven by dreams of glory, they are even more sensitive to them (Post 1980). Not just their inevitable physical decline but also the success of an envied peer can be a profound blow. The years leading up to and surrounding midlife as defined by society are the time of another peak in assertive leadership actions and, for some, for radical ideological revisions.

We have earlier observed the impact of Lenin as admired mentor to young Stalin. The life of Stalin provides a fascinating example of the constraints of the mentor relationship and the need to become one's own man (Tucker 1973; Post 1980). The two had a close relationship, fighting together in the revolutionary cause, but by age thirty-eight, in the era of becoming one's own man, Stalin was beginning to chafe under the restraint of Lenin's leadership. Their relationship became increasingly conflicted; at the height of his midlife transition, Stalin had an intense confrontation with Lenin, who shortly thereafter suffered an incapacitating stroke. Stalin had supplanted his mentor with a vengeance and had fully consolidated his power.

The aspiring revolutionary who, armed with idealism and a youthful sense of adventure, joins the cause in his late teens or early twenties may find himself increasingly cynical and disillusioned as he moves into his thirties. It has been observed that there are very few forty–year-old terrorists. After they have traveled a tortuous revolutionary path, what happens when those dreams of a brave new world are not yet realized?

The social psychologist Edward Klein provides an interesting example of a major change at midlife that occurred with an IRA terrorist he came to know (personal communication, 1983). Klein and Leonard Doob organized a number of Human Relations conferences that brought together Protestants and Catholics involved in the bloody conflict in Northern Ireland. The conferences forced individuals to engage in self-examination and enhanced their awareness of the humanity of the other side. One participant, who had been involved in terrorist activities since he was a teenager and was a demolition specialist, at age forty traded in his career in high explosives for a career as a social worker. He remained as committed to his cause as before, but he could no longer justify his deadly activities as serving that cause, and turned his energies to helping others.

What happens to deferred dreams of glory? What happens when the passage of time makes it increasingly clear that the dreams of one's youth, the dreams that have carried one throughout life, not only have not been achieved but will not be achieved? In the words of Langston Hughes again,

There's a certain amount of traveling in a dream
deferred . . . a certain amount of nothing in a dream
deferred . . . a certain amount of impotence in a dream
deferred. . . . There's liable to be confusion in a dream
deferred. . . . There's liable to be confusion when a dream gets
    kicked around

                                              Hughes 1974, 67

For some, the disappointment of shattered dreams and the consequent self-doubt and confusion can lead to a radical change in ideology. Angus McIntyre (1982) makes a compelling case that the narcissistic wound that Sir Oswald Mosely suffered when he did not become prime minister as rapidly as his personal timetable dictated led to his abrupt turn at midlife toward the ideology of fascism.

It is interesting to contrast the vicissitudes of narcissism in the middle years in two key senators who played important roles in American foreign policy: Wayne Morse and Key Pittman. Both served on the Senate Foreign Relations Committee; both distinguished themselves by their independence of mind and political sagacity; both clearly took pride in the important role they played in the American political scene. And both clearly had significant narcissistic elements in their personalities. However, Morse came to the end of his days with a sense of profound satisfaction in his achievements, while Pittman became progressively embittered and disillusioned, contributing to his own decline by drowning his despair in alcohol. Morse was very much "full of himself" and, despite criticism, had enough confidence in his own judgment to take a very lonely role early in the Vietnam War as one of only two senators to vote against escalating the war. Wilkins (1983) develops the interesting concept of Morse as a political mentor at a distance to a generation. On his deathbed, he expressed thanks for being able to serve (Davies 1983). Morse was driven to achieve, he had a personal quest, but his narcissism reflected a healthy self-esteem, and by all descriptions was an aspect of a basically healthy personality. His dreams were satisfiable; for him, playing the important role he did, with the satisfactions it brought, was "enough."

For Pittman (Glad 1983), in contrast, merely being chairman of the Senate Foreign Relations Committee was not enough. He had played an important behind-the-scenes role and provided wise counsel to Franklin Roosevelt, hoping to become a key foreign policy advisor to him. He wrote about his major advisor role well after it was clear that Roosevelt was not turning to him in a significant fashion—indeed, was not even consulting him on matters involving the Senate. He began to complain to members of Roosevelt's circle about this neglect, stressing that greater attention should be paid to senators.

Betty Glad's (1983) carefully documented record of Pittman's decline in influence makes it clear that Pittman's inability to restrain his expressions of dissatisfaction over the lack of recognition and attention paid to him contributed to the administration's further distancing itself from him. His narcissistic need for attention and recognition would not be stilled. Although Pittman did not criticize Roosevelt directly, he increasingly criticized those around him, behavior not designed to increase his acceptance in the inner circle. These attacks became more and more vituperative, more and more unbalanced, suggesting that at one level Pittman was saying, "If it weren't for you, I would be getting the recognition I deserve." This is somewhat reminiscent of the dynamics of the terrorists earlier described, who identify, blame, and attack outside forces as being responsible for their lack of success.

Glad (1983) provides fascinating documentary evidence to support her thesis that Pittman suffered from a narcissistic character disorder. In his diary, Pittman reveals the "split" earlier discussed when he describes two Key Pittmans: an idealized admired self and a baser self. Pittman both owns and disowns the baser aspect of himself—feelings and qualities that are inconsistent with his self-image but keep asserting themselves and impelling him to actions he later comes to regret. Always a heavy drinker, his alcohol consumption increased as his disappointment mounted, so that by the late 1930s he was drinking almost constantly. This led to a further unraveling as the alcoholism produced careless speech. During the late 1930s, on the eve of World War II, at a time when feverish diplomatic efforts were underway, without clearing his statement he made a public pronouncement that:

1. The people of the U.S. do not like the Government of Japan.
2. The people of the U.S. do not like the Government of Germany.
3. The people of the U.S., in my opinion, are against any form of dictatorial government, Communistic or Fascistic.
4. The people of the U.S. have the right and the power to enforce morality and justice in accordance with peace treaties with us. And they will. Our Government does not have to use military force and will not unless necessary. (Glad 1983)

Nontrivial words from the chairman of the Senate Foreign Relations Committee! Pittman's loose talk and alcoholism became the subject of conversation at cabinet meetings, where objects of his criticism, such as Harold Ickes, now took to the attack. As Glad (1983) notes, his drinking and shoot-from-the hip rhetoric led others to caricature and ridicule him. Former friends and supporters pulled away. His marriage deteriorated. His finances were in ruinous shape. The decline accelerated, and Pittman's judgment deteriorated to the point where he called on the president while drunk, pawed at him in a maudlin fashion, and suggested that he seize the British fleet. The gap between the dream and the reality widened all the more. Despite the clear evidence that he was ineffective and without influence, dreams of higher office flowered, and as it became clear that Roosevelt, who had broken with Vice President John Garner, would seek a third term, Pittman entertained the hope that Roosevelt would turn to him as his vice-presidential running mate. He died a broken man.

Although this is clearly the saga of profound alcoholic deterioration, it is alcoholism wed to narcissism, a combination often found in the narcissistic leader, whose narcissistic wounds beget increased alcohol consumption as balm to wounded ego, which begets destructive behavior, which leads to further narcissistic disappointment, and so forth. And the more unrealistic the dreams of glory, the deeper the wounds and the greater the need for alcohol's soothing balm.

The Late Adult Transition

The psychology of the period of old age should be of special interest to the field of political psychology, for a continuing concern in predicting governmental decisions and evaluating the potential for aggression is the judgment and emotional stability of the leadership, and aspects of the psychology of the aging period can affect these crucial attributes of leadership. During the decline of the Soviet empire, a striking number of leaders in the Communist world were in their late sixties and seventies. A striking number of Chinese Communist leaders were in their seventies and eighties. This section examines some of the normal psychological reactions of the later years, emphasizing the sense of increased urgency to accomplish one's goals. The next chapter, "The Psychopolitics of Illness in High Office," then describes the characteristics of early dementing illnesses, which, at first subtly, and later dramatically, can affect political behavior. Especially important are declining judgment and intellectual abilities, increased rigidity, an exaggeration of earlier personality reactions, and a tendency toward marked fluctuations in behavior.

The death in 1980 at age sixty of Feodor Kulakov of the Soviet Politburo highlighted the aged leadership of the Soviet Union; Kulakov, considered a prime contender to succeed Brezhnev, was among the youngest of the Soviet leaders. At that time, more than half of the full Politburo members were sixty-eight years old or older. The four top-ranking Soviet leaders, Leonid Brezhnev, Aleksey Kosygin, Andrei Kirilenko, and Mikhail Suslov, were all in their seventies. In Eastern Europe, there was the same preponderance of aging leaders. Most prominent was Marshal Tito of Yugoslavia, age eighty-eight.

In the People's Republic of China, more than half of the twenty-three full Politburo members were sixty-five or older. Of the five most senior leaders, three were veterans of the Long March and seventy years old or more: Marshal Yang Shangkun, age eighty; Deng Xiaoping, seventy-three; and Li Hsien-nien, seventy. Other Asian Communist countries had the same preponderance of aging leaders.

In considering the manner in which the psychological reactions of old age can contribute to irrational political behavior, perhaps the most important generalization to be made about the intellectual and behavioral capacities of aging individuals is that we can make no generalizations. Some individuals may show significant psychological or even physiological effects of the aging process as early as their fifties, while other individuals may function with no apparent decline in their intellectual or creative powers well into their eighties. In the world of arts and letters, we need only think of Sophocles, who was eighty-nine when he wrote *Oedipus at Colonus;* Goethe, who completed *Faust* at age eighty; and Michelangelo, who completed the *Pietà* at age eighty-four and served as architect to St. Peters until his death at eighty-nine. Particularly if an individual has had a rewarding and self-actualizing career, he may in old age contribute a dispassionate wisdom based on a lifetime's experience.

An example of a leader who performed extremely effectively, indeed often brilliantly, until just before his death at age seventy-eight is Chou En-lai. Yet, ironically, many of his leadership efforts were devoted to moderating the extreme reactions of the aged Mao Ze-dong, whose political leadership was significantly affected by the ravages of age.

Normal Psychological Reactions of the Aging Period

> Though he has watched a decent age go by,
> A man will sometimes still desire the world.
>
> Sophocles, *Oedipus at Colonus*

Even though there may be no evidence of physiological deterioration, some of the psychological reactions of individuals in their later years differ qualitatively from those of younger men. For many, the idea of losing their occupational status may be very threatening, particularly when their career has been an extremely rewarding one. This often leads to a sense of nostalgia, a tendency to see the present in terms of the past, to look to the past both for solutions and reassurance. The threat of loss of position and the increasing awareness of failing physical powers may lead some to react against being passive by becoming hyper-independent and preoccupied with demonstrating power and strength. This exaggerated demonstration of power may be necessary to deny the approaching ultimate powerlessness of death.

Time is of the essence. The same ambitions, wishes, feelings, yearnings, and desires that motivated the aging individual when younger are present in old age. It has been remarked by Martin Berezin, a specialist in geriatric psychiatry, that "old wishes never die; they don't even fade away." Although it is rare for aged individuals to think of themselves as old, as they become increasingly aware of the ebbing of time they often experience an increasing urgency to make their mark. They may ask, "What have I accomplished? How much time do I have left?"

There may be highly creative consequences from the psychological reactions to the perception that remaining time is short, for an individual may feel impelled to invest his or her remaining time with significance. This is movingly described by Michel de Montaigne:

> Especially at this moment, when I perceive that my life is so brief in time, I try to increase it in weight; I try to arrest the speed of its flight by the speed with which I grasp it, and to compensate for the haste of its ebb by my vigor in using it. The shorter my possession of life, the deeper and fuller I must make it. (*Essays*, bk. 1, 1580)

This sense of urgency in reaction to the perception of diminished time imparts an exaggerated quality to personality needs and drives, so that long-standing personality patterns and preexisting attitudes appear to be intensified. This sense of urgency is particularly true for individuals from cultures where a premium is placed on youth, ambition, and strength. Old age in such cultures can be particularly threatening.

In contrast, in cultures emphasizing strong family ties, where religious values stress tranquility and wisdom, the aged individual may be revered as a prophet and given a place of honor. In such countries, the approach of death may be accepted with equanimity, and therefore the distorting influence of advancing age on political behavior may be correspondingly diminished. Chou En-lai is a particularly striking example. He reacted quite stoically to the cancer of the stomach that ultimately took his life at seventy-eight, and from all outward indications was able to approach the tasks of government with his characteristic good judgment, balance, and intelligence.

Sclerosis in the Eastern Bloc: Aging Autocrats

The remarkable story of the dramatic collapse of the Eastern European socialist states is at one level the story of aging autocratic Communist leaders refusing to give up power and being unable to respond flexibly to the tides of political change. An aging, sclerotic political system led to the selection and retention of aging, sclerotic leaders. These leaders were unwilling to transform the system that so faithfully mirrored them.

The stagnation of leadership in the Eastern European states was even more pronounced than in the Soviet Union. In some cases, the same leader had been in place since shortly after the end of World War II when the Eastern European Communist governments had first been installed. The actuarial statistics for this group in terms of tenure and age was striking. The average age of the leadership of the Eastern European nations was seventy-six years at the end of their rule, while the mean duration of control of their countries was twenty-seven years. This is not a recipe for innovative responses to rapidly changing and unprecedented situations. These are the statistics not of stability but of stagnation.

For most of these leaders, the manner in which they came to power and exercised leadership inevitably linked them symbolically to totalitarian responses in the minds of their countrymen, even if they were otherwise disposed. This was particularly the case with Erich Honecker of East Germany, who erected the Berlin Wall; Gustav Husák of Czechoslovakia, who crushed the Prague Spring; and János Kádár of Hungary, who invited Soviet troops to crush the nascent revolution in his country in 1956.

The wisdom of the aged leader derives from having a long historical perspective with which to view events. The hazard is inappropriately labeling the present as an echo of the past, when the circumstances are quite different and call for new and innovative responses. With advancing age, leaders tend to see the present in terms of the past and to look to the past for solutions. At times of crisis in particular, aged leaders are apt to call upon the leadership behaviors that brought them success in their prime, and they may have difficulty in adapting to new situations that require new and creative solutions.

Another aspect may be worth considering when we contemplate aged men functioning in a leadership group, as was not infrequently the case in the last years of the Soviet Union and the Eastern bloc. The group-dynamic literature suggests a tendency for groups to seek consensus. Although individually there may be only minor problems with lack of flexibility, in a group setting the difficulties of the aging period may summate, with an inhibition of individual creativity and an increased tendency for rigid and inflexible decision making. This may well have contributed to the 1983 shooting down of the Korean airliner that strayed accidentally into Soviet air space, a decision made by the aged Soviet Politburo.

Effects of the Approach of the End of Life on the Narcissistic Leader

What happens to ambition unfulfilled? Does it wither in the grass, become the bone-dry dust of despair? Or, like a burning ember, does it smolder, only later to burst into flame? How the psychology of the late-adult transition affects a leader's response to frustrations and unfulfilled dreams at this stressful time of transition depends on the manner in which the leader negotiates earlier developmental phases and the nature of his or her psychology. Especially for narcissistic leaders driven by dreams of glory, it may be very difficult to cope with the end of a political career.

Leaders at the end of their years may increasingly become preoccupied that their lives are drawing to a close and that they have not yet fulfilled all of their ambitions, that they have not fully realized their dream. The impact of aging (Post 1973) is particularly stressful for narcissistic individuals, especially if they are consumed by a sense of mission. Their truncated personal timetables may lead to distortions in implementing political agendas as they try to fulfill their mission before time runs out.

It is instructive to contrast the last years of two of the giants who shaped the course of Chinese Communism—Mao Ze-dong and Chou En-lai.

No major historical event has but one cause, and the Cultural Revolution that gripped China in the late 1960s was a consequence of factional struggles, regional antipathies, personal conflicts, ideological differences, and bureaucratic competition. Yet no serious observer denies the impact, the determinative role, of the strong personal leadership of China's leader, Mao Ze-dong. He initiated the widespread disorder and near civil war, encouraged it while it was underway, legitimated it throughout, and he went to his grave in 1976, after the movement had run its disastrous course, still praising it.

The economic and political goals of both the Great Leap Forward and the Cultural Revolution were not necessarily misguided in the view of many China scholars. The problem was the pace at which Mao moved to actualize them. Given the state of societal inertia, the programs being enacted might well have required decades to accomplish rather than mere months. But Mao did not have decades. It was as if by an act of revolutionary will that he believed he could wrench China into the twentieth century and consolidate his revolution. Aged and aware that he had little time left, Mao reacted to impending death by imposing his personal timetable on his nation. It was Mao's intimations of mortality that contributed to the urgency with which he set these wrenching and destabilizing events in motion. Mao's perception that the time was short for accomplishing his goals could well have contributed to the destructive pace of the Great Leap Forward and the Cultural Revolution.

In Robert Jay Lifton's psychobiography of Mao, *Revolutionary Immortality* (1968), he argues that the Cultural Revolution was Mao's attempt to achieve immortality by identifying himself with a set of symbols that would live on beyond his death. Mao believed, with substantial justification, that his highly personalized revolution would be rejected by his successors. He feared that they would move closer toward the "imperialist" powers and work to dilute his strict communism, so that the revolutionary accomplishments of his life would not extend beyond his grave. For Mao, the meaning of his life could be ensured—and immortality achieved—only by becoming part of an ongoing revolutionary process. Continuing revolution became the essence of Mao's struggle against inevitable death. Though rejecting the divine, in striving to ensure perpetual pursuit of an egalitarian utopia, Mao sought to achieve a quasi-holy status.

Not every revolutionary leader, however, is so consumed at the end of his days. There are leaders in every political system that face their death bravely and seek to serve their people selflessly until the very end. By Mao's side until his own death was the loyal Chou En-lai. Reflective and judicious, Chou retained his emotional and political balance as he sought to moderate Mao's excesses, aiming to sustain the gains of the revolution without permitting its architect to destroy them. Only after he died was it revealed that Chou himself had been suffering from carcinoma of the stomach, a painful and debilitating disease, since 1972. Chou was stoic and self-contained until his death. He was first hospitalized in the spring of 1974, but the world did not hear of his ailment until later that summer. It was at that time that Deng Xiaoping was brought back into the power structure.

Chou and Mao offer contrasting political personalities whose reactions to the approach of the end of their years could not have been more different. Chou was psychologically mature, content within himself, and well organized. Mao was the epitome of the narcissistic charismatic leader, consumed by a messianic vision, a person to whom his reverential followers ascribed godlike status.

For the leader seeking glory, there is never enough glory, never enough time, and facing the end of life is intolerable. And thus it was that Mao Ze-dong, who, at the end of a remarkable revolutionary life, was clearly to be enshrined in the pantheon of history's great leaders, still did not feel fulfilled. Whatever the evaluation of the outside world, Mao's inner drive was undiminished, his ambition for revolutionary glory unfulfilled. Mao's appetite for glory and a role in history was insatiable. The specter of reaching the end of life before he had fully consolidated his revolution was intolerable, precipitating his terminal rush to glory.

Deng Xiaoping: Unable to Let Go, Reliving the Past

> Xiaoping, Xiaoping, in his 80s!
> Health OK, brain not sharp!
> Go home, quickly, go play bridge!"
>
> Poster in Tiananmen Square

> We still have a large group of veterans who have experienced many storms and have a thorough understanding of things. They were on the side of taking resolute action to counter the turmoil.
>
> Deng Xiaoping,
> reflecting on the events in Tiananmen Square in 1989

In considering political paranoia, it is sometimes difficult to determine whether an act was an example of hard-headed prudence, simple overre-action, or a reflection of paranoia. In fact, in a conspiratorial environment such as the Kremlin during the Soviet Union, the boundary between pru-dence and paranoia may be impossible to distinguish. The same sort of problem exists in determining whether an extreme action of an aging leader in a closed society in defense of his office or a cause close to his po-litical identity springs from rational calculation or is an irrational defense of a private self-identity. This problem in discriminating motivations is ex-emplified by Communist Party chief Deng Xiaoping's treatment of the prodemocracy youth movement in the People's Republic of China that ended, at Deng's orders, in the bloody massacre at Tiananmen Square.

At the conclusion of the Chinese Communist Party's National Congress in November 1987, the eighty-three-year-old Deng Xiaoping won interna-tional praise and admiration for engineering the first stable succession in China's modern history. Deng's efforts to consolidate and institutionalize the revolution and to transcend Mao Ze-dong's charismatic and highly personalistic rule dated back thirty-four years. At the 1956 party congress, when Deng was appointed general secretary, he emphasized the primacy of law and institutions and sought to curb the personal power of Mao. In giving up his own formal power thirty-one years later, Deng was, through his selfless example, personifying the issues he had championed throughout his life—the primacy of the country and its institutions over any one individual.

Premier Zhao Ziyang, who would now lead the forty-six–million-member party, indicated that Deng, even though he had given up his major positions of power, would retain considerable influence: "I have a high respect for Comrade Deng Xiaoping. I will often ask his advice so that I will be able to do things better."[3]

Deng had not given up all his positions, however, having chosen to retain control over China's People's Liberation Army and to remain as head of the party's Military Affairs Commission. As the architect of the economic reforms and China's most revered revolutionary veteran, Deng would continue to have ultimate decision-making power on major issues if he chose to exercise it.

In fact, despite his public postures of selflessness, Deng did not relinquish his hold on power. Only a year and a half later, it was Deng who made the decisions that led to the massacre in Tiananmen Square. It was Deng who rejected the anguished pleas of Zhao, who was at that time general secretary of the Communist Party, to negotiate with the demonstrators. It was Deng who threw his support to the hard-liner Li Peng, who had succeeded Zhao Ziyang as premier. It was Deng who was ultimately responsible for the decision to impose martial law, which led to the violence. And, in the aftermath, it was Deng who orchestrated the firing of his erstwhile protégé Zhao Ziyang.

Deng was supported in his decisions by the party elders, especially by his fellow octogenarian and close political ally Yang Shangkun, the Chinese president, a veteran of the Long March. On May 24, 1989, Yang made an important speech to the military commission explaining the decision to impose martial law, asserting that he and the other party elders "feel there is no way to retreat."[4] The speech demonstrates how aged leaders tend to oversimplify their interpretation of the present in terms of the past: "Back stepping will be the end of us. It will be the end of the People's Republic of China. It will be the restoration of capitalism, the goal which was sought by [U.S. Secretary of State John Foster Dulles]. After several generations, our socialism would be turned into liberalism." Yang's worldview was shaped and frozen in time forty years earlier. The generational succession struggle was epitomized in a joke circulating in China that the country's political crisis could be explained as "a bunch of eighty year olds telling a bunch of seventy year olds which sixty year olds should retire."

In the wake of Mao Ze-dong's disastrous policies, Deng had led the

movement to bring economic reform—the introduction of a market economy—to China. But it was to be economic reform under the strict control
of the Communist Party, whose leadership was not to be challenged. In
the communiqué announcing his dismissal, Zhao was accused of lending
support to the student protests, described as "turmoils" (a code word for
the upheavals of the Cultural Revolution). In so doing, he was guilty of
"splitting the party" and weakening the cardinal principles of Communist
Party primacy and opposition to bourgeois liberalization.[5] For Deng and
other members of the old guard, the student demonstrations and Zhao's
alleged support for them as well as his failure to submit to Central Committee discipline had threatened the primary role of the party and their
own authority.

There were, however, more personal reasons as well. To comprehend
fully the decision making leading to the tragedy at Tiananmen Square,
one must attempt to view the events from Deng's perspective. Deng
feared political disorder even more than he desired economic liberalization. He had good reason for doing so. A loyal follower of Mao Ze-dong
from the revolution's earliest days, Deng nevertheless suffered greatly
during the unchecked violence of the Cultural Revolution. During that
period, which seemed to pit young against old, Deng was stripped of his
rank and forced to "confess his errors" in a rite of public humiliation. His
son suffered a paralyzing spinal-cord injury when thrown from the second story of a building by Mao's young zealots, the Red Guards. Although Deng emerged from the Cultural Revolution with the reputation
of a hero, the emotional scars were deep.

The spectacle of the protesters in Tiananmen Square must have awakened painful memories of youth out of control violently rebelling against
their elders during the Cultural Revolution, in which Deng and his son
had been humiliated and injured. Never again should rebelling youth be
permitted to destroy the fabric of society, which depends so strongly on
Confucian traditions and unquestioned respect for the father's authority.
Never again should "turmoil" sweep the nation. This fear was not irrational on Deng's part nor on the part of his colleagues, some of whom had
suffered even more severely in the Cultural Revolution at the hands of
young people. Precisely because Confucian societies emphasize the subordination of youth to age, once that subordination is broken, the violence
of youth against authority becomes extremely dangerous.

During 1988 and the beginning of 1989, there was a great deal of social
unrest in China in response to the economic stress produced by Deng's
market reforms. Inflation was running at 30 percent, higher than in any
year since the Communist Revolution in 1949. Although the policies were
instituted by Zhao, they were clearly in response to Deng's leadership.

Student demonstrations began, and Deng, who for so long had been a hero to the youth of his nation, was now a target of blame. One placard read, "The Chinese people should not put their hope in a single benevolent emperor."

The event that catalyzed the youthful protestors in the spring of 1989 occurred on April 8. During a Politburo meeting, Hu Yaobang, the voice in the Politburo who was urging that the nation's youth succeed its aged leaders, was stricken with a heart attack. He died a week later.

In the summer of 1986, Hu had gone so far as to suggest that all of China's elderly leaders, including Deng, should retire. Hu's suggestion was rejected by an enlarged Politburo stacked with elderly leaders. As a consequence, Hu replaced Deng as the great hero to the nation's youth and was extolled for his courage in confronting the generation of aging leaders holding on to power. His fatal heart attack, occurring under such dramatic circumstances, sparked the powerful protests that followed. Within hours of his death, a poster appeared stating, "A great man has died, but false men still live." Hundreds, then thousands, of protesting students began to come to Tiananmen Square and other places of assembly around the country.

As the protests increased and the crowd in Tiananmen Square grew larger, Zhao argued for moderation and negotiation. But a hard-line editorial, "Take a Clear Stand against Turmoil," was drafted at the explicit instructions of Deng, condemning the student unrest and calling for a crackdown. Confirming that Deng's view of the crisis was determined by his past, each time the term "student movement" was used in the draft editorial, Deng substituted "turmoil," the pejorative used to describe the Cultural Revolution.

The threat to the primacy of the party and its maintenance of order was a threat to the core values of Deng, values shared with his elderly colleagues. If the leadership of the party was defeated by these young demonstrators, a new cultural revolution would result. To Deng and his close associates, that would have to be prevented at any cost.

Deng brought in troops from outside the Beijing military district, and the students were warned that violence was likely if they did not disperse. The students refused, the troops acted, and thousands of unarmed youth lost their lives in the violent confrontation that ensued. In the aftermath, Deng righteously reflected on the correctness of the regime's actions, emphasizing the need to avoid "turmoil" and celebrating the wisdom and experience of his aged comrades.

In fact, Deng himself seemed to be questioning his capacities and judgment. In a remarkable but little-noticed speech he made on November 18, 1989, to a group of officials, he warned them not to listen to him if he "starts to say crazy things as he gets older and becomes less clear-minded."[6] Could it be that he regretted the hard line that led to the tragedy at Tiananmen Square and wished that his subordinates had not listened to him, that he was recognizing that his age was affecting his leadership capacities, and that his judgment was compromised and had already failed him and his nation? Perhaps, but in a discussion with Secretary of State Henry Kissinger at about the same time, Deng indicated that he was not yet ready to retire, that he had too much to do, and that his leadership remained important.

History should record the tragedy at Tiananmen Square as the expression of conflict between generations, of youth impatient for change versus aged leaders holding on tightly to the reins of power lest everything they valued be destroyed. These leaders were trying to safeguard the accomplishments of their lifetimes, and given the behavior of youth during the Cultural Revolution, they had reason to fear the students in Tiananmen Square. But ironically, in the unwillingness of Deng Xiaoping and his old guard to retire and pass on the torch of leadership, they were tarnishing the very historical legacy they were hoping to preserve. Rather than go down in history as the great reformer who helped bring China into the modern world, Deng is apt to be remembered as the leader responsible for the massacre in Tiananmen Square, as the controlling aged leader who clung to power beyond his time.

Charles de Gaulle: Terminal Grandiosity

Charles de Gaulle identified himself with his country. He devoted his entire life to his country. De Gaulle's absolute faith in his own greatness meant that he never despaired of his country's eventual victory. There were many conquerors and would-be conquerors of France in de Gaulle's lifetime: the Germans, the Anglo-Saxons (as he referred to the Americans and the British), self-seeking French politicians, France's European partners, and the radical French youth of the 1960s. De Gaulle was to overcome them all.

De Gaulle's identification with his nation was shaped in his family home. His schoolmaster father was such an ardent nationalist that he never permitted any of his children to learn English. With the encouragement of his family, de Gaulle chose a military career, becoming an outstanding student at Saint-Cyr and at the École de Guerre.

Throughout his life, de Gaulle was a man who set himself apart. He chose his few friends with care. His biographer, Jacques de Launay (1968), has attempted to explain why de Gaulle always stood alone, to explain his apparent aloof arrogance. It was, he observes, not so much because de

Gaulle felt others to be his inferiors but because they were merely ordinary human beings, whereas de Gaulle believed himself to represent France. His motto, in effect, was "L'état c'est moi." This explanation, of course, confirms the lofty narcissistic pedestal from which de Gaulle viewed the world. This arrogant certainty conveyed a sense of strength to his followers, but it was the source of despair to his fellow Allied leaders during World War II. Churchill once remarked in frustration that the heaviest cross the Allies had to bear was the Cross of Lorraine, the symbol of France (Launay 1968; Werth 1966). This serene and stubborn grandeur not only supported de Gaulle after France's defeat by Germany but was his armor against the maelstrom of French politics.

> As for those whose profession was politics, who constituted the fauna of committees and congresses, they discovered what was to be their tragedy. This meteoric general, the product of Saint-Cyr and the École de Guerre, seemed to them the incarnation of all that was most hateful: the absolute preponderance of the State, the cult of the nation, the indifference to ideologies, the mistrust of political parties, plus an antagonism to them personally and a determination to dominate, to defy and if possible, to destroy them. The professional politicians understood on that day of the liberation of Paris that this man would be their tragedy. This staff of iron would not bend. They would have to take him or leave him, as we say, but the history that began that day, and that is still being made, would come down to this: each time they rejected him, they would be obliged to take him back, on pain of death. This insupportable man was an inevitable man. (François Mauriac, quoted in Isaak 1975)

De Gaulle was sixty-seven in 1958, when he agreed to become something very close to dictator of France in order to put down the revolt of French army officers in Algeria and so avoid a civil war. His leadership was strong and highly personal. During the next decade, the identification of France with de Gaulle was reaffirmed. To ignore either France or De Gaulle would produce a dramatic political action, making the stature of France and de Gaulle evident to all. But over this decade, his reactions were to become increasingly extreme.

Even the normal decline of once powerful abilities foreshadowing death is likely to create an overcompensation. Charles de Gaulle's inflammatory exhortations for an independent Quebec during the summer of 1967 were considered by his opponents to be the cries of a man on the edge of senility. One commentator even joked that "liberté, égalité, sénilité" was the motto of de Gaulle's government.

De Gaulle's actions, however, did not represent aberrational behavior in the face of senility. His actions were in continuity with his political style, attitudes, and behavior over the years, only more so. Le grand Charles was, if anything, grander than ever. He was beginning to parody himself.

Studies of the life cycle of political leaders do not support the notion that old age brings a mellowing (Post 1973, 1984). In fact, especially for narcissistic individuals, as a man grows older, he becomes more like himself. The same drives and needs that impelled the individual throughout his life are still present, only now the time is short, and for some the inhibitory effect of judgment is reduced. De Gaulle's exaggerated political behavior in the twilight of his political career is quite consistent with this pattern.

There was a direct relationship between de Gaulle's failing physical powers and his exaggerated political moves. Almost seventy-nine in 1967, he had progressively deteriorating eyesight. Three years earlier, in 1964, he had had prostrate surgery. Although he was by no means showing symptoms of senility, observers had noted he had lost his edge. Particularly when he was made aware of his diminished stature, either as a world leader or in a more personal sense when he was made forcibly aware of his failing power as a physically healthy and mentally alert man, he tended to behave in an exaggerated fashion to reaffirm his mastery. He would not be ignored. To the consummate narcissist, the end of the heroic life is unthinkable, a consummation devoutly to be denied. The weaker Charles de Gaulle felt physically, the more secondary France seemed politically, the more powerfully he seemed impelled to act politically, and the grander were his moves (Post 1973).

He had been in power in May 1968 when a student rebellion seemed for a while to threaten revolution. His supreme self-confidence, a reflection of his narcissistic personality, and his great political ability, had permitted him, until then, to stand his ground.

The student protest was particularly painful for de Gaulle, who thrived on public adulation. During the events of May his narcissistic belief in the indispensability of his own leadership came into conflict not only with his political perceptions but also with his grudging acknowledgement of his ill health. Should he remain a rod of iron and face down his opponents, or should he defeat them by sacrificing his own office?

De Gaulle chose the path of self-sacrifice in his nation's interest. He removed himself as an issue by permanently resigning his office. He deflected the protests into peaceful and legitimate channels by calling for national elections. He did what so few national leaders do when faced with illness and national revolt: he stepped aside. National disorder, and perhaps even revolution and civil war, were averted.

The narcissistic identification of a leader with his nation often makes it impossible for that leader to step aside. In the case of de Gaulle, it was that very identification that permitted him to step aside; for he recognized that the destiny of his nation, of his France, required it. But to be turned out of office by the nation to which he had given his life was painful, and he was to spend his remaining two years isolated and embittered. De Gaulle the private citizen died in the fall of 1970.

3

The Psychopolitics of Illness in High Office

Leaders, despite our wishes and their pretensions to the contrary, are merely flesh and blood creatures, as subject to the inevitable ravages of age and illness as the rest of us. Serious illness, both physical and mental, is an equal opportunity employer. It does not discriminate between the poor and the wealthy, between the man in the street and the VIP, between the private citizen and the public official. But when illness strikes the leader, unlike the man in the street, it poses a special problem, because the leader must be seen as strong and wise and in control. This image of strength and stability is critical to public confidence. Accordingly, there is a premium on concealing illness, or, if this is not possible, on minimizing the perception of the severity of impairment. Moreover, this need to preserve the image of health may cause leaders to avoid comprehensive diagnostic evaluation and treatment altogether or to undergo inadequate treatment secretly.[1]

Leader health and illness is all too rarely considered in evaluating and estimating leader decision making. Yet, even a cursory medical tour of the first half of the twentieth century, a period dominated by leaders of towering stature, makes startlingly evident that most of these towering figures were leading while ailing, and their illness may well have had an important, indeed critical, influence on their decision making.

Major Leader Illness in the First Half of the Twentieth Century

WOODROW WILSON'S MAJOR STROKE AND THE FIRST WOMAN PRESIDENT

A prime mover in the creation of the League of Nations, President Woodrow Wilson wanted the United States to enter the world peace organization as the capstone of his distinguished career of reform at home and abroad. Having returned from an exhausting effort at the Paris peace talks, where he failed to achieve the moderate conditions for the Versailles Treaty ending World War I that he so desperately sought, he was physically and psychologically depleted. The White House physician, Admiral Cary Grayson, counseled him to not undertake the grueling trip around the country necessary to mobilize support for Senate ratification of the League of Nations, but Wilson stubbornly refused. On the trip, Wilson suffered a debilitating stroke that paralyzed the left side of his body and severely impaired his intellectual functioning and ability to communicate, leading to an abrupt cancellation of his speaking tour.

Although Wilson's illness could not be concealed, its nature and the degree of the impairment could be, and was. Dr. Grayson reported that Wilson was suffering from nervous exhaustion and only needed a rest. During his period of recuperation, only three people had access to Wilson—his wife, Edith Wilson; his close personal aide, Joseph Tumulty; and Dr. Grayson. Issues requiring presidential decision were brought into the presidential bedroom by Tumulty, who also conveyed the decisions to key officials. But, in fact, the decisions made in the name of Wilson were being made by the troika of Mrs. Wilson, Tumulty, and Grayson. Afterward, Mrs. Wilson remarked, "You men make such a fuss. When Woody was ill, I had no difficulty running the country."

In the twilight of his distinguished political career, two failures were to cast a shadow over Wilson's accomplishments: the failure to achieve Senate ratification for his cherished League of Nations, and his inability to win moderate terms for the peace treaty after World War I. As a consequence of the harsh and punitive terms of the Versailles Treaty, Germany became an economic basket case, setting the stage for the rise of Adolph Hitler.

MacDonald and Hindenburg: Presenile Dementia

In the 1930s, two leaders were in positions to call attention to the danger posed by Hitler and to stem his rise to power, Ramsay MacDonald, prime minister of Great Britain, and President Paul von Hindenburg of the Weimar Republic of Germany. Both were suffering from presenile dementia and were unable to appreciate the danger posed by Hitler to the free world.

Ramsay MacDonald, prime minister of Great Britain in the early 1930s, was maintained in office by his party even though clearly demonstrating a mental incapacity, which almost certainly contributed to his failure to judge the growing threat posed by Hitler's rise to power. Indeed, evidencing the severity of his dementia, toward the end of his prime ministership

MacDonald became increasingly incoherent when he attempted to address Parliament.

President Hindenburg had become a national hero for his military leadership in World War I. In 1925, the hero of the Prussian forests was called back to serve as president of the republic. But by then, the solid and reliable military commander was suffering from many of the signs of presenile dementia. In his eighty-third year by 1930, he was "physically and mentally exhausted, hardly able to grasp, still less to solve, a political crisis for which he had neither training nor aptitude. . . . His stolidity for some time had been indistinguishable from inertia; the inertia now became a senile torpor" (Friedlander 1972).

When a ban on Nazi activity was rescinded at the suggestion of the ambitious and irresponsible Franz von Papen, the Prussian premier, Otto Braun, attempted to persuade Hindenburg of the dangers of this move, but "Hindenburg seemed so terribly uncomprehending," Braun said, unable to recognize that "he was being misled by unscrupulous men in such an infamous way" (Park 1986).

Hitler: Victim of Polypharmacy

Hitler himself was suffering from the indiscriminate pharmaceutical ministrations of his quack physician, Dr. Theodore Morell, known as the "meister-jabber" for the bewildering array of medications he administered to his patient. In his medical journals, Morell recorded no fewer than seventy-three medications he administered to Hitler, including a wide variety of sedatives, stimulants, hypnotics, tonics, vitamins, and hormones. Included in this pharmaceutical cocktail was extract of bull testis, hormones from the female placenta, several varieties of opium, belladonna, barbiturates, and steroids such as cortisone. He also gave his own golden Vitamultin tablets to Hitler, which he also marketed through his patent medicine company. The tablets contained methamphetamine. Hitler especially liked these pills. For his chronic sinusitis, Hitler began receiving the recommended treatment at the time, twice daily swabbings of the nasal membranes with a 10 percent cocaine solution. Because of his many meetings and unavailability for regular treatments, his ear-nose-throat physician devised a cocaine inhalator, which Hitler regularly employed. So, in the current jargon of the streets, Hitler was simultaneously taking "speed" and "coke."

How this pharmaceutical cocktail of methamphetamine, cocaine, and other stimulants affected his decision making is difficult to gauge. Methamphetamine alone has major deleterious effects on decision making, effects that would be augmented by cocaine. These include restlessness, excitement, irritability, impairment of judgment, and frequently paranoid ideas. It is interesting to consider the following description of Hitler's reactions in view of the possibility of significant influence of stimulant drugs:

> His fists raised, his cheeks flushed with rage, his whole body trembling, the man stood there in front of me, beside himself, and having lost all self-control. After each outburst of rage, Hitler would stride up and down the carpet edge, then suddenly stop immediately before me and hurl his next accusation in my face. He was almost screaming, his eyes seemed about to pop out of his head and the veins stood out on his temples. (L'Etang 1979, 8)

FRANKLIN DELANO ROOSEVELT: THE SICK MAN OF YALTA

In considering the effects of disability on the political leadership of Franklin Delano Roosevelt, the disabling effects of poliomyelitis with which he struggled throughout most of his political life comes readily to mind. But the illness that was particularly consequential was a serious decline in his physical health associated with cardiovascular and pulmonary illness that affected his decision making. This was obvious by December 1943 on his return from the Tehran Conference, when he appeared bone tired and his characteristic spark and vitality were missing. Evaluated at Bethesda Navy Hospital by a staff cardiologist, Dr. Howard Bruenn, Roosevelt was found to be suffering from congestive heart failure, significant hypertension, acute bronchitis, and long-standing pulmonary disease. Despite the gravity of Commander Bruenn's findings, his superior, the White House physician, Admiral Ross McIntire, issued a bland and reassuring medical communiqué to the effect that, for a man of his age, Roosevelt was in remarkably good health and ordered Commander Bruenn to not discuss the gravity of his findings with Roosevelt or Roosevelt's family, nor to reveal the seriousness of Roosevelt's condition to the public.

Roosevelt's eldest son and political advisor James bitterly remarked later that "I have never been reconciled to the fact that father's physicians did not flatly forbid him to run [in 1944]. . . . The fourth-term race in 1944 was Father's death warrant" (Roosevelt and Shalett 1975, 311, 313).

On Inauguration Day in 1945, John Gunther wrote, "I was terrified when I saw the President's face. I felt certain he was going to die. It was gray, gaunt and sagging, and the muscles controlling the lips seemed to have lost part of their function" (Gunther 1950, 31).

At the Yalta conference in February 1945, Roosevelt was obviously impaired by a combination of hypertension, arteriosclerosis, and congestive heart failure secondary to hypertension. Lord Moran, Prime Minister Winston Churchill's physician, observed:

> The President looked old and drawn; he had a cape shawl over his shoulders and appeared shrunken; he sat looking straight ahead with his mouth

open, as if he were not taking things in. Everyone was shaken by his appearance and . . . seemed to agree that the President had gone to bits physically . . . It was not only his physical deterioration that had caught their attention. He intervened very little in discussions, sitting with his mouth open . . . I doubt, from what I have seen, whether he is fit for his job here. He has all the symptoms of hardening of the arteries of the brain in an advanced stage, that I give him only a few months to live. (Moran 1966, 218, 223, 226)

Roosevelt died in April 1945 of a massive cerebral hemorrhage.

WINSTON CHURCHILL: PROPPING UP A FIGUREHEAD

Ironically, the same Lord Moran who so clearly observed that Roosevelt was near death at the Yalta Conference was later to play a leading role in propping up Winston Churchill in office in his last prime ministership, despite obvious progressive arteriosclerotic dementia. His physician had recognized Churchill's failing powers before his election in 1951, expressing doubts in his diary as early as 1947. He was concerned that Churchill's mind was no longer fertile and expressed "doubt whether he is up to the job." Yet he wrote in 1951 that his duty as a physician was to see that Churchill stayed in politics and stayed in office as long as possible—an interesting interpretation of the Hippocratic oath, apparently similar to that of Dr. McIntire, Roosevelt's physician, of whom Moran had been critical.

When he assumed the mantle of prime minister for the last time, in September 1951, Churchill was a sick old man, a veritable walking textbook of pathology, with significant illnesses affecting his heart, brain, lungs, gastrointestinal tract, skin, and eyes, and a medical history that included several episodes of pneumonia and cerebral ischemia, a heart attack, a major stroke, diverticulitis, and intermittent depression, which Churchill called "my black dog." Shortly after assuming office, his decline became evident to the inner circle. He was often unable to follow the flow of conversation, easily broke into tears, and was frequently irritable and short tempered. In June of 1953, with his putative successor, Foreign Minister Anthony Eden, himself sidelined with his third surgery for biliary tract disease, Churchill suffered a major stroke. The inner circle decided to conceal this illness from public view. Lord Moran supported the cover-up. The stroke accelerated a progressive dementia, which was magnified by frequent bouts of depression. Moreover, in his zeal to keep his patient going, Dr. Moran prescribed a bewildering variety of stimulants and sedatives, referred to by Churchill as "majors, minors, reds, greens and 'Lord Morans.' " Taken with alcohol, as was often Churchill's habit, these medications only further magnified his mental confusion.

JOSEPH STALIN: TERMINAL PARANOIA

Throughout his career, Stalin displayed a paranoid orientation. It can be argued that in the conspiracy-ridden Kremlin, a leader who was not highly suspicious and alert to betrayal would not long survive. At a party congress in 1923, Stalin declared:

> We are surrounded by enemies—that is clear to all. The wolves of imperialism that surround us are not dozing. Not a moment passes without our enemies trying to seize some little chink through which they crawl and do harm to us. (Tucker 1973, 460)

Always alert to danger, he ruthlessly eliminated enemies, real and imagined. The degree of his paranoid suspiciousness would have seemed pathological anywhere other than the conspiracy-ridden Kremlin, where to a significant degree it could be masked. Obsessed with a fear of assassination, before public appearances in Red Square he would have a million onlookers searched and searched again. In the 1940s, as his paranoia mounted further, some twenty-three million people lost their lives in the purges, according to Robert Conquest, as Stalin sought to eliminate all enemies of the state, real and imagined (Conquest 1973). Of course, in so acting, he was indeed generating enemies, confirming his paranoid suspicions. His chief of secret police, Lavrenty Beria, adroitly manipulated Stalin's growing paranoia. One suspicion whispered in Stalin's ear would be sufficient to eliminate a political rival. By 1953, Stalin was in a frank clinical paranoid state, obsessed with fear of a bizarre plot, the so-called Doctors' plot. The elements of this paranoid delusion were that a group of Jewish doctors in cooperation with the Western powers and their allies within the Soviet Union were scheming to murder Soviet leaders. A purge of major proportions was being planned when Stalin died of a massive cerebral hemorrhage.

Concealment of Leader Illness

As the histories of Wilson's, Roosevelt's, and Churchill's illnesses make clear, even in democratic systems the inner circle around the leader can successfully mask the degree of illness of their leader from public view. In considering the problem of disability in high office, there is a paradox: the more severe the disability, the less problematic it is in terms of the potential for political distortion of medical diagnosis and treatment. The acute disability—stroke, myocardial infarction, acute gastrointestinal bleeding—that is dramatic in onset and medically incapacitating cannot readily be concealed. It will almost certainly come to public notice, and medical treatment will be administered in the bright glare of public attention.

But it is the insidious illness, the subtle disability, not readily obvious, that in many ways is the most problematic for the political system. It is the gradual disability, subtle in its initial manifestations, that will be most easily concealed. When the onset is gradual and the symptoms are fluctuant, the leader is unlikely to present an obvious or consistent public image of medical impairment, even though the disability is evident to the inner circle. In such a circumstance, if the leader and his inner circle ignore how much the illness is compromising his decision making and effectiveness and carefully orchestrate his public appearances, the presence or degree of the disability can be significantly obscured. Such a situation can present to a conscientious leadership circle a choice between being loyal to what may be a temporarily ill leader and deceiving the public.

But there is another hazard as well. The insidious illness, gradual in onset, varying in degree, may not be readily apparent to the inner circle, including the president's physician. They may collectively "cast a blind eye" toward the disability, for the cost of recognizing it would be too high.

Distorting and Minimizing Presidential Illness

THE ATTEMPTED ASSASSINATION OF RONALD REAGAN

When President Reagan appeared at the window of his hospital room after the nearly fatal assassination attempt by John Hinckley in April 1981, the world watched in amazement, and the nation was cheered by the apparently rapid pace of his recovery. The nightly news regularly showed clips of a vigorous Reagan in good spirits. But, in fact, these moments were carefully chosen, and the president was seriously disabled:

> Reagan's closest advisers soon learned it was an act. The morning after Reagan's first and reassuring public appearance, the president limped from his bedroom to an adjoining room in the upstairs residence of the White House. He emerged slowly, walking with the hesitant steps of an old man. He was pale, and disoriented. Those who observed him were frightened. Reagan hobbled to a seat in the Yellow Oval Room, started to sit down and fell the rest of the way, collapsing into his chair.
>
> He spoke a few words in a raspy whisper and then had to stop to catch his breath. He looked lost. The pause wasn't enough and his hands reached for an inhaler, a large mask-like breathing device next to his chair. As he sucked in oxygen, the room was filled with a wheezing sound.
>
> Reagan could concentrate for only a few minutes at a time, then he faded mentally and physically, his wounded lung dependent on the inhaler. Dur-

ing the following days he was able to work or remain attentive only an hour or so a day.

The few who were granted access to the president were gravely concerned. This was supposed to be the beginning of the Reagan presidency, but at moments it seemed the end of the Reagan they knew. . . . His aides began to consider that his was going to be a crippled presidency—that it would, at its very beginning, devolve into something similar to Woodrow Wilson's at the end, a caretaker presidency, and that they would be reduced, or elevated, to a team of Mrs. Reagan's.

The senior aides were intent on protecting this terrible secret and their own uncertainty, at least until the prognosis was clearer. (Woodward 1987)

The aides did not consider invoking the Twenty-fifth Amendment, which governs what happens when a president becomes disabled. The net effect was that executive decisions were being made not by the elected vice president but by the inner circle of appointed officials. Nor was the Twenty-fifth Amendment invoked when President Reagan was undergoing abdominal surgery for cancer of the colon.

IMPACT OF POLITICAL CONTEXT AND LEADER PERSONALITY ON MEDICAL DECISION MAKING AND TREATMENT

The degree to which political considerations bear on decisions concerning executive capacity is strikingly illustrated by the manner in which President Reagan resumed the reins of power after surgery for colon cancer in 1985. Comments to the contrary notwithstanding, the Twenty-fifth Amendment was not officially invoked at this time, despite the exchange of letters between the president and Vice President Bush. Indeed, comments by White House staff at the time weakened the intent of this part of the amendment, which was to ensure the nation that an able leader was in charge.

President Reagan was disoriented after awakening from surgery, a nearly three-hour procedure. Herbert L. Abrams's meticulous research has documented the casual, ad hoc manner in which the decision was made that the president was competent to resume official authority (Abrams 1992). White House Counsel Fred Fielding, Chief of Staff Donald Regan, and White House Press Secretary Larry Speakes devised their own test. A two-sentence letter had been drafted for the president to sign in order to regain his office. If the president could understand the letter, did that mean he was sufficiently lucid to resume the presidency, they asked his surgeon. The surgeon responded, "Yup." (A surgeon may be the best judge of respiratory capacity, but surely not the best judge of cognitive capacity.) No other physicians, including the White House physician, were involved in this decision; no screening mental status exam was given; and no consideration was given to using even the simplest test of cognitive functioning. Nor was the president asked whether he felt able to resume the burdens of the presidency. It was believed that the sooner the president resumed the responsibilities of office, the sooner the public would be reassured. It was essentially a political decision.

During his recovery, the president was asked to sign a "special finding" authorizing the decision to ship arms to Iran in return for the hostages. A year later, when the Iran-Contra scandal broke, President Reagan claimed he could not remember the decision to ship arms to Iran, a decision made while he was recovering from surgery. During the Iran-Contra hearings, Attorney General Edwin Meese stated that President Reagan approved the shipment while "recovering from surgery and that his memory could have been impaired as a result of postoperative medication" (Abrams 1992). It was politically expedient to declare the president competent to regain the office immediately after the surgery, and it was politically expedient a year later to suggest the president's inability in order to exculpate him from responsibility for Iran-Contra.

Concealing presidential impairment was again to become an issue in the aftermath of the Iran-Contra scandal. When Senator Howard Baker took over the position of White House chief of staff, he decided to have an inquiry to determine what the flaws were in the White House decision-making process and asked an experienced aide, James Cannon, to systematically conduct an assessment. Cannon interviewed a number of senior White House officials who described an inattentive, often distracted president who appeared uninterested in his job: "All he wanted to do was watch movies and television at his residence" (Mayer and McManus 1988). Cannon was sufficiently concerned about this that in his report he recommended to Baker that he "consider the possibility that Section 4 of the Twenty-Fifth Amendment should be applied" because he had concluded that the president "was at the brink of being physically and mentally incapable of carrying out his responsibilities." Baker took the report seriously, and, accompanied by Cannon, he met with President Reagan the next day (Abrams 1992). After interviewing the president, he satisfied himself that there was no basis for such a consequential step, and the matter was closed. Note that no physician or psychologist was involved in making the judgment that the president was physically and mentally capable of carrying out the duties of the president; it was made by a political figure.

François Mitterrand: Metastatic Prostate Cancer

In January 1996, the former physician to President François Mitterrand produced quite a stir when he revealed that Mitterrand had concealed his prostate cancer for decades. Mitterrand had succeeded Valery Giscard d'Estaing in office; his predecessor, Georges Pompidou, had concealed from public view, with the connivance of his inner circle and his physicians, the bone marrow cancer, multiple myeloma, that ultimately claimed his life. On assuming the presidency in 1981, Mitterrand called in Dr. Claude Gubler and told him that he had prostate cancer that had spread to his bone and solemnly declared, "We must reveal nothing. This is a state secret to which you are bound." By November 1994, only six months before he would hand over the presidency to Jacques Chirac, Mitterrand was so ill he could not even stand up to receive visitors. At a press conference, asked why he did not reveal his serious illness and whether it hadn't affected his decision making, Mitterrand pointed to his forehead and declared, "My decision making is up here, and [pointing to his groin] my cancer is down there."

But of course this cannot be the case. Suffering from terminal illness must inevitably affect decision making.

John F. Kennedy: A Lifetime of Illness and Pain Concealed

Newly uncovered medical records reveal that illness—and a spectrum of powerful medications—played a continuing role throughout John F. Kennedy's life and political career. Kennedy concealed his illnesses throughout his life, and his family continued this concealment after his assassination. He first suffered from colitis as a teenager and probably began taking powerful corticosteroid medication then, medications with serious side effects, including duodenal ulcers and osteoporosis, from both of which Kennedy was to suffer.[2]

From 1940 on, Kennedy suffered from severe back pains, probably as a result of the steroid-induced osteoporosis. He made use of his father's influence to enlist in the Navy in the spring of 1941 without a physical examination. After leaving the service, in 1945, he was observed by a companion in Castle Hot Springs, Arizona, to look "jaundiced—yellow as saffron and thin as a rail," and in 1946 he was diagnosed as suffering from Addison's disease, a life-threatening insufficiency of the adrenal glands, a very serious illness requiring twice-daily steroid injections (Dallek 2003, 104).

He later developed osteoporosis and progressive degenerative back disease with vertebral collapse in his lower back, and by 1950 he was suffering from constant back pain. In April 1954, Lahey Clinic surgeons recommended a complicated surgical procedure that would place him at extreme risk because of the Addison's disease. Kennedy was told his chances of surviving surgery were only 50/50, but, according to his mother, he told his father that "he would rather be dead than spend the rest of his life hobbling on crutches and paralyzed by pain." After surgery was postponed three times in order to stabilize his endocrine system, in October 1959 he underwent surgery in New York's Hospital for Special Surgery. The three-and-a-half hour procedure was only a limited success.

From the middle of the 1950s on, Kennedy required extensive medication to manage his illnesses, including powerful narcotic medications such as codeine, Demerol, and methadone to control his back pain. He also took the stimulant Ritalin, barbiturates for sleep, and both major (Stelazine) and minor (meprobamate) tranquillizers for tension and anxiety. At times he was taking as many as eight different medications a day. From May of 1955 until October of 1957 he was hospitalized nine times—for a total of forty-five days—for back pain, colitis, weight loss, abdominal pain, and throat and urinary tract infections. The image of vigor he conveyed belied chronic pain and the powerful narcotic medication required to control that pain. Throughout his political career, Kennedy concealed his illnesses, and Bobby Kennedy, during JFK's run for the presidency, described his brother as being in "superb physical condition."

Before press conferences, he would often require "seven to eight injections of procaine in the back in the same sitting" from Dr. Janet Travell to control his pain, according to Dr. Jeffrey Kelman, a physician who reviewed his medical records.

But despite the plethora of physical illnesses and medications, Robert Dallek, author of *An Unfinished Life: John F. Kennedy, 1917–1963* (2003), concluded that the effects of the illnesses and their treatment did not incapacitate him. The detailed transcripts and recordings during the Cuban Missile Crisis reflect a Kennedy lucid and in firm command. But, as Dr. Lawrence Altman and Scott Purdum observe, at the time of the Cuban Missile Crisis "he was taking anti-spasmodics to control colitis; antibiotics for a urinary tract infection; and increased amounts of hydrocortisone and testosterone along with salt tablets to control his adrenal insufficiency and boost his energy."

In 1962, John Kennedy declared: "Life is unfair." Altman and Purdum note, with reference to Kennedy, that most citations of this epigram, unaware of the illness that plagued Kennedy's life, omit the words that follow: "Some people are sick and others are well."   .

As Dallek ironically observed, "The evidence suggests that Kennedy's physical condition contributed to his demise. On November 22, 1963, Kennedy was, as always, wearing a corsetlike back brace as he rode through Dallas. Oswald's first bullet struck him in the back of his neck. Were it not for the back brace, which held him erect, the second, fatal shot to the head might not have found its mark" (Dallek 2002).

Being a VIP Can Be Dangerous for Your Health

The above examples consider the dangers to government of concealing leader illness. But concealing leader illness can also be dangerous to the leader—indeed, it can have fatal consequences, as illustrated by the cases of former Governor Earl Long of Louisiana and President-elect Tancredo Neves of Brazil.

In what was to be his last hurrah, the sixty-five-year-old former governor Earl Long was running for a congressional seat in 1960 in a hotly contested election against a younger vigorous opponent. On the morning of Election Day, Long suffered a heart attack, leading his doctor to strongly recommend hospitalization—immediate treatment with anticoagulants, oxygen, and bed rest can often minimize the extent of damage and prevent serious complications. But Long, fearing that news of his heart attack could throw the election to his opponent, chose to stay at home, claiming indigestion. He did not enter the hospital until that evening, after the polls closed. The ruse worked, and Long won the seat by a narrow margin. But he never occupied the seat, for nine days later, the newly elected congressman died.

Tancredo Neves was elected president of Brazil on January 15, 1985, ending twenty-one years of military rule. Like Earl Long, he never was to occupy the seat of office. During the long interregnum between the day of the election and his inauguration, Neves began to suffer from gastrointestinal distress. After initially doctoring himself, he consulted with a physician who informed him he was suffering from diverticulitis, a common, and not particularly serious, inflammation of an intestinal pouch. When the illness did not respond to antibiotic treatment, the doctor recommended surgery. Fearing a coup would occur, and not trusting the vice president–elect, Neves decided to defer the surgery until after he had assumed the presidency on March 15. He nearly made it. On March 14, the eve of his inauguration, the diverticulum burst, leading to generalized peritonitis. What followed was almost a caricature of the disasters that can befall VIP patients.

Although the political capital of Brazil is Brasilia, the commercial and medical capitol is Sao Paulo. For political reasons, the family decided to have the emergency surgery performed in Brasilia. But when he came fully scrubbed to the operating table, the chief surgeon from Brasilia, awestruck by his VIP patient, discovered that he had left his glasses at home. He broke scrub, leaving his patient anesthetized upon the table, raced home with his driver to retrieve his glasses, and then began the first of what would be seven operations. The family, dissatisfied with the

Brasilian surgeon, had the surgical team from Sao Paolo flown to Brasilia, leading to an intense medical rivalry that was dubbed "the war of the princes" by the newspapers. The chief surgeon of the Sao Paulo team dryly remarked that the best medical equipment they had in Brasilia was the air shuttle to Sao Paulo. Complicating the situation, the hospital lost control to politicians and journalists who flooded the facility, and Neves's wife further complicated the matter by insisting that only male nurses care for her husband.

The Sao Paulo group finally was able to control the situation, and on March 15, Neves underwent a second three-hour procedure, conducted this time by the Sao Paulo surgeons, who immediately discovered that inadequate suturing by the first surgical team had led to serious complications with the abdominal wall breaking down. On March 26, Neves was medically evacuated to Sao Paulo, where he underwent a third procedure, a fourth on April 2, a fifth to treat two new abscesses, and a sixth. At this point he was in critical condition, and on April 6 required a tracheotomy to assist with breathing. Kidney abscesses then developed, requiring a seventh procedure on April 11. The next day, his kidneys shut down, and he was put on dialysis. Prayer meetings were held throughout the nation, with national "chains of energy" called for. On April 21, he died, never having been inaugurated.

The concern that optimal medical care could be politically fatal led both Long and Neves to conceal their illness and delay needed treatment, with the result that what they deemed would be optimal political care was medically fatal.

Broken Minds and Broken Hearts: The Effects of Illness on Leaders' Mental and Emotional Reactions

The American people want a president who is in full control of his mental faculties and emotional reactions, wise, knowledgeable, judicious, temperate, decisive. Disorders, both functional and organic, that impair the leader's decision making and judgment are the most stressful for the political system. These disabilities are the most difficult to evaluate and to manage, and the easiest to mask—a dangerous combination for the nation. Because of the collective need for the leader to be seen as decisive and in control, illnesses that affect the leader's mental processes and/or emotional reactions are especially threatening to the public. Accordingly, the perceived need to conceal is particularly strong for mental illness. Such was the case with the suicidal depression that tragically claimed the life of President Clinton's long-time friend and deputy White House counsel, Vincent Foster, in 1993. The ambitious Foster was seriously depressed but, aware of the stigma surrounding mental illness, had not entered treatment. When his body was found, he had with him an unfilled prescription for an antidepressant from his doctor in Little Rock and the names of three Washington-area physicians, whom he never consulted. In his last note he bitterly observed about Washington that "ruining people is considered sport." Despite major advances in medical science in understanding the etiology and treatment of depression, the victims of this serious mental illness continue to be stigmatized and are perceived by the public as weak and unstable.

The revelation of a VIP's psychiatric illness and treatment must be avoided at all costs, a lesson painfully learned during the 1972 U.S. presidential campaign. The Democratic Party's presidential nominee, Senator George McGovern of South Dakota, chose Senator Thomas Eagleton of Missouri to be his vice-presidential running mate. Ten days after the Democratic National Convention, aware that the Knight newspaper chain was about to break the story, Eagleton acknowledged that in his twenties he had been voluntarily hospitalized for depression and had undergone a series of electroshock treatments. The revelation produced a firestorm. Democratic prospects plummeted in the polls, and party leaders felt they had no choice but to remove Eagleton from the ticket, replacing him with Sargent Shriver. McGovern, perceived to be injudicious and ineffective as a leader, in part because he had initially chosen Eagleton to be his running mate, lost the election to Richard Nixon by a wide margin. Although the Eagleton episode occurred more than a quarter of a century ago, the passage of years has not done much to diminish the taint of mental illness.

JAMES FORRESTAL: SUICIDAL DEPRESSION

After serving for three years as Secretary of the Navy, James Forrestal was confirmed as the nation's first secretary of defense on July 27, 1947, named to this distinguished position by President Harry Truman. His was a clarion voice warning of the dangers from the Soviet Union. Before serving with distinction as secretary of the navy, he had achieved notable success in the private sector as an investment banker, having risen to the presidency of the investment banking firm Dillon, Read and Company by age forty-six. A man of immense ambition, Forrestal had been seen by some as a possible future presidential candidate. Sharing the widespread conviction that Governor Thomas Dewey of New York would win the presidency in the 1948 election, Forrestal had signaled his willingness to continue to serve in a Dewey administration, either as secretary of defense or secretary of state. After the Truman upset victory, a swirl of controversy developed over Forrestal's lack of faithfulness to the Democratic Party and his lack of financial support for the ticket, and he became the target of widespread media attacks on his integrity and loyalty.

Seeing his political future destroyed, Forrestal became seriously depressed and developed insomnia, loss of appetite with weight loss, and fatigue. He became increasingly paranoid as well.[3] The gravity of his illness was unrecognized by those around him, who thought he was suffering from "exhaustion." A workaholic, Forrestal remained in office, but President Truman isolated him from decision making, and the isolation only magnified his paranoia. When Truman informed Forrestal that Louis Johnson would replace him on May 1, Forrestal was shocked and became even more depressed and paranoid, with delusions that he was being pursued by Communist and Zionist agents. Rather than being admitted immediately to a psychiatric hospital, he was instead flown to a rich man's retreat, Hobe Sound, where the eminent American psychiatrist William Menninger diagnosed him as suffering from "combat fatigue." When he ultimately was admitted to the Bethesda Naval Hospital, rather than being treated on the psychiatric ward on the first floor, he was placed in the VIP suite in the hospital's tower. He committed suicide by plunging to his death.

Had he been treated like an ordinary seaman, this talented public servant might well have recovered from his suicidal depression. In many ways, Forrestal's death can be seen as a result of his high status. Before he leaped to his death, Forrestal copied in a notebook the melancholic chorus from Sophocles' play *Ajax*:

> Thy son is in a foreign clime
> Worn by the waste of time
> Comfortless, nameless, hopeless
> Save in the dark prospect of the yawning grave
>
> Oh, when the pride of Graecia's noble race
> Wanders, as now, in darkness and disgrace,
> Better to die and sleep
> The never waking sleep than linger on
> And dare to live when the soul's life is gone.

A psychiatrically trained medical corpsman would have recognized this as a literary suicide note, but the corpsman assigned to Forrestal paid no attention to the poignant despair conveyed by this selection.

Calvin Coolidge: Depression in the White House

Severe debilitating depression has been an occupant of the White House. As Robert E. Gilbert, a political scientist who has specialized in presidential illness, has persuasively demonstrated, President Calvin Coolidge's reputation for being a "do nothing" president in his second term was almost certainly the consequence of a severe depression precipitated by the death of his adolescent son (Gilbert 1988). In July 1924, just one month after Coolidge's nomination by the Republican National Convention as their candidate for president, Coolidge's favorite son, Calvin Jr., developed a blister after playing tennis on the White House grounds without wearing socks. The blister became infected. Young Coolidge developed septicemia, and three days later he died. President Coolidge fell into a profound grief from which he never recovered. In the judgment of Knight Aldrich, a psychiatrist who has studied the mental illnesses of political leaders, Coolidge's condition was a case of pathological grief (Aldrich 1996). He withdrew, became hypersomnolent, spending eleven hours sleeping each day of his second term; he was both irritable and disinterested. Gilbert's description is vivid:

> The President withdrew almost completely from interaction with Congress and showed little inclination even to participate in the activities of the departments of his own government. His workdays began to shrink in length and his naps grew considerably longer and more frequent. His shrewdness turned to disinterest; his involvement turned to indifference, and his well-developed leadership skills were abandoned.

Both Dwight Eisenhower and Lyndon Johnson suffered from heart attacks from which they recovered. Calvin Coolidge, on the other hand, never recovered from the broken heart occasioned by his son's death.

Altered Statesmen: Effects of Substance Abuse on Political Leaders

In looking at major leader illnesses in the first half of the twentieth century, we observed Adolph Hitler's polypharmacy and simultaneous treatment with methamphetamine and cocaine. We saw the bewildering array of medications administered to the failing Winston Churchill, which further compromised his mental incapacity. Clearly, there are serious consequences when the high and mighty become mighty high.

ANTHONY EDEN: BENZEDRINE ADDICTION

One reason the failing Churchill was sustained in office was that his putative successor, Anthony Eden, was suffering from the effects of a botched gall bladder operation, during the recovery from which he had become addicted to morphine and Benzedrine (amphetamine). While he was successfully weaned off morphine, he continued to rely on Benzedrine when he became prime minister in 1955. In October 1956, the British under Eden's leadership decided to join with France and Israel in a military intervention to attempt to prevent Egypt from nationalizing the Suez Canal. President Eisenhower's furious condemnation of Eden's decision led to a crisis in the British pound and forced the British to withdraw, an ignominious humiliation for the Eden government. Eden himself acknowledged that during the Suez crisis he "was practically living on Benzedrine" (Reeves 1991). One witness described him as being "almost in a state of exaltation at the time" (Giglio 1991). During this major international crisis, Eden was truly an altered statesman.

Although a concerned physician confided that "Anthony could not live on stimulants any more" (Henry 1970), the case emphasizes the dilemma for the physician to the prime minister, in this case Lord Charles Moran. When the prime minister shouts, "Where is Charles, I must have my Benzedrine," and the very future of the British Empire is seen to rest on the shoulders of the prime minister, it is very difficult, if not impossible, for the physician to say, "I am sorry, sir. You are the victim of substance abuse, and I cannot prescribe Benzedrine for you."

JOHN F. KENNEDY: CHEMICALLY ASSISTED VIGOR?

That John F. Kennedy concealed that he suffered from Addison's disease, an adrenal insufficiency that required treatment with steroids, probably from the time of his military service in World War II, is now well known. The severity of illnesses that dogged Kennedy throughout his life, and the variety of powerful medications prescribed to treat theses illnesses, as well as their concealment has only recently come to light, as was discussed earlier in this chapter.

In addition to the medication legitimately prescribed for Kennedy's spectrum of serious illnesses, the president, like Anthony Eden, almost certainly also abused amphetamines that he received from another physician. In effect this was physician-assisted substance abuse. This medication was administered to Kennedy unbeknownst to Dr. Janet Travell, the physician who treated his serious and extremely painful back disorder, for which he was receiving powerful narcotic medication.

Amphetamine abuse began among elite circles in the United States in the 1940s and 1950s (Bartlet 1966). Dr. Max Jacobson, a physician in New York City, became known to the glitterati as Dr. Feel-Good, for the energizing injections of amphetamine he gave them. Anthony Quinn, Cecil B. de Mille, Emilio Pucci, and Tennessee Williams were among his famous patients. Apparently, JFK also became a patient of Dr. Jacobson, whose license to practice medicine in New York was revoked in 1969. Secret Service records reveal no fewer than thirty-four visits to the White House by

Dr. Jacobson. On one occasion, JFK's brother Bobby, alarmed at the frequency of Kennedy's amphetamine tonic injections, implored, "Jack, you've got to stop taking that stuff. It's poisoning you!" Kennedy reportedly replied, "I don't care if it's horse piss. It makes me feel good. And I'm going to keep taking it."

Jacobson was flown to Berlin during the Berlin Wall crisis in 1963 in a private plane at Kennedy family expense. When Kennedy gave his famous "Ich bin ein Berliner" speech, he may well have been under the influence of amphetamines (Remmick 1991), his vitality enhanced by Dr. Feel-good's tonic.

Alcohol: The Lubricant of Politics

The substance most frequently abused by politicians is without question alcohol. It is the very lubricant that keeps the gears of Washington smoothly meshing. It is also frequently resorted to by politicians for self-medication for anxiety and depression. Chapter 2, in commenting on the consequences of frustrated dreams of glory, observed Senate Foreign Relations Chairman Key Pittman's alcoholic decline. More often than not, colleagues and staff will avoid dealing with a legislator or senior official's serious problems with alcohol until there is a public scandal. This is what befell the powerful chairman of the House Ways and Means Committee, Wilbur Mills, who was found frolicking while drunk in the tidal basin early one morning in 1974 with the stripper Fanny Fox. He was taken from the pool to Bethesda Navy Hospital for detoxification, and this episode effectively ended his political career.

Alcohol has figured prominently in Russian politics. The short-lived coup of August 19–21, 1991, by right-wing forces in the Soviet Union failed because of "the sheer incompetence of the coup leaders" (Remmick 1991), which in significant part was attributed to the heavy drinking of the coup leaders throughout. Boris Yeltsin was known to have a serious alcohol problem throughout his political life. On one occasion on a refueling stop-over in Ireland, with the green carpet rolled out to greet Yeltsin, he never appeared, reportedly because he was too inebriated. A number of the frequent disappearances and retreats to his dacha, which were politically paralyzing, were attributed to his need to dry out after alcoholic benders.

4

Terminal Leadership

Effects of Mortal Illness on Political Behavior

It's still the same old story,
The fight for fame and glory,
A case of do or die . . .

Carmichael, "As Time Goes By"

Life moves out of a red flare of dreams
Into a common light of common hours
Until age brings the red flare again.

William Butler Yeats

The leader who experiences physical illnesses, or sees the serious illness or death of an age peer, may have it vividly brought home that life is finite and time is running out. The resulting sense of urgency can affect decision making (Post 1980).

Leading a nation while facing terminal illness affects all aspects of decision making. But how it affects the leader will be a consequence of the nature of the leader's personality and the interaction between his own acceptance or denial of his illness and his attitude toward his own mortality—and the degree to which his dreams of glory have been fulfilled. Men and women are impelled to seek the highest office for diverse reasons. For some, it is merely to sit upon the throne and savor the perquisites of high office. For others, it is to wield the scepter of power. For still others, it is the quest for glory, to be inscribed in the pages of history.

Giving up the heroic life is inconceivable when a leader's entire sense of self is bound up in being revered, when the exercise of power is to compensate for inner insecurity. In contrast, a leader imbued with healthy self-confidence, with a sense of self apart from leadership and a sense of the life cycle and limited possibilities, recognizes that the exercise of his abilities must inevitably yield to the passage of time, as illustrated by

Chou En-lai's reactions at the end of his days. For others, like Mao Ze-dong, the prospect of death is a consummation devoutly to be denied, and the consequent rush to glory can be extremely destabilizing.

Death always comes too soon, but it is especially threatening when a leader's timetable to achieve his mark in history is abbreviated by the shadow of mortal illness. Confronted with the approaching end of life, a leader will experience a feeling of urgency to accomplish his goals for his nation before time runs out. The personal timetable takes precedence over the nation's timetable.

Rather than sink into despair, the specter of the end of life may ignite a terminal explosion in a frantic last-ditch attempt to ensure immortality. Such was the case with Mao at the end of his days. But Mao's terminal excesses in the Cultural Revolution almost exclusively affected his country. His terminal spasm pales by comparison with the international consequences of the political actions precipitated when the shah of Iran became seriously ill in 1973 (Zonis 1985, 154–55), an illness he concealed from his own people and from his American allies.

Terminal Urgency: The Shah of Iran's Quest for Glory

Marvin Zonis (1984) provides convincing evidence that the shah of Iran had a narcissistic personality structure, that underneath his grandeur were significant self-doubts. Mohammed Reza Pahlavi had been consumed by compensatory dreams of glory since his earliest years. He hoped through a sustained program of social and economic modernization to bring Iran into the twentieth century and become the leading influence in the Persian Gulf. His dreams for his nation—what he called the "White Revolution"—were spelled out in his 1960 book *Mission for My Country;* it detailed a plan to modernize his country that would require patient development over many decades. The shah saw his firm leadership as necessary to bring this ambitious plan to fruition. He wished to turn over the reins of leadership to his then-young son only when his mission for his country was accomplished, a strategic implementation that would require patience and persistence for many years.

Then in his early forties, the shah assumed that he would live into his seventies or eighties, with two, three, or even four decades to shepherd his country's advance into the twentieth century. But the shah learned he would not have decades to accomplish his goals. He became seriously ill in 1973. He declined alcoholic beverages, citing his "dyspepsia." He was observed to be gaunt and drawn, but that was assumed to be a consequence of the stresses of office. When his Iranian physicians found a massively enlarged liver and spleen, they called in French specialists, who diagnosed lymphocytic leukemia, a form of cancer of the white blood cells. At the urging of his Iranian physicians, however, they did not specify cancer but informed the occupant of the Peacock Throne (Cohn and Okie 1979) that he was stricken by Waldenstrom's macroglobulinemia, a rare and sometimes fatal blood disease.[1]

Even though the French physicians soft-pedaled his illness, the shah knew he was seriously ill. It was unlikely that he would live as long as ten years. Clearly, his plan for his country's development could not be accomplished in his lifetime.

He concealed his illness from his American allies, who were unaware that he was seriously ill, that he was attempting to lead his embattled nation through a crisis while he was dealing with the ravages of cancer and the debilitating effects of chemotherapy. The United States reposed all of its trust in the shah's ability to negotiate the stormy political waters of Iran as he had so often in the past. The United States banked on the shah to exercise effective leadership and resist the rising tide of discontent that threatened the stability of his regime. His inability to do so paved the way for the Islamic revolution that ultimately overthrew him.

The psychological effects of his illness had an even more important effect on his leadership than the debilitating physical effects of the disease and its treatment. Apprehending that he was seriously ill, and learning early in 1974 that he had cancer and that his lifespan would be foreshortened, meant that he would not have the requisite time to achieve the place he wanted in history.

Nineteen seventy-three, the year the shah became seriously ill, was the same year that the shah broke with the Organization of Petroleum Exporting Countries (OPEC), leading to a quadrupling of oil prices. The sudden infusion of vast oil revenues into an economy with a poorly prepared infrastructure led to massive societal dislocations and a revolution of rising expectations. The shah was playing a desperate game, gambling that he could speed up the White Revolution, yet control it, hoping to accomplish his goals in his few remaining years.[2] The forces he unleashed were powerful and there was massive societal discontent. Ayatollah Ruhollah Khomeini, who for years had been in political exile in France, skillfully mobilized the resulting discontent. Khomeini developed the most unlikely coalition of peasants and the *bazaari*, the merchant class. These disparate sectors of the polity were united only in their common hatred of the shah and their common desire to bring his rule to an end.

As protests became widespread, many urged the shah to deal with his opponents with an iron fist, as his father had. The ravages of his illness, the powerful medication he was taking, and American exhortations to observe the human rights of his opponents weakened his resolve. Moreover, the shah claimed that his obsession with the continuity of the throne significantly constrained him from employing the ruthlessness that the suppression of the Islamic revolt required. He told friends and allies in the final months of his rule that he was determined not to unleash the full force of the army and secret police against the Iranian people, because he hoped that some day Iran would turn again to his dynasty. After the victory of the Islamic revolution, he wrote from exile:

> I am told today that I should have applied martial law more forcefully. This would have cost my country less dear than the bloody anarchy now established there. But a sovereign cannot save his throne by spilling the blood of his fellow countrymen. A dictator can do it because he acts in the name of an ideology which he believes he must make triumphant, no matter what the price. A sovereign is not a dictator. There is between him and his people an alliance which he cannot break. A dictator has nothing to pass on: power belongs to him and him alone. A sovereign receives a crown. I could envisage my son mounting the throne in my own lifetime. (Ledeen and Lewis 1982, 119)

Like Mao Ze-dong, Shah Mohammed Reza Pahlavi would not let the approach of death frustrate his quest for immortality. But in his haste to accomplish his goals and hand over a fully accomplished White Revolution to his teenage son, the shah superimposed his personal timetable on the nation's timetable, and in so doing had destabilized Iran and paved the way for Khomeini's Islamic revolution. Consumed by urgency to accomplish his mission for his country in his few remaining years, the shah, in his headlong rush to glory, ensured instead the failure of that mission. Rather than reap the gratitude of the Iranian people for his dedicated leadership, he was to reap the whirlwind.

Terminal Control: Ferdinand Marcos of the Philippines

When a leader places great emphasis on strength and control, the onset of serious illness can be extremely threatening. Illness episodically affected the controlling Ferdinand Marcos from his twenties on, and it played a major role in his authoritarian rule. This case study is also a striking example of concealment of leader illness.

In August 1942, while fighting a guerrilla campaign in the jungles of the Philippines against the Japanese invaders, Marcos, then twenty-four, was afflicted with a mysterious fever and abdominal pain that left him bedridden for five months in a guerrilla camp. This illness was to recur in June

1943, leading to his hospitalization. His brother, a physician, diagnosed Marcos as suffering from an ulcer and from blackwater fever, a serious form of malaria that affects the kidneys. In 1944, a third episode was again diagnosed as blackwater fever. In retrospect, this may have been the onset of the disease of the connective tissue—systemic lupus erythematosus—that was to lead to kidney failure and ultimately claimed his life.

After the war, Marcos entered political life.[3] Intellectually acute, he demonstrated a subtle leadership style and a mastery of the political process, both domestic and international. He served in the House of Representatives from 1949 to 1959, was a senator from 1959 to 1965, and was president of the Senate from 1963 to 1965. At the age of thirty-seven, while a senator, Marcos married the beauty queen Imelda Romualdez, who was to play a very important role as a political wife and a political power in her own right. At the age of forty-seven, in 1965, Marcos was elected president of the Philippines.

The Communist insurgency of the New People's Army, which was to become a fixture of Philippine life, began in 1969. Its goal was to destabilize the regime through the use of violence. As Marcos was struggling to contain the mounting violence, he was also struggling with ill health. At age fifty-four, he was definitively diagnosed with lupus, and he secretly began to consult with a kidney specialist. Marcos questioned the doctors closely and learned of the grave prognosis. He insisted that the illness be kept a closely guarded secret. For the most part, he and his inner circle were successful in concealing from public view the existence, and later the gravity, of his illness.

In 1971, the same year he was diagnosed, Marcos initiated emergency steps to contain the increasingly violent activity of the rebels, suspending the writ of habeas corpus. In 1972, he imposed martial law. Although there had been significant insurgent violence, martial law was viewed by many as an unnecessarily harsh and disproportionate reaction. In 1973, Marcos further consolidated his political control, naming himself prime minister under the new constitution while remaining president under the old. Political opponents argued that Marcos was exploiting the political instability to justify his dictatorial bent. I believe there was also a more personal reason for the extremity of his actions. Facing the ebbing of his physical strength and the progressive loss of control over his body, Marcos needed to demonstrate his political strength and control.

By 1978, at age sixty-one, his illness was becoming more and more evident. He was having difficulty rising from his chair without assistance. The next year, the characteristic rash of lupus was explained away as a simple skin rash, but his face was puffy and he was suffering from arthritis of the hands, both symptoms of lupus. By 1980, his health had deteriorated further and his kidneys were failing, prompting U.S. specialists to recommend an immediate kidney transplant. The palace staff now knew of his illness, and word leaked to the press.

As his health declined, his leadership became more controlling. In September 1980, Marcos secretly signed the Public Safety Act, which gave him extraordinary powers; the next month, the government prepared to revive an old murder case against Benigno Aquino, his principal political adversary. In January 1981, he secretly signed the National Security Act. In anticipation of the visit of Pope Paul II, he lifted martial law, which had been in place for nine years, but the broad discretionary powers granted him under the Public Safety Act and National Security Act enabled him to exercise unconstrained power. Within the year, he had purged the government and military of anyone who threatened his rule.

As his control over his body continued to decline, Marcos took increasingly extreme measures to retain control of the government. During the summer of 1982, the sixty-four–year-old Marcos was hospitalized twice. He appeared on television to deny rumors of his failing health, but on a visit to Washington he had two dialysis machines available at the Philippine embassy. There was no longer any possibility of concealing that he was suffering from kidney failure and required regular dialysis to sustain him. Friends speculated that he was near death. Given the 1980 recommendation for an immediate kidney transplant, it is probable that he had been undergoing dialysis, a daily reminder of his mortality, at least since the late 1970s.

As is almost always the case, the illness exaggerated its victim's preexisting personality pattern. Throughout his political career Marcos had left nothing to chance. Trusting no one, he had developed competing sources of information and would frequently travel throughout the Philippines to ensure that he had the pulse of the people. But these sensible and practical methods of keeping informed were now denied to him. One of the consequences of Marcos's serious illness was the curtailment of his mobility; he rarely left Malapayang Palace.

Moreover, because of his vulnerability to infection, access to the ailing leader was sharply reduced. By now, the circle around the stricken president had contracted. Marcos had said that in the event of his death Army Chief of Staff General Fabian Ver would have "certain powers." His wife Imelda and General Ver controlled almost all the information that reached the largely bedridden leader. With Marcos rarely seen in public, it was unclear who was making decisions. For the last four years of his rule, the ailing Marcos and his constricted leadership circle represented a striking case of a captive king and his captive court.

The superstitious Imelda had been warned by a soothsayer of grave consequences should Marcos's political rival, Benigno Aquino, set foot on Philippine soil. In May 1983, she went to New York to warn Aquino not to return. In early August, decrees were issued affirming Marcos's right to imprison suspects in cases of subversion and deny them access to the courts. By now the disease was affecting Marcos's brain, and his mental processes were clouded. In August, he underwent an emergency kidney transplant.

The period immediately following a transplant is a critical one. To guard against rejection of the transplant, immunosuppressant drugs are administered that make the patient very susceptible to infection. The patient is usually kept in isolation during this period. Marcos was rumored to be semicomatose. Even if he had been reasonably alert, he would not have been able to make thoughtful decisions.

It was during this crucial recovery period, on August 21, that Aquino returned to the Philippines. He was assassinated as he was disembarking from the plane, but before he set foot on Philippine soil. Many, recalling the soothsayer's advice to Imelda, believed that she was behind the assassination. Aquino's killing was a catalytic event, creating widespread protests against the Marcos regime.

Marcos's immune system ultimately rejected the transplant, and he required continuing dialysis, but in September, his health status partially improved. He threatened once again to impose martial law. Tensions between the Marcos government and the United States over Marcos's authoritarian rule increased. In October, a civilian investigative panel called for the indictment of General Ver and others for the premeditated murder of Aquino. Although the United States pressed Marcos to relax his authoritarian control, in late October a regional secretary of the opposition party was assassinated.

With mounting public discontent and his health seriously compromised, from a rational standpoint Marcos might well have chosen to step down or to at least announce that he would retire for health reasons at the end of his term in 1987. But, no longer in control of his body, Marcos psychologically could not yield political control. To do so would have been to give up the fight for his life. On November 6, 1984, despite being seriously ill with terminal kidney disease, he announced that he would run for reelection in 1987. The elimination of leading opposition figures continued with the assassination of Manila Mayor Cesar Climaco.

Shortly after the announcement, Marcos disappeared from public view, giving rise to rumors that he was gravely ill. He underwent a second kidney transplant, and during the recovery he developed serious respiratory difficulties that required an emergency tracheotomy. On November 21, the opposition filed a motion for a caretaker government, and on December 3,

1984, the government confirmed that Marcos was seriously ill, the first official acknowledgment of the gravity of Marcos's illness.

Marcos's last year in office, 1985, was marked by increasingly blatant manipulation of the political system, as Marcos and his entourage frantically tried to hold on to power. Each violation of democratic norms further delegitimized his leadership. The evidence of his government's complicity in the Aquino assassination was so overwhelming that in February General Ver and others were indicted, amid widespread skepticism that the government would permit a fair trial. In August, Marcos proposed an early election, but then he reversed himself. During his years of iron control, an organized opposition had never been permitted to develop. Although the growing but factionalized opposition argued politically for this move before it had the opportunity to consolidate, Marcos's personal timetable was foreshortened, which probably also pushed him to try to secure his hold on power. Under intense U.S. and international pressure, Marcos decided to call a snap election for early 1986.

When the election was held in February, under close domestic and international monitoring, it was clear that Corazon Aquino, the widow of the assassinated martyr-hero Benigno Aquino, had won. However, with massive fraud, Marcos was declared the victor. The election was recognized as the final delegitimation of Marcos, and he was unseated in a bloodless coup led by Defense Minister Juan Ponce Enrile and General Fidel Ramos, the army's deputy chief of staff.

Ferdinand Marcos, his wife, Imelda, and their entourage fled the country, eventually to settle in Honolulu. Despite the support for Corazon Aquino and despite, or because of, his failing health, in January 1987 Marcos and his followers attempted a coup; but it was foiled by U.S. intervention.

In 1988, Marcos was diagnosed as chronically ill and unlikely to recover and so avoided trial in the United States. It is fitting that 1989, that remarkable year that saw the end of the careers of so many autocratic leaders in Eastern Europe, was the year in which the Marcos era ended as well. After a final ten months of hospitalization, during which he was often semicomatose and had numerous emergency surgical interventions, Marcos finally succumbed to cardiac, pulmonary, and kidney failure. So large was his reputation, so strong the support he still had, that Corazon Aquino refused permission for him to be buried in the Philippines.

Ferdinand Marcos had played a giant role in the history of his nation, but the magnitude of his achievements will be overshadowed by the desperate lengths to which he went at the end of his life to retain and then to regain control. Although complex political forces were at play, the shadow of serious illness influenced his entire twenty-three-year presidency and distorted his leadership during the last eight years of this period. The degree of his authoritarian control, the sustained period of martial law, the assassination of his archrival Benigno Aquino, the inability to relinquish the reins of power, the decision to run for another term in office, and the final, flagrant electoral fraud that precipitated the bloodless coup—these benchmarks in the decline of his leadership occurred as his health was failing.

Marcos strove with increasing desperation to hold on to political power as a way of holding on to life itself. At a number of junctures, had he been content to accept the verdict of the democracy he had helped to establish, he could have retired with honor, his reputation intact. But in the end, his judgment increasingly failed, and he behaved more impulsively, less judiciously, perhaps influenced or controlled by the frightened and greedy courtiers around him. The more desperate his moves, the greater the damage he did to his reputation in history. The more desperate his moves to hold on to control, the more impossible it became to yield power.

Terminal Machismo: Andreas Papandreou of Greece

For some narcissistic political leaders, the confrontation with mortality primarily produces instability in the leader's personal life, which in turn has secondary destabilizing political effects. Such was the case with Andreas Papandreou, prime minister of Greece in the 1980s.

Controversy surrounded Papandreou throughout his career. The son of George Papandreou, a highly popular prime minister, throughout his life Andreas seemed to be bent on establishing his own identity by opposing authority. He attended graduate school in economics at Harvard, and went on to teach economics at the University of Minnesota and at UC Berkley. Papandreou became a major force in U.S. Democratic Party politics, serving as a member of Adlai Stevenson's inner circle during his first unsuccessful run for the presidency.

It was during his academic career in economics that the thirty-three-year-old Andreas met and married an American woman, Margaret Chant. Despite, or because of, these strong American connections, Papandreou was to make anti-Americanism a rallying cry of his nationalist politics when he returned to Greece after the Greek military junta was overthrown, a theme he continued to use after he became prime minister in October 1981. Papandreou developed a reputation as a womanizer during his stormy thirty-seven year marriage to Margaret. Maintaining the facade of family propriety while pursuing extramarital affairs probably enhanced his popular appeal. As one Greek commentator observed, "We love love affairs. It's in our blood. But at the same time, we take the family very seriously. You don't fool around with that" (Cody 1988).

But Papandreou crossed the line from macho but stable family man to foolish old goat in his seventieth year, when he threw discretion to the wind in his headlong pursuit of a woman thirty-five years his junior, the former Olympic Airlines stewardess Dimitra (Mimi) Liani. It was the diagnosis of coronary artery insufficiency that would require a triple bypass operation that pushed Papandreou, a lifelong hypochondriac, over that line. His voluptuous mistress, and not his wife, accompanied Papandreou to London in the fall of 1988 for the required cardiac surgery. Without leaving anyone in Athens to mind the store, he spent two months in London, attempting to run the government by telephone from his hospital bed.

The prime minister became an object of ridicule. One of the jokes circulating throughout Greece was that Papandreou had added a new position to the *Kama Sutra*, the Indian erotic manual: one foot in the bed, the other in the grave. Photographs of his well-endowed mistress at a topless beach appeared in the Greek press. Political plays mocked the Papandreou government, focusing on the seventy-year-old prime minister's neglect of his official duties as he concentrated on his thirty-four-year-old mistress. Helen Vlachos, a senior Greek newspaper correspondent, commented, "Suddenly he has lost control. The Greek people who sort of admired the macho side of having an affair have begun to think this is too much" (Cody 1988).

After photographs of a postoperative Papandreou in London being led around by his mistress appeared in the Greek press, a diplomat observed that "the question became not that he was having an affair with a woman young enough to be his daughter, but that he was a doddering old man being manipulated by her" (Cody 1988). He brought his mistress to Parliament for the annual presentation of the budget. Putting the final scandalous nail in the coffin, Papandreou announced his intention to divorce his wife.

In concert with financial improprieties in his government and charges of corruption, his personal indiscretion led to a marked decline in his popularity. After getting 45 percent of the vote in the 1985 election, he lost the June 1989 election, receiving only 20.5 percent.

Terminal Stubbornness: P. W. Botha of South Africa

Loss of control is especially threatening to authoritarian personalities. Highly sensitive to position in the hierarchy, they are notably unreceptive to advice from subordinates. They have extremely strong needs for autonomy and tend to become resistant and oppositional in the face of strong pressure, which conveys a picture of stubbornness and rigidity, an absence of flexibility. Having a strong need to be right, they do not easily admit error or change positions.

On January 18, 1989, a week after his seventy-third birthday, South African President Pieter W. Botha suffered a "slight cerebral vascular incident" (*Washington Post*, January 19, 1989), that is, a mild stroke, which left him partially paralyzed on his left side. The rigid obstinacy and tenacity with which he clung to office for the next seven months also left his government paralyzed at a time when it required strong and flexible leadership.

The illness could not have struck at a less opportune time, for the government was facing

- mounting international and domestic pressure to dismantle apartheid;
- the problem of when or if to release jailed African National Congress leader Nelson Mandela, contrary to the wishes of the conservative Afrikaner population who feared for their survival;
- slowed economic growth and soaring inflation because of punitive international sanctions; and
- the transfer of control of South African-controlled Namibia to an independent government.

Botha's illness immediately kindled speculation that he would retire. Medical experts stated that even if he recovered quickly, it would be extremely dangerous for him to return to office—"If he wants to live to see his next birthday, he should immediately cut all the stress out of his life" (*Mcleans*, January 30, 1989).

Rumors during the preceding year that Botha was in poor health had gained force when he chose not to deliver the traditional New Year's message to the nation. In an interview in 1988, reflecting on the pressures of the office, Botha stated, "If I am to be honest, I have to say that you can only do this job while you are healthy. If my health is of such a nature that I cannot continue doing it, I myself will decide to go" (*Washington Post*, January 30, 1989).

But the first thing he did on returning to his official residence in Cape Town two weeks later to convalesce was to order that a desk be moved into his bedroom, making clear his intention to remain on the job. Ironically, Botha had come to office in 1978 after leading the effort to force the resignation of Prime Minister B. J. Vorster after financial improprieties in his government were revealed. Vorster had been suffering from a chronic blood disease for years and clung to office despite his poor health.

Known as "The Great Crocodile" for his imperious manner and total control of his government, Botha was not to relinquish that control easily. In early February, taking even his senior cabinet members by surprise, he abruptly quit as head of the National Party, but he resisted calls for his resignation as president and said he intended to serve out his term, elevating the presidency above partisan politics and making it "a unifying force in South Africa" (*Washington Post*, February 3, 1989). This, according to National Party sources, would fulfill his long-held dream of finishing his political career as a senior statesman, granting some power to the country's black majority of 23 million without taking power from the 4.5 million whites. In fact, the move created a peculiar political anomaly, essentially making it impossible for his successor as party leader, Frederik W. de Klerk, to lead effectively.

There was a growing sentiment within his party that Botha should resign the presidency too. But Botha defiantly announced that he would resume his official duties later that month. In making his announcement, he asserted, "I am not looking for power for the sake of power . . . I do not cling to posts. But now I am healthy" (*Los Angeles Times*, March 13, 1989).

Afrikaans newspapers, which traditionally reflected National Party views, suggested that the president should quit and allow de Klerk to guide the reform process. In a stunning rebuke to Botha's defiant stand, the 133 members of the parliamentary caucus of the ruling National Party, which Botha had led for eleven years, voted unanimously on March 13 to urge Botha to step aside so that de Klerk could replace him as state president. But on March 15, as promised, Botha returned to office, leading one senior party official to remark, "The Great Crocodile is going to fight this one out to the end, and I wouldn't be surprised if he manages to bite a couple of people where they sit before this thing is all over" (*Mcleans*, March 27, 1989).

Liberal newspapers had a field day with Botha's bulldog insistence on retaining his position. A South African business newspaper editorialized that "the spectacle of President Botha clinging to high office like a two-year-old to a toy has been so unedifying that it is hard to see how he can rescue much dignity" (*Los Angeles Times*, March 13, 1989). A South African daily ran an article under the headline "Botha Stands Alone" and editorially described Botha's defiance as "quite irrational. The real interests of this country . . . are certainly more crucial than the *quirks of a fading strongman reluctant to let go of power*" (*Los Angeles Times*, August 15, 1989, emphasis added).

Over the next several months, there was a standoff between Botha and de Klerk, and ill feelings between the two grew. A South African professor of political studies observed that "in the past five months, P. W. Botha has done everything he could to hamstring his successor. This shows how even astute leaders like P. W. Botha lose touch with reality. He clearly ought to have retired with honor after he had his stroke" (*Los Angeles Times*, August 15, 1989). A government-supported newspaper, the *Citizen*, referred to Botha as "totally unpredictable . . . yesterday's man" and urged de Klerk to "be strong in the showdown with the president" (*Los Angeles Times*, August 15, 1989).

Finally, on August 15, the embittered seventy-three-year-old president resigned. Appearing gaunt and nervous, he petulantly complained in his resignation speech that

> It is evident to me that after all these years of my best efforts for the National Party and for the government of this country . . . I am being ignored by ministers serving in my cabinet. I consequently have no choice other than to announce my resignation. (*Los Angeles Times*, August 15, 1989)

How sad, as a South African academic observed, that he could not have retired with honor after his stroke, for he had, during his eleven-year rule, made quiet but significant progress in granting increased power and political participation to the nation's black population while preserving the rights of the white minority. But his dream had not been achieved. Indeed, the *Star*'s editorial diagnosis was astute, for Botha was in fact "a fading strongman reluctant to let go of power" (*Los Angeles Times*, August 15, 1989).

The exercise of power and control gave meaning to Pieter Botha's life; to yield the reins of power was akin psychologically to forfeiting life itself. Portending as it did the end of life, the stroke must have threatened Botha. To acknowledge his incapacity as a leader was equivalent to yielding to death's embrace. In denying his incapacity and in fighting for his personal survival, Botha gravely damaged his nation.

Terminal Strength: Menachem Begin of Israel

Before he yielded to terminal despair, Prime Minister Menachem Begin had fought with single-minded devotion for his nation. Begin was a man of fragile health, whose leadership was punctuated by health reverses, including three heart attacks and a stroke. These were pointed reminders that his time was limited, and the dream he had cherished throughout his lifetime, a Jewish homeland at peace, was not to be achieved in his lifetime. Like Moses, he would not enter that promised land. But if he could not achieve an Israel at peace, then in the time remaining he would fight to ensure a secure Jewish state.

As each illness underlined the brevity of his remaining time, in the wake of serious illness came some of his most dramatic political moves. Two of his most controversial political actions not only occurred in relationship to illness but the decisions were actually made from his hospital bed!

In May, 1980, the popular Ezer Weizman resigned as defense minister, the culmination of fractious dispute within Likud inner circles. Weizman had pushed for a more flexible and conciliatory posture, of considering trading land for peace with the Palestinians, but Begin had rigidly resisted, insisting on the integrity of the biblical land of Israel.

In June 1980, Begin suffered a minor heart attack. While recuperating in the hospital, he became obsessed with the need to declare unambiguously to the world his commitment to the integrity of the biblical land of Israel. To his doctor's dismay, he received political advisors daily. From his hospital bed he crafted a statement that was read to the press on July 6:

> It is the national consensus and the policy of the Government of Israel that Jerusalem, which has been reunited as a result of a successful legitimate self-defense, will remain forever united, forever indivisible, and forever the capital city of the State of Israel by virtue of right. (*Middle East Report* 1980)

This was a highly provocative and unnecessary statement coming as it did during an American presidential campaign. It led to tension with the United States, Israel's strongest supporter. It also strengthened the hands of the Arab states who wished to perpetuate the state of hostility with Israel. They could point to Israel's intransigence to justify their own. When Begin was released on July 14, upon leaving the hospital he personally endorsed the statement and spoke again of his vision of Jerusalem as capital: "If the Arab countries recognize the State of Israel and Jerusalem as its capital, twenty Arab flags would fly in Jerusalem, the capital of Israel, which would be recognized by all the Arab countries." On November 26, 1981, Begin tripped in the bathroom of his home and fell. He suffered a fractured hip, a frequent affliction of the aged. The fracture required surgical repair, and the postoperative hospital stay was painful. But during this hospitalization, too, he was preoccupied with Israel's security. On December 14, the day of his discharge, Begin called an emergency meeting of the cabinet, and, still in his hospital bathrobe, announced the extension of Israeli law to the Golan Heights—the equivalent of annexation (Jerusalem Post 1980). The Golan Heights, which had been captured from Syria in the 1967 war, had long been a source of menace to Israel, with nightly rocket bombardments of the settlements below in the northern Galilee. Never again, vowed Begin, would Israel be exposed to that mortal danger. Once again, physical weakness had precipitated a politically "strong" response, an affirmation of Begin's lifelong creed, "I fight, therefore I am!"

Begin's aim was to establish an eternally secure Israel. Weak physically, he was demonstrating his strength as a leader. But politically, as with the annexation of East Jerusalem, this provocative policy of annexing the Golan Heights damaged Israel's standing in the West and his ability to deal with moderate Arab governments.

Terminal Denial: Mustafa Kemal Ataturk

Vamik Volkan (1980, 1982), in his psychobiographic analysis of Mustafa Kemal Ataturk, founder and first president (1923–1938) of modern Turkey, demonstrates the creative potential of narcissism when it is played out on the national scene. Unlike the "splitting" of the narcissistic terrorist who seeks to destroy the devalued and projected aspect of himself, Ataturk, through the vehicle of his "reparative leadership" of Turkey, healed the splits within his psyche. In so doing, he was idealized by the Turkish people who attributed godlike status to him and came to see him as immortal.

In his last year of life, Ataturk became increasingly itchy and began to scratch himself constantly. His followers were frantic. They called in one exterminator after another to rid the presidential palace of the insect infestation presumed to be responsible for their leader's misery, but to no avail. It was only when Ataturk left the country that his characteristic physical appearance made it obvious to a foreign physician that he was mortally ill. He had massive ascites (abdomen swollen and filled with fluid), severe jaundice, and was suffering from terminal cirrhosis of the liver, of which severe itching is a prominent symptom (Volkan and Itzkowitz 1984, 331–43). It was unthinkable to Ataturk, his inner circle (including his own physicians), and his followers that he could ever die. For "immortal Ataturk" and his followers, as for so many narcissistic leaders, the dreams of glory were insatiable.

Terminal Religiosity: Jafar Nimeiri, President of Sudan

A deathbed religious conversion is a not uncommon reaction to a confrontation with mortal illness. When it is a chief of state who belatedly turns to religion, and makes his terminal religiosity the basis of national policy, it can have painful consequences for his country.

In 1969, after years of an ineffective democratic government, thirty-nine–year-old Jafar Nimeiri led a group of military officers in a successful coups d'état and assumed the leadership of Sudan. As with all successful coups, specific circumstances determined its success. The coup occurred on the eve of Nimeiri's fortieth birthday. A press to action is a frequent reaction to the midlife transition (ages thirty-eight to forty-three); a disproportionate number of leaders who have assumed power by military coup have taken action during this period of psychological flux.

Although Nimeiri portrayed himself as a lifelong devout Muslim in his 1978 revisionist history *The Islamic Way, Why?*, throughout his life and career he had not been particularly devout. Nimeiri describes how he and his colleagues prayed to Allah before the coup, but in fact Nimeiri was a hard-drinking military man, and he and his colleagues were intoxicated on the night of the coup. (The *shari'a*, the codified Islamic law that governs the conduct of everyday life for devout Muslims, proscribes alcohol use.) In his initial speech on assuming power, there was no sense of mission, no mention of Allah, no description of Sudan as an Islamic republic. Rather, he described the new regime as neither Eastern nor Western but as a democratic-socialist regime working for Sudan's interests alone.

In the early years of his leadership, Nimeiri devoted his energies to dealing with Sudan's long-standing social, economic, and political problems. He met with considerable success and improved Sudan's position both domestically and internationally. His greatest accomplishment was the Addis Ababa agreement of 1972, which ended the seventeen-year civil war between the Islamic north and the largely Coptic Christian south. By exerting his influence against the Islamic fundamentalists and clerics, Nimeiri, espousing the belief that the south could remain culturally and religiously distinct, was able to craft a constitutional formulation that gave special recognition and protection to the south's unique status within a unified Sudan (*Al Sahada*, May 25, 1984). Article 8 specified autonomy for the south, with its own governmental and administrative structure, but most important were the guarantees of religious freedom. Article 16 declared that Islam is the religion of the Democratic Republic of the Sudan, but recognized that a large number of citizens professed belief in Christianity. The constitution guaranteed that "heavenly religions and the noble aspects of spiritual beliefs shall not be abused or held in contempt." It expressly forbade

> the abuse of religious and noble spiritual beliefs for political exploitation. . . . The State shall treat followers of religion and noble spiritual belief without discrimination and . . . shall not impose any restrictions on citizens or communities on the grounds of religious faith. (Khalid 1985)

Yet such discrimination and restrictions were exactly what occurred when Nimeiri became religiously obsessed in the face of mortal illness.

His zeal to impose his religious beliefs on his nation was initiated by his personal illness. As Nimeiri's health declined, the manifestations of his public religiosity grew more intense as he violated the Addis Ababa accord, dividing his country, and destroying the greatest achievement of his presidency. His leadership became increasingly personal and less institutional, and his Machiavellian manipulation of the factions within the system led to a progressive disintegration of the fragile unity he had achieved.

In the late 1970s, while still in his mid-forties, Nimeiri began to experience serious health problems. He experienced drowsiness and confusional episodes, described as temporary dementia, and collapsed on several public occasions. At first his illness was undiagnosed, but ultimately Nimeiri traveled to the United States and underwent a thorough medical evaluation at the Walter Reed Army Medical Center in 1979.

The comprehensive medical evaluation revealed that Nimeiri's longstanding diabetes mellitus was under poor control and that he had developed widespread arteriosclerosis, which was affecting the circulation to the heart and the brain. In addition to involvement of the coronary arteries, an arteriosclerotic plaque had led to obstruction of the internal carotid artery, which provides the main blood supply to the brain; this was the cause of his mental symptoms.

Nimeiri returned to Walter Reed in 1980 for a three-week checkup to treat his heart ailment and better regulate his diabetes. He returned later in 1980 for surgery to remove the clot obstructing the carotid artery. On returning from the 1980 procedure, he informed his aides that his maintenance medication sometimes affected his mental faculties and judgment. Early in 1981, he announced that he would retire in August 1982 because of illness. Nevertheless, by January 1982 he had reconsidered, claiming to be indispensable to Sudan's future, and declared himself president for life.

It was this siege of serious illness that prompted Nimeiri's turn to Islam. But Nimeiri was not content to apply this epiphany to himself alone. As he explained in his 1978 book *The Islamic Way, Why?*, the way of Allah was the way for all of Sudan, and if some did not see that way, they would be shown it, and made to walk it. Islamic law began to be forced on all Sudanese, regardless of their religion, and regardless of the constitution.

When Nimeiri's health problems began in the mid 1970s, his local physicians strongly recommended that he stop his alcohol consumption, which they believed was contributing to his medical condition. With the onset of serious illness, they told him that unless he stopped drinking immediately, he would be dead within six months. Nimeiri vowed to stop drinking. Not only did Nimeiri abstain, but he sent a circular entitled "Guided Leadership" to cabinet ministers and other senior officials instructing them to swear an oath to him that they would also abstain from drinking.

At the same time, Nimeiri, a deeply superstitious man, fell under the sway of Sufi Muslim mystics and, to the dismay of his cabinet officials, began to rely on witch doctors to divine the future and guide his policies. One of the holy men gave him a ring and walking stick to assure him divine protection.

Nimeiri's speeches at times demonstrated paranoia and an obsession with powerlessness. To compensate for his growing physical enfeeblement, he spoke of his total power, as if he were a law unto himself: "Beware, I am empowered by the Constitution to take any measures I deem necessary for the protection of the May revolution." Pointing to a guard, he said, "According to the Constitution, I can order this guard to shoot anybody and he would have to obey me" (Khalid 1985, 47).

Nimeiri's assumption of religious leadership was not confined to the boundaries of Sudan. In August 1981, he sent open letters to both President Assad of Syria and Mu'ammar Gadhafi of Libya, instructing them to leave Lebanon alone and enjoining them to side with Iraq in the Iran-Iraq War. They did not respond to his advice. When earthquakes struck Syria in December 1981, he sent a message to Assad, explaining the natural disasters as divine punishment.

> The news of the disaster which has afflicted Damascus has been conveyed to us. God gives reprieve but does not forget. What has happened in Damascus is the result of your disregard for God's law and your attempt to extinguish the fire of the Qur'an and the Light of Islam. Justice is the only way for establishing peace and the first principle of justice which God has decreed is the sanctity of human life and the futility of manslaughter without good cause and genocide without just trials. All these are against Islamic law. God, our destiny is in your hands. (*Al Ayan*, December 4, 1981; cited in Khalid, 212)

Further demonstrating both his lack of international political sensitivity and his proselytizing zeal, during a trip to the People's Republic of China he tried to convert the Chinese to Islam.

But while Nimeiri was increasingly religious and enjoining Sudanese officials to share his new-found piety, he had not yet strongly institutionalized Islamic practices into law, and many of his exhortations were greeted with a wink and a nod. This was to change abruptly in 1983, the year he again traveled to the United States for surgery. Before the trip, he talked to his military commanders about funeral arrangements. This forcible encounter with his mortality led to a major escalation in the pace of Islamization of Sudan.

In September 1983, without warning, he declared the shari'a, the legal code of Islam that prescribes conduct for all aspects of life, to be the law of the land, including the largely Coptic Christian south. He introduced the shari'a dramatically, by pouring millions of gallons of alcohol into the Nile. The shari'a was to be rigorously enforced, including flogging for possession of alcohol, hand amputation for theft, and the stoning to death of adulterous women. Previously, adultery had rarely been punished, for the shari'a requires four witnesses to the adulterous event. Nimeiri, however, invented a new offense, attempted adultery, which did not have the same witness stipulations.

Nimeiri fell increasingly under the sway of his spiritual mentors and was increasingly isolated from his secular advisors. His rule became more and more idiosyncratic, and so certain was he of the righteousness of his way that he would not tolerate criticism. Indeed, those who criticized his policies would find themselves not only out of a job but apt to be imprisoned.

Nimeiri became preoccupied with his own spiritual role for his nation, and his speeches increasingly evidenced that he had identified himself as the spiritual leader of his country, as its imam. Beginning all his speeches with verses from the Koran, he regularly referred to his mission for his country, making it clear that its goal was to "establish the religion [Islam] amongst your ranks" (*Al Sahada*, May 25, 1984).[4]

He prayed for God's help in carrying out his divinely ordained mission. He spoke about his enemies and the rumors they spread that he was ill by again quoting the Koran in such a way as to make it clear he identified himself with the Prophet.

The declaration of the shari'a as the law of the land, and Nimeiri's divisive policies, propagated under the sway of his religious advisors, led to great civil unrest, prompting him to declare martial law in April 1984. He indicated that those in the south who had risen against him were also enemies of God. Though he pledged to carry out the shari'a mercifully, the specifics of his policies suggested the opposite:

> Although Islam is the religion of forgiveness, the religion of brotherliness and the religion of honor and integrity, we will flog people publicly, we shall publish names in papers . . . because the Muslim hates to hear his name. . . . We shall continue to publish . . . to flog . . . continue to amputate hands . . . until we establish a righteous Islamic community. (*Al Sahada,* May 25, 1984)

Increasingly out of touch with his own people, and obsessed with his religious mission, Nimeiri continued to struggle with his health. In March 1985, he again traveled to Walter Reed for a thorough evaluation and treatment. While in Cairo en route to Khartoum, he learned that a coup d'etat had occurred and that he had lost his pulpit.

Searching for the kingdom of God, he lost his kingdom on earth, living out his days in exile.

Terminal Détente: Konstantin Chernenko

We have earlier observed the manner in which the intolerable prospect of the end of life for Mao Ze-dong contributed to the convulsions of the Cultural Revolution and how the prospect of death accelerated the shah of Iran's attempt to consolidate his place in history. Konstantin Chernenko had not yet made his mark in history when he was named secretary-general of the Soviet Communist Party. He, too, was to make efforts to achieve an honored place in his nation's history.

Unlike the dramatic efforts of Mao Ze-dong and the shah of Iran, Chernenko's efforts were gentle; for the most part he attempted to set a new tone. Enfeebled by lung and heart disease when he took office, his efforts were ultimately to no avail. But it was clear that facing the end of his life contributed to his raising his voice for détente and accord between the superpowers.

Well before 1984, Konstantin Chernenko had already developed emphysema, chronic obstructive pulmonary disease, and right-sided heart failure, conditions that could only be expected to become more severe and debilitating. Yet he was elected general-secretary of the Communist Party of the Soviet Union in 1984. The evidence is persuasive that he was elected not despite these major health problems but precisely because of them.

Despite discomfort with the illness-plagued reigns of Leonid Brezhnev and Yuri Andropov, the strife to succeed Andropov between supporters of the conservative Grigori Romanov and the liberal Mikhail Gorbachev was so intense and the forces so balanced that a deadlock resulted. The only other eligible candidate who was a member of both the Politburo and the Secretariat was the seventy-two-year-old Chernenko. The old guard— Dimitri Ustinov (76), Nikolai Tikhonov (79), and Andrei Gromyko (75)— were reluctant to accept a new generation of leadership and were chary of a leader as young as Gorbachev (52), yet they feared that Romanov would be insufficiently responsive to their own collective authority.

Accordingly, they pressed for the transitional Chernenko regime, believing that the previously undistinguished leader would demonstrate continuity with the policies of Brezhnev. It was, after all, his commitment to Communist ideology and a thirty-year association with Brezhnev that had brought him to the Kremlin. But Gorbachev and Romanov also supported a Chernenko interregnum, for neither had had time to shore up sufficient support.

Because Chernenko seemed most fulfilled in the role of follower, both the old and the new guard probably believed they had nothing to fear from his leadership and that they would be able successfully to manipulate him, especially in view of his failing health. Demonstrating that the regime was well aware of Chernenko's medical problems, the day after Andropov's funeral, Dr. Yevgeny Chazov, director of the Kremlin medical clinic, ran a computer search seeking information concerning pulmonary disorders, especially emphysema and asthma.

Prior to his election to the Soviet Union's highest position, Chernenko was best known as one of "the butchers of Stalin's great terror of 1937" (Solovyov and Klepikova 1986, 44–49). In Dnepropetrovsk, Chernenko, as deputy personnel chief of the NKVD, the Soviet secret police, played a leading role with his comrade-in-arms Leonid Brezhnev. This surely was not a predictor of a commitment to détente on assuming the Soviet Union's highest office, yet this is exactly what Chernenko was to develop.

Among the consensual leadership, Chernenko was the principal advocate for détente. I believe that the impact of the gravity of his health problems and his recognition that his career was previously undistinguished by notable achievements were major factors leading the failing Chernenko to marshal his faltering energies. Having not yet made his mark in history, he was determined to go down in history as the Soviet leader who eased tensions between the superpowers, who led the way in moving away from the spiraling nuclear arms race. He was determined to be viewed as the champion of détente.

In the year before his election as chairman, Chernenko was absent from official duties for three months because of bronchitis, pleurisy, and pneumonia. Demonstrating that health concerns were weighing on his mind and influencing his political perspective, as well, were a book by Chernenko that appeared that year, *Establishing the Leninist Style in Party Work*, and a major address he delivered to the CPSU Central Committee on June 14, 1983 (*Soviet Report*, June 14, 1986). The texts are strewn with references to vigor, vitality, struggle, superiority, and well-being, as well as wishes to enrich, strengthen, and succeed.

Although these statements were made in a political context, the choice of words contrasts with the failing health of the author. Chernenko commented, "Human health, vitality and mood depend not on medicine alone," and recommended that individuals attend to their health, through, for example, participation in sports (*Soviet Report*, June 14, 1986). This may have reflected a rueful retrospective wish for Chernenko, for whom each breath was a struggle. Chernenko had begun smoking at age nine, and despite his emphysema, continued to smoke nonstop. At a Polit-buro meeting during the Andropov years, Andropov personally rebuked Chernenko for fouling the atmosphere (Solovyov and Klepikova 1986, 44).

The regime was initially successful in concealing the gravity of Cher-nenko's health problems from the West, but the success was short-lived, and a public preoccupation with Chernenko's health status was to domi-nate his term in office, the third deathwatch in a row. His fragile health and diminished stamina were manifest in his public appearances shortly after he returned to Moscow in February 1984. In his inaugural speech, he spoke in short gasps, breathing very rapidly, and was barely able to raise his arms in a salute to Soviet troops marching past the reviewing stand. Foreign medical experts noted his shortness of breath, hunched shoul-ders, difficulty saluting, and irregular speech, all suggesting advanced pulmonary disease (*New York Times*, February 16, 1984).

Shortly after his inauguration, Chernenko delivered a major speech that addressed the Soviet-U.S. relationship. But the effect of his prepared words was overcome by his blatant difficulty in delivering the address. Not only was he breathing heavily throughout the speech, but a break in concentration, which resulted in his losing his place, was sufficiently con-fusing for Chernenko to cause him to overlook an entire page, the most crucial page of the text. He failed to recognize his error and continued with the address (*Newsweek*, March 12, 1984).

A month later Chernenko was seen in the Kremlin hospital, although it was reported that he was there to visit an ailing comrade, Tikhonov, rather than for his own health (*Soviet Report*, April 2, 1984). In May, during a meeting in Moscow with King Juan Carlos of Spain, Chernenko appeared frail and tired. He had to be assisted from his limousine by two aides, had trouble buttoning his coat, and moved around "like an automaton or a bear, with arms dangling and an absent-minded air" (*New York Times*, May 12, 1984). His hunched shoulders, uneasy breathing, and occasional difficulty in raising his arms confirmed the earlier impressions of ad-vanced emphysema. In another speech from which he omitted the key passages, he stumbled and stuttered, frequently lost his place, and showed labored breathing. During the opening session of an important congress in June, he had two "sick spells" in close succession, causing him to break off his speech twice (*Soviet Report*, June 26, 1984). After that, his speeches were read by announcers.

The more serious Chernenko's condition, the more intense were the ef-forts to cover it up. His emergency room visit and hospitalization were not initially reported. The official Moscow line was that the general-secretary was on holiday, but he was out of sight for more than a month, unusual considering his recent assumption of power. Belying Chernenko's "holiday," his son returned from Greece to the Soviet Union, and an official trip to France by Gorbachev was also cancelled with no explanation (*Soviet Report*, June 26, 1984). In the middle of February, Dr. Yevgeny Chazov, director general of the Soviet Cardiology Research Center, who had earlier claimed that his presence in the United States refuted the "rumors" of Chernenko's ill health, was recalled to Moscow (*Soviet Report*, February 7, 1985).

Chernenko developed heart irregularities, but the medical cover-up continued. Analysis of a late February photo purportedly showing Chernenko voting in a polling place showed that it had been taken in Moscow's Kuntsev Hospital. In a public appearance at the end of February, Chernenko sat slumped in a chair, exhausted, speaking with difficulty.

But after each hospitalization and period of illness, his speeches emphasized all the more strongly the need for peace among nations in the nuclear age, which would require the Soviet Union and the United States to work together toward that goal.

Konstantin Chernenko died on March 11, 1985. The autopsy showed chronic emphysema, an enlarged and damaged heart, congestive heart failure, and cirrhosis of the liver, which could have resulted either from alcoholism or from chronic heart failure (*New York Times*, March 12, 1985). The emphysema and heart failure would have caused chronic oxygen deprivation, which would have affected Chernenko's mental functioning and decision making.

His thirteen months in office were marked by advanced pulmonary and cardiac illness. Yet despite, or because of, his grave illness, during his brief period of leadership the climate between the Soviet Union and the United States noticeably improved. It was initially chilly, as epitomized by the Soviet boycott of the 1984 Olympics, which were held in Los Angeles, and the U.S. reaction to the banishment of the Soviet dissident scientist Andrei Sakharov. But Chernenko negotiated deals on trade and other exchanges and was ardent, if short of breath, in his speeches calling for reduction of tensions between the superpowers. Chernenko was no Gorbachev; health, temperament, and the politics of the period prevented him from doing more, but he did "not go gentle into that good night" but, rather, pushed for a major improvement in U.S.-Soviet relations until his last gasp.

Terminal Risk for Peace: Yasir Arafat and King Hussein

Just as Chernenko was moved at the end of his life to seek peace, Yasir Arafat, the chairman of the Palestine Liberation Organization (PLO) and later president of the Palestinian Authority, and King Hussein of Jordan, two leaders who were remarkably risk-averse, took a risk for peace after both confronted their mortality.[5]

The 1994 signing of the peace accord with Israel by King Hussein of Jordan was hailed as the crowning achievement of his life. The quintessential survivor, noted for his caution, Hussein had been praised for taking a risk for peace. The signing followed in quick succession the announcement that Yasir Arafat of the PLO, along with Yitzhak Rabin and Shimon Peres of Israel, had been awarded the Nobel Peace Prize. Who would have thought that Arafat, the master terrorist, would ever be hailed for his role in peacemaking? But who can forget the dramatic moment in the White House Rose Garden in September 1993 when Arafat reached out to grasp the hand of Rabin?

What precipitated these remarkable turnabouts? To be sure, the geopolitical circumstances in the Middle East had radically altered with the dissolution of the Soviet Union, so that the superpower rivalry was no longer being played out in the Middle East, and Syria had lost its Soviet patron. But like Hussein, Arafat, too, was the quintessential survivor, always leading with his finger squarely in the wind to ascertain the sentiment in the Palestinian movement and the Arab world. By no means was Arafat a risk taker.

Both Yasir Arafat and King Hussein of Jordan had survived over the years by carefully assessing political risks. Arafat, in his quest for an independent Palestinian nation, had never been willing to break from the radical absolutists in the Palestinian movement, nor had Hussein ever broken from major Arab constituencies. Yet both Arafat and Hussein had broken from their previous risk-averse patterns to take a risk for peace.

Although the role, histories, and characters of Arafat and the king could not be more different, they shared some features in common. As noted, both are remarkable survivors, both had been reluctant to take major political risks—and both encountered their mortality in 1992.

On April 5, 1992, a dazed Arafat was found in the Libyan desert twelve hours after his Russian-built private plane had crash-landed in a sandstorm. He was apparently uninjured, although the pilot was killed in the crash. The incident dramatically focused attention on the then sixty-two-year-old Arafat, who had devoted his life to the Palestinian cause, emphasizing not only that once again had he miraculously survived a brush with death, but also that he had no credible successor. Then in June, suffering from severe headaches, Arafat entered the King Hussein Hospital in Jordan, and it was discovered that he had bilateral subdural hematomas (blood clots under the membrane covering the brain) caused by the head injuries he had sustained in the plane crash. He underwent neurosurgery to remove the clots and relieve the pressure on his brain.

Arafat's decision to back Saddam Hussein in the Gulf War had severely diminished his stature in the Arab world and led to a major reduction in financial support. Moreover, the success of the *intifada* and the PLO's lack of accomplishment had weakened his standing among the Palestinian people.

Politically, there were many imperatives to make a dramatic move to regain his leadership prominence. There previously had been opportunities to achieve the beginnings of a political solution in pursuit of the long-sought goal of a Palestinian homeland, but before his near fatal accident, Arafat had not seized them, reluctant to make a move that did not have the support of the entire Palestinian movement. It was only after Arafat's plane crashed in the Libyan desert and his emergency surgery six weeks later to remove blood clots that he broke with the radical rejectionists and agreed to participate in the Oslo accord negotiations, leading to the Nobel Peace Prize. He had not yet achieved his goal of being the founding father of the independent Palestinian nation, and, having confronted his mortality, he took bold action to ensure his place in history.

In August 1992, at age fifty-seven, King Hussein of Jordan underwent surgery at the Mayo Clinic because of a narrowing and blockage of the left ureter. It was determined that a cancerous kidney was the cause of the blockage, and the left kidney was removed.

In November, a pessimistic-sounding Hussein told his nation about the cancer invading his kidney and ureter, and said that further treatment in the United States would be required. Saying that "the life of an enlightened people and a vibrant nation cannot be measured by the life of any individual," Hussein said the surgery had been successful, but that "every soul will meet its destined end."

In the same speech, he stressed that the Hashemite family "shall continue to bear the nation's standard generation after generation." Hussein, who traced his lineage back to the prophet Muhammed, had led the Hashemite kingdom since 1952. Stewardship of the holy Islamic sites in Jerusalem was considered a special responsibility of the Hashemite leadership. Fifteen-year-old Hussein was beside his grandfather, King Abdullah, on the steps of the Al Aqsa mosque in Jerusalem when his grandfather was shot to death by a Palestinian assassin. This event endowed young Hussein with a special sense of destiny. Jordan's entry into the 1967 Arab-Israeli War led to the loss of Jerusalem and the sacred mosques, a stain on Hussein's reputation.

Constrained by neighboring Syria and Iraq, Hussein had not risked alienating Jordan's Palestinian majority. Indeed, this was the principal motivation for his decision to back Saddam Hussein during the Gulf crisis. Before his cancer surgery, Hussein had been a notably cautious political actor.

But after 1992, both Hussein of Jordan and Arafat of the PLO were sitting crowned on the grave. When leaders with dreams of glory have been confronted with life-threatening illness, emphasizing the brevity of their remaining time, they may feel an urgency to establish their place in history and to take uncharacteristically bold moves. And Hussein and Arafat both took major risks, uncharacteristic in their careers, which have culminated in the signing of peace treaties with Israel—truly crowning achievements. For Arafat, it was to enshrine his name in the pages of history as the founding father of the Palestinian state. For Hussein, it was to remove the stain on his reputation of the loss of custody of the holy places.

Hussein continued on the path to peace, rising from his bed to make a crucial intervention at the Wye Plantation talks between Arafat and Israeli Prime Minister Benjamin Netanyahu just days before his death. Arafat has developed a parkinsonian tremor of the lips in the last several years, probably a consequence of the brain damage and neurosurgery he underwent in 1992, further emphasizing his mortality. After the failure of the Camp David II talks, Arafat reverted to his customary role as leader of the unified Palestinian resistance, the revolutionary fighter. But Arafat's internal clock is ticking, and his wish to be recorded as the founding father of the Palestinian nation could well impel him again to take a risk for peace.

Terminal Mental Incapacity

Acute organic illnesses affecting the central nervous system are much more alarming to the public than those in which mental functioning is unaffected. President Eisenhower's 1955 heart attack produced little alarm, but the stroke he suffered in 1957 produced great consternation, for initially his speech and thinking were affected. Major news columnists suggested that the president should delegate his responsibilities to Vice President Richard Nixon. Several commentators urged the president to resign, and the *New York Post* editorialized that it preferred having Nixon as president to having no president at all. Senator Wayne Morse suggested that the time had come for Eisenhower to step aside. Even White House staffers were gloomy and tense (Gilbert 1998). The impact of this particular illness, then, was particularly pronounced because the president's reasoning abilities seemed to be in question.

In addition to the problems of acute illnesses such as Eisenhower's in 1955 and 1957, a particularly vexing diagnostic problem concerns the gradual and progressive organic brain syndrome reflecting early Alzheimer's disease or multi-infarct dementia. In the previous chapter on the effects of the life cycle on political behavior, the impact of old age on psychological reactions in individuals without physiological deterioration was considered. But, as was illustrated in the brief medical history of some leaders during the first half of the twentieth century, aging political leaders can also suffer from the infirmities of old age, Alzheimer's disease, and other illnesses that produce senile dementia. Particularly in closed societies, without a free press and vigorous political opposition, leaders who were at one time effective can gradually slide into the mental incapacity of senility.

There is no one-to-one correlation between age and cerebral degeneration. Many individuals in their seventies and eighties function at a very high level with little or no impairment to their creative and intellectual capacities, while younger people may show significant interference with their functioning. But once the march of symptomatic cerebral arteriosclerosis or other presenile cerebral degeneration has begun, a pattern of functional disturbance usually follows that can be expected to become more severe.

Afflicted individuals demonstrate a progressive impairment in their capacity to think abstractly. Thinking becomes more concrete, rigid, and inflexible. There is a tendency to see things in black and white terms as the ability to discriminate nuance and subtle shades of difference diminishes. Responses become less flexible and more stereotyped, so that afflicted individuals are seen as becoming more "stubborn." It is difficult to change a mental set. For a leader suffering from organic brain damage, it might be difficult to stop a plan once it is set in motion, despite compelling evidence and advice to the contrary. There is a general decline of intellectual capacities. Concentration and memory, particularly recent memory, are usually especially affected. There is an associated impairment of judgment. Impulses that had earlier been checked by the restraints of judgment may now be more easily expressed. Thus, an individual may behave more aggressively or be more easily provoked. Emotional reactions in general become less well controlled; afflicted individuals are irritable, easily provoked to anger, tears, or euphoria, and are more sensitive to slight. Depressive reactions are common.

Earlier Personality Reactions Become Exaggerated

Aging individuals do not tend to mellow with increasing age. Rather, earlier personality traits tend to intensify. As with normal aging individuals, the basic personality and lifestyle remain intact, but long-standing attitudes and drives are expressed in an exaggerated way. The characteristically distrustful person may become frankly paranoid. The Soviet Union and the People's Republic of China provide striking examples. Always distrustful, Joseph Stalin in his last years was in a clinically paranoid state, blatantly exemplified in "the doctors' plot." Similarly, during the Cultural

Revolution, it was striking to observe the number of individuals loyal to Mao from the days of the Long March who fell from his favor and were politically disgraced.

Good Days and Bad Days

Afflicted individuals have both good days and bad days. The course of cerebral arteriosclerosis is often characterized by wide fluctuations but is invariably downhill. For some, the decline is gradual, while for others it may be quite precipitous. The disparity between observations made on good days and bad days has on occasion led to slanted conclusions concerning the mental state of the individual. Thus, if a senior official observed Mao Ze-dong on one of his better days, when he was more alert and in reasonably good contact with reality, there would be a tendency to invalidate the reports of poor health. On the other hand, sometimes observations of a leader made during a period of particular fatigue or confusion have led the observer to underrate the capability of the leader to function. What is particularly important is to assess the entire pattern and to neither overrate nor underrate the individual's capabilities on the basis of one particular observation. If one can with some certainty diagnose cerebral arteriosclerosis, even though an individual may appear alert on a particular occasion, the other features already enumerated, in particular the decline of intellectual abilities and problems with judgment, nevertheless can be assumed to be operating.

Denial of Disability

A particular problem with aging individuals whose capacities have been affected by age is their tendency to deny the extent of disability. When a leader manifests this denial, it may lead him to grasp the reins of power more tightly at the very time when he should be relinquishing them. Although the circle surrounding a leader may often be able to insulate him from decision-making responsibilities during periods of disability, it is a rare subordinate who, distressed about poor decisions being made by his superior, will confront him with this knowledge, especially if some of the irritability and distrust and capricious decision making often seen in aging individuals are also in evidence. When one contemplates the difficulties in addressing the subtle encroachments of age upon judgment and leadership functioning, one must recognize the manner in which the characteristics of the office can support denial and obscure leadership difficulties.

This emphasizes the importance of considering the relationship between individual irrationality and the nature of the leadership circle. Considering the increased suspiciousness, emotional irritability, and denial of disability often characteristic of people with cerebral arteriosclerosis, it should not be surprising to note that there would be a natural tendency for the leadership group to foster distorted perceptions of political reality. If the somewhat suspicious leader becomes frankly paranoid so that "those who are not with me are against me," the subordinate who actively disagrees with the leader may find himself out of a job or worse. Thus, some of the psychological qualities of the aging period may promote a sycophantic leadership circle that is unwilling to differ with and upset the leader. Another group aspect may be worth considering when we contemplate aged men functioning in a leadership group. The group dynamic literature suggests a tendency for groups to seek consensus. Although individually there may be only minor problems with lack of flexibility, in a group setting the difficulties may summate, with an inhibition of individual creativity and an increased tendency for rigid and inflexible decision making. This may well have contributed in 1983 to the shooting down of the Korean airliner that strayed accidentally into Soviet area space, a decision made by the aged Soviet Politburo.

Terminal Paralysis: The Soviet Gerontocracy

In a hierarchical, highly authoritarian system, the illness of the leader decapitates the state. To be sure, in the Soviet Union, there was a tradition of consensual decision making, but the Communist Party's general-secretary had an extremely powerful role. Prior to—and setting the stage for—the vigorous transformational leadership of Mikhail Gorbachev, the Soviet Union was virtually paralyzed by a succession of aged, ailing leaders.

LEONID BREZHNEV

Born in December 1906, Leonid Brezhnev became head of state in 1960 at the age of fifty-three and was elevated to Communist Party general secretary in 1964. He was to remain in this position for eighteen years, dying just before his seventy-sixth birthday.

After a heart attack in 1975, Brezhnev's health deteriorated and he was never again the same. For several years before his death, Brezhnev was suffering from generalized arteriosclerosis, including the arteries of the brain. This led to the deterioration of his intellectual functioning and his leadership. He was progressively infirm and had trouble speaking. His workload was significantly reduced, and for the last two years of his life he was essentially a figurehead.

Boris Yeltsin, who became president of Russia in 1991, has vividly described Brezhnev's leadership in his final years. This contains a description par excellence of the syndrome of "the captive king and his captive court":

> Here's a typical example of how the country was run in those days. We needed to get a top-level decision on the construction of a subway system. Sverdlovsk was, after all, a city of 1,200,000 inhabitants. We needed permission from the Politburo, and I decided to go to Brezhnev. . . . I had been told how to handle him, so I prepared a text to which he had only to add his signature for approval. I went into his office and we talked for literally five or six minutes. . . . He was incapable of drafting the document himself. He said to me, "Just dictate what I should write." So of course I dictated it to him: "Instruction by the Politburo to prepare a draft decree authorizing the construction of a metro in Sverdlovsk." He wrote what I had said, signed it, and gave me the piece of paper. Knowing that even with Brezhnev's signature, some documents might be misplaced or disappear altogether, I told him, "No, you should call your aide." He summoned an assistant, and I said to Brezhnev, "Give him your instructions that he must first enter the documents in the registry and then take the necessary official steps to ensure that your instructions to distribute it to the Politburo members are carried out." He did all this; the aide collected the papers; and Brezhnev and I said good-bye.
>
> The incident was typical and revealing. In the last phase of his life, Brezhnev, in my opinion, had no idea what he was doing, signing, or saying. All the power was in the hands of his entourage. He had signed the document authorizing the construction of the Sverdlovsk metro without giving any thought to the meaning of what I was dictating. Granted, as a result of that signature a good deed was done . . . But how many of the rogues and cheats, indeed plain criminals, who surrounded Brezhnev exploited him for their own dishonest purposes? How many treaties or decrees did he calmly, unthinkingly sign, bringing riches to a few and suffering to many? (Yeltsin 1990)

While the circle around him made accommodations, there was a virtual paralysis of leadership in the face of Brezhnev's growing incapacity. He died in 1982 at the age of seventy-five. There was pressure for a more youthful successor, but factional disputes led to the appointment of another aged and ailing leader to succeed Brezhnev—Yuri Andropov, who had served as Brezhnev's KGB director for fifteen years.

YURI ANDROPOV

At the time he was designated to succeed Brezhnev in November 1982, the sixty-eight-year-old Andropov was already seriously ill with kidney disease. The leadership paralysis characteristic of Brezhnev's last years was to continue during Andropov's brief reign, which was, for the most part, a deathwatch. His term of office was punctuated by lengthy medical absences. Pallid and frail when he was elected general-secretary of the Soviet Communist Party, Andropov was in power for only fifteen months, of which the last six were spent in the hospital. He died at age sixty-nine of kidney failure.

The factional striving led to the appointment of yet another aged, ailing leader as a transitional figure, Konstantin Chernenko, whose reaction to the approach of death, by becoming a leading advocate for détente, was described previously.

The Psychological Impact of Facing the End of Life

Being faced with the end of life—whether because of the impact of mortal illness or the passage of years—inevitably requires a leader to assess his accomplishments. This assessment, and the reaction to the threatened loss of power, will depend significantly on his personality and political psychology. The controlling autocrat and the narcissist will have particular difficulty in yielding the throne of power.

For the autocrat, such as Erich Honecker, the throne of leadership is the seat of power and control. To yield that throne is to lose control. Paradoxically, the pressure from below is for greater participation and greater control over people's destiny. Only by responding to that pressure and yielding a greater degree of control to the people can autocratic leaders hope to retain their positions. But the very psychological and political forces that contribute to a controlling style of leadership make it impossible to share, to yield even partially, and a powerful struggle for control ensues.

Narcissists are often successful in achieving power, in large part because they appear totally self-sufficient. But under the arrogant, self-confident facade the narcissist is consumed by self-doubt and feelings of inadequacy, which drive him in a never ending quest for attention and approval. It is because of this insatiable drive for admiration and glory that the end of the heroic life is unthinkable for the consummate narcissist.

No amount of success can fill that inner void. Even Mao Ze-dong, at the end of a remarkable revolutionary life, clearly to be enshrined in the pantheon of history's greatest leaders, or the shah of Iran, who brought his country to the edge of modernization, were not fulfilled. Whatever the evaluation of the outside world, their inner drive was undiminished, their driving ambition for glory unfulfilled.

Seeking symbolic immortality is not unique to political leaders. What is unique is the availability of resources to achieve those ends. And when they succeed, like Caesar and Napoleon, Gandhi and Churchill, their fantasies of symbolic immortality will be realized.

The degree of control the leader exerts over his nation's resources varies greatly from system to system. Whether the leader stays past his time and, in terminally holding on to power, destroys the achievements of a lifetime will depend on the nature of the political system and the relationship of the leader to the political system.

Captive Kings and Captive Courts

The issue of ailing leaders in the seat of power is not merely a matter of historical interest. Leaders are flesh and blood, subject to the vicissitudes of the life cycle, prone to illness, and inevitably subject to the passage of their years. How leaders and their political systems react to illness and aging will continue to have tremendous consequences for society. If the leader and his inner circle conceal the illness, profound distortions in leadership dynamics and decision making can occur as the captive king and his captive court become locked in a destructive and often fatal embrace.

At first they are plotting together to conceal the leader's illness, for the ailing leaders and their inner circles need one another to survive. And, it should not be forgotten, especially in closed societies, that the alternative to being in power may be prison or death. Increasingly, however, the leader is propped up as a figurehead, with the inner circle ruling in his name. This was the case with Ayatollah Khomeini and with Mao Ze-dong at the end of their periods of rule.

Special hazards are posed by aging autocrats who hang on to power and by leaders who are consumed by dreams of glory and are struck by illness before they have fulfilled what they believe to be their destiny. Dreams of glory are responsible for some of civilization's greatest achievements, but the intemperate reactions of aging and ailing leaders to the ebbing of their power and the frustrated dreams of their youth have been responsible for some of history's most tragic excesses.

5

The Impact of Crisis-Induced Stress
on Policy Makers

No matter how well trained the military crew, in the stress of combat errors in perception and judgment occur that can have tragic consequences—a fact given pointed emphasis by the after-action report of the mistaken downing of an Iranian civilian airliner by the U.S. Navy combat frigate *Vincennes*:

A military investigation of the shooting down of an Iranian civilian airliner last month [July 1988] found that crew error arising from the psychological stress of being in combat for the first time was responsible for the disaster . . . Radar operators on the *Vincennes* mistakenly convinced themselves that the aircraft they had spotted taking off from the airport in Bandar Abbas, Iran, was hostile and intended to attack the *Vincennes*.

With the perceived threat fast approaching, they wrongly interpreted what they saw on their radar screens in a way that reinforced this preconceived notion. These misinterpretations were then passed on to Capt. Will C. Rogers III, the ship's commanding officer, and led him to conclude that his ship was in imminent danger.

Military psychologists say that soldiers and sailors in their first battle suffer immense stress before and during the fighting and may confuse perceptions with reality. Soldiers often shoot at shadows or at each other on their first night in a combat zone. Pilots in their first air engagements sometimes misread their instruments and fly in the wrong direction.

A navy officer who served with the riverine forces in Vietnam said, "Stress can override your faculties. You see what you want to see and hear what you want to hear." . . . This appears to have happened to some crew members aboard the *Vincennes*.

"Stress is something military medicine pays a lot of attention to," said a doctor at the Walter Reed Medical Center in Washington, D.C. "We concentrate on the effects of stress on individuals who have been exposed to prolonged periods of combat. We pay less attention to what is probably the highest stress point of all, the period immediately preceding and during first combat." (*New York Times*, August 3, 1988)

If this is true of well-trained military personnel in conventional combat, what of senior government officials in a crisis situation? Consider the exemplary leadership displayed by New York Mayor "Rudy" Giuliani in the wake of the al Qaeda attack on the World Trade Center on September 11, 2001. But what of senior government officials in a nuclear crisis? It is by definition a "first combat" of an extraordinary sort for which no prior training of a fully realistic character is possible; the magnitude of the stress on the decision makers and the consequences of errors in judgment are incalculable.

This chapter will draw attention to the psychophysiology of decision making under both acute and prolonged stress; the interaction between personality and crisis behavior; the interaction between individual personalities and the decision-making group; and the interaction between personality and the organizational context. It is at the nexus between these subsystems—the individual, the group, and the organization—that distortions of crisis decision making are most apt to occur (Holsti and George 1975).

Scholars from different disciplines generally agree as to what constitutes a crisis. The elements characteristically enumerated include a perceived threat to major values and some danger of a war. Moreover, crises often (although not always) have one or more other characteristics that can add to the stress of the decision maker. They include time urgency, ambiguity or uncertainty, and surprise or uniqueness. The political scientist Ole R. Holsti, for example, finds two elements concerning which there is broad agreement—a severe threat to important values and finite time for coping with the threat—and adopts this as his working definition (Holsti 1976). He also mentions the elements of surprise and probability of armed conflict, while Paul T. Hart identifies threat, urgency, and uncertainty (Rosenthal, Hart, and Charles 1989).

Effects of Crisis-Induced Stress on Individual Decision Makers

> Since we live in an age in which individual reaction may bear on the fate of mankind for centuries to come, we must spare no effort to learn all we can and thus sharpen our responses.
>
> Richard Nixon, 1960

The literature on crisis decision making, including the role and performance of individual decision makers, is extensive.[1] The comprehensive review by Holsti, which builds on concepts identified in his earlier book, *Crisis, Escalation, War*, is particularly clarifying. He disaggregates four major analytic perspectives: the nation-state, the bureaucratic organization, the decision-making group, and the individual decision maker. He systematically considers different dimensions of each level of analysis, differentiating the character of decisions made in crises versus "normal" situations as well as the constraints on rational decision making. But in considering the individual decision maker, he concludes that "the personality and other correlates of performance under stress are at best imperfectly understood" (Holsti 1976).

That this terrain is for the most part terra incognita is curious, because the importance of personality as a variable in considering crisis reactions has not been overlooked. Fred Greenstein (1987) makes an important distinction between action dispensability and actor dispensability, and notes that crises are occasions when the performance of the actor will regularly be of central significance. Likewise, Sidney Hook (1943) distinguished between eventful and event-making leaders. Margaret Hermann (1976), in identifying eight conditions in which leader personality affects foreign policy decisions, emphasized the importance of crises. In considering contributions to political behavior, M. Brewster-Smith (1968) considered the interaction of person and immediate situation. Yet, in examining political behavior in crises, the consideration of the individual is, for the most part, undifferentiated. How different personality structures affect reactions to crises has not been systematically considered. I will try to reduce this deficiency in our understanding of crisis behavior by differentiating the role of person and personality.

Indeed, there is no one-to-one relationship between crisis (as defined by threat to national values) and stress (as experienced by the individual). What threatens one individual and, hence, becomes a source of stress for him or her may differ considerably from what is threatening to another. Consider, for example, Menachem Begin, for whom political conflict with the Arab world—being besieged from without—was like a tonic, yet criticism from within Israel—particularly from within his own party—was a major source of stress. Thus, in stipulating threat as a characteristic of crises, from the individual perspective it should be amended to "perceived" threat. The flow chart from Alexander L. George shown in figure 5.1 illustrates the importance of distinguishing between the properties of the stimulus situation and the perceptions of the actor.

Several aspects of the sequence delineated by George (1986) are worth emphasizing. "Perception of threat to values" is the first element following the initial stimulus. But whose values? Although definitions of crisis characteristically refer to national values, there may be a considerable dis-

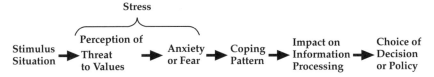

Figure 5.1. Impact of Stress on Decision Making

crepancy between the national values being threatened and personal values. Moreover, the term "coping pattern" in effect refers to the organized pattern of defense mechanisms. Although the pattern of defenses precipitated by a crisis is not identical to an individual's characteristic pattern of defensive organization—their personality—it is derivative. Under stress, characteristic defense patterns intensify. Thus, different personality types will react differently to stress.

Let us first consider in summary form aspects of individual crisis decision making at the level of the undifferentiated person—that is, without taking personality differences into account. Being under stress does not necessarily adversely affect performance. The feeling of being at the height of his powers that Richard Nixon describes during his periods of crisis has a foundation in the literature of social psychology. The early stress response has been demonstrated to improve performance; but as stress mounts, performance degrades. This is illustrated in the well-known "inverted *U*," as shown in figure 5.2.

The manner in which performance degrades under conditions of continuing stress has been studied. Major attention has been directed to cognitive aspects of decision making and the role of belief structures, with less attention paid to motivational aspects. In examining "hot" cognitive processes (the quality of cognition in emergency situations, a term coined by R. P. Abelson [1963]), Irving L. Janis (1972, 1989; Janis and Mann 1977) has made major contributions to our understanding of decision making in general and crisis decision making in particular. In contrast to optimal decision making, which he terms "vigilant decision making," Janis has identified major patterns of impaired decision making that can affect the decision maker operating under the stress of crisis. Of particular importance are the patterns of defensive avoidance and hypervigilance. Because of the anxiety attending crucial decisions, some individuals will avoid decisional conflicts by unduly procrastinating or by not defining the situation as a crisis—hence, defensive avoidance. Hypervigilance, in contrast, is a much rarer state; it is a near panic-like state in which there is a marked deterioration of judgment and impairment of cognitive efficiency.

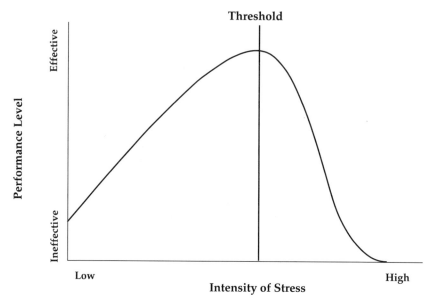

Figure 5.2. Effects of Stress on Performance

A severely stressed individual is prone to suffer various types of impairment of cognitive functioning—perceptual distortions, exaggerated coping mechanisms, and flawed cognitive processes. Many of the following traits, which have been described as characterizing impaired decision making in crisis situations, are subsumed under the overarching patterns described by Janis:

1. A truncated time span, with major attention being devoted to the immediate and diminished attention to long-range consequences of the action;
2. A perceived requirement for decisional closure, which may in turn lead to premature action or, conversely,
3. in searching for certainty, a tendency to irrational procrastination;
4. Cognitive rigidity—a tendency to maintain a fixed mind-set and not be open to new information;
5. A tendency to reduce cognitive complexity and uncertainty;
6. A reduction of the range of options considered;
7. In considering options, a tendency to "bolster"—that is, to upgrade factors that support the favored action prescription and downgrade factors militating against;
8. A tendency to view the present in terms of the past;

9. A tendency to seek familiar patterns, to relate the critical events to mental schemata or scripts;

10. Diminished creativity;

11. A tendency toward the fundamental attribution bias—to see the other's actions as being precipitated by internal (psychological) causes rather than external circumstances (example: my adversary's actions show he is malevolently out to destroy us, rather than that he is protecting himself from external threat); and

12. A corresponding tendency to fall into the actor-observer discrepancy—that is, to see the external situation as the cause of one's own behavior without attending to one's own internal psychological motivations.

Crisis Reactions and Personality Structure

Reflecting the imbalance in the literature discussed earlier, the majority of the reactions to crisis-induced stress that are catalogued above concern belief systems, cognition, and intellectual functioning. Emotional and interpersonal reactions also, of course, affect decision making in crisis situations, although they are less frequently addressed. By and large, however, the literature does not address the question of which leaders—leaders with what kinds of personality structure—are particularly apt to experience which kind of reaction and under what circumstances.

Let us consider the challenge of decision making in an atmosphere of ambiguity, a frequent feature of crisis situations. The tolerance of individuals for ambiguity varies considerably and is related to personality. Compulsive personality features, to a moderate degree, are frequently found in successful executives and leaders. Compulsive individuals are characteristically uncomfortable with uncertainty and handle ambiguous situations very differently from, for example, action-oriented individuals who react intuitively. The action-oriented decision maker who reacts viscerally—intuitively—will not be burdened in the same manner as the compulsive decision maker. The hazard for this type of action-oriented decision maker is a premature decision to act, driven by the need to act and by discomfort with inaction, when judicious delay could provide a much more definitive assessment of the situation without unduly delaying a response—that is, rational procrastination as distinguished from irrational procrastination in search of certainty, which is often the pitfall of the compulsive decision maker.

At what point in an escalating crisis the leadership defines the situation as being of critical proportions is extremely important and can vary considerably depending on a number of factors, including but not limited to the personality dispositions of the principal decision makers. Delay in diagnosing the criticality of a situation can, of course, have disastrous consequences, but to prematurely or incorrectly appraise a situation as critical can also have unfortunate consequences. Consider, for example, the Cuban Brigade crisis of the Carter years, when intelligence information concerning the presence of a Soviet brigade in Cuba precipitated a crisis mentality in the government. As an array of diplomatic and military moves was being considered at the highest levels, it was eventually recognized that the information was not new, that the Soviet unit was a construction brigade that had been present in Cuba for more than a decade assisting with a variety of engineering projects, and the "crisis" quickly disappeared. I will discuss three leader personality types and characterize their differing reactions to crisis situations on the basis of their cognitive, affective, and interpersonal differences. Two of the types—the compulsive personality and the narcissistic personality—are frequently found in the ranks of leaders; the third, the paranoid personality, is found much less frequently but is included because aberrant reactions of paranoid individuals under stress can have catastrophic consequences.

In describing only these three personality types, I am not suggesting that this is an all-inclusive typology. Moreover, the personality patterns as described are rarely found isolated from other personality traits. Indeed, well-balanced individuals are not easily categorized, for a measure of psychological health is the capacity to call on a broad array of psychological coping mechanisms, or ego defenses, rather than being limited to a narrow repertory of ego defenses, as is the case in personality disorders.

Each of the three personality types described has a characteristic cognitive style. George (1974) has usefully observed that differing cognitive styles per se can contribute to the quality of decision making in the interval preceding a full-blown crisis when exaggerated coping mechanisms can be expected to be mobilized.

While drawing on David Shapiro's (1965) depictions of the compulsive and paranoid cognitive styles, the following personality descriptions are also derived from the Diagnostic and Statistical Manual of the American Psychiatric Association (DSM IV). These descriptions are of severe personality disorders, not of healthy personalities; personality dysfunction of the magnitude described would be incompatible with sustained effective leadership. But to the extent that individuals do have significant compulsive, narcissistic, or paranoid elements in their personalities (as many successful individuals do), under stress these traits can be expected to magnify, and they can approach the extreme descriptions portrayed.

THE COMPULSIVE PERSONALITY AND CRISIS DECISION MAKING

Compulsive personality characteristics are frequently encountered in successful government and business executives, scientists and engineers, scholars, and military leaders. Indeed, core features of this personality type—organizational ability, attention to detail, and emphasis on rational process—often contribute to their success. For such individuals, thinking is dominant over feeling, with a need to keep strong feelings—such as anxiety and anger—under control. Such individuals approach decision making on the basis of logical reasoning and reach solutions only after attempting to consider all aspects of the problem at hand.

Crises, however, do not easily lend themselves to such orderly thought processes, and when these compulsive characteristics become intensified under pressure, they can become disabling and be manifested as preoccupation with detail, inability to see "the big picture," and indecisiveness. Under pressure to decide on the basis of only partial and imperfect information, a compulsive decision maker can become paralyzed with doubt, vacillating between alternatives and resembling Tevya in *Fiddler on the Roof*—"Well, on the one hand . . . , but, on the other hand . . ." Because the compulsive personality suffers from an inordinate fear of making a mistake, he seeks to find that one extra fact that would help achieve certainty. Thus, the compulsive decision maker may procrastinate, reluctant to make a mistake, and this irrational procrastination in the quest for certainty can, in effect, become a decision to not act.

Moreover, during the final stages of decision making, compulsive personalities tend to isolate themselves, worrying "conscientiously" over the alternatives. The individual's advisers become providers of information and sources of input but are not fully incorporated into the decision-making process. Thus, it is not uncommon for the compulsive decision maker to remain in this splendid isolation until emerging to announce a decision, which is now final and not open to constructive criticism by subordinates. Indeed, the rash subordinate who tries to get his boss to reconsider may reap the whirlwind, for with the decisional agony ended, the leader has experienced great relief, and reopening the process would be to plunge again into an agony of indecision.

This decisional agony can be forestalled if there is a rule to apply, if there is a formula or standard operating procedure the situation seems to fit—hence the importance both of training and of organizational and psychological processes, which can facilitate high-quality decisions. But the compulsive decision maker, under stress, may shoehorn a unique situation into a familiar shape that has its own clear (but in this case inappropriate) procedural rules and thus make a flawed decision with dangerous consequences.

Even when the compulsive person does make a decision, after this agonizing doubt and anxious worrying over all of the possibilities and permutations, the decision is often not the product of the judicious weighing that has taken place but rather is the consequence of a frantic impulse, either because of a tight time limit or because of the need to end the tortured search for a decision. It is very important for members of the compulsive leader's circle to weigh in before a decision is reached, for the ideas and judgments arrived at after conscientious deliberation are overvalued by the compulsive; once he or she has reached a decision, the compulsive will react to criticism of it as if it were a personal attack.

The nexus of the individual personality and the decision-making group can generate considerable interference with optimal decision making. Unfortunately, much of the social psychology literature on group decision making has little relevance to the realities of the political-military decision-making group. This literature, and the experimental situations from which it derives, characteristically assumes that the participants are equal, but in most decision-making groups power is unequally distributed. Accordingly, the decision-making dynamics of such groups will be strongly affected by the manner in which participants relate to superiors, peers, and subordinates. Location in the interpersonal hierarchy is of great importance to compulsive individuals who are preoccupied with their relative status in dominant-submissive relationships. Indeed, many characteristics of the authoritarian personality are explained by these aspects of the compulsive personality. They can be extremely responsive to the wishes of their superiors and highly competitive with peers, and they may insist on both peers and subordinates submitting to their will, tending to be oblivious to the resentment they create in others. Such behavior obviously can have a disruptive, harmful effect on the group process of decision making.

THE NARCISSISTIC PERSONALITY AND CRISIS DECISION MAKING

If the ranks of leaders were stripped of individuals with narcissistic personality features, they would be seriously depleted, for the upper levels of government and industry are filled with successful narcissists. After all, at one level narcissism is nothing more than extreme self-confidence, and the wedding of self-confidence and ability is what creates success.

But narcissism to an extreme can be disabling. As with the compulsive personality disorder, the personality flaws of the full-blown narcissistic character disorder are so severe as to be inconsistent with sustained effective leadership (Kernberg 1975). The differences, however, between individuals with significant narcissistic personality features and those with the full-blown character disorder are differences of degree, not of kind; under stress, mild narcissistic characteristics can become extreme and, temporarily, can resemble the full-blown picture.

Characteristics of the narcissistic leader have been considered in detail in earlier chapters. Here I emphasize only those characteristics that can have a deleterious effect on crisis decision making.

Some narcissistic leaders will so crave adulation that they surround themselves with individuals who learn that it is necessary to uncritically assure the leader of the excellence of his or her plans, and protect them from knowledge of public discontent and other criticisms of their policies. In effect, the self-esteem maintenance function dominates, and the leader is surrounded with sycophants. Even though a narcissistic leader is psychologically "normal" according to all psychological tests and is fully in touch with psychological reality, a narcissistic leader who has selected his inner circle on this basis may be totally out of touch with political reality. There are reports that this was true of Egyptian President Sadat toward the end of his rule. Despite his international success, he was extremely sensitive to criticism. When the Egyptian peasants rioted over the price of bread, an expression of their discontent with Sadat's economic policies, Sadat's advisers informed him of the bread riots but assured him they were caused by Communist agitators. Similarly, for well-founded reasons, Iraqi President Saddam Hussein's advisers were reluctant to offer constructive criticism of Saddam, for to do so was to risk losing not only their jobs but their lives.

Optimally, the adviser close to the narcissistic leader will manage both to shore up the leader's self-esteem and help him to appraise political reality accurately. Examples of such healthy advisory relationships include Theodore Sorensen and John Kennedy, Colonel Edward House and Woodrow Wilson, and Louis Howe and Franklin D. Roosevelt. This is not meant to imply that Wilson, Kennedy, and Roosevelt were full-blown narcissistic characters, but a reading of psychobiographic materials suggests there were significant narcissistic elements in their personalities. The special relationships they had with their close advisers were by all accounts healthy and candid. By no means sycophants, these advisers shored up the leaders' self-esteem while helping them to gauge political reality.

Because narcissists are so vulnerable under their grandiose facade, it is difficult for them to acknowledge ignorance and, accordingly, to accept information or constructive criticism of their ideas. This contributes to the tendency of narcissists to surround themselves with sycophants who tell them what they want to hear, rather than what they need to hear.

Narcissists place overly high value on their own judgments and tend to overestimate the probability of success for their plans. Indeed, the narcissistic tendency to be overly optimistic may contribute to the group appraisals described by Janis (1972) under the rubric of "groupthink."

Because of their difficulties in empathizing with others, narcissists have a difficult time putting themselves into the mind of an adversary. Because they tend to identify themselves with the nation, they have a difficult time in separating national interest from self-interest. Thus, for the narcissist, the operant questions are not "What are the threats to my country, and what can be done to counter them?" but "How can I use this situation to enhance or protect my own reputation?"

The conscience of the narcissist is dominated by self-interest. Nevertheless, the narcissist's self-image is of a principled and scrupulous person who, if he has reversed himself, did so because of circumstantial changes. Thus, a narcissist communicates utter sincerity and trustworthiness, so the unwary can be completely taken in. The narcissist seems to be completely sincere, and indeed, at that moment, he is. In negotiating with a narcissist in a crisis situation, it would be well to recall Ronald Reagan's admonition, "Trust, but verify." Two contemporary leaders with severe narcissistic personality disorders, Saddam Hussein and Kim Jong Il of North Korea, who violated their commitments to stop their weapons of mass destruction programs, are prime examples of this.

In characterizing practitioners of "hardball politics," Lloyd Etheredge (1979) is describing a variant of the narcissistic personality often encountered in the corridors of power. For these individuals, image and career enhancement are always primary values.

Crises do not eclipse this personality tendency—on the contrary, for hardball politicians, crises are opportunities to seize the moment. It was probably the hardball narcissistic personality that a cynical senior government official had in mind when he defined a crisis to me as "an optimal opportunity for a bureaucratic power player to gain senior level visibility and maximize his promotion potential." Thus, as he went on to say, the primary interest for such an individual is who goes to the White House for the morning meeting. Because gaining access to power is a primary value for such an individual, knowledge becomes power—a precious commodity to be held tightly and used for one's own advantage.

These special characteristics of narcissistic leaders' psychology and interpersonal relationships affect their leadership behavior and decision making in general, but particularly in crisis situations. Response to such situations will largely be determined by whether a narcissistic leader is surrounded by sycophants or whether he or she has advisers who can help them accurately assess the nature of their adversary, evaluate the completeness of their plans, and make midcourse corrections.

THE PARANOID PERSONALITY AND CRISIS DECISION MAKING

The essential features of the paranoid personality are a pervasive and long-standing suspiciousness and mistrust of people in general. The paranoid is always expecting plots and betrayal and sees himself alone, surrounded by enemies. This derives in part from an exaggerated need for autonomy. In such a dangerous world, it is best to trust no one.

Suspiciousness is the sine qua non of the paranoid. Paranoid individuals are hypersensitive and easily slighted; they continually scan the environment for clues that confirm their original assumptions, attitudes, or biases. Individuals who are highly suspicious constantly search for evidence to confirm their conclusions. They seize on evidence that confirms their suspicions and reject disconfirming evidence. Psychologically healthy individuals can abandon their suspicions when they are presented with firm contradictory evidence. The paranoid, in contrast, has a fixed conclusion of danger in search of evidence.

Paranoids tend to be rigid and unwilling to compromise. In a new situation, they tend to lose appreciation of the total context as they pursue their fixed conclusion of danger.

The paranoid will become hostile, defensive, and stubborn when presented with evidence that contradicts his or her suspicions. Trying to breach the rigidity of the paranoid can produce unfortunate consequences. Well-meaning attempts to reassure or reason with a paranoid person will usually provoke anger, and the helpful one can become the object of suspicion and be seen as disloyal. This wary hypervigilance and readiness to retaliate often generate fear and uneasiness in others. One treads lightly and carefully around a paranoid and "walks on eggshells," lest one provoke anger.

The paranoid's view of an adversary is both strong and central. The world is seen as highly conflictual and the adversary is seen as evil, an immutable threat to one's own and the national self-interests. An adversary's overture of friendship will be seen as confirmation of the adversary's treachery, as an attempt to lull one's own side into a false sense of complacency. In a crisis situation, the paranoid will not see the adversary as being eager to avoid conflict but rather will attribute malevolent motivations and construct a worst-case scenario. This in turn pushes the paranoid to preemptive action, convinced that persuasion and compromise are impossible.

Fortunately, severe paranoids of the kind described above usually do not last long in a hierarchy, at least in an open society. In a closed society, the paranoid—as exemplified by Saddam Hussein or Joseph Stalin—can structure the environment to confirm his suspicions. More muted, often better controlled, manifestations of these behaviors are seen in individuals who manage generally to function effectively, although the underlying personality gives a particular style to their behavior. Indeed, in a highly competitive bureaucracy, a touch of paranoia with its heightened readiness to see bureaucratic rivals around every corner can be adaptive and help the individual to survive the bureaucratic wars.

But, as noted earlier, under crisis-induced stress, paranoid personality traits of a moderate degree become exaggerated and can become dysfunctional. Thus, the somewhat suspicious individual, whose suspiciousness is not usually of pathological proportions, can, under stress, become frankly paranoid. Several journalistic and memoir accounts of the last days of the Nixon presidency suggest that there was serious concern within the inner circle that the effects of the Watergate crisis on Nixon were so severe that his reactions could not be trusted, with particular concern for the so-called nuclear suitcase that always accompanies the president. Emergency measures were instituted to limit his capability of instituting conflict. In particular, procedural safeguards were instituted that required validation by senior officials before direct orders by the commander-in-chief, especially orders to use nuclear weapons, could be enacted (Kissinger 1979; Woodward and Bernstein 1976).

In considering the relationship between personality styles and crisis-induced stress, we should not limit our attention to leaders in open societies—to the principal U.S. and Western decision makers. What of their opposite numbers in closed societies? In a conspiratorial milieu, having paranoid traits is not only *not* dysfunctional, it is necessary for survival. Stalin is an interesting case in point. To have failed to be on guard and plot-conscious in the conspiracy-ridden Kremlin would have been to be out of touch with reality. Stalin's antennae for enemies were finely tuned. This additional edge of suspiciousness undoubtedly played a major role in his survival. But over time the ranks of identified enemies were swollen with imagined enemies. Moreover, the paranoid fears induced a self-fulfilling prophecy, for Stalin's paranoid political behavior toward imagined enemies created enemies in actuality. Robert C. Tucker's (1973) psychobiography of Stalin provides persuasive details concerning Stalin's state of mind at the end of his life. At the time of the so-called doctors' plot there seems little doubt that Stalin was in a clinically paranoid state and that his fears were being manipulated by Lavrenti Beria to secure his own position and eliminate bureaucratic rivals.

When individuals with strong paranoid propensities, such as Stalin, occupy major leadership roles, their characteristic reactions can have major consequences for political behavior, especially in crisis situations. Accounts of Hitler under stress, both on the eve of the Normandy invasion and on other occasions as the political-military situation was further unraveling, suggest that the dynamics sketched above were very much in play. The greater the stress, the more rigidly Hitler held on to his construction of the world. To attempt to present him with new information or to persuade him to change his mind was not only to risk explosive wrath but even the possibility of expulsion from the ranks of advisers, court martial, or worse. This would inhibit even the most self-confident of advisers. But given the strong psychological need to please authority that characterized many of these individuals, the premium on not disturbing or angering the Fuehrer took precedence over fully expressing one's assessment of the situation. This example, while striking, is by no means unique. It emphasizes the point that in considering the effects of personality on crisis reactions, one must consider the interaction between different personalities in the decision-making hierarchy.

Decision Makers and Their Support Groups

> Representative Les Aspin, the chairman of the House Armed Services Committee, asserted that a safety officer destroyed a Navy Trident 2 submarine missile by mistake. "There's always someone who doesn't get the word," Mr. Aspin said, "and in this incident it was the man with his finger on the button."
>
> "Missile Blast Called Deliberate,"
> *New York Times*, October 14, 1988

The decision maker does not make decisions in splendid isolation but in relation to a chain of command. The interplay of personalities can influence both the information on which the decision maker acts and the manner in which the decisions are implemented.

The following two examples illustrate subordinates who were inhibited because of a combination of bureaucratic and psychological reasons from "getting the word" to the principal decision maker.

In *Victims of Groupthink*, the study by Irving Janis of the influence of group dynamics on decision making in the Bay of Pigs case, there is an interesting illustration of the problems in reopening a decision when decisional closure has been reached by the principal decision maker, and of the difficulties for the subordinate in groups in which power is distributed unequally. As the final countdown for the invasion of Cuba was proceeding, then-Undersecretary of State Chester Bowles expressed grave reservations to Secretary of State Dean Rusk about the wisdom of the plan. Rusk informed Bowles that the president had already made up his mind and that contrary opinions would not be welcome. Bowles felt unable to make his reservations known to Kennedy, and his opposition to the plan was only to surface after the operation had disastrously failed. Although it was attributed to protocol, Bowles's reluctance to push the matter further in the face of Rusk's admonition can be seen as deference to the superior authority of both Rusk and Kennedy.

Another example of the manner in which sensitivity to hierarchical relationships can adversely affect the quality of decisions is reflected in an episode that occurred in the State Department crisis task force during a terrorist hostage crisis in Southeast Asia. The chair of the task force received an urgent cable from the field that required an immediate decision by officials at the senior policy-making level; lives were in jeopardy. The chair's immediate superior, the deputy assistant secretary of state, would normally have conveyed the message to the senior officials, but he could not be located. The chair delayed forwarding the cable for some forty-five minutes, because he did not want to make an "end run" around his superior, the deputy assistant secretary. The chair of the crisis task force did not wish to place the deputy assistant secretary in the embarrassing position of having his superior, the senior policy official, know the information before he did. Although the delay did not produce loss of life, what was uppermost on the chair's mind was avoiding embarrassing his boss and avoiding his displeasure.

Both of the above circumstances have been characterized as demonstrating the manner in which sensitivity to hierarchical relationships can influence decision making. In neither circumstance is there any reason to believe that the key participants were suffering from a personality disorder. But in a decision node comprised of a principal decision maker and his decision support staff or circle of advisers, all of the participants have personalities, and many of the personality traits described above will be present in varying degrees. Individuals with significant compulsive traits tend to be especially concerned with hierarchical relationships, and will be especially concerned with the reactions of the principal decision maker. The possibility of upsetting a somewhat paranoid leader or a vulnerable narcissistic leader is likely to magnify the anxiety of a highly deferential subordinate who has problems dealing with authority and who, accordingly, may well conceal adverse information rather than risk his superior's wrath.

There are important interpersonal implications of each of the personality types described above when the individual is acting in relation to superiors, peers, and subordinates. In the social science literature concerning group decision making, there has been no systematic examination of how decision groups with differential distribution of power and authority function nor of how different personality types affect the function of such groups.

Psychophysiologic Considerations

One of the most interesting and, at first blush, perplexing characteristics of reactions by an individual leader to crises concerns the discrepancy between subjective self-reports by the leader and objective descriptions by observers. The experience of the stress of crisis decision-making is often described by the person engaged in it in the most glowing terms. A striking example is found in the introduction to Richard Nixon's *Six Crises* (1960):

> From my own experience, the bigger the problem, the broader its consequences, the less does an individual think of himself. He has to devote his entire concentration to the much larger problem which confronts him. The natural symptoms of stress in a period of crisis do not become self-destructive as a result of his worrying about himself but, on the other hand, become positive forces for creative action.
>
> No one really knows what he is capable of until he is tested to the full by events over which he may have no great control.
>
> Courage—or putting it more accurately, lack of fear—is a result of discipline. Any man who claims never to have known fear is either lying or else he is stupid. But by an act of will he refuses to think of the reasons for fear and so concentrates entirely on winning the battle.
>
> Experience is a vitally important factor. When a man has been through even a minor crisis, he learns not to worry when his muscles tense up, his breathing comes faster, his nerves tingle, his stomach churns, his temper becomes short, his nights are sleepless. He recognizes such symptoms as the natural and healthy signs that his system is keyed up for battle. Far from worrying when this happens, he should worry when it does not. Because he knows from experience that once the battle is joined, all these symptoms will disappear—unless he insists on thinking primarily of himself rather than the problem he must confront.
>
> A man who has never lost himself in a cause bigger than himself has missed one of life's mountaintop experiences. Only in losing himself does he find himself. Only then does he discover all the latent strengths he never knew he had and which otherwise would have remained dormant.
>
> Crisis can indeed be agony. But it is the exquisite agony which a man might not wish to experience again—yet would not for the world have missed. (xviii)

Some individuals may even seek out and create crises as a way of feeling a sense of mastery, of channeling their own aggressive and combative instincts. Commenting on Nixon's reactions to crisis, J. D. Barber (1972) observes that for the "active-negative" (neurotically driven to prove himself) Nixon, involvement in a crisis imbued him with a sense of power. Accordingly, Barber posits an adversarial, crisis-seeking bent in Nixon.

Gary Sick, the principal White House aide for Iran during the Iranian Revolution and the hostage crisis, was by all accounts highly effective in his crucial National Security Council staff role. His book about his experiences includes a discussion of the effects of sustained crisis-induced stress (1986). At times, the long hours and sustained pressure were debilitating, but he also describes aspects of his reactions during that prolonged crisis in terms reminiscent of Nixon's "mountaintop" experiences. Sick served on the National Security Council staff under Presidents Ford, Carter, and Reagan, but he regarded the long days and nights when he was at the center of the Iran hostage crisis as the very acme of his government service—an occasion when he functioned at the height of his powers. Other experiences paled by comparison.

The operational definition of crisis at the Department of State is any situation that calls into being a crisis task force. When a task force is created, key players from numerous bureaus within the department are recruited. Considered by many an onerous task, service on such task forces is sought after by others. They describe the excitement and high-tension involvement in glowing terms and are described by their peers as "action junkies." The choice of the term "action junkies" is not accidental, for they are seen as being addicted to the excitement of crises, and their ordinary duties seem pale and lifeless by comparison.

The euphoria and the feeling of being at the height of one's powers reported by Nixon, Sick, and State Department crisis task force members reflect in part the natural high that accompanies stress. It partly results from the discharge of adrenal hormones, an important psychophysiologic response to stress described by Hans Selye (1976) and others. The same hormones that mobilize the body's defenses in a "fight-flight" pattern characteristically produce a heady, euphoric feeling. Figure 5.3 is a version of Selye's illustration of the mind-body connection and reactions to stress updated by E. L. Rossi (1987).

Note particularly the central role of the adrenal glands, the endocrine glands that secrete adrenal steroids that play so central a role in the body's fight-flight reaction. Note that these steroids affect mental and emotional processes.

Let us now take a closer look at the relationship between increased levels of stress and an individual's performance. Early in a crisis, one's alertness is magnified, and certain kinds of performance may be improved. However, the so-called "inverted U," shown in figure 2, usefully captures what experimental studies reveal—an early heightening of decision-making ability and performance that may be followed, if stress increases beyond a certain point, by a decline in judgment and performance. But the emotional effects of the discharge of corticosteroids (adrenal hormones)

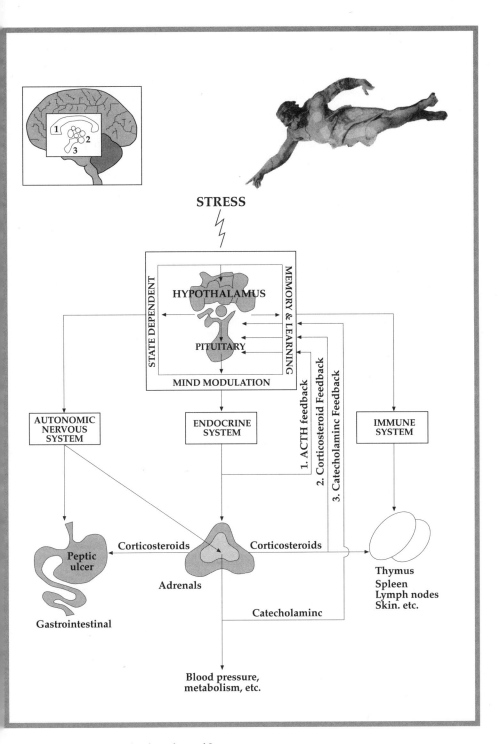

Figure 5.3. The Psychophysiology of Stress

will convey a feeling of being at the height of one's powers, even when objective performance measures demonstrate the contrary. Adrenal hormones magnify feelings of mastery and optimism, a combination of feelings that can clearly lead to miscalculations. The subjective feeling and self-report of heightened abilities should be distrusted.

One of the characteristics of "groupthink" identified by Janis (1972) is being overly optimistic about the likelihood of success. He sees it as a consequence of unusually high group cohesion, a necessary condition for the concurrence-seeking that serves as a way of coping with the stress of crisis decision making. The psychophysiologic explanation presented here does not compete with that of Janis, but suggests that the observed over optimism may be multiply determined. In addition to Janis's social psychological explanation, the psychophysiology of stress as well as the narcissistic overvaluation described earlier may contribute to this characteristic phenomenon and probably interact with it. Thus, the adrenaline high produced by stress may well magnify the already present tendency toward optimism in a consensus-seeking group of high-level decision makers abundantly endowed with narcissistic personality traits.

One statement in Nixon's (1960) long discourse on the effects of crisis-induced stress on decision makers—repeated here to emphasize the deleterious consequences of crisis-induced stress on decision making—needs to be distrusted:

> When a man has been through even a minor crisis, he learns not to worry when his muscles tense up, his breathing comes faster, his nerves tingle, his stomach churns, his temper becomes short, his nights are sleepless. He recognizes such symptoms as the natural and healthy signs that his system is keyed up for battle. Far from worrying when this happens, he should worry when it does not.

Nixon's statements to the contrary, the combination of sleeplessness and irritability that frequently affects individuals operating in crisis decision groups can have serious consequences. It is in the crisis task force, where twenty-four-hour coverage of the critically defined situation is implemented, that psychophysiology, personality, and group and organizational dynamics come dramatically into play. Individuals experienced in running crisis task forces, recognizing the adverse effects of sleep deprivation, have established procedures for ensuring that individuals serving on task forces have adequate sleep, recreation, and down time away from the emotional pressure cooker of the crisis task force operations center. Thus, when a round-the-clock task force has been established, the first job of the task force director is to establish rosters and watch schedules and shifts. A major responsibility of the task force director is to ensure that the members adhere to the discipline of these schedules; he will sometimes have to literally force the members to leave the operations center.

Although this discipline is effective with mid-level employees, senior officials will rarely adhere to the discipline of shifts, and the task force director, who is usually a subordinate, will often feel inhibited from insisting that his or her superior leave. Indeed, insofar as they are not only senior in rank but often in age as well, it may well be these very individuals who most need adequate sleep and who can function least well in the face of fatigue. Stories abound of senior officials during crises walking around like "living zombies"—taking in information but being utterly unable to make decisions—with a consequent paralysis of decision making, because their subordinates feel unable to make decisions on their own while the senior officials are present. Add to the sleeplessness the irritability to which Nixon refers and recall the deferential attitude of certain personality types, and one has a recipe for impaired decision making.

The subject of deference to irritable authority underlines the inaccuracy of another of Nixon's characterizations of crisis decision making. He says that personal concerns disappear in the face of crisis and describes a noble selflessness. Although there is a widespread notion that personal and bureaucratic rivalries disappear during crises and that everyone pulls together to cope with the common emergency, in fact, nothing could be further from the truth, and bureaucratic fault lines are frequently magnified by a crisis.

When the nature of the crisis is such that senior participants feel unable to delegate to their juniors, the potential for adverse effects of sleep deprivation and aberrant individual reactions is magnified and the symptoms delineated above can become exaggerated. Such would surely be the case in a nuclear crisis, such as the Cuban Missile Crisis. Reports from the 1988 meeting in Moscow of some of the original Soviet and U.S. participants in the Cuban Missile Crisis and their relatives or knowledgeable staff suggest that the decision-making process was very far from the idealized model of judicious governmental decision making many have considered the deliberations of the ExCom to be (Allen, Blight, and Welch 1989). One of the participants described their thinking as badly flawed and said it was only a miracle that a disaster did not occur.

By the fourth or fifth day of the crisis, many were experiencing exhaustion and impaired reasoning processes. Soviet ambassador to the United States Anatoly Dobrynin's account of his meeting with Robert Kennedy, if correctly recalled by Nikita Khrushchev (1970), is revealing: "Robert Kennedy looked exhausted. One could see from his eyes that he had not slept for days. He himself said that he had not been home for six days and nights. 'The President is in a grave situation,' Robert Kennedy said, 'and he does not know how to get out of it. We are under very severe stress.' " Arthur Schlesinger (1978) reports Robert Kennedy's observation that the magnitude of the stress led Secretary of State Dean Rusk to have "a virtually complete breakdown mentally and physically," although James G. Blight and David A. Welch's (1988) research leads them to disagree with this assessment of Rusk's reaction.

Sleeplessness and irritability can have a further deleterious consequence. Sleeping pills may be turned to for insomnia, minor tranquilizers such as Valium for anxiety or irritability, and stimulants such as amphetamine compounds for fatigue. One particularly destructive sequence is to alternate so-called downers (sedative or tranquilizing medication) with uppers (stimulants). Each of these medication classes can affect reaction time, judgment, and other cognitive functions. For example, Halcyon, a frequently used sleeping pill, often produces retrograde amnesia, that is, an inability to recall events that occurred before the drug-induced sleep. Among the initial effects of amphetamines, which make them attractive to a leader in a crisis situation, are increased alertness, lessened fatigue, feelings of well-being, and lessened need for sleep. In a crisis, an individual who is "high" on amphetamines may be insufficiently cautious or unduly optimistic. Amphetamines not only give their takers a grossly overvalued sense of their own competence but the feelings of well-being can mount to the point of euphoria, exaltation, and grandiosity. Suspiciousness and irritability are frequently in evidence as well, and these stimulants can also produce paranoid reactions.

As detailed in chapter 3, a number of important twentieth-century leaders, with the assistance of their physicians, abused stimulant and other medications. One of President Kennedy's personal physicians, Dr. Max Jacobson, assisted the president in abusing amphetamines (Greenberger 1972). British Prime Minister Anthony Eden described himself as "living on Benzedrine" during the Suez Crisis. Irritable to the extreme, he would fly into rages at the very mention of Nasser's name, and his decision making was judged to be highly erratic. Hitler's erratic reactions may well have been exacerbated by the concoction of medications prescribed for him by his physician, Dr. Theodore Morell, widely viewed as a quack (L'Etang 1979; Park 1986). Hitler was simultaneously taking amphetamines and cocaine, a dangerous combination that would have had very deleterious effects on his decision making.

Because of the rank of the senior official, the physician may be loath to decline to prescribe the medications he requests or demands. In the midst of the Suez Crisis, with the very fate of the British Empire resting on the prime minister's shoulders, it would be an intrepid physician who would resist his VIP patient's demand for Benzedrine.

In addition to taking prescription medications, individuals under stress may self-medicate, turning to alcohol to help them fall asleep and to calm their nerves. The question of alcohol abuse was raised prominently during the confirmation hearings for Secretary of Defense–designate John Tower in 1981. Several senators said that the secretary of defense's position in the nuclear decision-making chain of command heightened the importance of whether he turned to alcohol under stress. Tower was not confirmed for the position.

So far, I have only considered issues of personality and psychophysiology. What are the effects of the aging process on crisis reactions? Although "wisdom is with the aged and understanding in length of days" (Job 12:12), rapid tactical decision making is difficult for individuals in their sixties and seventies, even if they are not hampered by illness. What, then, can be said about the decision-making ability of aged, ailing individuals? What if such an individual is a major leader? What can be said about a decision-making group composed of aged leaders?

Consider crisis decision making during the latter years of the Brezhnev era, when the average age of the Politburo was 73.5 years and several of the key leaders were manifestly suffering the incursions of age and probably suffering from moderate hardening of the arteries of the brain (cerebral arteriosclerosis). When the Korean airliner, the KAL-007, wandered into Soviet airspace, was the aging senior leadership involved in the decision that led to the shoot-down?

Despite Nixon's heroic claim of selflessness in the face of crisis, human vulnerability does not disappear in times of stress. To the contrary, although moderate levels of stress usually improve the performance of most individuals, at least initially, human frailties are magnified at the individual, group, and organizational levels when acute, prolonged stress and fatigue are experienced; psychological fault lines are widened, and the greater the stress, the more magnified the responses.

The result can be major distortions in communication and the syndrome of groupthink. Conversely, irritability and exaggerated psychological reactions can contribute to a badly divided, fractious group. Moreover, the psychophysiology of acute and chronic stress in turn can lead to abuse of prescription medications and alcohol, which adds a further complicating dimension.

A war-threatening crisis or a conventional war that could escalate to nuclear confrontation would surely lead to massive stress. There is no reason to believe that the magnitude of the crisis would somehow immunize decision makers from experiencing the almost unimaginable level of stress of a nuclear crisis.

What are the implications—and prescriptions—that follow from the preceding analysis? In the military, selection and training are the twin pillars for the identification and preparation of military officers responsible for decision making under combat stress. In selecting our leaders and senior civilian officials, a major criterion should be a demonstrated capacity for effective and judicious decision making under stress.

Our leaders and senior officials should regularly participate in training simulations to become familiar with crisis decision making and to identify and remedy individual, group, and organizational vulnerabilities under stress.

Military psychologists note that such simulations can never fully prepare participants for combat because "the excitement factor is missing in such drills, because regardless of the realism of the simulation, it is just that, a simulation of the real thing," but, nevertheless, training simulations can make the unimaginable imaginable. Political-military simulations and exercises are regularly conducted by governments, East and West, but world leaders and their most senior officials are often too busy to participate. Yet, it is they who will be exercising that awesome responsibility should the unimaginable become reality. The very highest officials, including civilian officials, should be participating in such exercises within their own governments and alliances.

Moreover, we should now be considering what could not have been conceived of until recently—developing and conducting political-military exercises and war games in collaboration with our potential adversaries. By permitting the participants to see the distortions in decision making caused by crisis-induced stress, including the misinterpretations of the adversary's intentions, such exercises could have extremely constructive consequences in sensitizing the participants and helping to avoid inadvertent war.

6

The Mind of the Terrorist

There is no universally accepted definition of terrorism, because defining an individual or group as terrorist is a pejorative judgment.[1] Terrorism is defined in Title 22 of the United States Code, Section 2656f(d), as "premeditated, politically motivated violence perpetrated against noncombatant targets by sub-national groups or clandestine agents, usually intended to influence an audience." Symbolic in intent, the terrorist act is designed to influence an audience beyond the immediate victims, including members of the victims' class, the government, and society. It is political theater, a vicious species of psychological warfare using violence as communication. Terrorism falls into the spectrum of low-intensity conflict, relying on the methods and strategies of unconventional warfare in targeting women and children, businessmen, tourists, and other noncombatants to gain exposure, pressure governments, and extort concessions, such as the release of prisoners or changes in domestic or foreign policies.

Diversity of the Terrorist Spectrum

Terrorism is not a homogeneous phenomenon. There is a broad spectrum of terrorist groups and organizations, each of which has a different psychology, motivation, and decision-making structure. Indeed, one should not speak of terrorist psychology in the singular, but rather of terrorist psychologies. This chapter might more accurately be titled "The Minds of Terrorists," for within the spectrum of terrorist groups is a variegated assortment of terrorist psychologies, although there are certain psychological themes in common.

Figure 6.1 depicts the broad spectrum of terrorist types. The top tier differentiates criminal and pathological terrorism from political terrorism. Criminal terrorism refers to groups using terrorist techniques to support

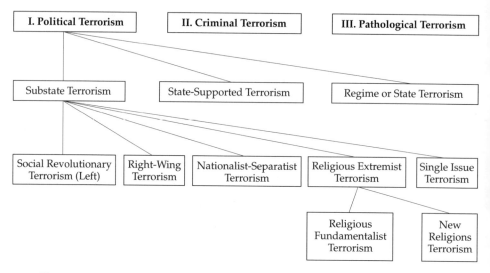

Figure 6.1. Spectrum of Terrorism

criminal goals, such as the narco-terrorists of the Andean nations of Latin America who carry out terrorist acts in support of the narco-trafficantes of the drug cartels. When they assassinate a judge in Colombia, it is to intimidate other judges to keep them from enforcing the law against the narcotics traffickers. The lines are blurring between political and criminal terrorists in this region, for many of the narco-terorists are from what were originally social revolutionary groups that still nominally espouse their Marxist cause. Studies of political terrorist psychology do not reveal severe psychiatric pathology (Post 1990). In fact, political terrorist groups do not permit emotionally disturbed individuals to join them because they are a security risk. Seriously disturbed individuals tend to act alone.

In the middle tier, it is important to differentiate among state terrorism, state-supported terrorism, and substate terrorism (Schmid 1984).

State terrorism refers to the use of terror by the government, with the state turning its resources—police, judiciary, military, secret police, and so forth—against its own citizenry to quell domestic opposition to its policies and suppress dissent, as exemplified by the "dirty wars" in Argentina in the 1970s and 1980s, when regime opponents were "disappeared." When Saddam Hussein used nerve gas against his own Kurdish citizens, this was an example of state chemical terrorism.

State-supported terrorism refers to situations in which a state provides logistical, financial, and training support for a terrorist organization to further its foreign policy goals. State-supported terrorism is of major concern to the United States. The U.S. Department of State designated Iran, Iraq, Syria, Libya, Cuba, North Korea, and Sudan as state sponsors of terrorism in 2002. In these situations, when states are acting through terrorist groups, the government will constrain the group acting under their influence or control because of a fear of retaliation.

Substate terrorism, also known as terrorism from below, refers to acts of terrorism perpetrated by nonstate actors. In the lower tier, a diverse group of substate terrorist groups is specified: social revolutionary terrorism, nationalist-separatist terrorism, right-wing terrorism, religious-extremist terrorism (subsuming both religious fundamentalist terrorism and terrorism perpetrated by nontraditional religious groups), and single-issue terrorism.

Social revolutionary terrorism, also known as terrorism of the left, refers to groups seeking to overthrow the capitalist economic and social order. Drawing on the "propaganda by the deed" tradition of the European and Russian anarchists of the late nineteenth and early twentieth centuries, these groups are exemplified by the European "fighting communist organizations" active throughout the 1970s and 1980s, among which were the Red Army Faction in Germany and the Red Brigades in Italy. Although social revolutionary terrorist groups have experienced a significant decline over the last two decades, paralleling the collapse of Communism in Europe and the end of the Cold War, social revolutionary terrorism and insurgency are still underway, as exemplified by the Japanese Red Army (JRA); the Maoist Sendero Luminoso (the Shining Path) and the Tupac Amaru Revolutionary Movement (MRTA) in Peru, and several Columbian terrorist groups that are also associated with narco-terrorism, as exemplified by the Revolutionary Armed Forces of Colombia (FARC); and the Zapatista Army for National Liberation (EZLN) of Chiapas, Mexico.

These are complex organizations, however, not groups per se. The decision-making locus is outside of the action cells. In these secret organizations, there is a tension between security and communication. This leads to rather more decision-making latitude for the action cells than might be present in a more open organization. Policy guidelines may be laid down, but specific planning concerning the target and the tactics is delegated to the group.

Insofar as these groups are seeking to influence their society, they would be significantly constrained from indiscriminate acts that cause significant casualties among their own countrymen or cause negative reactions in their domestic and international audiences. But these groups could rationalize acts against government or symbolic capitalist targets.

Nationalist-separatist terrorism, also known as ethnonationalist terrorism, includes those groups fighting to establish a geographically separate political state based on ethnic dominance or homogeneity. The Provisional Irish Republican Army of Northern Ireland (PIRA), the Liberation Tigers of Tamil Eelam (LTTE) of Sri Lanka, the Basque Fatherland and Liberty (ETA) in Spain, and the radical groups seeking to establish a Palestinian homeland, such as Fatah, the Popular Front for the Liberation of Palestine (PFLP), and the Abu Nidal Organization, are prominent examples. Nationalist-separatist terrorists are usually attempting to garner international sympathy for their cause and to coerce the dominant group. Thus ETA is attempting to pressure Spain to yield to its demands for an independent Basque state. The causes espoused by nationalist-separatist terrorist groups are particularly intractable, for resentment of the dominant ethnic group has been conveyed from generation to generation (Post 1990). Hatred has been "bred in the bone." In these organizations, the young revolutionaries of these nationalist-separatist terrorist organizations are often extolled as heroes within their communities, for their mission reflects their people's cause. Nationalist-separatist groups operating within their nation are particularly sensitive to the response of their internal constituency, as well as of their international audience. This constrains acts so violent or extranormal as to offend their constituents, as exemplified by the bombing by the Real IRA (a splinter group of the Provisional IRA) in Omagh in 1998 that killed twenty-nine people, most of them women and children. The resulting uproar from their Irish constituents was so intense that the Real IRA apologized and forswore future violence.

Religious-extremist terrorism comprises both religious fundamentalist terrorism and "new religions" terrorism. In both cases, religious belligerents are defending their faith against enemies of their faith, responding to the interpretation of scripture by radical clerics who endorse killing in the name of God. Among all of the "people of the book"—Jewish, Christian, and Muslim—there are extremists seeking to "force the end." "New religions" include groups such as Aum Shinrikyo, which was responsible for the 1995 sarin gas attack in the Tokyo subway.

In the beginning of the modern era of terrorism, ushered in by the radical Palestinian seizure of the Israeli Olympic village during the 1972 Munich Olympics, two types of groups dominated the terrorist landscape—social revolutionary terrorists and nationalist-separatist terrorists. Their goal was to call the world's attention to their cause. They regularly claimed responsibility for their acts; indeed, there were often multiple claims. Then, in the late 1980s and early 1990s, this changed. No responsibility was claimed for upward of 40 percent of terrorist acts. These were the acts of radical religious fundamentalist terrorists. They were not interested in influencing the West or calling attention to their cause. They were interested in expelling the West and its corrupt secular modernizing values. And they did not need to claim responsibility for their act. They did not require a CNN story or a *New York Times* headline to identify who was responsible, for they were "killing in the name of God" and God already knew. Nor are religious fundamentalist terrorists ambivalent about their acts of violence. They are "true believers"; as instructed by their radical clerics, be they ayatollahs, rabbis, or priests, they believe that their acts have been sanctified by religious authority.

Only a small minority of religious fundamentalists turn to the path of activism. Most groups withdraw passively, waiting for the arrival of the messiah and the subsequent redemption. Others strive to combat the immoral forces in the world, to demonstrate their piety to the world. These "spiritual belligerents" (Hazani, forthcoming) individually and collectively confront society aggressively in terms of their religious doctrine. Living in a subjective polarized reality, an "us versus them" world, they display a paranoid attitude and a Manichean dichotomization of the universe.

Religious belligerents are not confined to closed religious cults but are found within the ranks of the great religions. The dichotomization of the universe depicted in scripture is fertile soil for the spiritual belligerent, justification for their aggression. A sharp division of the moral universe between good and evil is one of the principal attributes of the three largest monotheistic religions that originated in the Middle East—Judaism, Christianity, and Islam. This is a world of light and darkness, in constant warfare with evil, its members having an unambiguous responsibility to fight on God's side.

Ardent practitioners of these faiths, committed to the literal word of God, are able to find ample justification in their texts for militant aggressive defense of their beliefs. When "truth" is conveyed by an authoritarian religious leader, such as Khomeini or Osama bin Laden (who, in fact, has no religious credentials), all doubt is relieved for the true believer. It provides justification for the rigid moralistic conscience to attack the nonbeliever. It can justify aggression to the point of killing.

Right-wing terrorism comprises those groups seeking to maintain an extant political order or to return society to an idealized "golden age" of the past. Examples include neo-Nazi groups, such as the Aryan Nations, and groups espousing racist ideology, such as the Ku Klux Klan.

Single-issue terrorism represents groups acting on a single issue, such as the environment or animal rights.

The Underlying Psychology of Terrorism

The principal argument of this chapter is that political terrorists are driven to commit acts of violence as a consequence of psychological forces, and that their special psycho-logic is constructed to rationalize acts they are psychologically compelled to commit. Individuals are drawn to the path of terrorism in order to commit acts of violence; their special logic, which is grounded in their psychology and reflected in their rhetoric, becomes the justification for their violent acts.

Considering the diversity of causes to which terrorists are committed, the uniformity of their rhetoric is striking. Polarizing and absolutist, it is a rhetoric of "us versus them." It is rhetoric without nuance, without shades of gray. "They," the establishment, are the source of all evil in vivid contrast to "us," the freedom fighters, consumed by righteous rage. And, if "they" are the source of our problems, it follows ineluctably in the special psycho-logic of the terrorist that "they" must be destroyed. It is the only just and moral thing to do. Once one accepts the basic premises, the logical reasoning is flawless.

What accounts for the uniformity of the terrorists' polarizing and absolutist rhetoric? My own comparative research on the psychology of terrorists does not reveal major psychopathology, agreeing with the finding of Martha Crenshaw (1981) that "the outstanding common characteristic of terrorists is their normality." Her studies of the National Liberation Front (FLN) in Algeria in the 1950s found the members to be basically normal. Nor did K. Heskin (1984) find members of the IRA to be emotionally disturbed. In a review of the *Social Psychology of Terrorist Groups*, C. R. McCauley and M. E. Segal (1987) conclude that "the best documented generalization is negative; terrorists do not show any striking psychopathology."

Nor does a comparative study reveal a particular psychological type, a particular personality constellation, a uniform terrorist mind. But although a diversity of personalities are attracted to the path of terrorism, examination of memoirs, court records, and, on rare occasions, interviews suggests that individuals with particular personality traits and personality tendencies are drawn disproportionately to terrorist careers.

What are these traits, these personality characteristics? Several authors have characterized terrorists as action-oriented, aggressive individuals who are stimulus hungry, seeking excitement. Particularly striking is the reliance placed on the psychological mechanisms of externalization and splitting, psychological mechanisms found in individuals with narcissistic and borderline personality disturbances. It is not the intent of this essay to imply that all terrorists suffer from borderline or narcissistic personality disorders, or that the psychological mechanisms of externalization and splitting are utilized by every terrorist. It is my distinct impression, however, that these mechanisms are found with extremely high frequency in the population of terrorists, particularly among the leadership, and contribute significantly to the uniformity of terrorists' rhetorical style and their special psycho-logic.

Splitting is one of the defense mechanisms of individuals with a damaged self-concept. Individuals who rely on splitting and externalization look outward for the source of their difficulties. They need an outside enemy to blame. This is a dominant mechanism of the destructive charismatic, such as Hitler, who projects the devalued part of himself onto the interpersonal environment and then attacks and scapegoats the enemy without. Unable to face his own inadequacies, the individual with this personality style needs a target to blame and attack for his own inner weakness and inadequacies.

Such individuals find the polarizing, absolutist rhetoric of terrorism extremely attractive. "It's not us—it's them. They are the cause of our problems" provides a psychologically satisfying explanation for what has gone wrong in their lives. And a great deal has gone wrong in the lives of individuals who are drawn to the path of terrorism. Research in the field of political terrorism continues to suffer from a poverty of data that would satisfy even the minimal requirements of social scientists. Perhaps the most rigorous and broad-based investigation of the social background and psychology of terrorists was conducted in the late 1970s and early 1980s by a consortium of West German social scientists under the sponsorship of the Ministry of the Interior. They examined the life course of 250 terrorists—227 left wing and 23 right wing. Their analysis of the data from their study of the left-wing terrorists from the Red Army Faction and the June 2 Movement is particularly interesting. The authors found a high incidence of fragmented families. Some 25 percent of the leftist terrorists had lost one or both parents by the age of fourteen; loss of the father was found to be especially disruptive. Seventy-nine percent reported severe social conflict, especially with the parents (33 percent), and the father, when present, was described in hostile terms. One in three had been convicted in juvenile court. The authors concluded that the group of terrorists whose lives they had studied demonstrated a pattern of failure both educationally and vocationally. Viewing the terrorists as "advancement oriented and failure prone," they characterized the terrorist career as "the terminal point of a series of abortive adaptation attempts."

The findings from clinical interviews and memoirs tend to confirm the sociological impressions. In his psychoanalytically oriented interviews of incarcerated Red Army Faction terrorists, Lorenz Bollinger (1981) found developmental histories characterized by narcissistic wounds, and a predominant reliance on the psychological mechanisms of splitting and externalization.

To be sure, each terrorist group is unique and must be studied in the context of its own national culture and history. It would be very unwise to generalize to other terrorist groups from the observed characteristics of West German left-wing terrorists. Franco Ferracuti conducted a similar study with Red Brigade terrorists in Italy, using politically active youth as controls. He found that the terrorists did not differ strikingly from their politically active counterparts in their family backgrounds. His principal conclusion was that the network of friendships was the main determinant
√ of whether the youth ended up in a terrorist group, a youth gang, or the drug culture. He, too, found an absence of gross psychopathology, but also observed the personality characteristics described above. The West German study and the Ferracuti study both were analyzing sociological patterns in social revolutionary terrorists who had broken from their families and chosen an underground existence as they pursued their war with the establishment.

This is in vivid contrast to nationalist-separatist terrorists, such as radical Palestinian terrorists of the Abu Nidal Organization and the Popular Front for the Liberation of Palestine—General Command; the Provisional Irish Republican Army; and Basque Fatherland and Liberty (ETA). In these organizations, the young revolutionaries are often extolled as heroes within their communities, for their mission reflects their people's cause. Among incarcerated Palestinian terrorists that my group has been interviewing, the regularity with which Palestinian youth chose to enter these groups was striking.[2] The responses of the interview subjects indicated, in sum, "Everyone was joining. Everyone was doing it. It was the thing to do." They have heard the bitterness of their parents and grandparents in the coffeehouses in Jordan and the occupied territories.

But for some of the nationalist-separatist groups, there is data to suggest sociologically marginal individuals chose this path. Robert Clark's studies of the social backgrounds of the nationalist-separatist terrorists from ETA are revealing. ETA members are sociologically marginal, with a much higher proportion (44 percent) coming from mixed Basque-Spanish parentage than is characteristic of the unusually homogeneous Basque region, where only 8 percent of the families have mixed marriages. Moreover, the offspring of these mixed marriages are reviled as "halfbreeds" or "mongrels." This suggests that these outcasts are attempting to "out-Basque the Basques," to demonstrate their authenticity through their acts of terrorism.

The social and generational dynamics of the social revolutionary (anarchic-ideologue) terrorists such as the Federal Republic of Germany's Red

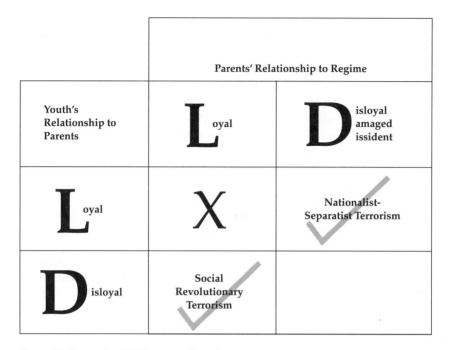

	Parents' Relationship to Regime	
Youth's Relationship to Parents	**L**oyal	**D**isloyal **D**amaged **D**issident
Loyal	X	Nationalist-Separatist Terrorism ✓
Disloyal	Social Revolutionary Terrorism ✓	

Figure 6.2. Generational Pathways to Terrorism

Army Faction and Italy's Red Brigades differ strikingly from the dynamics of the nationalist-separatists such as the Palestinian group Fatah and ETA of the Basques. As is depicted in figure 6.2, the social revolutionary terrorists, through their acts of terrorism, are striking out at their parents' generation. They are disloyal to the generation of their families that is loyal to the regime. They are seeking to heal their inner wounds by attacking the outside enemy. One of the West German social revolutionary terrorists bitterly described his parents' generation as the generation of "corrupt old men who gave us Auschwitz and Hiroshima." This is in vivid contrast to the generational dynamics of the nationalist-separatists, who are carrying on the mission of their parents and grandparents who were wounded by the establishment. They are loyal to families that are disloyal to the regime, were damaged by the regime. They have heard the bitterness of their families and are carrying on their families' cause. Their acts of violence are acts of revenge against the regime or establishment that damaged their parents.

The theme of loyalty to a family that has been damaged by the regime is well illustrated by Omar Rezaq, an Abu Nidal terrorist tried in federal district court in Washington, D.C., in 1996. I interviewed Rezaq for seventeen hours during my service as expert on terrorist psychology for the Department of Justice in connection with his trial for the federal crime of skyjacking. Rezaq, a member of the Palestinian terrorist Abu Nidal Organization, had played a central role in seizing the EgyptAir plane that was forced down in Malta in 1985. Rezaq shot five hostages—two Israeli women and three Americans—before a botched SWAT team attack by Egyptian special forces led to fifty-plus casualties. Convicted of murder in a Malta court, after seven years Rezaq was given amnesty and released. But subsequently he was arrested by FBI agents for the federal crime of skyjacking.

The defendant epitomized the life and psychology of the nationalist-separatist terrorist. A coherent story emerged after seventeen hours of interviews and a review of thousands of pages of documents. The defendant did not believe that what he was doing was wrong: from boyhood on Rezaq had been socialized to be a heroic revolutionary fighting for the Palestinian nation. Demonstrating the generational transmission of hatred, he can be considered emblematic of many from the ranks of ethnonationalist terrorist groups.

Rezaq's mother was eight years old and living in Jaffa when the 1948 Arab-Israeli War broke out, forcing her family to flee their home for the West Bank where she and her family lived in refugee camps. The mother's displacement from her ancestral home by Israel was an event of crucial importance, which became a key element in the family legend. Born in 1958, Rezaq spent his childhood in the West Bank village where his grandfather was a farmer.

In 1967, when Rezaq was eight, the 1967 Arab-Israeli War broke out, and the family was forced to flee once again, this time to a refugee camp in Jordan. There young Rezaq attended a school funded by the United Nations; his teachers were members of the Palestine Liberation Organization (PLO). In 1968, the battle of Karameh occurred, in which Yasir Arafat led a group of Palestinian guerrillas who fought a twelve-hour battle against a superior Israeli force, galvanizing the previously dispirited Palestinian population. The spirit of the revolution was everywhere, especially in the camps, and the PLO became a rallying point. In Rezaq's words, "The revolution was the only hope."

In school, Rezaq was taught by his teacher, a PLO member whom he came to idolize, that the only way to become a man was to join the revolution and to regain the lands stolen from his parents and grandparents. In the mornings, he was exposed to a basic elementary school curriculum, but in the afternoons, starting at age nine, he was given paramilitary training and ideological indoctrination.

He joined Fatah at age seventeen, and subsequently became a member of the Abu Nidal Organization. When he carried out the skyjacking, it was the proudest moment of his life. He was fulfilling his destiny. He was carrying on his family's cause.

For both nationalist-separatist and social revolutionary terrorists, becoming a terrorist may represent an attempt to consolidate a fragmented identity. Data comparable to that acquired by the German research team is not available for Muslim and Palestinian terrorists, but our colleagues who have closely followed Middle Eastern terrorist groups share the impression that many of the members are marginal and that belonging to these fundamentalist or nationalist groups powerfully contributes to consolidating psychosocial identity at a time of great societal instability and flux.

To summarize the foregoing, terrorists as individuals for the most part do not demonstrate serious psychopathology. Although there is no one personality type, it is the impression that there is a disproportionate representation among terrorists of individuals who are aggressive and action oriented and place greater than normal reliance on the psychological mechanisms of externalization and splitting. Many terrorists come from the margins of society and have not been particularly successful in their personal, educational, and vocational lives. The combination of the personal feelings of inadequacy with the reliance on the psychological mechanisms of externalization and splitting make especially attractive a group of like-minded individuals whose credo is "It's not us; it's them. They are the cause of our problems."

The Power of the Group

Although not everyone who finds his or her way to a terrorist group shares the characteristics described above, to the degree that many in the group do, it gives a particular coloration to the group. For many, belonging to the terrorist group may be the first time they truly belonged, the first time they felt truly significant, the first time they believed that what they did counted.

As Wilfred Bion has persuasively demonstrated, when the healthiest of people find their way into a group, the power of group dynamics is impressive indeed. When a group has a disproportionate number of individuals with fragmented psychosocial identities with a strong need to strike out against the cause of their failure, extremely powerful forces result.

In assessing the dynamics of the terrorist group, it is important to differentiate among terrorisms. Both structure and social origin are of consequence. Of particular importance to structural analysis is identifying the locus of power and decision-making authority. In the autonomous cell, the leader is within the cell, with all his warts and blemishes visible. These cells tend to be emotional hothouses, rife with tension. In contrast, in well-differentiated organizations, such as the Red Brigades in Italy, the action cells are organized within columns, and policy decisions are developed outside of the cells, although details of implementation are left to the cells.

The different social origins and psychosocial dynamics of nationalist-separatist terrorists and anarchic ideologues have already been described. Their group dynamics differ significantly as a consequence. Nationalist-separatist terrorists are often known in their communities and maintain relationships with friends and family outside of the group. They can move in and out with relative ease. In contrast, for the anarchic-ideologues the decision to cross the boundary and enter an illegal underground group is an irrevocable one, what the Germans call *der Sprung* (the Leap). Group pressures are especially magnified in the underground group; the group is the only source of information and confirmation, and, in the face of external danger and pursuit, the only source of security. The resultant group pressure cooker produces extremely powerful forces, particularly (1) pressures to conform, and (2) pressures to commit acts of violence.

Given the intensity of the need to belong, the strength of the affiliative needs, and, for many, the as yet incomplete sense of individual identity, terrorists tend to submerge their own identities into the group, so that a kind of group mind emerges. The group cohesion that emerges is magnified by the external danger, which tends to reduce internal divisiveness to unity against the outside enemy. Doubts about the legitimacy of the group's goals and actions are intolerable to such a group. The individual who questions a group decision risks the wrath of the group and possible expulsion. Indeed, the fear is even more profound, because, as the German terrorist Michael "Bommi" Baumann observed, "The only way out of the terrorist group is feet first—by way of the graveyard." The way to get rid of doubt is to get rid of the doubters. Extreme pressure to conform has been reported by all who have discussed the atmosphere within the group. What an interesting paradox, that these groups whose ethos is so intensely against the authorities should be so authoritarian.

The group ideology plays an important role in supporting this conformity-inducing group environment. When questions are raised, the absolutist ideology becomes the intellectual justification. The ideology becomes the scripture for the group's morality.

Questions have often been raised as to how individuals socialized to a particular moral code could commit such violent antisocial acts. Insofar as the individual submerges his identity into the group, the group's moral code becomes the individual's moral code. As Crenshaw has observed, "The group, as selector and interpreter of ideology, is central." What the group, through its interpretation of its ideology, defines as moral is moral and becomes the authority for the compliant member. And if the ideology states that "they are responsible for our problems," to destroy "them" is not only viewed as justified but can be seen to be a moral imperative.

The Psychology of Religious Violence

Killing in the name of God runs like a scarlet thread through the major events of the final decades of the twentieth century, a burning fuse that exploded on September 11, 2001. When the guilty verdict was announced at the trial of the Islamic fundamentalist terrorists for the 1993 bombing of the World Trade Center—which killed six people, injured more than a thousand, and caused property loss in excess of $500 million—the defendants shouted in unison, "Allah Akbar!" (God is great). When Dr. Baruch Goldstein massacred twenty-nine Muslim worshippers in the Tomb of the Patriarchs in Hebron in 1994, he believed he was on a divine mission and was hailed as a saint by hard-line Israeli settlers, as was Yigal Amir, the twenty-five-year-old religious extremist responsible for the assassination of Israeli Prime Minister Yitzhak Rabin. Michael Griffin, the "pro-life" activist convicted in the 1993 murder of Dr. David Gunn, the attending physician at the Pensacola, Florida, Women's Clinic, also believed that he was acting in support of his faith. So did Rachelle Shannon, who attempted to murder Dr. George Tiller in his Wichita, Kansas, abortion clinic later in 1993. Shannon, like Griffin, pled not guilty, because trying to kill a perceived murderer was justifiable to them.

In each of these cases, the perpetrator of the violence was striking out at perceived enemies, at threats to his or her belief system. It was defensive aggression against the enemy without. The true believer's sense of self rests on the integrity of his belief system (Hoffer 1951). Accordingly, those perceived as threatening that belief system, by words or deeds, pose a fundamental threat to the psychological integrity of the true believer. For the passionate true believer, it is not the beliefs that provide the passion. To the contrary, the rigid beliefs are providing a sense-making container for powerful feelings. These powerful feelings, which threaten to overwhelm the individual, require the beliefs. Because attacks on those beliefs threaten that tenuous control, such attacks provoke a passionate, often violent, response.

In both Judaism and Christianity, there are some who believe literally in Scripture, be it the Old Testament or the New Testament. Within each fundamentalist belief, there are two sentiments—the quietist and activist. The majority is quietist, awaiting the arrival of the messiah. The activists seek to "force the end," believing that they can hasten the arrival of the messiah by acts of piety. This "duty" to force the end is a major justification of religious fundamentalist terrorism. God's will must be realized now, and so unbelievers are a threat that must be eliminated, either by forced capitulation or by destruction.

Fundamentalist Muslims too believe in the literal sacredness of the Koran, and some are inspired to strike out violently against those who threaten their faith. Islam, in particular, has been closely intertwined with violence since its very beginnings.[3]

Killing in the Name of Allah

> Fight ye the chiefs of unfaith . . . Will
> ye not fight people who violated their
> oaths, plotted to expel the messenger, and
> were the first to attack you?
> Do ye fear them? Nay, it is Allah
> whom ye should more justly fear;
> if ye believe. Fight them and Allah will
> punish them by your hands.
>
> Koran (9:12–14)

This sura (verse) of the Koran is one of many that advocate violence against unbelievers and apostates. While jihad means persistence or struggle, radical Muslims, referring to the fourth jihad—the jihad of the sword—emphasize the waging of holy war, which they believe is an obligation of every Muslim. The Koran dictates that Muslims should go to war only in the name of Allah.[4] At the final judgment, the warrior who has given his life for the faith will, according to the Koran, spend eternity "in gardens of bliss."

An important source of inspiration to militant Islam is Muslim Brotherhood leader Sayid Qutb, who declared, before he was executed by the Nasser regime in 1965, that there was a "war to be waged in the name of Islam" (Taheri 1987, 34). This refrain was echoed by the Iranian Islamic scholar Ayatollah Fazlallah Mahallati, who wrote in 1980 that a Muslim who saw Islam insulted and did nothing would "end up in the seventh layer of Hell," but if he harmed or killed the offender his place would be "assured in heaven." An Islamic state is a state of war until the whole world sees and accepts the light of the True Faith (Taheri 1987, 17).

Ayatollah Khomeini not only justified striking out at the enemies of the true faith but made it obligatory to do so. In a June 5, 1983, radio broadcast, Khomeini said: "I would like to warn the governments of the Islamic countries not to repeat their past mistakes but extend the hand of brotherhood to each other. With humility toward God and relying on the power of Islam, they should cut the cruel hands of the oppressors and world-devouring plunderers, especially the United States, from the region."

His ideology is appealing on a highly personal level. In effect, he instructed Muslims that their personal trauma will be resolved through violent action for which they will be rewarded; they can resolve their personal existential crises by pursuing political-military action against "illegitimate" regimes. Even though ruled by Islamic leaders, moderate modernizing Islamic regimes, such as Egypt and Morocco, were a threat to Khomeini's expansive vision and became the target of his systematic strategy to destabilize them. They were viewed as corrupt and nonauthentic Islamic regimes that had sold out to the West.

For Khomeini, there was either good or evil, true believers versus the followers of Satan; there were no shades of light and dark. Corruption, in Khomeini's absolutist view, could not be reformed, it had to be destroyed. Radical Islamists inspired by Khomeini cite suras in support of their beliefs.

> And slay them wherever ye catch them, and turn them out from where they have turned you out. . . . Such is the reward of those who suppress the faith. (2:190–193)
>
> Fight and slay the pagans wherever ye find them. . . . But if they repent and establish regular prayers . . . then open the way for them, for Allah is oft-forgiving. (9:5)

For those committed to this interpretation of Islam, conducting this struggle is not a choice. Muslims are divinely commanded to "strive and fight in the cause of Allah with their goods and their persons." Fighting is also a test set by God to let the Muslims demonstrate their piety, and those who die in the holy cause are assured a favored place in heaven.[5]

Hezbollah — The Party of God

With the support of Iran, in 1982 a group of Lebanese Shi'ite Muslims formed a revolutionary party dedicated to establishing an Islamic state in Lebanon. After the Koranic injunction "And verily the party of God is sure to triumph," they called themselves "the party of God" (Hezbollah). Hezbollah leaders Ayatollah Sayyid Muhammad Husayn Fadlallah and Husayn al-Musawi provided the "moral logic" requiring kidnapping, assassination, and other terrorist acts (Kramer 1990). The extraordinary circumstances of the extremity of Islam's degradation justified extraordinary means. The value of martyrdom was extolled in Fadlallah's speeches and writings. He regularly observed in his sermons that "there is evil in everything good and something good in every evil."

Hezbollah and other Iranian-backed Islamic extremists based in Lebanon were responsible for taking thirty-seven American and other

Westerners hostage in 1982. The last American was freed in 1991. Hostage taking violates the Koran, which emphasizes hospitality toward strangers, but Fadlallah's clerical followers justified the extraordinary measure, asserting "just as freedom is demanded for a handful of Europeans, it is also demanded for the millions of Muslims."[6]

Iranian-backed radical Shi'ite Muslims were also responsible for the 1983 suicide truck bombing of the U.S. Marine barracks in Beirut in which 241 Marines were killed. This ushered in a wave of suicide bombings by Shi'ite Muslims that lasted from the spring of 1983 until the summer of 1985. Fadlallah offered a remarkable justification for suicide, which is strictly prohibited by the Koran. Ingeniously arguing it was really a matter of timing, Fadlallah asserted that killing oneself as a means of killing an enemy "differs little from that of a soldier who fights and knows that in the end he will be killed."[7]

The calls to destructive action by Khomeini and Fadlallah are part of Shi'ite doctrine. Shi'ites have long been considered the more violent, intense, populist, and the least compromising of the two major divisions in Islam. It is important to emphasize the complex, infinitely variegated texture of Islam, and that the justifications of violence in the Koran cited by Khomeini and Fadlallah were selected from this rich tapestry and used by them to justify their goals. These goals and justifications appealed to their followers, but by no means were they universally approved by Muslims. A similar call to violence can be found in the rhetoric of the majority Sunni.

Muhammad Abdel Salam Faraj, leader of al-Jihad, the Sunni Islamic group responsible for the 1981 assassination of President Sadat of Egypt, justified Sadat's murder as the fulfillment of a sacred obligation (Jansen 1986). He claimed that the religious obligation to struggle when Islam is in danger was a "neglected duty"—the title of his book. The devout Muslim, according to his interpretation, cannot rest until the shari'a governs all human conduct, and this goal may require killing unbelievers, as prescribed by the Koran.

Hamas: Violence against the Enemies of God

> Israel will be established and will stay established until Islam nullifies it as it nullified what was before it.
>
> martyred imam Hasan al-Banna[8]

The genius of Khomeini was in conceptualizing a radical ideology based on a particularistic interpretation of the Koran, justifying violence in pursuit of the Islamic state. Hamas, the radical Islamic Resistance

Movement, justifies the unity of radical Islam with Palestinian nationalism and absolved violence on the basis of an absolutist and paranoid worldview.

Established during the *intifada* (a Palestinian civil revolt against Israeli occupation of the territories captured by Israel in the 1967 war that began in December 1987), Hamas traces its origins to the Muslim Brotherhood in Palestine, which was founded in 1928.[9] The Brotherhood sought to revitalize Islam and to establish an Islamic state with no distinction between religion and the state. Its members considered Palestine a permanently and exclusively Muslim land, so designated by God. It is the duty of Muslims to liberate the entirety of the Holy Land from non-Muslim authority. According to the founder and "supreme guide" of the Muslim Brotherhood, Sheikh Hasan al-Banna, "It is the nature of Islam to dominate, not to be dominated, to impose its law on all nations and to extend its power to the entire planet" (quoted in Taheri 1987).

When the intifada spontaneously erupted in 1987, Sheikh Ahmad Yasin convened a group of Muslim Brotherhood leaders. They decided to establish a nominally separate organization to participate in the intifada. This would provide deniability should the revolt fail but would permit them to claim credit if it succeeded. They called the organization "Hamas," which means "zeal," "force," and "bravery" in Arabic. HAMAS is also an acronym for Harakat al-Muqawama al-Islamiyya (the Islamic Resistance Movement).

The Hamas charter (Maqsdi 1993) identifies Islam with Palestinian nationalism and the destruction of Israel. Article 13 emphasizes the Brotherhood's belief that "giving up any part of the homeland is like giving up part of the religious faith itself."

Paranoid rhetoric pervades the Hamas charter. The conspiratorial foundation of this "religious cause" is spelled out in detail in Article 22:

> The enemy planned long ago and perfected their plan so that they can achieve what they want to achieve. . . . So they worked on gathering huge and effective amounts of wealth to achieve their goal. With wealth they controlled the international mass media—news services, newspapers, printing presses, broadcast stations and more. . . . With money they ignited revolutions in all parts of the world to realize their benefits and reap the fruits of them. They are behind the French Revolution, the Communist Revolution, and most of the revolutions here and there. . . . With wealth they formed secret organizations throughout the world to destroy societies and promote the Zionist cause; those organizations include the freemasons, the Rotary and Lions clubs, and others. . . . With wealth they controlled imperialistic nations and pushed them to occupy many nations to exhaust their natural resources and spread mischief in them. . . .

They are behind the First World War in which they destroyed the Islamic Calipha and gained material profit, monopolized raw wealth, and got the Balfour Declaration [which laid the groundwork for the creation of Israel]. They created the League of Nations so they could control the world through that organization. They are behind the Second World War . . . and set down the foundations to establish their nation by forming the United Nations and Security Council instead of the League of Nations in order to rule the world through that organization.

There is not a war that goes on here or there in which their fingers are not playing behind it.

Article 32 of the charter cites as the authoritative source for this international Jewish conspiracy the anti-Semitic counterfeit, the "Protocols of the Learned Elders of Zion":

Today it's Palestine and tomorrow it will be another country, and then another. The Zionist plan has no bounds and after Palestine they wish to expand from the Nile River to the Euphrates. When they totally occupy it they will look towards another, and such is their plan in the "Protocols of the Learned Elders of Zion."

Just as Khomeini saw modernizing Arab leaders as a threat to his cherished Islamic republic, so too the extremist Hamas saw the more moderate Palestine Liberation Organization and the peace process as a threat to their mission to free the Holy Land from non-Muslim rule.[10]

Thus, the use of violence in the defense and expansion of Islam is not only accepted but embraced by a significant sector of the Muslim political community.

Killing in the Name of Jehovah

Just as radical Muslims are impelled to violent acts in defense of their faith, so too messianic Zionist settlers have become militant warriors in defense of the Promised Land and their faith. Some Orthodox Jews have seen the permissive modern age as a profound threat and have responded by withdrawing into tightly knit communities. Others see Israel as the promised kingdom of God, Eretz Yisrael.

Avraham Yitzhak Hacohen Kook was the chief rabbi of Palestine in 1948 at the time of the British mandate. While many orthodox Jews had turned away from secular political Zionism and rejected the concept of the Jewish state, Kook conceived of a union of the divine idea and nationalist sentiment, and his followers were to become spiritual belligerents in the pursuit of the kingdom of Israel.

The 1967 Arab-Israeli war was a singular moment in the history of Israel.[11] Israel's dramatic victory brought about the reunification of Jerusalem. The result was the return of the Old City and the West Wall of the ancient temple, among the most sacred sites in Judaism, and of biblical Judea and Samaria (the West Bank of the Jordan River) in addition to the capture of the Golan Heights and the Sinai Peninsula. There was a resurgence of pride and religious Jewish identity for the largely nonreligious Zionist nationalists. The boundaries of Israel were now essentially those of biblical Israel. So overwhelming was the victory that to many religious Jews it seemed like a miracle.

Six years later, however, in October 1973, the Yom Kippur War shattered the illusion of Jewish invulnerability. Israel was not defeated, though at one stage the country was on the precipice of defeat. The ruling Labor government was pressed from within Israel and by the United States to relinquish occupied territory to achieve peace with Arab neighbors and defuse the explosive situation. This threatened to undo God's will in the view of Rabbi Kook and his followers. In February 1974, they founded Gush Emunim (Movement of the Faithful), dedicated to fulfilling the biblical prophecy of the Promised Land, committed to not yielding "one square millimeter" of the land that in their view belonged to the Jews by virtue of the covenant between God and his chosen people. Gush Emunim began to establish settlements in the occupied territories, trying to establish "facts on the ground" to guarantee that none of the God-given land would be relinquished as part of any peace negotiations. Their intent was to annex the occupied territories.

The Likud government's 1977 land-for-peace negotiations with Egypt were seen as a betrayal by Gush Emunim that threatened to delay the arrival of the Messiah, an arrival foreshadowed by regaining the Promised Land in the 1967 war. The Camp David accords and the 1979 peace treaty, which entailed the return of the Sinai, confirmed the betrayal.

In 1980 a group of radicals within Gush Emunim reacted to attacks by Palestinians on the settlements by initiating a campaign of counterterror. In May 1980, a group of Gush Emunim settlers was gunned down while leaving the synagogue in Hebron. The government deported three Arab leaders to Lebanon. Considering the government's response feeble, the Gush radicals booby-trapped the cars of three West Bank Palestinian mayors, seriously wounding them. The Israeli government did not press an investigation, and no punishment occurred. Violence flared again in 1983 after a yeshiva student was killed in Hebron. The radicals again retaliated, killing three Palestinians in the Islamic university in Hebron. After Israeli buses were attacked in 1984, the Gush radicals were about to plant bombs on five Arab buses when Israeli security arrested the conspirators.

With their arrest and interrogation, a plan of alarming dimensions was revealed. The Gush underground intended to dynamite one of the holiest sites in Islam—the Dome of the Rock in Jerusalem—which sat atop the Temple Mount, the holiest Jewish site, the location of the First and Second Temples and, when the Messiah arrived, the site of the Third Temple.

A group of ardent messianic Jews formed the Gush Emunim underground. They reasoned that the intensely religious Zionist Menachem Begin could not have voluntarily yielded part of Eretz Yisrael in the Camp David concessions. Therefore, this was an act of God, reproaching the Jewish people. But for what? The offense, they concluded, must be the continuing presence of the "abomination," the Dome of the Rock, on the Temple Mount. Accordingly, the removal of this blemish was required to ensure the Messiah's arrival on earth.[12] The object of the destruction of the Al Aqsa mosque and the Dome of the Rock was to transform the secular state of Israel into the kingdom of Israel, which "will be no more an ordinary state."[13]

If carried out, the bombing of the Islamic holy sites surely would have precipitated the most extreme Arab reaction, perhaps a major war. This was a possibility that the Gush Emunim underground welcomed. Their leaders estimated that the destruction of the Dome of the Rock "would arouse hundreds of millions of Muslims to a jihad sweeping all mankind into an ultimate confrontation. . . . Israel's victorious emergence from this longed for trial by fire would then pave the way for the coming of the Messiah" (Gideon Aran, cited in Keppel 1994, 168). War or no war, the goal of this plan was to demonstrate their faith, to prepare for the rebuilding of the temple by "cleansing" the Temple Mount of the "abomination" and to "force the end."

THE FIGHTING JEW

In 1994, Dr. Baruch Goldstein massacred twenty-nine Muslim worshippers in the Tomb of the Patriarchs in Hebron in 1994. He was a devoted follower of the Jewish-American activist Rabbi Meir Kahane, whose book *Never Again!* is an exposition of "the fighting Jew," grounded in Old Testament and Talmudic commentary.

Kahane started with the unexceptional Talmudic statement that "if one comes to slay you—slay him first" (Berachot 58). This principle is simply one of self-defense. A second Kahane principle also seems unexceptional: "Ahavat Yisroel," love of Israel (Kahane 1971, 150). Kahane cites the Old Testament verse "Thou shalt not stand idly by your brother's blood" (Lev. 19:16) and the Talmudic commentary that states that if a person "sees someone pursuing his comrade with the purpose of killing him, he is free to save a life through killing the pursuer" (Sanhedrin 73). Kahane and his followers drew on many other commentaries, such as Maimonides' exhortation to wage "obligatory war" against Jewish enemies (Maimonides, *Hilchot Melachim*, 5:1), the duty of Jews to lay down their own lives for another Jew (Maimonides, *Hilchot Rotzeyasch*, 1:6), and the obligation of Jews to be skilled in war.

In Kings of Israel Square in Tel Aviv, at a peace rally attended by more than one hundred thousand people on November 4, 1995, Israeli Prime Minister Yitzhak Rabin, winner of the 1994 Nobel Peace Prize, was assassinated. The assassin was not a Palestinian terrorist but a twenty-seven-year-old Orthodox Jewish law student at Bar-Ilan University and a member of Israel's extremist religious right. When he was arrested, Yigal Amir told police, "I acted alone on God's orders. I have no regret" (Thomas 1995). Shortly after the arrest Avishai Raviv, leader of the outlawed right-wing group Eyal, to which Amir belonged, said in a television interview that his group "admires the lad [Amir] for his sincerity, for standing behind his words. . . . This man Rabin is responsible for the murder of hundreds of Jews" (Kifner 1995). He was referring to the ideology of the extreme right, which holds that the government's agreement to cede control of parts of the West Bank is a surrender of the Jews' biblical heritage and poses a mortal threat to Jews by creating a haven for Palestinian terrorists. Subsequently Raviv and other members of Eyal were arrested, and officials announced that the assassination was the result of a conspiracy.

As the peace process advanced, the stridency of the rhetoric in Israeli's extreme religious right increased to incendiary proportions. The land-for-peace terms of the Oslo agreement meant relinquishing Israeli control over the West Bank of the Jordan River, called Judea and Samaria by the religious right. The militant Orthodox opponents of the Rabin government believed that the land had been given to the Jewish people by God, and for the secular government to give away the Promised Land was in violation of God's command. Extremists had branded Rabin a "traitor" and "murderer," and effigies of Rabin in a Nazi uniform were prominent at right-wing rallies. This inflammatory rhetoric was not confined to the extreme right. Opposition Likud Party chairman Benjamin Netanyahu had invoked the threat of a Palestinian state on Israel's border in a speech shortly before the assassination: "You, Mr. Prime Minister, are going to go down in history as the Prime Minster who established an army of terrorists" (Schmemann 1995a).

At the interrogation, Amir stated he killed the prime minister to prevent the handing over of land to the Palestinians. A member of Eyal, the outlawed offshoot group of the Kach party founded by Meir Kahane, he asserted that he had followed Jewish religious law in shooting Rabin. He called Rabin a "pursuer," quoting the Talmudic commentary so frequently cited by Kahane that states that a person is obligated "to kill an assailant who poses a mortal threat, to save a life through killing the pursuer." "According to Jewish law," Amir asserted at his hearing, "the minute a Jew betrays his people and country to the enemy, he must be killed . . . I've been studying Talmud all my life, and I have all the data" (Greenberg 1995). Commenting on the interrogation, Police Minister Moshe Shahal said that the assassin was influenced by militant rabbis who effectively issued a death warrant for Rabin and Shimon Peres, the former foreign minister who had negotiated the Oslo accords, by invoking the "pursuer's decree" of Jewish religious law, which morally obligates a Jew to kill someone who poses a mortal danger to him. The rabbis had regularly stated that Rabin's policies posed a mortal danger to Israel and the Jewish people (Schmemann 1995b). At a meeting of religious nationalist leaders after the assassination, a prominent West Bank rabbi observed that "There are those among us who still say that Rabin deserved death because of the injunction [in Jewish law] regarding someone who wants to kill you" (Williams 1995, A35).

Fellow students at Bar-Ilan University recalled a Talmudic colloquy of several days duration among Amir and his yeshiva classmates several months earlier in which Amir had drawn on the twelfth-century Law of Kings. Amir had asserted that Rabin qualified for a *din rodef*, the "judgment of the pursuer," entitling a righteous man to kill him, because Rabin was poised to spill the blood of other Jews by giving up control of the West Bank.

Amir had devoted his life to the study of the Old Testament and the Talmud. He was a true believer whose extreme religious ideology was central to his self-concept. The abandonment of Judea and Samaria by the secular Rabin government was a threat to the psychological integrity of Amir and other ardent Jews of the extreme right. He struck out, finding justification for his act in the religious writings he had studied.

Statements from the Old Testament and the Talmud, pillars of moral force, have been drawn on to justify violence, to provide a religious rationale for striking out with defensive aggression against the enemies of one's faith. Some Jews, like some Muslims, have drawn on their holy literature to justify killing in the name of God. Christians have done the same.

Taking Life to Preserve It: Pro-life Extremist Violence

Since the 1973 *Roe v. Wade* Supreme Court decision, which largely legalized abortion, it has been the political issue that has galvanized fundamentalist Christians in America. Until 1973, abortions were illegal in most states, and this prohibition had general religious support. The massive changes in the direction of personal choice in the Western world in the 1960s resulted in the abandonment of many restrictions—especially regarding sexual practices—and also in a decline in the status of many institutions, especially religious ones. Fundamentalist Protestants suffered more from this status decline than any other group. The abortion issue struck a strong emotional chord with them. It was an issue on which they could receive support from their erstwhile antagonist, the Catholic Church, and one that many nonfundamentalists and non-Catholics felt uneasy about.

The abortion issue has resulted in more violence, including murder perpetrated by Christians, than any other religiously connected issue since the Crusades. It is ironic that the issue that has led some religiously inspired extremists to murder has been the preservation of life.

Members of the "pro-life" antiabortion movement believe that human life begins at conception, so that there is no moral difference between killing a fetus and killing an infant. By this reasoning, abortionists are not only murderers, they are child murderers, mass murderers in most cases. Pregnant women who have an abortion are killing their own child. The concept of abortion as murder has led the movement's extremists to liken the legalization of abortion to genocide, to a "resurrection of the spirit of Nazism." Holocaust rhetoric is prominent among antiabortion activists. A position paper of the fundamentalist Bible Tabernacle states: "The response of Bible-believing Christians has been almost the same as it was in Hitler's Germany. Those who claim to believe their Bibles have responded to the abortion holocaust in America by doing little if anything" (Melton 1989, 53; see also Chu and Clary 1994, A1, A19).

Following the logic of their beliefs, antiabortionists have used violence against abortion clinics and doctors who perform abortions. Soon after their arrest for three Christmas Day firebombings of abortion clinics in Pensacola, Florida, in 1984, two young Christian fundamentalist defendants, James Simmons and Matthew Goldsby, said that God had instructed them to bomb the clinics. The young perpetrators called the bombs "a birthday gift for Jesus" (Blanchard and Prewitt 1993, 51). They planted their first bomb in a clinic in June 1984, escaping undetected. In their view, their escape was a sign from God that what they had done was right and encouraged them to plan the Christmas bombing of the Pensacola clinic (39, 46, 60).

David Gunn, medical director of the Pensacola [Florida] Women's Medical Services Clinic, was assassinated by abortion activist Michael Griffin in March 1993. Griffin, a member of Rescue America (an extreme antiabortion organization), told police that he had acted for God (Allen 1994, 12).

This level of violence had been building for over a decade. The beginning of the movement, in 1973, was characterized by mild protests, with the throwing of stink bombs, cementing of clinic locks, blockades of clinic entrances, and so forth. From 1982 to 1992, in connection with the anti-abortion movement in the United States, there were

- 32 bombings
- 54 incidents of arson
- 76 cases of assault and battery
- 129 death threats
- 296 acts of vandalism against abortion providers.

Between 1987 and 1993, there were 33,000 arrests, mostly for nonviolent protests.

Although few of the official pro-life organizations openly condone violence, one group that has actively advocated it is the Army of God, which has published a handbook detailing ways to commit terrorism without being captured while causing the largest impact (Hed, Bowermaster, and Headden 1994, 55).

Paul Hill, leader of Defensive Action, stated, "The police use force to protect abortionists. Abortion is murder, and murderers deserve to be executed." Defensive Action is "a small group of about 30 pastors and church leaders from across the country who have signed a declaration proclaiming the Godly justice of taking all action necessary to protect unborn life." Hill, a former minister who had been defrocked by the Presbyterian church, insisted that "executing abortion providers was a moral imperative" (Allen 1994, 14).

Protestant fundamentalists seldom draw on pre-Reformation doctrine to support killing abortionists. David C. Trosch of Mobile, Alabama, a fundamentalist minister, has, however, defended killing abortion doctors as "justifiable homicide," citing the writings of St. Augustine and St. Thomas Aquinas, and stating, "There is full human life, by Christian common belief, in the womb following conception. They are persons worthy of defense, like any born person, and they must be defended by any means necessary to protect them, including the death of the assailants, which in this case would be the abortionists and their direct accomplices" (Niebuhr 1994).

Roman Catholic Archbishop Oscar H. Lipscomb criticized Trosch in a letter of pastoral instruction, citing the biblical commandment against killing, stressing that citizens must not usurp the role of civil authorities. Trosch dismissed the archbishop's arguments, stating that God's law supersedes civil law. He wrote to the Vatican, warning of "coming catastrophes" that would wipe out a fifth of the world's population. He wrote to members of Congress warning of a possible civil war with "massive killings" of abortion doctors. Asked if he would not feel guilty if his sermons and speeches incited someone to murder an abortion doctor, Trosch responded, "Defending innocent human life is not murder. You're comparing the lives of morally guilty persons against the lives of manifestly innocent persons. That's like trying to compare the lives of the Jews in the incinerators in Nazi Germany or Poland or wherever with the lives of the Gestapo." He also made an analogy to the French Resistance in World War II: "When they killed their enemy soldiers, did anybody ever admonish them? In fact, they were considered heroes" (Niebuhr 1994, 12; see Allen 1994, 16, 17, 76 for other examples).

Right-Wing Terrorism under a Pseudo-Christian Ideology

THE CHRISTIAN IDENTITY MOVEMENT: PSEUDO-HISTORY AND RACISM

> [The Jews are a] half-breed, race-mixed,
> polluted people not of God. . . . They are
> not God's creation. [They are] the
> children of Satan, the serpent seed line.
>
> Jarah Crawford,
> proponent of the Identity Bible

When racist groups such as the Aryan Nations and the Ku Klux Klan can provide a religious as well as a racist rationale for their program, it enhances their moral footing and broadens their appeal.[14] The whites to whom they appeal typically come from a fundamentalist Protestant background. Identity Christianity is a pseudo-Christian belief system that combines traditional elements of fundamentalist Protestantism with a paranoid explanation and set of required actions based on this paranoid worldview. This combination has so distorted its traditional Protestant elements as to make the relationship almost unrecognizable, converting a religion of love into one of hatred. But its appeal rests in large part on the fact that it is preached from the pulpit with religious authority and there is a lineal connection to Christian doctrine.

The Identity Church claims that the Bible teaches the racial superiority of Aryans (defined as those of Nordic and Alpine racial background, principally the inhabitants of the Scandinavian and Germanic countries as well as the British Isles, though for the most part any gentile white person is included). Its members denounce Jews and blacks, claiming that they are on the spiritual level of animals. Identity Christians also claim that Aryans are God's chosen people and that Jesus was not a Jew. Apocalyptic in their rhetoric, proponents of Christian Identity call on their fellows to fight in "these final days." They believe that

- Aryans are descendants of the lost tribes of Israel and are the true "chosen people." They have a special calling and are on earth to do God's work.
- Jews are not descendants of the biblical Israelites but are the offspring of Satan, descended from Satan's seduction of Eve in the Garden of Eden.
- The apocalypse is approaching. The final battle will be between the Aryans, the forces of good, and the forces of evil under the direction of the Jews. It is the God-given task of the Aryans to warn of the dangers the Jews and the blacks represent and to destroy them.

The theory of the Satanic origin of the Jews became fully developed in the 1960s and began to circulate broadly in Christian Identity circles. This theory is the ideological foundation of the political agenda of Christian Identity:

- God distinguished between two types of beings according to their paternity. Some, called Adamites, were descended from Adam and were human. Others, called Pre-Adamites, were created separately, long before Adam, and were less than human. Referred to as the "mud people," they include blacks and people of color.
- The serpent in Genesis's story of the Fall was not a reptile but an intelligent "humanoid" creature associated with the Devil, if not the Devil himself.
- Original sin consisted of Eve's sexual relationship with this "serpent."
- Because of this liaison, the world contains two "seedlines." One (Adam's seedline) consists of the descendants of Adam and Eve. The other (the serpent's seedline) consists of the descendants of Eve and the serpent/Devil.
- Cain, the product of Eve's liaison with the "serpent," was a historical figure associated with evil in general and the Devil in particular, and passed his propensity for evil to his descendants (Barkun 1994, 150–51).

Thus, the Identity Christians trace a line of Jewish descent from the serpent/Devil who seduced and impregnated Eve in the Garden of Eden. In some versions, the issue of this union, Cain, was the first Jew. His line passed through the Edomites and the south Russian Khazars to contemporary Jews. Christian Identity thus combines the delusions of a world Jewish conspiracy with that of a cosmic satanic conspiracy (136–37).

This dehumanization of the Jews justifies acts of violence against them; such acts can be freely committed without violating biblical injunctions. In the following creedal statement of the Aryan Nations and the Church of Jesus Christ Christian, proponents of Christian Identity speak of a "final solution" in which the Jewish people, the seed of Satan, are obliterated in a religious war:

> We believe that there are literal children of Satan in the world today. These children are the descendants of Cain, who was a result of Eve's original sin, her physical seduction by Satan. . . . [T]here is a battle and a natural enmity between the children of Satan and the children of the Most High God . . . We believe that there is a battle being fought this day between the children of darkness (today known as Jews) and the children of light (God), the Aryan race, the true Israel of the Bible. (189)

THE PARANOID RADICAL RIGHT AND DEFENSIVE AGGRESSION

Right-wing extremism is not an organized movement with clear identifying characteristics.[15] Rather, it should be viewed as a mosaic containing groups and organizations with themes in common and with differences. White supremacist and neo-Nazi elements are major but not uniform themes, as are "survivalist" and antigovernment themes, united under a common banner of patriotism and religion. Not all right-wing organizations rely on religion, but Christian Identity does provide a theological justification for many right-wing extremist groups. In particular, it draws together religious fundamentalism and racism, providing a religious rationale (that Jews control America with the intent of destroying the white race) both for a "race war that would deliver our people and achieve total victory for the Aryan race" and for groups opposing the exercise of governmental control and power.[16]

The tenets of Identity Christianity described earlier have been made all the more extreme by right-wing extremists and are a rich basis for paranoid political activists of the radical right to support an extreme political agenda:[17]

- Anglo-Saxons are the true descendants of the Israelites of the Old Testament with whom God made his covenant, and they are His chosen people. They are the last true defenders of the faith, and the United States is the true State of Israel, the last bastion against evil.
- God's laws are absolute and the only ones that people are obligated to follow. Because His laws have been disregarded, the United States is on the brink of disaster and Armageddon is imminent. Loyalty is

not owed to institutions that violate these laws. America's laws, especially, are invalid because the United States government is controlled by Jews, a "Zionist Occupational Government" (ZOG). The news media and economic institutions are also directed by Jews.

- Three types of people exist. Whites (God's chosen) are of a higher order than either Jews (the "Seed of Satan") or blacks (the "mud people"). Because members of the last group have no souls, they are subhuman and represent "false starts" before God perfected whites. They also are manipulated by Jews against the Aryans.

- Because Jews are the children of the Devil, they are responsible for all the evil that has occurred throughout history and are the spiritual and moral enemies of white Christians. Armageddon will be a military confrontation between God's chosen (the Aryan race) and the forces of Satan (Jews, blacks, and other minority groups).

- For white Christians, there are no practical distinctions among race, religion, and nationality. (Wood 1996, 217–34, drawing on Finch 1983)

The doctrine of Identity Christianity can be easily dismissed, but all religious doctrines are bizarre to those who do not believe in them. The fact that Identity Christianity locates its origins in a major religion—Christianity—and offers a pseudohistorical rationalization means that it contains the sense-making appeal that a destructive paranoid movement requires.

Christian Identity and its activist arm, Aryan Nations, tell its members that they must endure the apocalypse on earth and help prepare for it through paramilitary and survival training (Ostling 1986; Barkun 1990). In the Aryan Nations' Hayden Lake, Idaho, compound, white supremacist groups gather each July to receive paramilitary training and indoctrination in Identity Christian principles. They refer to their organization as the Church of Jesus Christ Christian (as opposed to "Jesus Christ Jew"). Robert Butler was the founder and leader of both the Aryan Nations and the Church of Jesus Christ Christian.

The Aryan Nations magazine, *Calling Our Nation*, has accused Jews of committing human sacrifice. In publications and speeches it elaborates on the satanic Jewish conspiracy, which, in the words of George Stout, leader of the Aryan Nations in Texas, exerts control over "the world's political system through the Babylon system of banking, finances, and economics" (Barkun 1994, 190).

Inspired by Christian Identity doctrine, Robert Mathews, a leading lieutenant of Robert Butler, in 1983 formed his own group, the Order, a violent neo-Nazi cult that also calls itself "The Brotherhood of Silence" and the "White American Bastion." Mathews recruited Gary Yarborough into the Aryan Nations in 1979 from an Arizona prison, where he belonged to a white racist group called the Aryan Brotherhood. Yarborough became Butler's bodyguard and Mathews's principal lieutenant. The major preoccupation of The Order is the danger of "Genocide of the White Race" at the hands of "the Devil's children," the powerful Jewish conspiracy that they believe controls the United States through its domination of the media and banks. The Order's obsession with the Zionist Occupational Government (ZOG) is not only defensive aggression but is fueled by projection—a desire to destroy the Jews.

Members of the Order swear an oath of violence in pursuing an Aryan victory over the Jew. They claim "no fear of death, no fear of foe" in doing "whatever is necessary to deliver our people from the Jew." Members of the Order, "true Aryan men," face "the enemies of our faith and our race," invoke "the blood covenant" and declare they are in "a state of war" and will not cease their struggle until they "have driven the enemy into the sea" (Barkun 1994, 229–30). To finance a guerrilla campaign that it hoped would lead to an uprising by the white population against the Zionist-controlled government, the Order embarked on a campaign of bank robberies and counterfeiting. The most dramatic crimes committed by the Order were the July 1984 robbery of a Brinks armored car (which netted $3.8 million); the destruction by arson of a synagogue in Boise, Idaho; and the 1984 murder of Alan Berg, a Jewish Denver-based talk radio host (Barkun 1994, 228).

After the murder of Berg, the FBI traced Yarborough and confronted him on October 18, 1984, near his home in Sandpoint, Idaho. Yarborough fired at the FBI agents and fled. When his house was searched, police found an array of terrorist and racist tracts, including a list of "enemies of the Aryan people" listing prominent California jurists, journalists, and entertainment figures, as well as explosives and weapons, including the Berg murder weapon (Lake 1985, 103).

One of the largest groups in the radical Christian right is the Posse Comitatus, which is fiercely opposed to government and believes there is no legitimate public official above the level of sheriff.[18] The extremist group began as the Citizen's Law-Enforcement Committee, a tax protest organization formed in 1969 in Portland, Oregon, to challenge the authority of the federal government over the local government. After the Posse Comitatus was born in Oregon, William Potter Gale organized a branch in Glendale, California, calling it the U.S. Christian Posse Association. The national Posse Comitatus was formally organized in Michigan in 1972.

Over the next ten years, chapters were formed in nearly every state, focusing on tax protest, providing legal assistance to tax evaders, and advocating local constitutional authority. They sought to avoid taxes by establishing tax-exempt Christian Identity churches. In their view, the county level is the legitimate seat of government, hence the Posse Comitatus (literally "power of the county"). Believing that all legal rights derive from the U.S. Constitution and its first ten amendments, the Magna Carta, the Bible, the Articles of Confederation, and common law (Yaeger 1994, 17), Posse members are violently opposed to state and federal laws that they consider unconstitutional, and refuse to pay state and federal taxes. They have declared the Internal Revenue Service and the income tax "Communist and unconstitutional." The "Jew-run" federal government, in the view of the Posse, has usurped the powers assigned to it. Posse doctrine advocates firearms and survival training in preparation for Armageddon, the approaching nuclear holocaust that is the goal of the "Communist-Jew run government."

Perhaps reflecting the group's antipathy to central authority, there is no leader or central governance. Rather, the various posses constitute a leaderless national organization of loosely affiliated chapters, often under other names.[19] The average Posse member tends to have strong religious beliefs, be a tax protestor, a loner, and self-employed. Most hate blacks and Jews. To join, a person must be white and Christian and state that they are patriotic, of good character (in Posse terms), and interested in the preservation of law and order as that is understood by Posse members.[20]

The legitimacy of killing federal officials is regularly cited in Posse documents. "Killing in the defense of freedom," members were advised, "is not murder any more than a soldier killing in war" (Lake 1985, 22; also see Barkun 1994, 110).

The mail order catalogs of these groups provide an insight not only into what they believe but also demonstrate the common thrust of the movement. The catalogues of the Christian Patriots, a group identified with the Posse Comitatus, and of the National Vanguard, a West Virginia neo-Nazi group, for example, carry many of the same books. A best-seller is *The Turner Diaries* (1980), written by William Pierce under the pseudonym Andrew McDonald. Pierce served as an assistant to George Lincoln Rockwell, chief of the American Nazi Party, in the late 1960s, sold "Negro control equipment" from his home, and was a mentor of Robert Mathews, the founder of the Order. A physicist, Pierce left academia in the 1960s to crusade against Jews and blacks. Pierce, who died in 2002, said he would like "to see North America become a white continent" and asserts that "there is no way a society based on Aryan values can evolve peacefully from a society which has succumbed to Jewish spiritual corruption."[21]

First published in 1980, *The Turner Diaries* is regularly referred to by white supremacist groups and anti gun-control militias and is considered the "bible" of the extreme right. The plot is a paranoid triumphalist fantasy. It describes America eighteen months after all private ownership of guns has been outlawed by the Cohen Act. The central character, the Aryan hero Earl Turner, recounts his role in overthrowing the U.S. government in the 1990s by a "Great Revolution." Turner is a member of a clandestine group, the Organization, whose goal is to restore white control of the United States by killing nonwhites and Jews. In the final section of the book, millions of American Jews, blacks, Latinos, and "race traitors" are killed on "The Day of the Rope." California is liberated by exploding a nuclear bomb and hanging from lampposts thousands of blacks and Jews, as well as "White women who were married to or living with Blacks, with Jews, or with other non-white males." The book describes the fate of thousands of these women at the triumph of the white nation: their mass hanging, each necklaced with a placard proclaiming "I defiled my race" (Pierce 1980, 210). The book, which has attracted a wide following in right-wing circles, has sold more than two hundred thousand copies. Other offerings by the Christian Patriots include Holocaust denial literature such as Arthur Butz's *The Hoax of the Twentieth Century* and Richard Harwood's *Did Six Million Die?* as well as Henry Ford's *The International Jew* and Carleton Putnam's *Race and Reason*.

The themes of this literature have a familiar paranoid flavor. They identify a threat to the existence of Christian white society, mostly from Jews and blacks. Jews are portrayed as a malevolent force controlling nearly every aspect of life and growing ever more powerful. Blacks, on the other hand, an inferior species, threaten to destroy white society by racial mixing that produces "mongrelization." Again we see the posture of defensive aggression, "provoked" by the powerful conspiracy that threatens to engulf the victim. It is necessary to defend against the dangers posed by Jews and blacks. Often added to this list of corrupters are homosexuals and foreigners. Note the attribution of power and danger to "them"— "they" must be destroyed before "they" destroy us.

The radical right—a broad aggregation of organizations tied together by common delusional fears and not central leadership—displays the paranoid themes of external control (Jews and the federal government) manifested in a desire to overthrow the government of the United States, destroy those that they call non-Aryans, and restore an ideal America. The psychological dynamic is that of defensive aggression: I must destroy you before you destroy me.

The Militia Movement: Fighting the "New World Order"

The bomb that destroyed the federal building in Oklahoma City on April 19, 1995, not only claimed 168 lives, it also shattered the widespread illusion that "it can't happen here," that the United States was immune to domestic terrorism.[22] The massive explosion demonstrated that a great danger existed within American society, in the very heartland of the United States. The devastating explosion was perpetrated by American citizens consumed with rage against the federal government. A troubling mindset within the American political landscape was brought forcibly to Americans' attention—that of the paranoid radical right, especially the militia movement.

The ideas that identify and the social processes that unite organizations can be far more paranoid than their members. The militias demonstrate how unexceptional personal beliefs can be carried to paranoid lengths under the stimulation of a paranoid organization. The right to bear arms is a constitutional right upheld by the courts and adhered to by mainstream political groups. A distrust of government, especially the central government, is America's oldest political tradition and one strongly espoused across the political spectrum.

For many of the most active militia members, the advocacy of these established liberties reaches paranoid lengths. The three themes militias share are a strong belief in the right to bear firearms, intense distrust and fear of the federal government, and collective paranoid beliefs. Statements of John Trochmann, cofounder of the Militia of Montana, capture these three themes. Trochmann claims to have been the victim of death threats intended to deter him from uncovering the hidden plot by "one-world" government authorities to disarm average citizens, violate their constitutional rights, and destroy America's sovereignty (Kovaleski 1995, A13). In Trochmann's view, an armed citizenry is the most important defense against this usurpation, and so armed resistance is necessary to any government effort to disarm Americans (Trochmann, quoted in Goshko and Swardson 1995, A22). Trochmann and others in the militia movement cite the killing by federal agents of the wife and child of Idaho white supremacist Randy Weaver in a confrontation in Ruby Ridge, Idaho, in 1992 as proof of the lengths to which the federal government will go to disarm its citizens. They also regularly cite the attack by the Bureau of Alcohol, Tobacco and Firearms on the Branch Davidian compound in Waco, Texas, to disarm David Koresh and his followers of their weapons, and the subsequent siege by the FBI, which ended in a fiery tragedy. The Ruby Ridge attack and the siege in Waco have assumed almost mythic significance for the militias.

The federal government, according to the conspiracy theories shared by many of the militias, seeks to control the lives of citizens and will crush those who resist, including by sending in United Nations troops (Schneider 1994, A1). Fiercely independent and resenting control of any kind, militia members believe the federal government will destroy American democracy. These self-styled patriots believe that well-armed, grassroots paramilitary organizations offer the only protection against the tyranny to come. The intensive paramilitary training of the militias is for defense against the secret elites that plan an apocalyptic takeover of the United States, under the auspices of the United Nations or NATO.

One of the suspects in the Oklahoma City bombing, Timothy McVeigh, was deeply influenced by *The Turner Diaries*, which he bought in quantity and sold below his cost at gun shows to spread the word. In the novel, one of the first and most dramatic acts of the Organization is to blow up the FBI building in Washington with a fertilizer bomb—the same explosive used to destroy the federal building in Oklahoma City. In Montana, three weeks before the Oklahoma City bombing, a militia official threatened several government officials, warning, "There cannot be a cleansing without the shedding of blood" (Egan 1995, A1).

According to some militia members the bar codes on federal highway signs are secret codes for the United Nations army when it moves in to take over the country. They also speak of surveillance by black helicopters and satellites. The surveillance is maintained through signals sent to the orbiting satellites from microchips implanted in their buttocks during their military service.[23] McVeigh spoke with conviction of his belief that he had a biochip in his left buttock.

What shall we make of individuals who read secret meanings into bar codes on highways signs, imagine surveillance helicopters hovering overhead, and believe they have microchips implanted within them? If an individual were to report such ideas in a clinician's office, he would be diagnosed promptly as suffering a severe paranoid disorder. But groups adhere to these beliefs and claim they are "common knowledge." Such beliefs—held by otherwise sane and sensible persons—are more a reflection of group dynamics than of individual psychopathology. The members hear their leaders repeat these "facts" and are exposed to common messages in both print and electronic media. Like the rest of us, they obtain their reality checks by comparing their beliefs with those of their associates. Wanting to belong, they do not question the group's beliefs. Once a paranoid belief system in established in a group, it is nearly impossible to dislodge.

The fact that the militias fantasize about and fear technology has not meant that they do not use it for their own purposes. Militia members, for example, exchange advice, "intelligence," and political views through Internet bulletin boards such as the Paul Revere Net, the American Patriot Fax Network, and the Motherboard of Freedom. Gaining full access to these networks requires commitment. One has a welcoming message that states: "We are a network of doers, not whiners or fakers" and then asks newcomers whether they are willing to provide safehouses, training areas, and supplies to "patriots." An item running on the alt.conspiracy Usenet was headlined "Clinton Orders Okla. Bombing?" (Kentworthy and Schwartz 1995, A22). The Aryan Nations Liberty Net is a national neo-Nazi computer network, which, among other things, provides a list of Anti-Defamation League offices, as well as an enemies list of those who "have betrayed their race [and will] suffer the extreme penalty" (quoted in Lake 1985, 98).

Although only a minority of the militias are explicitly racist, forty-five militias in twenty-two states have links to white supremacist groups (Doskoch 1995). Some militias have close links to the Christian Identity movement, whereas others have no apparent relationship to it.

Some militias are more extreme in their actions than others. In testimony before Congress on June 15, 1995, in connection with the April 19 bombing of the federal building in Oklahoma City, five leaders of the militias described themselves as ordinary people who loved the Constitution, feared government abuse, and owned guns only to protect themselves. They stated that the government was using "weather-control techniques so the new world order could starve millions of Americans" and had caused up to eighty-five Midwestern tornadoes to disorient heartland America, and that there were actually two bombs that destroyed the Oklahoma City federal building, which were accidentally detonated by the government itself. The head of the Michigan Militia accused the lawmakers of being part of the "corrupt, oppressive tyranny in government" and identified the CIA [as] "the grandest conspirator behind all this government" (Janofsky 1995; Mintz 1995).

WMD Terrorism

In considering which groups in the spectrum of terrorist groups might be inclined to carry out acts of chemical, biological, or radiological/nuclear (CBRN) terrorism, it is important to differentiate the spectrum of such acts as well. Terrorist acts can be divided into six types:

1. Large-scale casualties with conventional weapons
2. CBRN hoax
3. Conventional attack on a nuclear facility
4. Limited scale CBW attack/radiological dispersal
5. Large-scale radiological dispersal/CBW attack
6. CBRN (super-terrorism), in which thousands of casualties may result.

The crucial psychological barrier is not the choice of weapon but the willingness to cause mass casualties, and this threshold has already been crossed by some groups.

Writing in *Disorders and Terrorism*, the report of the Task Force on Disorders and Terrorism, more than twenty years ago, R. W. Mangle distinguishes four means by which terrorists attempt to achieve their goals.[24] He observes that there is a distinct difference between discriminate and random target selection. Whereas discriminate target selection can be used in support of bargaining or to make a political statement, random targeting is associated with the motivation to cause social paralysis or to inflict mass casualties.

In evaluating the risk for use of CBW weapons, it is useful to employ this distinction in differentiating among terrorist groups, or the impact of the act on internal or external constituents. Some groups might well consider CBW attacks only in a bounded area, limiting casualties, which would significantly militate against negative reactions from their constituents, both local and international. These groups would be significantly constrained against such acts in a region in which the group's constituents might well be adversely affected as a result of physical proximity to the area of attack. These bounded acts are specified as discriminate. Indiscriminate attacks, in contrast, are attacks in which no consideration is given to the selection of specific victims, or the impact of the act on internal or external constituents.

For each of the terrorist group types described above, there are varying constraints against the use of CBRN weapons and against mass casualty terrorism and "superterrorism."

Social Revolutionary Terrorists.   Insofar as these groups are seeking to influence their society, they would be significantly constrained from indiscriminate acts that cause significant casualties among their own countrymen, or cause negative reactions in their domestic and international audiences. But discriminate acts against government or symbolic capitalist targets could be rationalized by these groups.

Nationalist-Separatist Terrorists.   These groups will be significantly constrained from acts that indiscriminately involve mass casualties and will negatively affect the group's reputation with their constituents and their international audience. But discriminate acts against their adversary, in areas where their constituents are not present, can be rationalized. Just as the rash of suicide bombings in Tel Aviv and other predominantly Jewish cities in Israel was implemented by absolutist Palestinian groups (some of which were radical Islamists as well) in order to reverse the peace process, the prospect of tactical CBW weapons in such areas is quite conceivable. Such discriminate attacks could also be implemented in revenge against U.S. targets. But a CBW attack in Jerusalem by secular Palestinian terrorists that might affect their own constituents is considered highly unlikely.

Radical Religious Fundamentalist Terrorists.   These organizations are hierarchical in structure; the radical cleric provides interpretation of the religious text justifying violence, which is uncritically accepted by his "true believer" followers, so there is no ambivalence concerning use of violence that is religiously commanded. These groups are accordingly particularly dangerous, for they are not constrained by Western reaction, indeed are driven to expel secular modernizing influences and by revenge against the West, which has been focused upon the United States. They have shown a willingness to perpetrate acts of mass casualty terrorism, as exemplified by the bombings of Khobar Towers in Saudi Arabia, the World Trade Center, the U.S. embassies in Kenya and Tanzania, the U.S.S. *Cole*, and the mass casualty terrorism on a scale never seen before in the coordinated attacks on the World Trade Center in New York and the Pentagon in Washington, D.C. Osama bin Laden, who is responsible for these events, has discussed the use of weapons of mass destruction in public interviews. Thus, in contrast to the previous two groups, the constraints against CBRN mass terrorism are not present and they are considered especially dangerous.

Right-Wing Terrorism.   Because of this dehumanization of their enemies, discriminate attacks on target groups, such as blacks, or, in Europe, on enclaves of foreign workers, are justified by their ideology. Because of their delegitimation and dehumanization of the government, discriminate attacks on government facilities are certainly feasible by such groups, including attacks on the seat of the federal government, Washington, D.C., as represented in *The Turner Diaries.*

Right-Wing Community of Belief.   Many of the case studies of chemical-biological terrorism developed by the Center for Non-Proliferation Studies at the Monterey Institute for International Studies—the first group of which was published as *Toxic Terror*—were committed by individuals hewing to a right-wing ideology, but not belonging to a formal group or organization per se. The case study by Jessica Stern of Larry Wayne Harris, a former neo-Nazi, is a case in point. Timothy McVeigh is an exemplar of such individuals seeking to cause mass casualty terrorism, using conventional weapons. McVeigh was enthralled by *The Turner Diaries.* At the time of his capture, highlighted pages from this bible of the radical right were found in his car. Individuals in this category are a significant threat for low-level CBW attacks, but, because of resource limitations, probably do not represent a threat of mass casualty CBW terrorism.

The role of the Internet in propagating the ideology of right-wing extremist hatred is of concern, for an isolated individual consumed by hatred can find common cause in the right-wing Web sites, feel he is not alone, and be moved along the pathway from thought to action, responding to the extremist ideology of his virtual community.

We ought not forget that the horrors of 9/11 represented conventional terrorism and that the incarcerated radical Islamist terrorists interviewed under the auspices of the Smith Richardson foundation,[25] while open to considering CBRN weapons, for the most part said "Just give me a good Kalashnikov" and several indicated that the Koran prohibited the use of poisons.

Implications for Counterterrorist Policy

Because terrorisms differ in their structure and dynamics, counterterrorist policies should be appropriately tailored. As a general rule, external force is counterproductive when the terrorist group is small and autonomous. When the autonomous cell comes under external threat, the external danger reduces internal divisiveness and unites the group against the outside enemy. The survival of the group is paramount because of the sense of identity it provides. Terrorists whose only sense of significance comes from being terrorists cannot be forced to give up terrorism, for to do so would be to lose their very reason for being. To the contrary, for such individuals, violent societal counterreactions reaffirm their core belief that "it's us against them and they are out to destroy us." A tiny band of insignificant individuals has been transformed into a major opponent of society, making their "fantasy war," to use Ferracuti's apt term, a reality. Left to their own devices, these inherently unstable groups will probably self-destruct.

Similarly, for terrorist organizations that define violence as the only legitimate tactic for achieving their goals, outside threat and a policy of reactive retaliation cannot intimidate the organizational leadership into committing organizational suicide and ceasing to exist—which is what ceasing committing acts of political violence would be if that is the group's sole purpose.

For complex organizations dedicated to a cause, such as that of Basque separatism, where an illegal terrorist wing operates in parallel with a legal political wing as elements of a loosely integrated larger organization, the dynamics and the policy implications are different. If the overall organizational goals—in this case Basque separatism—are threatened by societal reactions to terrorism, one can make a case that internal organizational constraints can operate to constrain the terrorist wing. However, insofar as the terrorist group is not fully under political control, this is a matter of influence and partial constraint. As noted earlier, the ETA has its own internal dynamics and continues to thrive despite the significant degree of autonomy that the Basques have already achieved.

Terrorist groups that are state supported and directed are, in effect, paramilitary units under central governmental control. The individual, group, and organizational psychological considerations discussed so far are not especially relevant. The target of the antiterrorist policy in this circumstance is not the group per se but the chief of state and the government of the sponsoring state. Because the survival of the state and national interests are the primary values, retaliatory policies can have a deterring effect, at least in the short term. But even in this circumstance, to watch children shaking their fists in rage in the aftermath of the U.S. bombing attack on Libya—in retaliation for a Libyan-sponsored terrorist attack on U.S. troops in a Berlin disco—suggests such tactics are contributing to raising generations of terrorists.

Just as political terrorism is the product of generational forces, so too it will be here for generations to come. When hatred is bred in the bone and passed from generation to generation, the signing of a "Good Friday" accord (Northern Ireland) or the Oslo accords (Israel and Palestine) will not suddenly end the deeply rooted hatred. *There is no short-range solution to the problem of terrorism.*

Political terrorism is not only a product of psychological forces—its central strategy is psychological. For political terrorism is, at base, a particularly vicious species of psychological warfare. Up until now, the terrorists have had a virtual monopoly on the weapon of the television camera as they manipulate their target audience through the media. Countering the terrorists' highly effective media-oriented strategy through more effective dissemination of information and public education must be key elements of a proactive program.

Terrorists perpetuate their organizations by shaping the perceptions of future generations of terrorists. Manipulating a reactive media, they demonstrate their power and significance and define the legitimacy of their cause. To counter them, effective education and dissemination of objective information is required.

In the long run, then, the most effective way of countering terrorism is

1. *to inhibit potential recruits from joining the group.* Once an individual is in the pressure cooker of the terrorist group, it is extremely difficult to influence him or her.
2. *to produce tension within the group.*
3. *to facilitate exit from the group,* by providing pathways out of terrorism through amnesty programs. Through an effective amnesty program, the *pentiti* program, the Italian government significantly eroded the hold of the Red Brigades on its members.
4. *to reduce external support for the group and its leader.* At the present

time, alienated Islamic youth are attracted to radical terrorist groups such as Hamas and al Qaeda, and Osama bin Laden is a romantic hero. Accordingly, the goal is to marginalize al Qaeda as a group and delegitimate bin Laden as a leader.

To reemphasize, one does not counter the vicious species of psychological warfare that is terrorism with smart bombs and missiles. One counters psychological warfare with psychological warfare. And the fourfold strategy outlined above represents an integrated strategic psychological operation program.

The goal of this fourfold strategy is not to eliminate terrorism. One cannot eliminate terrorism without eliminating democracy, as witness the period of the "dirty wars" in Argentina, which was considered state terrorism. A healthy democracy must tolerate dissent. Rather, this strategy is designed as a continuing process to reduce the frequency of terrorism so as to interfere as little as possible with our democratic way of life.

7

The Loss of Enemies

Fragmenting Identities and Ethnic/Nationalist
Hatred in Eastern Europe

How rapidly—and tragically—was the celebration of freedom occasioned by throwing off the yoke of Communist rule in the former Soviet Union and Eastern Europe succeeded by a wave of ethnic-nationalist conflicts, expressed at its violent genocidal extreme in the identity war in Bosnia, in which ethnic cleansing became policy.[1] Tragic, but predictable, for the loss of enemies is destabilizing, and the chaos left in the wake of the departing Communist enemy provided fertile soil for hate-mongering demagogues to exploit centuries-old hostilities.

The revival of hostility among existing groups with a history of conflict is not surprising. Nor, given the long-standing history of anti-Semitism in these nations, would it be surprising to see the revival of anti-Semitism in post-Communist Eastern Europe, *if there were Jews there.* The fact that anti-Semitism has revived so powerfully in the absence of Jews demonstrates the power of the paranoid dynamic and the associated need for enemies. When the real enemy disappears, the need for enemies becomes intensified, and in the absence of real enemies they will be created.

There is a readiness in the human psyche to fear strangers and seek comfort with the familiar. Under duress, stranger anxiety and fear of the other mount, and the paranoid capacity to project hatred is mobilized. Such anxiety is produced not only by unknown persons but also by unfamiliar places, foods, and sounds. Significant others—parents, teachers, peers—sponsor "suitable targets of externalization" for the developing child, and "group-specific externalizations" tie the children together (Volkan 1988, 32). The strangeness of some things (and the comforting familiarity of others) take on political significance as the child grows into adulthood.

This fear of the stranger and projection of hatred onto the other are the psychological foundations of the concept of the enemy.[2] The crystallization of the shared comfort of the familiar is the psychological foundation of nationalism.

Vamik Volkan has drawn on both his psychoanalytic training and his own life history to illustrate this process, constructing a bridge from the family to the nation and the development of the sense of national identity:

> In Cyprus [Volkan's birthplace], although Greeks and Turks lived side by side for centuries until 1974, when the island was divided, they remained— and still remain—mutual antagonists. A Greek child learns from what his mother says and does that the neighborhood church is a good place; he unconsciously invests in it his unintegrated good aspects and feels comfortable there. The same mechanism, fueled by his mother's influence, makes him shun the Turkish mosque and minaret, in which he deposits the unintegrated bad aspects of himself and important others. He is more himself when playing near his church and distancing himself from the mosque. . . . Although the child would have his own unique individualized psychological makeup, he would be allied to other children in his group through the common suitable target of externalization . . . that affirms their ethnic, cultural, and national identity. (32–33)

As personal identity consolidates, it incorporates elements of national identity. The sense of comfort and belonging spreads to the national flag. Those who oppose the nation, or desecrate the flag, may threaten one's sense of self. This helps explain the rage engendered in the United States, for example, by flag burning, and the emotional force behind the proposed constitutional amendment making desecration of the flag a federal crime. Especially under stress, we cling all the more tightly to those symbols of our national, racial, ethnic, or religious identity that have become psychologically incorporated as part of our self-concept. They are in effect self-objects.[3] This is illustrated by the talismans with ethnic symbols worn by Palestinians living in the Gaza Strip:

> Like songs often repeated among the Arabs, they are shared only within the in-group, providing a magical [psychological] network for maintaining group narcissism under adverse conditions as well as contributing to the self-esteem of individual Arabs. It is not enough for Palestinians in the Gaza Strip simply to be aware of their Arabic identity; they need to exhibit its symbols in order to maintain their self-esteem. (Volkan 1988, 36)

The profusion of American flags in the wake of September 11 is another graphic example of self-objects. After our nation was attacked, we clung all the more tightly to symbols of our national identity. We are comforted by familiarity and cling tightly to those like us. This contributes to a sense of group and self-cohesion.

But this requires differentiating ourselves from strangers. They are necessary for our process of self-definition. To say that "these things are specially good and are specially part of me" is to say that "those other things are specially bad and not part of me, are part of others." The self, and objects with which the self has identified (such as one's ethnic group or political party), are idealized; other objects (such as historical adversaries of one's ethnic group or political party) are viewed as dangerous persecutors and are demonized.[4] The absorption ("introjection") of the good cultural symbols is expressed thus: "I must be good because my people's history—which is part of me—is good, our food is delicious, our religious buildings are impressive, our architecture is beautiful," and so on. The converse also occurs: "All those others, especially those I see around me and with whom my group has lived, are bad—their history is one of deception and violence, their food is inferior, their architecture is ugly," and so on. All badness is outside, all goodness inside. The self and the familiar group are idealized; the stranger is demonized. Such racial or ethnic or religious identifications have helped produce great poetry and music, and have stimulated self-sacrifice in the interest of fellow group members. But it has also created the fertile field from which wars and massacres have grown. Pride in one's heritage often manifests itself as destructive narcissism and political paranoia. In a world of friends and enemies, there is a splitting of good and evil, of self and not-self.

This tendency to idealize the in-group and demonize the out-group can never be eradicated. The germs of that more primitive psychology remain within the personality, ready to be activated at times of stress. Otherwise psychologically healthy individuals can be infected by paranoid thinking when the friendly group with which they are identified is attacked or when economic reversals occur.[5]

Thus enemies are necessary for self-definition, which makes it necessary to have enemies in our midst. Creating bad others is a necessary part of a child's acquiring a distinct identity, but insofar as a national identity becomes part of one's personal identity, deep-seated feelings that transcend childhood become fixed within one's social personality. For some people, the bad objects remain true enemies. A mature, integrated person learns that those enemy objects are at most adversaries, or things which are distasteful, and not objects to be hated or destroyed. Under overwhelming social stress, however, even mature individuals and groups can return to the paranoid position and experience these internalized bad objects as true enemies.

A "good enough enemy" (Stein 1987, 188–89) is an object that is available to serve as a reservoir for all the negated aspects of the self. It serves the valuable function of stabilizing the internal group by storing group projections. The enemy thus provides cohesion for the social group, especially the social group under stress. Because it is representations of the self that are being projected, there must be a recognized kinship at an unconscious level. We are bound to those we hate.

Yet at the same time there must be a recognizable difference to facilitate the distinction between "us" and "them." An important aspect of the development of group identity is shared symbols of difference, symbols on which to project hatred. The more "different" the stranger in our midst, the more readily available that person is as a target for externalization.[6] The enemy whom we are certain is a despicable "other" is littered with parts cast out from the self (Stein 1987, 193). We project onto "them" what we disown in ourselves. It becomes a part of their projected identity.

The need for an unconscious kinship is responsible for the "familiar enemy." The Greeks and the Turks, as Volkan points out, have lived near each other for centuries. So have India's Muslims and Hindus; Bosnia's Serbs, Croats, and Muslims; Northern Ireland's Catholics and Protestants; and, in the twentieth century, Israel's Arabs and Jews. They remain feared—but familiar—strangers. Thus those groups from which we most passionately distinguish ourselves are those with which we are most inseparably bound. We end where they begin (Stein 1987, 103).

This identity-creating process—a psychological necessity—results in the world being divided among groups with varying degrees of animosity, excessive self-regard, and fear of others. We need enemies to keep our treasured—and idealized—selves intact. Enemies, therefore, are to be cherished, cultivated, and preserved; if we lose them, our self-definition is endangered and our cherished group is threatened.

The Psychopolitics of Hatred: Searching for New Enemies, Reviving Old Hatreds

The events in Eastern Europe since the collapse of Communist rule bear tragic testimony to this need for enemies. Even some hardened observers of Balkan politics believed that the antagonisms among Croats, Serbs, and Muslims had been permanently blunted by the decades of peaceful Communist rule. The revival of ferocious ethnic wars in the early 1990s demonstrated that deep-seated fears and anger had not died but had merely been suppressed by the powerful leaders of the socialist state. When the outside enemy disappeared, the need for enemies produced a bloody revival of ancient hatreds. The revival of age-old tensions in Eastern Europe in the wake of the dissolution of the Soviet empire is a special case of the destabilizing consequences of losing one's enemy.

Lenin saw the inculcation of loyalty to the Soviet Union as a crucial task in institutionalizing the revolution. To develop an identity as "new Soviet man" required the suppression—indeed, the destruction—of other loyalties and identities, nationalist and religious. Even family loyalties were seen as reactionary vestiges, a view carried to its most dreadful extreme with the celebration of Pavel Morozov as a hero of the Soviet Union for denouncing his family to the authorities as counterrevolutionaries.

This ruthless stamping out of national identity was extended to the socialist nations of Eastern Europe in the wake of World War II. In the pursuit of the new socialist man, for forty years expressions of nationalist identity were forbidden to the people of Central and Eastern Europe—the intensely nationalist Poles, Hungarians, Bulgarians, Rumanians, the Czechs and Slovaks of Czechoslovakia, and the Serbs, Croats, and Muslims of Yugoslavia. In this exaggerated emphasis on one identity, and attempted forcible elimination of other identities, the essential quality of identity—difference—was attacked. Such destruction nearly always fails, and it did in Eastern Europe. In totalitarian regimes this leads to a duality of identity—the publicly espoused identity (new socialist man) and the private identity (see Eros 1991). The regime's intense pressure on private life led to an extensive erosion of private identity, which can occur in three ways:

1. through repression of identity elements that have been deemed undesirable;
2. through the transformation of undesirable identity elements into negative identity fragments (the "self-criticism" in Communist China is an example of such enforced transformations); and
3. through marginalization of private identity, "squeezing certain identity elements to the margins of awareness, thereby rendering them seemingly insignificant." (Eros 1991)

The Communist regime's attack on these private identity elements did not destroy them. Rather, the social basis of private identity was forced underground. Allusion became "the mother tongue of collective experience."

In the fall of 1989, that most remarkable season of freedom, with bewildering rapidity the Communist empire collapsed, and in Eastern Europe, one socialist government after another was overthrown as the long-suppressed peoples rose up in democratic protest. It was an exultant moment: Free at last!

Within a few years, however, that spirit of exultation was replaced by the revival of age-old hatreds in exaggerated form, as Serbs slaughtered Croats, Slovaks asserted their autonomy and split from Czech lands, and hatred of minorities was given free rein, often becoming a major theme in political campaigns.

This result is not surprising. After forty years of enforced suppression of national identity, at last these intensely nationalist people were free, free to express in intensified form the core of their identity—difference— and with it expressions of hatred of the "other." As one mocking, anonymous poem put it, "Free at last / Free to choose / To eat at MacDonald's / And hate the Jews."

More than difference was expressed, for the intensity with which hated groups were blamed for the troubles of the in-group was remarkable. A particularly painful example is found in Poland. Before World War II, Poland was the center of world Judaism, with a population of over three million Jews. About 2.9 million perished in the Holocaust. Today, fewer than 10,000 of the estimated 38 million population of Poland is Jewish, and their average age is over seventy. This annihilation of Jewry was particularly severe in Poland's capital, Warsaw. Approximately 30 percent of the population of Warsaw was Jewish when the Nazis invaded. As a consequence of the Holocaust, there are now only three to four hundred Jews in Warsaw.

Poland not only has fewer Jews than in 1939, it also has fewer other minorities. Hitler's murder of the Jews, the expulsion of the Germans from East Prussia and Silesia, and the shift westward of the Ukrainian border made Poland perhaps the most ethnically and religiously homogeneous country in Eastern Europe. Although Poland retains its historical memory of "enemy" minorities, it has almost none within its borders. Absent the Communist leaders, absent traditional enemies, who could be blamed when things went wrong (and initially they went very badly indeed)? The answer was, of course, Jews! Reports of anti-Semitism surfaced almost immediately after 1989. Monuments and cemeteries were desecrated, with swastikas painted on gravestones (Harden 1989 A1, A19). On the monument to the fighters of the Warsaw ghetto who fought against the Nazis was inscribed "the only good Jew is a dead Jew" (Brumberg 1991, 72). The largely nonexistent Jewish population was blamed for Poland's economic distress, with an invocation of the international Zionist conspiracy. A Polish academic, Krystyna Kersten, characterized this as "anti-Semitic paranoia" in a country where practically no Jews are left but where "the public imagination" is nonetheless "obsessed by the Jewish presence in the government, in parliament, in the press, in television, and God knows where else" (Shafir 1991, 9). A poll conducted in the early 1990s found that a quarter of the Polish population believed that Jews exercised too much influence, even though they recognized that Jews constituted only a small part of the population. Only 3 percent of those interviewed found it acceptable to have Jewish neighbors.[7] The pollster, Slawomir Nowotny, commented on the intensity of the anti-Semitism in the face of the virtually absent Jewish population. He dubbed the phenomenon "platonic anti-Semitism," observing that if love without sex is platonic love, then anti-Semitism without Jews is platonic anti-Semitism.[8] Nowotny saw the power attributed to the Jews as a reflection of the powerlessness of the populace and the need for someone to blame.

Polish government leaders, who were having difficulty coping with massive socioeconomic dislocation and widespread discontent, fanned the flames of anti-Semitism. In August 1990, Lech Walesa, the leader of Solidarity, clarified that his earlier charge that a gang of Jews "had gotten hold of the [country's] trough and is bent on destroying us" applied not to "the Jewish people as a whole" but only to those "who are looking out for themselves while not giving a damn about anyone else" (*Gazeta Wyborcza*, June 24, 1990, cited in Brumberg 1991). In the 1990 election campaign, Walesa asserted he was "clean" because he had no Jews among his ancestors. He said he was "100 percent Pole" (Brinkley 1991, A5). During the 1991 political campaign, Walesa's main opponent was Tadeusz Mazowiecki, who was "accused" at a press conference of being Jewish.[9] Not recognizing the anti-Semitism in its response, the Catholic Church defended Mazowiecki, asserting that they had gone back through two hundred years of church records of Mazowiecki's family and found "not a drop of Jewish blood."

In Romania, too, there is anti-Semitism without Jews. Before World War II, there were upward of one million Jews in Romania. Today, there are 17,000, most of them elderly. More than four hundred thousand Romanian Jews were killed during World War II by Germans and Rumanian security forces, and the climate under President Nicolae Ceaușescu fostered a large emigration to Israel.

Romanian politics were distinctly anti-Communist in the interwar period. Most of the Communist Party's support came from the disaffected minorities, including Jews, Hungarians, and Bulgarians. Hostility toward the now departed Communist leaders has been accompanied by blaming Jews and Hungarians. This "Communist equals Jew" as rationalization for anti-Semitism was demonstrated in the manifesto of the National Defense League, made public during a violent demonstration in April 1990 (Shafir 1991, 24). The leaflet began with a declaration that the Communists had "sown only blood and woes" and that "blood calls for blood." It then attacked the National Salvation Front, a political party, as having been "bought by the Bolsheviks and the international Jewish conspiracy." The manifesto declared that the Jews, under the direction of Moses Rosen, the chief rabbi of Romania, have a "secret mission . . . in your new communist government . . . of setting up a new form of communism and socialism for the benefit of the Jewry."

Anti-Semitic articles have appeared in national newspapers, and an anti-Semitic organization, the Legion of the Archangel Saint Michael (later renamed the Iron Guard), has been revived. A message from the anticommunist Iron Guard Army declared that its goals were to save the country and to reconstruct it on the sound basis of the "purity of the Rumanian soul, which has been poisoned then just as it is being poisoned now. . . . The crucifixion of the Legion was followed by the crucifixion of Romania itself! Today, when Romania's desperation is almost as great as Christ's desperation on Golgotha . . ." (Shafir 1991, 27). The pamphlet ended with the words, "Our time has finally come. Heil Hitler. We shall be victorious." There were swastikas in all four corners. An article by a former submarine commander, Captain Nicolae Radu, claimed that Israel planned to turn Romania into a Jewish colony, that Jews were plotting with the International Monetary Fund to turn Romanians into street sweepers, that the Jews control the Romanian government, and that they brought Communism to Romania (Champion 1991, A1, 4).

Elie Wiesel, the Nobel Prize–winning chronicler of the Holocaust, was taunted at a talk in Iasi, Romania, commemorating the deaths of eight thousand Jews by the Romanian Army and police in 1941. Before the war, of Iasi's ninety thousand residents, forty thousand were Jews. Today, only nine hundred remain. A woman disrupted the meeting, shouting "It's a lie. The Jews didn't die. We won't allow Romanians to be insulted by foreigners in their own country" (Kamm 1991, A1). In April 1991, the Romanian Chamber of Deputies rose in a minute of silence in tribute to the memory of Marshal Ion Antonescu, the dictator executed as a war criminal who allied Romania with Germany and ordered the deportation and killing of thousands of Jews.

A similar tribute was paid to another major participant in the Holocaust, Father Tiso, a Catholic priest who was president of Slovakia during the one period it was an autonomous nation, 1939–1945. Under Tiso's leadership, Slovakia was allied with Germany. In an attempt to "cleanse" its population, Slovakia paid the Germans five hundred crowns for each Jewish man, woman, and child deported to the death camps. Tiso was convicted of war crimes and executed. A cross was consecrated and erected on his grave in March 1991 on the occasion of the fifty-second anniversary of the Slovak Republic by Slovak National Unity, a new, intensely nationalist political force whose central goal is the creation of an independent Slovak state.[10] "It was not the first time in history when power humiliated the law and justice and an innocent man had to die," the eulogist said. During the rally, the eulogy was interrupted by cries of

"Glory to Tiso," "Long Live Slovakia," and "Enough of Havel." On a visit to Bratislava, Czechoslovakian President Vaclav Havel had been attacked by a crowd that called him "King of the Jews." When Israeli President Chaim Herzog visited Czechoslovakia, the Slovak fascist party erected a plaque on Tiso's birthplace. The resurgence of nationalism was coupled with an intense resurgence of the feelings associated with the brief period of national independence—fascism and anti-Semitism.

The Deformation of Personality after Forty Years of Socialism

More than identity was suppressed under forty years of Communist regimes. Peter Huncik, a psychiatrist who served as special assistant to President Havel, has written about the "deformation of personality" after forty years of socialism. Huncik observes that the socialist masters systematically extinguished initiative, and by emphasizing the primacy of state authority the Communists created a climate that socialized a passive, dependent populace with the expectation that the state would take care of them. The populace blamed the omnipresent authority for society's shortcomings, with a marked atrophy of individual responsibility. With the disappearance of that authority, the resentful and dependent populace had to find a target to blame, Huncik believes.

The readiness to externalize blame is another social-psychological consequence of forty years of Communist rule. For one of the legacies of Communism was societal paranoia (see Schifter 1990). The massive security organizations throughout the Communist bloc led to pervasive fear and distrust and an erosion of communality. The inability to trust friends and even family created deep scars and an atrophy of mutuality and sharing.

What happens when that all-powerful authority disappears, when the caretaking enemy is gone? As Communist governments were overthrown, leaving social and economic chaos in their wake, it was at last safe to express the long pent-up anger at the Communist leaders. For many, Communist equals Jew was an equation in the collective psychology.[11]

Anger and blame went to the departing enemy. But new enemies must be found as well, and old enmities were revived. A Czech journalist told me that "the politics of Slovakia is looking for an enemy—everybody who is different."

In the Czech lands—Bohemia and Moravia—there is some anti-Semitism, but the most intense feelings are directed at Gypsies. The intense resentment of the large Gypsy population may have defused feelings that otherwise might have been directed at Jews. The Gypsies have been the object of brutal attacks by young toughs, but the attitudes of ethnocentric resentment are maintained by the Czech intelligentsia as well. A Czech diplomat, shaking his head in disgust, stated:

> They [the Gypsies] are responsible for most of the crime. They are lazy and shiftless and don't hold regular jobs. And they have all of these children. It makes me angry that there are these special welfare programs for them, when the money should be going to the hard-working people of this country.[12]

Similar feelings were expressed in Hungary where there is also strong anti-Gypsy feeling. When the main opposition party in Hungary called attention to the plight of the Gypsies, it was characterized in leading newspapers as "the party of the gypsies and the Jews," and it lost support because of its principled stand.

The intensity of nationalist passions and the violence sometimes associated with them has several roots. After decades of suppression under Communist rule, the intense expression of nationalism represents an exaggerated search for identity, which, as we have seen, depends fundamentally on difference. At the same time, forty years of Communist rule led to "a deformation of personality," characterized by societal paranoia, an atrophy of personal responsibility and initiative, and an expectation of being cared for, however badly, by the totalitarian state. With the disappearance of that leadership, the populace is floundering. The long-sought freedom is frightening, as it emphasizes individual identity and responsibility, long-suppressed qualities.

When the powerful disappear, the powerless do not easily succeed them. There must be someone to blame for the chaos left behind. Who is behind the devastating economic dislocation? Being accustomed for so long to (justly) blaming their own government, it was an easy transition to continue to externalize blame. If, as in Poland, there is no clear internal enemy, one will be created from the country's social history. The political and economic instability in Eastern and Central Europe in the wake of the loss of the Communist enemy is ripe territory for demagogues to exploit the paranoid dynamic and to create scapegoats. Throughout the region, demagogues have provided meaning for the distressed population by identifying new enemies and reviving old enmities.

8

Hate-Mongering Leaders in the Former Yugoslavia

Radovan Karadzic and Slobodan Milosevic

Since the collapse of the Communist empire in 1989, a major crisis has affected the states of the former Soviet Union and the Warsaw Pact nations of Eastern Europe. In this unstable period, the climate has been ripe for hate-mongering leaders to exploit the tensions within their nations. This chapter presents two brief profiles of hate-mongering leaders in the former Yugoslavia.

The following profile of Radovan Karadzic, which is drawn from an article published in 1997 for a readership of forensic psychiatrists, addresses the question of how a physician, sworn under the Hippocratic oath to do no harm, could orchestrate a campaign of ethnic cleansing.

Radovan Karadzic: Poet of Death

As it became clear that a principal architect of ethnic cleansing in Bosnia was a psychiatrist—a disturbing echo of the Nazi doctors—I felt compelled to develop a political psychology profile of Radovan Karadzic to make sense of how a physician dedicated to saving human life could implement a policy of genocide.[1] As I was collecting and analyzing material, I was approached by another psychiatrist, Kenneth Dekleva, who traces his family origins to that conflict-ridden region, and who was similarly intrigued. We decided to collaborate in studying the political psychology of Karadzic, as well as the role of physicians in genocide, and also to develop a political psychology profile of the overall architect of the tragic conflicts in Bosnia and Kosovo, Slobodan Milosevic.

The year 1990 was a landmark one for Dr. Radovan Karadzic, self-styled president of the Bosnian Serbs. It was the year he assumed the leadership of the Serbian Democratic Party (SDS) in Bosnia, marking the transition from psychiatrist to political leader. And that year he also published his third volume of poetry, *Crna Bajka* (The Black Fable), a collection of dark and violent poems of which this passage from "A Morning Hand-Grenade" is representative:

> At last I am bereft
> Of all benefactors
> I glow like a cigarette's ember
> Touching neurotic lips:
> While others search me out
> I wait in dawn's hiding place
> This glorious opportunity
> To suddenly forsake all
> That this epoch has bestowed upon me
> And I hurl a morning hand-grenade
> Armed with the laughter
> Of a lonely man
> With a dark character.

In 1993 the American Psychiatric Association resolved that "Dr. Karadzic's actions as a political leader constitute a profound betrayal of the deeply humane values of medicine and psychiatry," citing his "brutal and inhuman actions as the Bosnian Serb leader."

The year 1994 was also a landmark. In 1994 the Russian Writers' Union bestowed the prized Mikhail Sholokov Award on Karadzic. And in 1994 a U.N. Security Council report concluded that "grave breaches of the Geneva Conventions and other violations of international humanitarian law have been committed in the territory of the former Yugoslavia on a large scale." The report emphasized that "so-called ethnic cleansing and rape and sexual assault, in particular, have been carried out by some of the parties so systematically that they strongly appear to be the product of a policy" perpetrated by the Bosnian Serbs in order to "ethnically cleanse" Bosnia of non-Serbian populations. On July 25, 1995, the International Criminal Tribunal for the Former Yugoslavia indicted Karadzic and Gen. Ratko Mladic, the Bosnian Serb military commander, and twenty-two others for war crimes, citing the killings and mass deportations of civilians and the seizing of hostages for use as human shields.

Karadzic has been called "one of the most misunderstood men in the world." Until his political involvement began in 1990, he was a psychiatrist and writer of poetry. What manner of man is this psychiatrist, poet, troubadour, political leader . . . and now indicted war criminal?

Little is known about the childhood of Karadzic, a descendant of the Serb reformer Vuk Karadzic. Not a Bosnian, he hails from a small village in Montenegro, a stronghold of Serb nationalism, a land described as a "crucified wilderness" and a land of "utter destitution and forlorn silence." One of three children, he was born to a poor peasant family on June 19, 1945, at the end of a war in which more than one million Yugoslavs perished.

At the age of fifteen, Karadzic moved to Sarajevo in search of better opportunities. The peasants did not easily assimilate into urban life, but Karadzic was accepted, for at age seventeen he joined the Communist Party, and in 1965, at age twenty, he began his study of medicine at the University of Sarajevo, later specializing in psychiatry. Accounts of his student days indicate a penchant for drinking and gambling. His gambling is of interest, given his propensity for risk taking as a political leader.

In 1968, he became swept up in the worldwide student movement, leading to his ouster from the Communist Party, although recent accounts hint that he was an informer, a young man who was well-connected, "the man to call." Later he was ostracized from the student movement.

During this time, he married Dr. Ljiljana Zelch (a well-to-do Bosnian Serb and also a psychiatrist), with whom he has two children. She characterized him as "a serene man, albeit melancholic, sensitive, and inclined toward politics and protest." She has described him as "a poetic soul" who wooed her with his poetry in which "he sang of life, of the unattainable, and of man's fate."[2]

His dark poetry provides intriguing glimpses of the man beneath the political mask, reflecting the powerful emotional currents that have influenced his leadership, and conveying his lifelong search for self-definition.

This odyssey led him to Columbia University in 1974 and 1975, a most unusual interruption of his medical career, suggesting doubts about his chosen profession. Biographic accounts indicate that he studied poetry at Columbia University that year. Karadzic, who speaks fluent English, told an American journalist of his love of Walt Whitman, explaining that his reading of American poetry helped him to appreciate "the need of Americans for a national myth."

The publication of his first two works at a young age suggests a unique drive and literary precocity. In his afterword to Karadzic's second book of poetry, the Bosnian poet Mark Vesovic refers to Karadzic as "among the most gifted of a younger generation of poets in Sarajevo." Karadzic boasted that he was "destined to become one of the three most important poets writing in the Serbian language." He has received many awards for his poetry. (Following the presentation of one literary award, two well-known Montenegrin poets—both previous awardees—returned their awards in protest.)

There has been little examination of Karadzic's creative writings in the English-speaking world. Karadzic speaks of his need to write "because it is through poetry that a nation defends itself." His poetic language may represent—more than his psychotherapeutic language or even his current political language—the language of self, and a way of identifying with the most salient symbols of his culture. Themes of darkness, death, violence, and destruction are prominent in his poetry; the Montenegrin poet Jevrem Brkovic observes that "none of his poetry is free of themes of death, knives, and bullets."

In *Ludo Koplje* (The Wrathful Spear, 1968), Karadzic's symbolic spear "divide[s] those witnessing, satiated with madness." But intermingled with poems of death, destruction, and decay are poems of longing and mournful regret. "The Road to Decline" is eerily premonitory and uncanny, given Karadzic's later foray into politics. He writes of "the well-trammeled path . . . [which] twists before you and leads you unto the wall and its heights of self-destruction," a hallowed path where he will become "a knight with no vassals."

In the title poem of his second book of poetry, *Pamtivek* (From Time Immemorial, 1971), Karadzic writes of a Christ-like figure who has the power to seduce, remember, dazzle, and destroy. This image is strengthened in his third volume when it becomes clear that Karadzic sees himself as having a messianic role in Bosnia's history.

During the Bosnian war some of the greatest poets of our time—including the Nobel laureates Joseph Brodsky and Czeslaw Milosz—wrote elegies for Sarajevo. But in his poem "Sarajevo," written twenty-one years before the war began, Karadzic with uncanny prophecy invokes a Sarajevo beset by plague, calamity, and destruction:

> I hear that a calamity really falters toward
> Its transformation into an insect—as if fated:
> It pulverizes the insect like the ruinous hand
> Transforming silence into his self-same voice
>
> The city lies ablaze like a rough lump of incense
>
> Wherein the haze of our awareness twists,
> The cite implodes in latent emptiness
> A stone's crimson death
> Bespeaks the house's blood-soaked tide.
> Plague!

Tranquillity. A squadron of white poplars
Marches in formation. The tempest's wind
Lifts up the chaos of our soul
At times human, at times breathtakingly divine

I speak of the dawning of a tempest's roar
What shapes the metal in the forge?
That's it—like fear transformed in its web
It searches in memory for a clue.

Following his return from the United States in 1975, Karadzic settled down, building his career as a psychiatrist and working in various clinical settings in Sarajevo, where many of his patients were Muslims. Later accounts note his relationship with the Sarajevo soccer team, as the team psychiatrist, in which he treated the players with "group hypnosis" in order to instill "a winning attitude." He had a Muslim boss, Dr. Ismet Ceric, with whom he was close for many years; a Muslim also served as the best man at his wedding. Reflecting the unique ethnic and cultural tapestry of Sarajevo, Karadzic lived in a neighborhood populated by Serbs, Croats, Muslims, and Hungarians.

The decade from 1975 to 1985 appears to have been a period of career consolidation for Karadzic, one of financial stability and vibrant intellectual life. But in 1985, the forty-year-old Karadzic was convicted of fraud and misuse of public funds involving a housing loan. He served eleven months in prison, when he was freed by a Serbian judge in Sarajevo. Allegations have also been made that Karadzic ran "a profitable racket selling false prescriptions and providing false medical diagnoses to help people collect insurance or pension benefits." The self-serving, unscrupulous manner in which he betrayed his medical trust can be seen as a template for the devious manner in which he reversed commitments during the conflict in Bosnia. He has a capacity to convey sincerity and then reverse himself without apparent discomfort.

The conviction and imprisonment must have been intolerable for Karadzic, a radical break from his august past. Karadzic salved his wounded ego by claiming he was a political prisoner. It was the system that was corrupt and at fault.

The psychiatrist Dr. Jovan Raskovic had an important influence on Karadzic in his transition from psychiatrist/poet to politician. Dr. Raskovic was the founder of the Serbian Democratic Party in Croatia and the author of *Luda Zemlja* (The Crazy Nation), a discussion of the psychodynamics of various ethnic groups in the former Yugoslavia.[3] Such rationalizations, couched in reductionist psychoanalytic language, have found their way into propaganda used by the Serb leadership to incite feelings of victimization related to genocidal violence, earlier in Bosnia, later in Kosovo. Later Karadzic would state that "myth is very dangerous at a political level. If we deal with politics by myth, we can have disaster." It may be precisely in this realm that psychiatrist-politicians Drs. Raskovic and Karadzic helped shape the political landscape of Yugoslavia in 1990 and 1991, as well as subsequent developments.

Karadzic's complete shift into politics in 1990 and the emergence of his political persona parallels that of the remainder of Yugoslavia and Eastern Europe in 1990; it was a reaction to internal disorganization, and, in Karadzic's case, a projection of his internal conflicts onto a larger political stage. In 1990 Dr. Karadzic published *Crna Bajka*, his first book of poetry since 1971. It had a different tone from his earlier work, with a stronger emphasis on the epic of the Serbian nation and its attendant myth, as well as an obsession with themes of blood and violence. Karadzic's "dictionary of fear" exalts violence and reveals an obsession with weapons, prominent in "A Man Made of Ashes":

> His world turned upside down
> And through his memory like a honeycomb
> A bullet,
> A slender bullet, majestic bullet.

In "Gavrilo Princip," he writes of madness, decay, hemorrhage, destruction, rot, and of Gavrilo Princip's shot that would purge a corrupted Europe and invoke Serbian dreams of glory. (Princip, a Serbian nationalist, assassinated the Archduke Francis Ferdinand, heir apparent to the throne of the Austro-Hungarian Empire, in Sarajevo in 1914, an act that led directly to the outbreak of World War I.)

> We are sick of the foggy image of brother,
>   God and predecessor
> The death is diluted and cheated
> But the mighty one has severe eyes
> It is never going to cover its cataract
> Never without bullets
> Insanity, stop!

In "On the Summit of Mount Durmitor" he writes of a journey toward "heights of dreams and glory."

Karadzic's poems reveal his embrace of myth, demonstrating a fusion of his personal Homeric myth with a collective myth of greater Serbian redemption. Karadzic identifies himself with Serbia and views himself as having a heroic role in Serbian history. His grandiose self-image is reflected in his poetic reference to his name: "Since people were not allowed to call God by his real name they called him Radovan," that is, "he who brings joy." In several of his poems he seems to identify himself with the deity.

Karadzic's sense of destiny and identification with Serbia is transformed in his language into a collective language of myth, which merges with that of sacrifice: "I am willing to sacrifice this entire generation, if it means that future generations [of Serbs] will live better." By 1994 he could state that "the Serbian people are about to reach their centuries-old goal of creating a unified Serb state." Group therapist to his wounded nation, Dr. Karadzic set himself the task of healing the collective sorrow of the Serbian people, fitting his dreams of glory with the collective dreams of the Serbian people.

From glory to disgrace, Karadzic now stands accused of war crimes including ethnic cleansing, genocide, mass rape and sexual assault, and the destruction of the Bosnian Muslim culture. He is now reviled by his former supporters.

The themes of his poetry seem to presage those of his political leadership, as though Karadzic had already reflected on and embraced the experiences described in his poetry. Karadzic ruefully acknowledges this premonitory prophetic quality, and speaks of it arising out of his sense of being "trapped in the depths of historical mire," and of his poetry as representing his answer to his sense of confusion and torment. That these themes of exile and return, death and destruction, pervade Karadzic's poetry from his earliest literary musings suggests this is a self-fulfilling prophecy, and when the poet turned political leader, he wrote his conflicts on the pages of Bosnia's tragic and tormented history.

> *Postscript: Radovan Karadzic has remained at large within Bosnia since his formal indictment by the War Crimes Tribunal in 1995. Initially aided by weak rules of engagement, which prohibited international peacekeeping troops from actively pursuing war crimes suspects, and then by an established network of loyal supporters, Karadzic continues to roam freely through the Bosnian countryside.*

Slobodan Milosevic: Heroic Nationalist Leader, War Criminal

> *This profile was completed in the spring of 1999 as the NATO air campaign was beginning against Serbia. It was distributed through*

the United States Information Agency (USIA) to appropriate embassies abroad.

The Kosovo crisis was defined by the brutality of Operation Horseshoe, a Yugoslav police and military crackdown against the Kosovo Liberation Army in Kosovo, where forty thousand troops "ethnically cleansed" and murdered civilians while rendering thousands of Kosovar Albanians (who make up 90 percent of Kosovo's population) homeless.[4] With the assistance of Russian and Finnish intermediaries, NATO's bombing campaign finally forced Yugoslavia's President Slobodan Milosevic to accept the NATO terms. But despite the massive bombing of Yugoslavia by the NATO alliance—which destroyed Yugoslavia's infrastructure—Milosevic remained as entrenched as ever and, indeed in the short term, was politically strengthened by the conflict. The NATO alliance now faces the delicate and awkward task of creating a lasting peace in Kosovo on the basis of an agreement negotiated with an indicted war criminal. Insight into Slobodan Milosevic's personality and political behavior will be crucial to the future of NATO's military and diplomatic efforts to create peace in the Balkans.

Previous portraits of Milosevic have emphasized both his cunning and ruthlessness, as well as his worldliness and charm. American media accounts of the 1995 peace negotiations in Dayton, Ohio—which led to a peace agreement in Bosnia—noted how Milosevic serenaded American negotiators, drank Johnnie Walker Scotch, cursed in colorful American epithets, waxed eloquent about his love of New York and American coffee, and became misty eyed when difficult compromises were reached. Milosevic conveyed the impression—seconded by the U.S. negotiator, Ambassador Richard Holbrooke—of a leader with whom the United States could reason and negotiate. The negotiations over Kosovo were described by Finland's Martti Ahtisaari (one of the architects of the Kosovo peace agreement) as "businesslike," and news photos of Milosevic showed a smiling leader who appears unruffled and in control of himself and events surrounding him. Milosevic's charm is rooted in deception, for his charm is malignant, that of a man whom Warren Zimmerman, the former U.S. ambassador to Yugoslavia, called "the slickest con man in the Balkans" and "a man of extraordinary coldness." He has also been called "an apparatchik" and has been vilified as "the Butcher of the Balkans."

Slobodan Milosevic was born in 1941 in wartime Serbia, the son of a Montenegrin theologian and a Serbian Communist schoolteacher, both of whom committed suicide during his young adulthood, as did his favorite uncle, a general in Yugoslav military intelligence. This depressive genealogy has led many, wishfully, to speculate that when he was on the ropes,

Milosevic too would follow the path of suicide. But when he is in crisis situations, his tendency is to externalize, identify enemies as the cause of his problems, and lash out at them.

Milosevic grew up in Pozarevac, where he met his wife Mira Markovic, who later became a sociologist, columnist, university professor, and head of her own powerful political party, the Union of the Yugoslav Left. She, too, had a tragic side to her childhood. Her mother, a partisan fighter, reportedly paused for a day in the forest to give birth to Mira and then resumed her wartime duties. Captured by the Nazis and tortured, according to Mira, she died in a concentration camp. Slavoljub Djukic's definitive biographies of Milosevic present a less heroic story, which has tainted Mira's image, a story she hotly disputes. According to Djukic, Mira's mother was executed by the partisans for betraying her partisan comrades under torture by the Nazis. Mira (which was also her mother's nom de guerre) has striven to buffer her heroic image by emphasizing her partisan roots, regularly calling attention to the fact that her father and mother were leading partisan cadres and that her mother's cousin was Tito's wartime secretary and lover.

Two wounded souls, she and Milosevic have been inseparable since adolescence. Mira Markovic's diaries and interviews—serialized in the Yugoslav media over the past several years—are notable for their surreal quality. She considers herself—in contrast to her husband—an ideologue, a feminist, and a Marxist. Her political power is formidable. She has functioned not only as Milosevic's intimate confidante but also as a political and social critic. It is said that she wrote the majority of Milosevic's most electrifying speeches (collected and sold as a best-seller) during the late 1980s, which led to his rise to power. Because of her visibility and perceived influence, she has been a lightning rod for criticism of the Milosevic regime. Her diaries and interviews reveal a unique vanity and self-absorption, which has led to her being reviled for her insensitivity and to her being characterized as Serbia's Lady Macbeth. The Lady Macbeth analogy is an apt one, for she is in many ways considered tougher than her husband—the steel in his spine—calling to mind the soliloquy by Lady Macbeth in act 1, scene 5, where she reflects with concern on the weakness of her "dearest partner of greatness," which she fears will inhibit his pursuit of power: "Yet do I fear thy nature, it is too full o' the milk of human kindness to catch the nearest way . . . Thus thou must do if thou have it . . . Hie thee hither that I may pour my spirits in thine ear, and chastise with the valor of my tongue all that impedes thee from the golden round." Most observers agree that without Mira Markovic's guidance and sleight of hand, there would be no Slobodan Milosevic as we know him today.

Since the formation of her party—the Union of the Yugoslav Left—in

1993, most persons of power within the Milosevic government—his inner circle—have been members of her party or else persons related to Milosevic or his wife. This web of influence extends through the media, government, the foreign ministry, the intelligence services, the military, and the world of commerce and banking.

Milosevic's vocation began quietly. After his graduation from law school in Belgrade, he labored in various local and state bureaucratic jobs as an administrator and international banker, revealing little of the charisma and ruthlessness that characterized his later rise to political power in the 1980s. Championed by his mentor, Ivan Stambolic, Milosevic climbed steadily in the Communist Party hierarchy. In 1984, after being elevated to head the Serbian Communist Party, Stambolic promoted Milosevic to the position he had just vacated, as leader of the Belgrade Communist Party. When Stambolic became president of Serbia in 1986, Milosevic was again promoted to Stambolic's vacated position, this time as head of the Serbian Communist Party.

Milosevic showed the cunning of a chess master; his skill in maintaining his power reveals a Machiavellian side that had remained unseen except by his most intimate associates in the factional world of Yugoslav Communist Party politics.

His wife has written that he was neither ideologue nor nationalist. It was only late in his career that Milosevic found his political voice and became a champion of Serbian nationalism. In the late 1980s, he tapped into the reservoir of Serb nationalist myth to fan ethnic hatreds and became the catalyst behind the destructive conflicts in Slovenia, Croatia, Bosnia, and Kosovo, in which hundreds of thousands died and millions of refugees were "ethnically cleansed" or displaced from their homes. According to Stambolic, in 1987 Milosevic was "transformed and set afire by Kosovo," a region of Yugoslavia with a long history of ethnic tension. Kosovo—90 percent of whose residents are ethnic Albanians—is hallowed ground to the Serbian people. It is the site of the mythologized 1389 battle of Kosovo Polje, where the Serbs were defeated by the Ottoman infidel. Many of medieval (Orthodox) Serb Christendom's holiest sites are in Kosovo. It also holds regions rich in undeveloped mineral resources. Sent to Kosovo by Stambolic in order to quell the ethnic unrest, Milosevic, defying Stambolic's instructions, inflamed the nationalist passions of the Kosovar Serbs. In a 1987 speech in Kosovo that helped catapult him to power, Milosevic spoke eloquently to a group of disgruntled minority Serbs living in Kosovo—"this is your country"—of Serb land, homes, fields, gardens, and memories. To not fight for what belongs to Serbs—he told his enthralled listeners—would be to "disgrace your ancestors and disappoint your descendants." He evoked the spirit of Prince Lazar, the hero of the battle of Kosovo Polje, who refused to yield to the overpowering might of the Ottoman invaders, vowing that it was better to die in glory than to live in shame.

Within a year of his promotion to head the Serbian Communist Party, Milosevic turned against his former mentor, accusing him of anticommunist and anti-Serbian policies, and by 1989 had displaced Stambolic as president of Serbia. During his rise to power in Serbia, Milosevic revealed consummate political skills and a remarkable talent for organization. By 1989 he had stoked the fires of Serb nationalism—primarily in Kosovo and Vojvodina (an area of Serbia with a large Hungarian minority)—to acquire political power in Serbia. A shrewd manipulator of symbols, as the 600th anniversary of the famed battle approached, Milosevic took the mummified remains of Prince Lazar, placed them in a coffin, and brought them to countless rallies throughout Serbia. In a legendary rally in Vidovdan on June 28, 1989—the 600th anniversary of the battle of Kosovo Polje—he spoke boldly before one million Serbs of "battles and quarrels," reminding his euphoric followers that "the Kosovo heroism does not allow us to forget that at one time we were brave and dignified." This theme of martyred courage in defying an overpowering enemy was to be replayed again and again during the Kosovo conflict. In 1989 he revoked Kosovo's autonomy, an action that led to the crisis there.

A consummate survivor, Milosevic is driven for the most part to preserve and magnify his power, rather than by ideology or financial gain. During and subsequent to his initial rise to power, Milosevic revealed himself as a consummate politician, with Teflon-like qualities that allowed him to repeatedly weather domestic political opposition, international outrage, economic sanctions, and the destruction of the former Yugoslavia to emerge as a key power broker in the 1995 Dayton peace agreement. This, despite acting Secretary of State Lawrence Eagleburger's declaration in 1992 before the International Conference on the Former Yugoslavia naming Milosevic, Karadzic, and Bosnian Serb General Ratko Mladic as war criminals. His tenacity showed in the 1996–97 Zajedno rallies, where he withstood months of defiant demonstrations by upward of two hundred thousand people in the streets of Belgrade who were protesting local elections widely believed to have been stolen by Milosevic and his cronies.

Again and again, Milosevic has proved himself to be a master of betrayal. A list of political associates with whom he has collaborated—and later betrayed—reads like a Who's Who of Yugoslav political, military, and intellectual life: Ivan Stambolic, Vojislav Seselj, Radovan Karadzic, Milo Djukanovic, Borisav Jovic, Mihailo Markovic, Dobrisa Cosic, Vuk Draskovic, Jovica Stanisic, Gen. Momcilo Perisic, and Milan Panic. His political flexibility and ability to bring formerly sacked colleagues such as Vojislav Seselj and Vuk Draskovic back into his government has been striking. Milosevic has always skillfully used the politics of fear and propaganda in ways that show him to be a calculating pragmatist rather than an ideological visionary. While utilizing the language of myth to foment ethnic hatred, Milosevic has always cleverly fallen back on legalistic formalities—coupled with near-complete control of the media—to achieve and maximize his political standing. His tenacious defiance of NATO centered largely on legal issues of sovereignty rather than nationalist myth, although he has utilized historical symbols with great effectiveness in mobilizing public opinion in his favor and against NATO. Besides his reliance on the Kosovo myth to seize power in the late 1980s, during the NATO bombing (including that which occurred on April 6, 1999) he cleverly revived the symbolism of the Nazi war machine's bombing of a defenseless Belgrade on April 6, 1941, when Yugoslavia refused to capitulate to the demands made by the fascist aggressor during World War II.

As earlier observed, in 1992 acting U.S. Secretary of State Lawrence Eagleburger (also a former U.S. ambassador to Yugoslavia) suggested that Milosevic should be among those indicted for war crimes and genocide under UN auspices, but it was not until June 1999 that the International Criminal Tribunal for the Former Yugoslavia finally indicted Milosevic—as well as several of his closest aides and henchmen—for war crimes. Milosevic had previously betrayed the fundamental principles of the Dayton peace agreement by harboring and refusing to hand over other previously indicted international war criminals such as Gen. Ratko Mladic, Dr. Radovan Karadzic, Gen. Milo Mrksic, and Col. Veselin Sljivancanin. In a further snub of The Hague tribunal, Mrksic, Sljivancanin, and Gen. Dragoljub Odjanic were promoted following their indictments.

A masterful manipulator of images, during the NATO campaign Milosevic managed to transform himself from the ethnic-cleanser of Kosovo to the martyr-hero of Belgrade, identifying himself with Prince Lazar. He adroitly manipulated both the Western media and internal Yugoslav opinion during the Kosovo crisis, calling attention to Serb civilians who had been maimed and killed in the NATO bombing in hospitals, schools, and cities. By referring to President Clinton as "Hitler" and NATO as "Nazis," he evoked the memory of the courageous stand against overwhelming odds by Serbs during World War II, and identified himself with Tito, the heroic partisan leader. He used such symbolism to awaken unified resistance behind his defiant banner.

After Milosevic finally agreed to NATO's terms, many Serbs celebrated the suspension of the air campaign, proclaiming victory. Milosevic declared that they had preserved Kosovo's sovereignty and that the issue of autonomy for Kosovo was no longer on the table. Reminiscent of Saddam

Hussein during Operation Desert Storm, Milosevic praised the courage of his people in standing up to a superior foe. In celebration, many Serbs echoed the above sentiments, proclaiming that they survived eighty-eight days of bombing while "resisting the whole world."

The devastation of Kosovo and Serbia proper, as well the exodus of Kosovar Serbs from Kosovo, led to calls for Milosevic's resignation by the powerful Orthodox Church. As the magnitude of destruction to Serbia caused by the reckless leadership of Milosevic sinks in, Milosevic and his wife (his only true confidante and closest advisor) may someday be seen as more akin to the Ceaucescus, whose policies led to the destruction of modern-day Romania. Milosevic's policies, with their residue of nationalist mythology remade and exalted, may someday be seen by the Serbian people as a hoax, imbued with cruelty and suffering.

Milosevic's indifference to the suffering of others—including the suffering of his own people—is striking. Milosevic is a shrewd manipulator, however, and he has a notable capacity for patience for enduring popular disapproval and weathering the storm.

But Milosevic, having made betrayal into political mastery, may have finally run out of persons whom to betray. In the months leading to the Kosovo crisis, he purged top military personnel as well as his chief of security services. Observers surprised by this would do well to remember his purge of thirty-eight Yugoslav Army generals prior to the 1992 Bosnia campaign. The indictments of several of his closest associates for war crimes will lead to his further political isolation; some of those indicted associates might be tempted to curry favor with prosecutors in The Hague. The indictment of Serbian President Milan Milutinovic—who is closely allied with Mira Markovic and is a member of her party—is particularly important, suggesting that the Hague tribunal indictments have focused not only on Milosevic but also on Milosevic's inner circle.

Milosevic's rule has left a trail of unsolved murders of high-profile persons connected to him and his family. Recent publicity about Milosevic's family appears to have burst the bubble surrounding his purported austerity and asceticism. He and his wife—not previously portrayed as corrupt—are said to have millions squirreled away in foreign bank accounts. Their daughter also owns her own radio/TV station, and their son—a race car driver notorious for consorting with Belgrade's criminal underworld—owns several discotheques in Serbia and reportedly has made millions smuggling whiskey and cigarettes.

Serbia's economy and political culture are in tatters. The NATO bombing destroyed Serbia's infrastructure, but Milosevic had long since destroyed any semblance of a civic political, cultural, and economic life. But more tragically, Milosevic's policies have led to the emigration—a brain drain—of over two hundred thousand young Serbs to the West since 1991. Milosevic's Serbia has become a surreal and frightening labyrinth. Yugoslavia, a country that fought with the Allies in two world wars, a country that gave us the genius of Nikola Tesla, and a country that fostered the literary gifts of Nobel laureate Ivo Andric is now known throughout the civilized world for ethnic cleansing.

Formulaic approaches in dealing with Slobodan Milosevic are fraught with difficulty. NATO military intervention has paradoxically strengthened Milosevic while weakening his opposition, allowing him to resurrect his forsaken charisma as the defender of the Serbs against NATO; he has once again tapped into Serb mythology to bolster his heroic stature and further his power. But Milosevic's political survival has in many ways been a pyrrhic victory. Milosevic—known as both "the arsonist and the fireman"—will need new crises to thrive and survive politically. As long as Milosevic is in power, there will always be new "Kosovos" in the lives of his countrymen.

For Milosevic, there is only one prize, his postwar political power in Yugoslavia, and this requires deflecting attention from the poisoned fruits of his leadership, through the creation of new crises. Montenegro may present an opportunity for further crisis creation, especially should his former supporter, Milo Djukanovic, the president of Montenegro, attempt a rapprochement with the West. Having closely watched the maneuvers of Saddam Hussein after the Iraqi defeat in the 1991 Gulf War and knowing how difficult it would be for NATO to resume military action against Yugoslavia, so too Milosevic can be expected to thwart and undermine the terms of the recent Kosovo agreement. A viable long-term strategy for peace in Kosovo demands the creation of meaningful democratic institutions in Serbia, and the healing of a generation's political and economic scars. For Slobodan Milosevic, peace would be the greatest and most dangerous crisis of all. Only then does he run the risk that the Serbian people may finally consign him to the halls of justice and the history books, lest he consign—yet again—the Balkans to the flames of his malignant and apocalyptic visions.

Postscript: Despite having been officially indicted in 1999 by the War Crimes Tribunal on the Former Yugoslavia on war crimes charges for atrocities committed by Serb forces in Kosovo, Milosevic remained in power until October 2000. Following student uprisings and national unrest, and the election of a new president, Milosevic was removed from office. The following spring Serbian authorities arrested Milosevic. Under increasing international pressure, including the threat of losing loans if they did not comply, Serbian authorities turned Milosevic over to The Hague in June 2001. By the end of 2001, the tribu-

nal had issued formal indictments against Milosevic for atrocities committed in Croatia and Bosnia as well as in Kosovo.

Milosevic has simultaneously denounced the legitimacy of the international court while acting as his own defense counsel. The prosecution is scheduled to complete its case by early spring 2004 at which time Milosevic will begin his formal defense.

9

Narcissism and the Charismatic Leader–Follower Relationship

This chapter examines the political psychology of the tie between leaders and followers. Drawing on the psychology of narcissism, it relates the charismatic leader to the "mirror-hungry" personality and the charismatic follower to the "ideal-hungry" personality.[1] The sense of grandiose omnipotence of the leader is especially appealing to his or her needy followers. In contrast to "reparative charismatics" who heal their nation's wounds, a hallmark of destructive charismatic leaders is absolutist polarizing rhetoric, drawing their followers together against the outside enemy. I distinguish the psychologically healthy follower rendered temporarily needy by societal stress from the mirror-hungry follower who only feels whole when merged with the idealized other.

The victory of the Islamic Revolution in Iran did not fulfill Ayatollah Khomeini's messianic aspirations. Still driven by dreams of glory, the aged ayatollah relentlessly pursued his greater goal of one "united Islamic Nation" under his guidance (Zonis 1985). The fundamental political, economic, and social changes, and the violence and havoc that the revolution unleashed are vivid testimony to the powerful forces that can be mobilized by charismatic leader–follower relationships. Osama bin Laden similarly forged a powerful bond with his alienated followers, resulting in the powerful events of September 11, 2001. Indeed, Khomeini can be considered an intellectual mentor and model for bin Laden. The Islamic revolution and the radical Islamic terrorism of al Qaeda are pointed reminders that such relationships are not merely interesting relics of a bygone era—the era of "great men"—but continue to play an important, and often determining, role in world affairs.

It will be observed that I speak not of charismatic leaders but rather of charismatic leader–follower relationships. I will be elaborating the political psychology of this tie between leaders and followers, attempting to identify crucial aspects of the psychology of the leader that, like a key, fit and unlock certain aspects of the psychology of their followers. In delineating this lock and key relationship, I will draw on emerging understandings of the psychology of narcissism.

When Max Weber (1922) first introduced the concept of charismatic authority, he addressed the psychology of the followers, but only in cursory fashion. He considered the determinant of the relationship between the charismatic leader and his followers to be the compelling forcefulness of the leader's personality, in the face of which the followers were essentially choiceless and felt compelled to follow. Schiffer (1973) has observed that later commentators on the phenomenon of charismatic authority have also focused disproportionately on the magnetism of the leader, failing to make the fundamental observations that all leaders—especially charismatic leaders—are at heart the creation of their followers. A notable exception to this criticism is the work of Ulman and Abse (1983), who studied the mass suicide at Jonestown, a settlement of the People's Temple in Guyana where the followers of the Reverend Jim Jones, most of them U.S. citizens, drank poisoned Kool-Aid at his direction in 1978. They emphasized the psychological qualities of the followers that render them susceptible to the force of the charismatic leader and lead to collective regression. They draw attention to the relationship between the psychological qualities of narcissistically wounded individuals and charismatic leader–follower relationships.

In her review of the subject, Wilner (1984) has observed that the concept of charisma has been much abused and watered down since Weber first introduced it. The media often use charisma as synonymous with popular appeal, whereas Weber defined charismatic authority as a personal authority deriving from "devotion to the specific sanctity, heroism or exemplary character of an individual person and of the normative patterns or order revealed or ordained by him." To operationalize the concept, Wilner surveyed the vast (and often contradictory) literature on charismatic leadership and then defined it as a relationship between a leader and a group of followers that has the following properties:

1. The leader is perceived by the followers as somehow superhuman.
2. The followers blindly believe the leader's statements.
3. The followers unconditionally comply with the leader's directives for action.
4. The followers give the leader unqualified emotional support.

Each of these properties relates to a perception, belief, or response of the followers. But Wilner nevertheless devotes most of her scholarly energies to analyzing the leaders who elicit these responses, paying scant attention to the psychology of the followers. Thus Wilner has committed the same sin of omission as the authors of the earlier reviews criticized by Schiffer (1973). Indeed, she relegated Schiffer's pathbreaking psychoanalytic exploration of charisma and mass society to an extended footnote, where he shares the distinguished company of Erik Erikson and Sigmund Freud, whose work on group psychology is noted but dismissed.   ·

In particular, Wilner dismisses as interesting—but unproven—hypotheses that "in times of crisis, individuals regress to a state of delegated omnipotence and demand a leader (who will rescue them, take care of them)" and that "individuals susceptible to (the hypnotic attraction of) charismatic leadership have themselves fragmented or weak ego structures."

In my judgment, there is indeed powerful support for these hypotheses. Clinical work with individuals with narcissistic personality disorders, the detailed studies of individuals who join charismatic religious groups, and psychodynamic observations of group phenomena all provide persuasive support for these hypotheses concerning the psychological makeup and responses of individuals susceptible to charismatic leadership—the lock of the follower for the key of the leader.

The central features of the development and phenomenology of the narcissistic personality help us understand the nature of charismatic leader–follower relationships. In discussing the vicissitudes of the life cycle in chapter 2, I presented descriptive material on the narcissistic personality, drawing especially on the Diagnostic and Statistical Manual IV of the American Psychiatric Association and the work of Vamik Volkan. Let me now take a brief excursion through the exotic landscape of narcissism, emphasizing in particular the consequences of the wounded self and how they relate to the charismatic leader–follower relationship. I will draw particularly on the works of Heinz Kohut (1971, 1977, 1978, 1984), Otto Kernberg (1975, 1976, 1984), and Vamik Volkan (1976, 1980, 1981, 1982, 1984 [Vamik and Itzkowitz]).

This is meant only as a brief sketch of the central personality features, not a thorough explication of the arcana of narcissism. In particular, this overview does *not* pretend to delineate the differences between the schools of Kohut and Kernberg. Suffice it to say that a separate "healthy" line of narcissistic personality development is a central feature of the self-psychology of Kohut, whereas Kernberg believes that the narcissistic personality develops only in response to psychological damage inflicted early in the course of development, and hence is always a pathological development. Like Volkan, I find the psychogenetic formulations of Kernberg more congenial. Nevertheless, in this essay I draw heavily on Kohut, particularly on his clinical observations. Although Kohut and Kernberg depict narcissistic transferences similarly, Kohut's formulations of the mirroring and idealizing transferences are particularly elegant, and an elaboration of the narcissistic transferences is essential to this examination of charismatic leader–follower relationships.

In the earliest stage of development—the stage of primary narcissism— the infant does not distinguish between himself and others. He experiences the external world—his mother—as part of himself. He is not just the center of the universe—he *is* the universe. As the young child experiences the frustrating reality of the external world's less-than-perfect response to his needs, he begins to differentiate himself from it. The child is demoted from being the universe to becoming merely its center. Two psychological constellations develop as ways of restoring a sense of completeness.

The first is the ideal or grandiose self. The "mirroring" response of the mother—her admiration and attention—allows the child to feel special and highly valued. This treasured position is maintained by an important psychological mechanism—splitting. The very young child is unable to tolerate the bad aspects of himself and his environment and to integrate them with the good ones into a realistic whole. He splits the good and the bad into the "me" and the "not me." By rejecting all aspects of himself and his situation that do not fit his ideal or grandiose self, the child attempts to maintain it.

The child's second mechanism for remedying frustration and incompleteness is to attach himself to an ideal object (Kernberg), or idealized parental image (Kohut), which derives particularly from the father. This is the fantasized image of the all-powerful, all-knowing, all-giving, all-loving parent. The child gains his own sense of being complete and worthwhile by experiencing himself as connected to or united with his idealized object. In Crayton's (1983) formulation, "If I am not perfect, I will at least be in a relationship with something perfect."

If the child is traumatized during this critical period of development, his emerging self-concept is damaged, leading to the formation of what Kohut calls "the injured self." Such damage can occur in several ways. Children rejected by cold and ungiving mothers may be left emotionally hungry, with an exaggerated need for love and admiration. A special form of rejection is overprotection by the intrusive narcissistic mother. She cannot let her child individuate because she sees him as an extension of herself. Her own sense of perfection seems to depend on her child's perfection.

Formation of the "injured self" results in two personality patterns that have particular implications for our study of charismatic relationships.

The first is the mirror-hungry personality. These individuals, whose basic psychological constellation is the grandiose self, hunger for confirming and admiring responses to counteract their inner sense of worthlessness and lack of self-esteem. To nourish their famished self, they are compelled to display themselves in order to evoke the attention of others. No matter how positive the response, they cannot be satisfied, but continue seeking new audiences from whom to elicit the attention and recognition they crave.

The second type is the ideal-hungry personality. These individuals can experience themselves as worthwhile only so long as they can relate to individuals whom they can admire for their prestige, power, beauty, intelligence, or moral stature. They forever search for such idealized figures. Again, the inner void cannot be filled. Inevitably, ideal-hungry individuals find that their gods are merely human, that their heroes have feet of clay. Disappointed by discovering defects in their previously idealized object, they cast him aside and search for a new hero, to whom they attach themselves in the hope that they will not be disappointed again.

The phenomenon of the charismatic leader–follower relationship is surely too complex to lend itself to a single overarching psychodynamic personality model. In addition to features of the leader, the followers, and their relationships, one must take into account complex sociocultural, political, and historical factors. Nevertheless, I believe elements of the narcissistic transferences just described are present in all charismatic leader–follower relationships, and in some charismatic leader–follower relationships are crucial determinants.

In certain of these cases, the complementarity between the two transference postures is so striking that it is extremely tempting to relate the two principal actors in this relationship—leaders and followers—to these postures. In the balance of this chapter, I will yield to that temptation and relate charismatic leaders to the mirror-hungry personality and charismatic followers to the ideal-hungry personality. I do so in the service of illuminating certain elements of the psychology of charismatic leaders and their followers, not as an all-encompassing explanation of all charismatic leader–follower relationships.

The Charismatic Leader as Mirror-Hungry Personality

Mirror-hungry leaders require a continuing flow of admiration from their audiences to nourish their famished selves. Central to their ability to elicit admiration is an ability to convey a sense of grandeur, omnipotence, and strength. Individuals who have had feelings of grandiose omnipotence awakened within them are particularly attractive to individuals seeking idealized sources of strength. They convey a sense of conviction and certainty to those who are consumed by doubt and uncertainty. This mask of certainty is no mere pose: so profound is the inner doubt that a wall of dogmatic certainty is necessary to ward it off. For them, preserving grandiose feelings of strength and omniscience does not allow for expressions of weakness and doubt. The mechanism of splitting is of central importance in maintaining their illusion.

The Language of Splitting Is the Rhetoric of Absolutism

There is the me and the not me, good versus evil, strength versus weakness. Analysis of the speeches of charismatic leaders repeatedly reveals such all-or-nothing polar absolutism.

Either-or categorization, with the charismatic leaders on the side of the angels, is a regular characteristic of their evocative rhetoric. Consider these words of Robespierre: "There are but two kinds of men, the kind that is corrupt and the kind that is virtuous." By the virtuous, as Bychowski (1948) notes in *Dictators and Disciples*, Robespierre means those who thought as he did—his main criterion for judging the morals of others became the extent to which they agreed with his ideas. Bychowski has observed the predominance of the theme of strength and weakness in Hitler's speeches: the emphasis on the strength of the German people, the reviling of weakness, the need to purify the race of any contamination or sign of weakness. But what could be the barrier to the German people achieving its full measure of greatness? "If we Germans are the chosen of God, then they [the Jews] are the people of Satan." (This is very similar to the rhetoric of Osama bin Laden.) Here the polarity is between good and evil, between children of God and the people of Satan:

> "Look at our splendid youth . . . I do not want anything weak or tender in them." Hitler invokes the cult of strength and reviles weakness. "One must defend the strong who are menaced by their inferiors," he asserts, and then indicates that "A state which, in a period of race pollution, devotes itself to caring for its best racial elements must someday become the lord of the earth." The fear of appearing weak is projected upon the nation with which he identifies.

Being on the side of God and identifying the enemy with Satan is a rhetorical device found regularly in the speeches of charismatic leaders. Ayatollah Khomeini continued to identify the United States as "the great Satan" as did Saddam Hussein. Wilner sees this as an identifying feature of the speeches of the charismatic leader that heightens his identity as a leader with supernatural forces. In another example, Wilner (1984) has observed the frequency of biblical references in the speeches of Franklin Delano Roosevelt. In the second inaugural address, for example: "We of the Republic pledged ourselves to drive from the temple of our ancient faith those who had profaned it . . . our Covenant with ourselves did not stop there." And, in the stirring conclusion, "I shall do my utmost to speak their purpose and do their will, seeking Divine guidance to help us and everyone to give light to them that sit in darkness and to guide our feet into the way of peace." As Wilner points out, not only is the authority of the Bible invoked but also there are suggestions of God speaking through the mouth of the prophet Franklin. He identified himself with Moses, as well, when he asked, "Shall we pause now and turn our back upon the road that lies ahead? Shall we call this the promised land?"

The invocation of divine guidance and use of biblical references are the currency of American political rhetoric, and no politician worth his salt would ignore them. What is the difference between the politician whose use of such rhetoric rings false, as hollow posturing, and the politician whose religious words inspire? Is this related to Wildenmann's distinction between charisma and pseudocharisma?[2] The narcissistic individual, who indeed consciously believes that he has special leadership gifts and accordingly has a special role to play, may utilize religious rhetoric much more convincingly. Most convincing of all is its use by leaders like Ayatollah Khomeini and Osama bin Laden, who are genuinely convinced they have a religious mission to perform.

Although the ability to convey belief is an important asset, real belief is most convincing. This is also true of the polarization of good and evil, *we* versus *them*. Again, although it is a common political tactic to attempt to unify the populace against an outside enemy, the rhetoric of polarization is most effective when, as in the case of Hitler, *they* are absolutely believed to be the source of the problem, *they* are evil, and to eliminate *them* is to eliminate *our* problems. Phyllis Greenacre observed that in order to be effectively charismatic it is a great asset to possess paranoid conviction.[3] Although there is no necessary relation between charisma and paranoia, when the two are linked some of the most fearful excesses of human violence in history have occurred (Robins 1984).

A leader's posture of total certainty is very attractive to one besieged by doubt. Indeed, this posture is necessary to ward off the inner doubt of the leader, too. In one of his last essays, Kohut began to consider the implications of self-psychology for group psychology and historical phenomena. He summarized the characteristics of the individual who is especially suitable to become the admired omnipotent model:

> Certain types of narcissistically fixated persons (even bordering on the paranoid) . . . display an apparently unshakeable self-confidence and voice their opinions with absolute certainty. . . . Such individuals' maintenance of their self-esteem depends on the incessant use of certain mental functions . . . they are continually judging others—usually pointing up the moral flaws in other people's personality and behavior—and, without shame or hesitation, they set themselves up as the guides and leaders and gods of those who are in need of guidance, of leadership, and as a target for their reverence.

Indeed, the degree of moral righteousness is often quite extraordinary. Kohut goes on to observe that the psychological equilibrium of such charismatic leaders is of "an all or nothing type: there are no survival potentialities between the extremes of utter firmness and strength on the one hand, and utter destruction on the other" (Kohut 1985, 198).

It is important to reemphasize that such individuals have disowned and projected on the environment all of the unacceptable weaknesses and imperfections within themselves. Psychologically, they cannot permit themselves to recognize that the source of their feared destruction is not from without but from within. The mirror-hungry personality is held together by this rigid shell of apparent total self-confidence to keep profound inner doubt from breaking through. For the charismatic leader with paranoid characteristics who is projecting his inner aggression, the rhetoric becomes the basis for justifying attacking the outside enemy: "We (I) are not weak. The problem is out there, with them. By destroying them, by expelling them (the weakness within me) from our midst, we (I) will be the strong people we want to be." And each time the admiring crowd shouts its approval in response to this externalizing rhetoric, the leader's facade of certainty is strengthened and his inner doubts assuaged.

There is a quality of mutual intoxication in the leader's reassuring his followers who in turn reassure him. One is reminded of the relationship between hypnotist and subject. Manifesting total confidence, the hypnotist instructs his subject to yield control to him and to suspend volition and judgment. To watch the films of Hitler's rallies and focus on his hypnotic use of language—the repetition of simple phrases, building to a crescendo, the crowd echoing his phrases—is to watch hypnosis on a large scale. Observers of the powerful mesmerizing effect of Hitler on his followers at the mass rallies have likened him to a hypnotist who placed his entire audience into a trance. Even those present at the rallies who did not understand German described themselves as coming under his hypnotic sway. And most striking of all, it was also autohypnosis, as Hitler apparently entered a trance state, mesmerized by the enraptured responses of his mesmerized followers.

But the power of hypnotists ultimately depends on the eagerness of their subjects to yield to their authority, to cede control of their autonomy, to surrender their will to the hypnotist's authority.

The Core Follower as Ideal-Hungry Personality

Let us turn now to an examination of the psychology of the admiring crowd of hypnotic subjects—the ideal-hungry followers, without whose uncritical response the charismatic leader would be but an empty shell, "full of sound and fury, signifying nothing." It is those ideal-hungry followers, narcissistically injured personalities, who are the core followers in charismatic leader–follower relationships and are permanently prone to enter the ranks of admiring followers. Like a "lock and key" relationship, they are attracted to "mirror hungry" leaders. Each needs the other to nourish his famished self. Even in the quietest of times, charismatic leader–follower relationships develop. What are the characteristics of the ideal-hungry followers? Damage to the self-concept during early childhood development tends to leave individuals permanently psychologically scarred, with an enduring need to attach themselves to a powerful, caring other. Incomplete unto themselves, such individuals can only feel whole when in relationship, attached, or merged with this idealized other. The charismatic leader comes to the psychological rescue of the ideal-hungry followers. Taking on heroic proportions and representing what the followers wish to be, he protects them from confronting themselves and their fundamental inadequacy and alienation. The leader's success becomes the follower's success, a succor to his self-esteem.

Marc Galanter's studies of charismatic religious groups confirm the hypothesis that narcissistically wounded individuals are especially attracted to charismatic leader–follower relationships.[4] The more lonely and isolated individuals were before joining the Unification Church, the more apt they were to affiliate themselves strongly and stay through the entire recruitment process. They tended to suspend individual judgment and follow unquestioningly the dictates of the leader. Moreover, the more psychological relief that was experienced on joining, the less likely the individual was to question the leader's requirement for actions and behavior that ran counter to his or her socialization.

Societal Crisis Produces Temporarily Overwhelmed Followers

In addition to those wounded personalities drawn to charismatic relationships, there are those who are, by virtue of external circumstances, temporarily drawn to join the ranks of charismatic followers. At moments of societal crisis, otherwise mature and psychologically healthy individuals may temporarily come to feel overwhelmed and in need of a strong and self-assured leader. But when the historical moment passes, so too does the need. Few would omit Winston Churchill from the pantheon of charismatic leaders. The sense of conviction and assuredness he conveyed provided a rallying point to Great Britain and the Allies during their darkest hours. During the crisis, Churchill's virtues were exalted and idealized. But when it passed and the need for a strong leader abated, how quickly the British people demystified the previously revered Churchill, focused on his leadership faults, and cast him out of office.

Indeed the process of idealization carries within it the seeds of disillusion. And the intensity of disengagement from the charismatic leader can be every bit as powerful as the attraction, a reflection of the cyclic course of history and the changing needs of the populace.

Charismatic leader–follower relationships require not only the congruence of a particular leader with a particular followership but also a special historical moment. In *The Sociology of Religion* (1922), Max Weber characterized a time of societal readiness for revolutionary change and a charismatic revolutionary leader. Throughout his years of exile in Iraq and France, Ayatollah Khomeini retained a loyal following. His basic personality, leadership style, and rhetoric were consistent over the years. But it was only when the shah of Iran hastened the pace of societal change in hopes of achieving his "White Revolution" before he died (Post 1984), thereby creating massive societal dislocation and disrupting the social order, that the ideal-hungry followers and the special historical moment were also present, and the charismatic leader–follower relationship blossomed and grew.

Charismatic leader–follower relationships do not only develop at such historical moments. Rather, they are particularly apt to occur at those times when the ranks of dependent followers will be swollen by normally self-sufficient individuals who have temporarily been rendered psychologically vulnerable by external events.

Repetitive Patterns of Group Behavior

The observations of Wilfred Bion (1961) concerning repetitive patterns of group behavior add further to our understanding of the forces mobilized in followers by charismatic leaders. Bion's work has been elaborated by the Tavistock Institute in Great Britain and the A. K. Rice Institute in the United States through their conferences on the role of "Leadership, Authority, and Responsibility in Organizations." Working with psychologically healthy executives, educators, and health care professionals, the staffs of these organizations continue to reconfirm the observations Bion first made with psychiatric inpatients in military hospitals in Great Britain. He noted that no matter how healthy the individuals, when they come together in a group they behaved as if they were acting on the basis of shared basic assumptions. He described three psychological states by which group members act as if they are dominated. He calls these three "basic assumption" groups the dependency group, the pairing group, and the fight-flight group. The dependency group turns to an omnipotent leader for security. Acting as if they do not have independent minds of their own, the members blindly seek directions and follow orders unquestioningly. They tend to idealize and place the leader on a pedestal, but when the leader fails to meet the standards of omnipotence and omniscience, after a period of denial anger and disappointment result. In the pairing group, the members act as if the goal of the group is to bring forth a messiah, someone who will save them. There is an air of optimism and hope that a new world is around the corner. And the fight-flight group organizes itself in relationship to a perceived outside threat. The group itself is idealized as part of a polarizing mechanism, while the outside group is regularly seen as malevolent in motivation. The threatening outside world is at once a threat to the existence of the group and the justification for its existence.

If it is true that mature and psychologically healthy individuals regularly fall into these states when they function in a group setting, psychologically scarred individuals and individuals under stress are particularly apt to demonstrate these patterns. For alienated and marginal individuals, who tend to externalize the source of their own failures—for the narcissistically wounded ideal-hungry individuals described by Kohut (1977, 1978)—the psychological attractiveness of these states is overwhelming.

All three of these basic-assumption states (which Bion termed "groups") regularly characterize the followers in charismatic leader–follower relationships. The skillful charismatic leader intuitively shapes and induces these states in his followers. Some may be attracted to the charismatic religious cults described by Galanter, others to the path of terrorism, as I have noted elsewhere (Post 1984a), and, especially in times of societal stress, some may be attracted to the banner of charismatic political leaders.

When one is feeling overwhelmed, besieged by fear and doubt, it is extremely attractive to be able to suspend individual judgment and repose one's faith in the leadership of someone who conveys with conviction and certainty that he has the answers, that he knows the way, be it Reverend Moon or Reverend Jim Jones, Adolph Hitler or Ayatollah Khomeini. Particularly through skillful use of rhetoric, such a leader persuades his needy audience: "Follow me and I will take care of you. Together we can make a new beginning and create a new society. The fault is not within us but out there, and the only barrier to the happiness, peace, and prosperity we deserve is the outside enemy out to destroy us."

A bonus for potential followers lured by the siren song of the leader's strength and conviction comes from the promise, "Join my followers and you will no longer be alone." These followers draw strength from sharing their allegiance with others; the identity of follower becomes a badge of honor, a statement of membership in a collective self. In having merged themselves with the collective other, the success of the followers becomes *their* success.

For isolated individuals with damaged self-esteem and weak ego boundaries, the sense of "we" creates and imparts a coherent sense of identity. For such individuals, the self and the "we" are fused so that the self is experienced *as* the relationship. They tend to merge themselves with the group. In a figurative manner, we can speak of the development of a "group mind" or "group ego." The group becomes idealized, and the standards of the group, as articulated by the leader, take over and become the norm. This helps explain the startling degree to which individuals can suspend their own standards and judgment and participate in the most violent of actions when under the sway of the psychology of the group, if persuaded that the cause of the group is served by their actions. Even that most basic of human needs—the drive for self-preservation—can be suspended in the service of the group, as was horrifyingly evidenced by the phenomenon of Jonestown.

The Destructive Charismatic and the Reparative Charismatic

In citing the phenomena of Jonestown and Germany under Hitler, I may falsely convey the impression that charismatic leader–follower relationships are only a force for human destructiveness. They will be destructive if the narcissistically wounded leader rages at the world for depriving him of "mirroring" and enlists his followers in attacking it. This is the destructive charismatic, as exemplified by Hitler.

By contrast, charismatic leader–follower relationships can also catalyze a reshaping of society in a highly positive and creative fashion, what Volkan (1984) has termed "reparative leadership." In his study of Kemal Ataturk of Turkey he persuasively demonstrated that the narcissistically wounded mirror-hungry leader, in projecting his intrapsychic splits on society, may be a force for healing. Such leaders seek a sense of wholeness through establishing a special relationship with their ideal-hungry followers. As they try to heal their own narcissistic wounds through the vehicle of leadership, they may indeed be resolving splits in a wounded society.

Just as temporarily needy individuals may attach themselves to an idealized object at trying moments in their personal psychological development, so too a temporarily needy nation may seek the leadership of an idealized object at trying moments in its historical development. And just as the object of individual veneration is inevitably dethroned as his worshippers achieve psychological maturity, so too the idealized leader will be discarded when the moment of historical need passes, as evidenced by the rise and fall of Winston Churchill.

But whatever the fluctuations in the external circumstances of whole populations, within them there will always be individuals whose internal needs lead them to seek out idealized leaders. And when these ideal-hungry followers find a mirror-hungry leader, we have the elements of a charismatic leader–follower relationship. These relationships can be looked on as peculiar aberrations, as cults, during times of relative societal repose. Microscopic in scale at first, in times of social crisis these powerful relationships can become the nuclei for powerful transforming social movements, as was the case with the reparative revolutionary leadership of Kemal Ataturk, Mahatma Gandhi, and Martin Luther King Jr., and the destructive charismatic leadership of Adolph Hitler, Ayatollah Khomeini, and Osama bin Laden.

10

Fidel Castro

Aging Revolutionary Leader of an Aging Revolution

The following profile of Fidel Castro was presented in the fall of 1994 to a conference sponsored by the United States government on the outlook for Cuba. It was published in Problems of Post Communism *(spring 1995) under the title "Aging Revolutionary in an Aging Revolution: A Political Psychology Profile of Fidel Castro."*

The protracted crisis Fidel Castro has been facing since the collapse of Communism in the Soviet Union and Eastern Europe is perhaps the gravest in his forty years of revolutionary leadership. Nearly all the stunning events of 1989 were major setbacks for Castro: the prodemocracy forces in Eastern Europe that deposed one Communist regime after another; the unraveling of the Soviet Union and the Warsaw Pact; Soviet president Mikhail Gorbachev's tilt away from revolutionary adventurism; Moscow's subsequent abandonment of Cuba; and the stunning electoral defeat of Castro's allies in Nicaragua. Domestically, the aging revolutionary faces a restive young generation that is not imbued with the previous generation's uncritical awe of Cuba's charismatic leader and is dissatisfied with the poor quality of life that continues to decline.

At sixty-eight, Fidel Castro now finds himself increasingly isolated internationally. Faced with unmistakable evidence that his revolution has failed at home as well as abroad, Castro has few options to regain a sense of revolutionary efficacy. How has the aging revolutionary responded to this prolonged winter of discontent, and what does the future hold? Will he once again prevail as he has so frequently throughout his remarkable career? Has Castro mellowed with age, so that the intensity of the revolutionary flame that once burned so brightly within him has now diminished? And will he accordingly adapt to the changed political reality he faces? Will he yield power? Or will the increasingly isolated maximum leader, shorn of his previous support, develop a siege mentality and strike out aggressively at his perceived enemies in Cuba and elsewhere?

Divining this complicated leader's reactions to these unprecedented stresses requires an understanding of:

- Castro's political personality;
- his characteristic reactions to crises; and
- the impact on him of so many dreams unfulfilled after so many years of revolutionary struggle.

Narcissism and Destructive Charisma

Fidel Castro is in many ways exemplary of the narcissistic personality—a personality type frequently encountered in prominent political leaders. Indeed, if the ranks of politicians were stripped of narcissistic personalities, they would be perilously thinned. Castro is a unique individual who does not fully fit into any diagnostic category, but a review of his characteristic pattern of functioning suggests that narcissistic elements form a core aspect of his personality.

On the surface narcissists appears totally self-sufficient. But, as discussed in chapter 9, under their arrogant, self-confident facade, they are consumed with self-doubt and feelings of inadequacy, which drive them in a never-ending quest for the attention and approval of an admiring audience.

Over the years the power of the charismatic leader–follower relationship between Castro and the Cuban people has been almost palpable. Early in his career, Castro seemed to gain strength from the admiring response of the crowd during his long, impassioned speeches. It was as if an electrical charge flowed between Castro and his audience and he was energized by it.

Central to the ability of the mirror-hungry leader to elicit a continuing flow of admiration from his audience is his ability to convey a sense of grandeur, omnipotence, and strength. Individuals who have had feelings of grandiose omnipotence awakened within them—and there is persuasive biographic and phenomenological evidence that Castro is such an individual—are particularly attractive to individuals seeking idealized sources of strength. This is the basis of Castro's charismatic appeal.

As also discussed in chapter 9, there are two kinds of charismatics—reparative and destructive. A reparative charismatic heals his own psychological wounds as he heals those of his society, while a destructive charismatic unifies his people by blaming an outside enemy. Like Hitler, Castro is an exemplar of the destructive charismatic. The United States has been the external enemy for Castro. Externalizing rhetoric that takes no personal responsibility for leadership failures is central to Castro's destructive charisma, as he blames the Yankees to the north for all of Cuba's problems. Thus the economic embargo has played into Castro's political and psychological hands. It justifies blaming the United States for Cuba's woes.

Destructive charismatic leadership is associated with a particularly dangerous kind of narcissistic personality—malignant narcissism. Combining extreme grandiosity with a paranoid outlook, an absence of conscience, and a willingness to use whatever aggression is necessary in the service of his own needs, Castro is a prime example of a malignant narcissist. So insatiable is his drive for glory that he will go to any lengths to achieve it, and he demonstrates remarkable perseverance when many other leaders would have given up. Failure is unthinkable.

The end of the heroic life is inconceivable for the consummate narcissist; this is why narcissists, convinced of their own superiority and accordingly that they are indispensable, rarely relinquish power voluntarily. When the narcissistic leader, consumed with dreams of glory, is faced with undeniable evidence that his mission cannot be achieved, precipitous actions may lead to tragedy. As we saw in chapter 3, the Cultural Revolution is an example of such a headlong rush to glory by the aging Mao Ze-dong, who hoped to consolidate the Chinese Communist revolution in his lifetime. The messianic leader's dreams of glory cannot be satisfied, and such individuals do not mellow with age. Indeed, with the passing years, achieving those heroic goals takes on an increased urgency.

Past Reactions to Setbacks

When a revolutionary personality with strong oppositional features succeeds in overthrowing the establishment and becomes the establishment, how does he respond to domestic failures that lead to internal criticism and loss of popular support? Castro turned to "exporting the revolution." His customary response to domestic economic stagnation and popular discontent has been to engage in revolutionary activities abroad with the encouragement and support of his Soviet patron. He struck out rhetorically at the United States, blaming it for his country's economic difficulties. When faced with criticism, he has frequently blamed scapegoats, silenced critics, and repressed dissenters.

One can detect a rhythm to Castro's political actions and excesses over the years. In the face of setbacks, he is first briefly "down" and then bounces back, often with a grandiose scheme. Such was the case of the ten-million-ton sugar quota he decreed in 1969–70, an impossible goal set as if it could be accomplished by sheer force of will. In the process of driving the Cuban people to achieve this goal, Castro seriously distorted the economy. In the wake of this debacle, he lashed out at two European social democrats, K. S. Karol and Réné Dumont, who had criticized his arbitrary and personalistic leadership. Similarly, in the late 1980s, after a decade of armed subversion in Central America and interventions with tens of thousands of Cuban troops in Africa had produced few results, Castro turned against a powerful and popular military leader, General Arnaldo Ochoa Sanchez. The trial and imprisonment of Ochoa for corruption and involvement in narcotics trafficking illustrate his penchant for scapegoating, but also eliminated a potential threat to his power.

Castro's ability to improvise has often permitted him victories, or it has at least significantly ameliorated setbacks. Such was the case with the 1980 Mariel boat lift. Initially, the magnitude of the exodus was a profound embarrassment for Castro, but through masterful manipulation and improvisation, he transformed the event into a foreign policy problem for the United States, reaping public relations benefits. His adroit manipulation in 1994 of "Mariel II," the most recent flood of refugees leaving Cuba, demonstrated that Castro has not lost his tactical dexterity and creative improvisational capacity to manipulate the U.S. media and government. Facilitating the exodus of discontented Cubans, he again managed to place the United States on the defensive, forced Washington to deal with him, and highlighted the embargo as the central cause of his country's economic difficulties, while deflecting attention from his leadership failures.

The negative side of Castro's ability to improvise is an impulsive cast to his behavior, a tendency to intemperate responses that had previously been moderated by some of his close long-standing advisers. Indeed, his leadership circle has always included two factions, militant radicals and a more moderate group able to contain some of Castro's excesses. Particularly important to Castro was Celia Sanchez, with whom he maintained a close relationship for more than twenty years. He was also close to Dr. Renée Vallejo, a surgeon, who joined him in the Sierra Maestra and later became his personal physician. Both have died, Sanchez of cancer and Vallejo of a rare disease. Adding to his isolation was the suicide in the early 1980s of two earlier collaborators, Haydee Santamaria, who had been with Castro since the 1953 attack on the Moncada Barracks, and Osvaldo Dorticos Torrado, president of Cuba in 1959 and a senior party official and vice-president under Castro. Castro is no longer able to obtain wise counsel from those who were able to soften his excesses, a dangerous loss indeed.

"Socialism or Death"

In the winter of 1989, as economic and political pressures mounted, and the Soviet Union and one Eastern European state after another yielded to the pressures to liberalize, Gorbachev urged Castro to open up the Cuban system and refrain from foreign involvements. But the fiercely independent Castro did not take kindly to Gorbachev's unsolicited advice.

Instead, the defiant Castro vowed, "Socialism or death!" Declaring that "socialism is facing the worst crisis in its seventy-year history," Castro emphasized Cuba's role as the last stronghold of socialism. He vowed:

> Whether there is war or a special period, this is the most important time in our country's history, and one of the most important in the world—even though a giant counterrevolutionary wave is taking over the world, we will struggle, resist, and set an example—we will live for the revolution or we will die defending the revolution. (FBIS, July 1990)

Castro declared "a special period in a time of peace," resembling a wartime mobilization. The Cuban economy was gravely damaged by the collapse of the subsidized trading relationship with Eastern Europe, but Castro girded for the even more difficult times ahead. The end of the preferential barter relationship with the Soviet Union, which had shored up the Cuban economy over the years, and the need for hard currency, contributed to a major economic crisis. There were shortages of basic foodstuffs, such as flour and eggs, and increasingly harsh rationing restrictions were imposed, including a limit of nine ounces of meat a month. Castro responded to the sharp cutback in petroleum supplies by rationing oil and reducing electricity supplies. The gasoline shortages and difficulty in obtaining spare parts led Castro to order two hundred thousand bicycles from China and to replace mechanized farm equipment with teams of oxen and bulls.

To achieve economic self-sufficiency through agriculture, Castro established model agricultural regions in the countryside. Civilian brigades that included housewives were dispatched to work in these agricultural regions. The military was also enlisted in this effort, and students were asked to leave their campuses and head for the fields. Reminiscent of China's "rustication" movement, it was by all accounts a return to the nineteenth century. Castro exhorted his people to join in the defense of the nation, saying: "We must save the homeland. We want always to have a free and independent homeland instead of a Yankee colony. We must save the revolution. We must save socialism. Socialism or death! We will win!" Since 1991, most of his speeches have ended with this defiant phrase.

Castro's rhetoric has emphasized his role in history and that of Cuba as the last stronghold of socialism. In a December 16, 1991, speech, he proclaimed: "We will not become a colony again, nor [will we] return to capitalism. It is too much garbage, too repulsive, too intolerable ever to return to. It is clear that we are involved in a battle for survival." And he gave clear voice to his intention to continue his revolutionary struggle in an interview with Ann-Louise Bardach published in the March 1994 *Vanity Fair*: "It is not my fault that I haven't died yet. My vocation is the revolution. I am a revolutionary, and revolutionaries do not retire."

Unfulfilled Promises

But man cannot live on ideology alone, and fiery rhetoric cannot fill empty stomachs. The population was acutely aware of the collapse of Communism in Eastern Europe and of the euphoria that accompanied the reunification of Germany. Visits of thousands of family members and Radio Marti broadcasts had informed Cubans of the quality of life in the West. The gap between unfulfilled promises and reality cannot be sustained forever on rhetoric alone.

As opposition mounts and the voices of criticism become louder, Castro has become more repressive, more aggressive. He declared that counter-revolutionaries have no human rights. In July 1990 seven members of the Cuban opposition, the Democratic Unity Movement, were sentenced to up to seven years in prison for talking to foreign journalists; in October of that year, human rights activists were sentenced to six years "for subversive propaganda and illegal association." The leaders of four of the five known Cuban human rights groups remain in detention without being charged.

Castro is surely aware that his position is in jeopardy. Although he has responded to this stress by increasing his aggressive speech and actions, he has also made some grudging gestures in the direction of economic reform. The National Assembly rewrote the Cuban constitution in July 1992 to say that the state owns the "fundamental"—not "all"—means of production. And it gives decentralized state enterprises more autonomy, allowing them to import and export as self-financing enterprises. Castro has also, to a degree, opened up the Cuban economy to foreign investment, especially oil and tourism. But with tourism and its Western-standard hotels, restaurants, shops, and resorts, Castro's police separate foreigners from Cubans. With the exception of high-ranking party members, Cubans may not partake of the tourist hotels and their amenities—an interesting repeat of the 1950s under Cuban President Fulgencio Batista, which produced the resentment later exploited by Castro.

Outlook

Castro has a remarkable penchant for dramatic surprises. The absence of a moderating group within his inner circle has increased the danger of his striking out rashly, although, over time, he has usually maintained a focus on self-preservation. Could this tendency lead to an opening to the United States out of desperation? There have already been hints of such a disposition, but militating against this is the fixed role of the United States as his prime enemy and the usefulness of his charismatic rhetoric to unite his followers by blaming the Yankee imperialists for his failures.

Castro surely was impressed by the fate of the Sandinista government in Nicaragua and of East European leaders when they participated in free elections, and he will not repeat their mistake. He certainly will not reverse his lifelong commitment to Communism in favor of open political processes. Revealing a royal self-concept, Castro shrugged off a reporter's inquiry concerning free elections: "England does not elect a chief of state—they have one—Elizabeth I think is her name. Japan has the emperor."

Castro has stated his intention to remain at the helm of Cuba, in words that reflect his heroic self-image:

> I wish they were right that political leaders should retire at age sixty: The problem is not only retiring but being able to retire. In these very difficult times, to resign or propose that they should look for someone else to perform my duties, they would say that I am the greatest traitor in the world. . . . I insist that fighting for the cause that is Cuba is to fight for something a lot greater than Cuba. It is to fight for the world's great cause. The obstacles we are overcoming can rightly be compared to the Red Sea that Moses crossed.[1]

But Moses never entered the Promised Land, and perhaps this biblical reference hints that Castro recognizes that his lifelong revolutionary quest will not be fulfilled. The pressures on him are immense. Driven by dreams of glory, he will not yield the seat of power. Nor will he be content to wait quietly as the turbulent course of history unfolds. Castro's and Cuba's (in his mind they are one) isolation and evidence of his declining popular support will be particularly threatening for him. Opportunities and financial support for compensatory foreign adventures are no longer available, which may mean increasing repression of dissidents at home, striking out at critics, and identifying scapegoats for his failures. A pragmatist and a survivor, he will undoubtedly move further toward a market economy. But these moves will be largely cosmetic, for to abandon the state-directed economy would be to invalidate his career-long endeavor, and this he cannot and will not do. Yet given his lifelong capacity for creative response to crisis, and his remarkable survival instincts, the resourceful Castro probably has a few surprises left in store.

Postscript

This profile was prepared in the summer of 1994 when Castro was sixty-eight. The passage of years has not dimmed the force of Castro's personality or altered the patterns earlier sketched.

Throughout the intervening period, Castro simultaneously pursued two tracks: adroitly playing to the international community to end the embargo, while never loosening his iron grip on Cuba. On January 1, 1999, in a speech commemorating the fortieth anniversary of the Cuban Revolution, the ever-defiant Castro stridently echoed the declaration "Socialism or death!" that he made years earlier on the occasion of the speech announcing a "Special Period in a Time of Peace" on the occasion of the collapse of the Soviet Union. In the speech, he stated, "More than three and a half centuries of colonialism and almost sixty years of hateful Yankee neo-liberal domination began to be definitively annihilated on that first of January [1959], and Cuba became from then and forever a free territory." Shortly thereafter, President Clinton rejected Senator John Warner's recommendation to establish a commission to review U.S. policy toward Cuba.

For ten successive years, Castro won overwhelming support for a UN resolution to lift the embargo. Usually only the United States with Israel and one or two other nations voted against the resolution. But during this period, there was little evidence of genuine easing and opening of the tightly controlled society.

As economic conditions continued to deteriorate, in August 1994 Castro declared an open immigration policy. That month a new boatlift began, and 32,000 Cubans were picked up by the Coast Guard and taken to the U.S. naval base at Guantanamo. That September, an immigration agreement between Cuba and the United States was reached, with an agreement for a minimum of 20,000 immigrants each year. In May 1995, because of the flood of illegal immigrants seeking to flee the Castro regime, an immigration agreement was reached between the United States and Cuba, providing for the direct return of rafters to Cuba.

Heating up the anti-Castro campaign of Cuban exiles, in July 1995 a small private plane belonging to Brothers to the Rescue flew over Cuba, dropping anti-Castro fliers and bumper stickers. Exile operations intensified in January 1996, as planes belonging to Brothers to the Rescue flew over downtown Havana at low altitudes dropping leaflets calling for

Cubans to oppose their government. This led to Castro's decision to crack down on exile groups. And in February, Cuban MIGs shot down two Brothers to the Rescue planes over international waters, with the death of four exiles, leading to increased U.S.-Cuban tension. President Clinton in March of that year signed the Helms-Burton Act, which imposed penalties on foreign companies doing business in Cuba, permitting U.S. citizens to sue foreign investors who use American-owned property seized by the Cuban government, and denying entry into the U.S. of such foreign investors.

In January 1995, a class B Internet license was granted to Cuba, permitting Cubans access to the Internet, and in January 1996, the official Cuba Web site, Cubanet, was launched, to try to combat the public exposure to anti-Cuba information on the World Wide Web, to which the Cuban people now had limited access.

In November 1996, Castro was received by Pope John Paul II at the Vatican, leading to an invitation by Castro, accepted by the Pope, to visit Cuba, with its large Catholic population. In February 1998, the long-planned and eagerly anticipated visit by Pope John II to Cuba took place. The pope used the occasion to call for increased human rights in Cuba.

After a U.S. defense intelligence report issued in November 1997 concluded that "Cuba does not pose a significant military threat to the United States or to other countries in the region," in March 1998 senior U.S. military officials urged further contacts with Cuban military counterparts. Later that spring, European countries again called for an end to the embargo, saying that provisions of the Helms-Burton Act might violate international law.

Such exile groups as the Cuban American National Foundation (CANF) continued to call for enforcing a strict economic embargo, and CANF sponsored a terrorist campaign, claiming "we don't consider these actions terrorism because people fighting for liberty cannot be limited by a system that is itself terrorist." But there was evidence that Castro's continuing campaign was paying off; a poll of Cuban-Americans conducted by the *Miami Herald* in June of that year indicated a shifting tide of public opinion, with a majority under the age of forty-five supporting establishing a national dialogue with Cuba, while those over forty-five opposed such an opening.

On November 25, 1999, Elián Gonzalez was rescued at sea two or three days after a boat bound for Florida capsized, killing his mother and ten others. The ensuing drama lasted for seven months, with the U.S. government ultimately returning young Gonzalez to his father in Cuba, despite intense opposition to the move by anti-Castro exiles. During this period, Castro was remarkably restrained, letting the drama play out, and only after the return of Gonzalez did he weigh in, capitalizing on the notoriety of Gonzalez and his father.

That year was marked by a further loosening of the media climate. Heretofore only CNN and AP had bureaus in Cuba, but in September Castro gave permission to both the *Dallas Morning News* and the *Chicago Tribune* to open bureaus in Havana. But the opening to the media and the earlier access to the Internet were tactical gestures, for in the spring of 2003, while U.S. forces battled Saddam's regime, stung by the rising tide of criticism, the Castro government made a series of raids across Cuba, arresting eighty opposition leaders, journalists, and human rights activists who had spoken out against Castro. They were arrested under Article 91 of the Penal Code for acting against "the independence or the territorial integrity of the State." Some of them were also charged with violating Law 88, which carries the penalty of twenty years in prison for anyone convicted of supporting or collaborating with the U.S. economic embargo on Cuba. In closed trials in early April, they were convicted and sentenced in some cases to more than twenty years. Characteristically, the optimal way to still the voices of criticism was to arrest and imprison the critics.

Now seventy-seven years old, Castro's diminishing support and the rising tide of criticism will not alter or soften his fiery leadership. To the contrary, he can be expected to continue to lead in the manner that has characterized him throughout his forty-four years in power. While he will play to the international community, making cosmetic moves to show a loosening of control, he will not relinquish his iron grip on Cuba, as evidenced by the arrests and sentencing of critics in 2003. And, as he suggested in 1994, "he will not go gentle into that good night."

11

Saddam Hussein

"Saddam Is Iraq, Iraq Is Saddam"

The core profile of Saddam Hussein that follows was developed in August 1990 following the invasion of Kuwait. It was presented twice in December 1990 in testimony to hearings on the crisis in the Gulf to the House Armed Services Committee and the House Foreign Affairs Committee. Originally printed in the Congressional Record *(December 5, 1990), it was subsequently published in 1991 as "Saddam Hussein of Iraq: A Political Psychology Profile"* (Political Psychology *12, no. 2). A subsequent brief article, "Saddam Hussein: Afterword"* (Political Psychology *12, no. 4), reviewed the course of events in light of the original profile. This is reflected on pages 223–25.*

In October 2002, as the drums of war were beating ever more loudly, a major update was developed for a conference sponsored by the U.S. Air Force Counterproliferation Center (reflected on pages 225–38). It was subsequently augmented in collaboration with Amatzia Baram, a leading Israeli scholar on Iraqi history, and published in November 2002 as " 'Saddam Is Iraq, Iraq Is Saddam': A Profile of Saddam Hussein and Iraq's Strategic Culture," and distributed to senior U.S. officials. This essay was included in Know Thy Enemy: Profiles of Adversary Leaders and Their Strategic Cultures, *edited by Barry Schneider and Jerrold Post (U.S. Air Force Counterproliferation Center, 2002).*

Identified as a member of the "axis of evil" by President George W. Bush, Saddam Hussein's Iraq continues to pose a major threat to the region and to Western society. Hussein has doggedly pursued the development of weapons of mass destruction, despite UN sanctions imposed at the conclusion of the Gulf War in 1991. To deal effectively with Saddam Hussein requires a clear understanding of his motivations, perceptions, and decision making. To provide a framework for this complex political leader, a comprehensive political psychology profile has been developed, and his actions since the 1991 Gulf War have been analyzed in the context of this political psychology assessment.

Saddam Hussein, president of Iraq, has been widely characterized as "the madman of the Middle East." This pejorative diagnosis is not only inaccurate but also dangerous. Consigning Saddam to the realm of madness can mislead decision makers into believing he is unpredictable, when in fact he is not. An examination of the record of Saddam Hussein's leadership of Iraq for the past thirty-four years reveals a judicious political calculator who, although he is by no means irrational, is very dangerous.

Saddam Hussein, "the great struggler," has explained the extreme nature of his actions as president of Iraq as necessary to achieve "subjective immunity" against foreign plots and influences. All actions of the revolution are justified by the "exceptionalism of revolutionary needs." In fact, an examination of Saddam Hussein's life and career reveals this is but the ideological rationalization for a lifelong pattern in which all actions are justified if they are in the service of furthering Saddam Hussein's needs and messianic ambitions.

Painful Beginnings—The "Wounded Self"

Saddam Hussein was born in 1937 to a poor peasant family near Tikrit, some one hundred miles north of Baghdad, in central-north Iraq. But the central lines of the development of Saddam Hussein's political personality were etched before he was born, for his father died of an "internal disease" (probably cancer) during his mother's pregnancy with Saddam, and his twelve-year-old brother died (of childhood cancer) a few months later, when Saddam's mother, Sabha, was in her eighth month of pregnancy. Destitute, she attempted suicide. A Jewish family saved her. Then she tried to abort herself of Saddam, but she was prevented from doing this by her same Jewish benefactors. After Saddam was born, on April 28, 1937, his mother did not wish to see him, strongly suggesting that she was suffering from a major depression. His care was relegated to Sabha's brother (his maternal uncle), Khayrallah Talfah Msallat, in Tikrit, in whose home Saddam spent much of his early childhood. At age three Saddam was reunited with his mother, who in the interim had married a distant relative, Hajj Ibrahim Hasan. Hajj Ibrahim, Saddam's stepfather, reportedly was abusive psychologically and physically to young Saddam.

The first several years of life are crucial to the development of healthy self-esteem. The failure of the mother to nurture and bond with her infant son and the subsequent abuse at the hands of his stepfather would have profoundly wounded Saddam's emerging self-esteem, impairing his capacity for empathy with others, producing what has been identified as "the wounded self." One course in the face of such traumatizing experiences is to sink into despair, passivity, and hopelessness. But another is to etch a psychological template of compensatory grandiosity, as if to vow, "Never again, never again shall I submit to superior force." This was the developmental psychological path Saddam followed.

From early years on, Saddam, whose name means "the One who Confronts," charted his own course and would not accept limits. According to his semiofficial biography, when he was ten he was impressed by a visit from his cousin who knew how to read and write. He confronted his family with his wish to become educated, and when they turned him down, because there was no school in his parents' village, he left his home in the middle of the night, making his way to the home of his maternal uncle Khayrallah in Tikrit in order to study there. It is quite possible that in the approved biography Saddam somewhat embellished his story, but there is no mistaking his resentment against his mother and stepfather that emerges from it.

Khayrallah Inspires Dreams of Glory

Khayrallah was to become not only Saddam's father figure but also his political mentor. Khayrallah had fought against Great Britain in the Iraqi uprising of 1941 and had spent five years in prison for his nationalist agitation. He filled the impressionable young boy's head with tales of his heroic relatives—his great-grandfather and two great-uncles—who gave their lives for the cause of Iraqi nationalism, fighting foreign invaders. He conveyed to Saddam that he was destined for greatness, following the path of his heroic relatives and of heroes of the radical Arab world. Khayrallah, who was later to become governor of Baghdad, shaped young Saddam Hussein's worldview, imbuing him with a hatred of foreigners. In 1981, Saddam republished a pamphlet written by his uncle, "Three Whom God Should Not Have Created: Persians, Jews, and Flies."

Khayrallah tutored Saddam Hussein in his view of Arab history and the ideology of nationalism and the Ba'ath Party. Founded in 1940, the Ba'ath Party envisaged the creation of a new Arab nation by defeating the colonialist and imperialist powers and achieving Arab independence, unity, and socialism. Ba'ath ideology, as conceptualized by its intellectual founding father, Michel Aflaq, focuses on the history of oppression and division of the Arab world, first at the hands of the Ottomans, then the Western mandates, then the monarchies ruled by Western interests, and finally by the establishment of the "Zionist entity." Thus inspired by his uncle's tales of heroism in the service of the Arab nation, Saddam has been consumed by dreams of glory since his earliest days, identifying himself with Nebuchadnezzar, the king of Babylonia who conquered Jerusalem in 586 B.C., and Saladin, who regained Jerusalem in 1187 by defeating the Crusaders. But these dreams of glory, formed so young, were compensatory, for they sat astride a wounded self and profound self-doubt.

Saddam was steeped in Arab history and Ba'athist ideology by the time he traveled with his uncle to Baghdad to pursue his secondary education. The school he attended, a hotbed of Arab nationalism, confirmed his political leanings. In 1952, when Saddam was fifteen, Gamal Abdel Nasser led the Free Officers' revolution in Egypt and became a hero to young Saddam and his peers. As the activist leader of Pan Arabism, Nasser became an idealized model for Saddam. Only by courageously confronting imperialist powers could Arab nationalism be freed from Western shackles.

At age twenty, inspired by Nasser, Saddam joined the Arab Ba'ath Socialist Party in Iraq and quickly impressed party officials with his dedication. Known as a "street thug," he willingly used violence in the service of the party, and was rewarded with rapid promotion. Two years later, in 1958, apparently emulating Nasser, General Abdul Karim Qassem led a coup that ousted the Iraqi monarchy. But unlike Nasser, Qassem did not pursue the path of socialism and turned against the Ba'ath Party. The twenty-two-year-old Saddam was called to Ba'ath Party headquarters and given the mission of leading a five-man team to assassinate Qassem. The mission failed, reportedly because of a crucial error of judgment by Saddam. But Saddam's escape to Syria, first by horseback across the desert and then by swimming a river, has achieved mythic status in Iraqi history. During his exile, Saddam went to Egypt to study law, rising to the leadership ranks of the Egyptian Ba'ath Party. He returned to Iraq after 1963, when Qassem was ousted by the Ba'ath Party, and was elected to the National Command. Aflaq, the ideological father of the Ba'ath Party, admired young Hussein, declaring the Iraqi Ba'ath Party the finest in the world and designating Saddam Hussein as his successor.

Rivalry with Assad to be Supreme Arab-Nationalist Leader

Despite—or rather because of—fellow Ba'athist Hafiz al-Assad's success in taking control of Syria, Saddam confronted the new Syrian Ba'ath leadership at a party meeting in Iraq in 1966. The split and rivalry persist to this day, for there can be only one supreme Arab nationalist leader, and destiny has inscribed his name as Saddam Hussein.

With the crucial secret assistance of the military intelligence chief, Abdul Razzaz al Nayef, Saddam mounted a successful coup in 1968 against the military leadership of Iraq, and the Ba'ath Party was again in control, with Saddam's senior partner, his cousin Brigadier General Ahmed Hassan al-Bakr, serving as president, and Saddam as the power behind the scenes. In "gratitude" for services rendered, within two weeks of the coup, Saddam arranged for the capture and exile of Nayef, and subsequently ordered his assassination.

This act was a paradigm for the manner in which Saddam has rewarded loyalty and adhered to commitments throughout his career. He has a flexible conscience: commitments and loyalty are matters of circumstance, and circumstances change. If an individual, or a nation, is perceived as an impediment or a threat, no matter how loyal in the past, that individual or nation will be eliminated violently without a backward glance, and the action will be justified by "the exceptionalism of revolutionary needs." Nothing must be permitted to stand in "the great struggler's" messianic path as he pursues his (and Iraq's) revolutionary destiny, as exemplified by this extract from Saddam Hussein's remarkable "Victory Day" message of August 8, 1990, when Iraq occupied Kuwait:

> This is the only way to deal with these despicable Croesuses who relished possession to destroy devotion . . . who were guided by the foreigner instead of being guided by virtuous standards, principles of Pan-Arabism, and the creed of humanitarianism . . . The second of August . . . is the legitimate newborn child of the struggle, patience, and perseverance of the Kuwaiti people, which was crowned by revolutionary action on that immortal day. The newborn child was born of a legitimate father and an immaculate mother. Greetings to the makers of the second of August, whose efforts God has blessed. They have achieved one of the brightest, most promising, and most principled national and Pan-Arab acts.
>
> Two August has come as a very violent response to the harm that the foreigner had wanted to perpetrate against Iraq and the nation. The Croesus of Kuwait and his aides become the obedient, humiliated, and treacherous dependents of that foreigner . . . What took place on 2 August was inevitable so that death might not prevail over life, so that those who were capable of ascending to the peak would not be brought down to the abysmal precipice, so that corruption and remoteness from God would not spread to the majority . . . Honor will be kept in Mesopotamia so that Iraq will be the pride of the Arabs, their protector, and their model of noble values. (FBIS *Near East Report*, August 8, 1990)

Capable of Reversing His Course

Saddam's practice of revolutionary opportunism has another important characteristic. Just as previous commitments must not be permitted to stand in the way of his messianic path, neither will he persist in a particular course of action if it proves to be counterproductive for him and his nation. When Saddam pursues a course of action, he pursues it fully; if he meets initial resistance, he will struggle all the harder, convinced of the correctness of his judgments. But should circumstances demonstrate that he has miscalculated, he is capable of reversing his course. In these circumstances, he does not acknowledge he has erred but only that he is adapting to a dynamic situation. The three most dramatic examples of his revolutionary pragmatism and ideological flexibility are in his ongoing struggle with his Iranian enemies (whom he called "Persians," following his uncle's model).

Hussein Yields to Iran to Quell the Kurdish Rebellion

Saddam forced a mass relocation of the Kurdish population in 1970. In 1973, he declared that the Ba'ath Party represented all Iraqis, that the Kurds could not be neutral, and that the Kurds were either fully with the people or against them. Indeed, this is one of Saddam's basic principles: He who is not totally with me is my enemy. The Kurds were therefore seen as insidious enemies supported by foreign powers, in particular the Iranians. In 1973, the Kurdish minority, supported by the shah of Iran, rebelled. By 1975, the war against the Kurds had become extremely costly, with sixty thousand Iraqis killed in one year alone. Demonstrating his revolutionary pragmatism, despite his lifelong hatred of the Iranians, Hussein's urgent need to put down the Kurdish rebellion took (temporary) precedence. In March 1975, Saddam signed an agreement with the shah of Iran, stipulating Iranian sovereignty over the disputed Shatt al-Arab waterway in return for Iran's ceasing to supply the Kurdish rebellion.

The loss of the Shatt al-Arab waterway continued to rankle, and in September 1980, sensing weakness and confusion in the Iranian leadership after the Iranian Revolution, Saddam invaded Khuzistan Province, at first meeting little resistance. One of his first acts was to cancel the 1975 treaty dividing the Shatt al-Arab waterway. After Iraq's initial success, Iranian resistance stiffened and began to inflict serious damage not only on Iraqi forces but also on Iraqi cities. It became clear to Saddam that the war was counterproductive.

ATTEMPTS TO END THE IRAN-IRAQ WAR

In June 1982, Saddam reversed his earlier militant aggression and attempted to terminate hostilities, offering a unilateral ceasefire. Khomeini, who by now was obsessed with Saddam, would have none of it, saying there would be no peace until Saddam Hussein no longer ruled Iraq. The Iran-Iraq War continued for another bloody six years, taking a dreadful toll estimated at more than a million. In 1988, an indecisive ceasefire was agreed on, with Iraq sustaining an advantage, retaining control of some seven hundred square miles of Iranian territory and control of the strategic Shatt al-Arab waterway. Saddam, who maintained half a million troops on the disputed border, vowed he would "never" allow Iran sovereignty over any part of the disputed waterway until Iran agreed to forgo its claim to it. Saddam declared he would not agree to an exchange of prisoners, nor would he withdraw from Iranian territory. But revolutionary pragmatism was to supersede this vow, for he desperately needed the troops that were tied up in the dispute.

On August 15, 1990, Hussein agreed to meet Iranian conditions, promising to withdraw from Iranian territory, agreeing to an exchange of prisoners, and, most importantly, agreeing to share the disputed Shatt al-Arab waterway. "Never" is a short time when revolutionary pragmatism dictates, which was important to remember in evaluating Saddam's 1990 vow to never relinquish Kuwait, and his continued intransigence to Western demands.

REVERSAL OF HOSTAGE POLICY

The decision to release all foreign hostages fits this pattern. Following the invasion of Kuwait on August 2, 1990, Saddam systematically seized the citizens of the United States and many other nations. This occurred in both Kuwait and Iraq and continued for several months. Demonstrating how out of touch he was with world opinion, Saddam, trying to convey an image of himself as kindly father figure to the diplomat families he characterized as "guests," patted the head of an obviously terrified boy, making it clear that the families were there under duress. The image was featured on international media, and produced widespread horror.

Many of the hostages were moved to strategic sites in Iraq, including armaments factories, weapons research facilities, and major military bases, to be used as human shields. This mass act of hostage taking was condemned by nations throughout the world, and the UN Security Council adopted Resolution 644, demanding that Iraq release the hostages. Eventually realizing that this policy was counterproductive, Saddam eventually reversed himself and released the hostages, starting with the women and children. By December of that year, all the Western hostages were freed, but many Kuwaitis remained in captivity.

As with other misdirected policies in the past, Saddam initially pursued his hostage policy with full vigor, despite mounting evidence that it was counterproductive. When it became clear to him that it was not protecting him from the likelihood of military conflict, as initially conceived, but was actually unifying the international opposition, he reversed his policy. His announcement followed an especially strong statement by Secretary of State James Baker concerning the use of "decisive force," but the anger of his former ally, the Soviet Union, was undoubtedly important as well. Moreover, the timing was designed not only to play on perceived internal divisions within the United States but also to magnify perceived differences in the international coalition, a demonstration of his shrewdly manipulative sense of timing.

A Rational Calculator Who Often Miscalculates

The labels "madman of the Middle East" and "megalomaniac" are often affixed to Saddam, but there is no evidence that he is suffering from a psychotic disorder. He is not impulsive, acts only after judicious consideration, and can be extremely patient; indeed he uses time as a weapon. Although he is psychologically in touch with reality, he is often politically out of touch with reality. Saddam's worldview is narrow and distorted, and he has scant experience outside of the Arab world. His only sustained experience with non-Arabs was with his Soviet military advisors, and he reportedly has traveled outside of the Middle East on only two occasions—a brief trip to Paris in 1976 and another trip to Moscow. Moreover, he is surrounded by sycophants who are cowed by his well-founded reputation for brutality and who are afraid to contradict him. He has ruthlessly eliminated those he has perceived as threats to his power and equates criticism with disloyalty.

In 1979, when he fully assumed the reins of Iraqi leadership, one of his first acts was to meet with his senior officials, some two hundred in number, of which there were twenty-one whose loyalty he questioned. The dramatic meeting of his senior officials in which the twenty-one "traitors" were identified while Hussein watched, luxuriantly smoking a Cuban cigar, has been captured on film. After the forced confessions by a "plotter" whose family had been arrested, the remaining senior officials were complimented for their loyalty by Saddam and rewarded by being directed to form the execution squads for the twenty-one disloyal officials.

In 1982, when the war with Iran was going very badly for Iraq and Saddam wished to terminate hostilities, Khomeini, who by then was personally fixated on Saddam, insisted there could be no peace until Saddam was removed from power. At a cabinet meeting, Saddam asked his ministers to candidly give their advice. The minister of health suggested that Saddam temporarily step down and then assume the presidency again after peace had been established. Saddam reportedly thanked him for his candor and ordered his arrest. The minister's wife pleaded for her husband's return, saying her husband had always been loyal to Saddam. Saddam promised her that her husband would be returned. The next day, her husband's body was returned to her in a black canvas bag, chopped into pieces. This powerfully concentrated the attention of the other ministers who were unanimous in their insistence that Saddam remain in power, for it emphasized that to be seen as disloyal was not only to risk losing one's job but could forfeit one's life. Thus, Saddam is deprived of the check of wise counsel from his leadership circle. This combination of limited international perspective and a sycophantic leadership circle has in the past led him to miscalculate.

Hussein's Malignant Narcissism

Saddam Hussein's pursuit of power for himself and Iraq is boundless. In fact, in his mind, the destiny of Saddam Hussein and Iraq are one and indistinguishable. His exalted self-concept is fused with his Ba'athist political ideology. Ba'athist dreams will be realized when the Arab nation is unified under one strong leader. In Saddam's mind, he is destined for that role.

In pursuit of his messianic dreams, there is no evidence he is constrained by conscience; his only loyalty is to himself. When there is an obstacle in his revolutionary path, Saddam eliminates it, whether it is a previously loyal subordinate or a previously supportive country.

In pursuing his goals, Saddam uses aggression instrumentally. He uses whatever force is necessary, and will, if he deems it expedient, go to extremes of violence, including the use of weapons of mass destruction. His unconstrained aggression is instrumental in pursuing his goals, but it is at the same time defensive aggression, for his grandiose facade masks underlying insecurity.

Although Saddam Hussein is not psychotic, he has a strong paranoid orientation. He is ready for retaliation, and, not without reason, sees himself as surrounded by enemies. But he ignores his role in creating those enemies and righteously threatens his targets. The conspiracy theories he spins are not merely for popular consumption in the Arab world but genuinely reflect his paranoid mind-set. He is convinced that the United States, Israel, and Iran have been in league for the purpose of eliminating him, and he finds a persuasive chain of evidence for this conclusion. His minister of information, Latif Jassim, who was responsible for propaganda and public statements, has probably helped reinforce Saddam's paranoid disposition and, in a sense, is the implementer of his paranoia.

It is this political personality constellation—messianic ambition for unlimited power, absence of conscience, unconstrained aggression, and a paranoid outlook—that makes Saddam Hussein so dangerous. Conceptualized as malignant narcissism, this is the personality configuration of the destructive charismatic, who unifies and rallies his downtrodden supporters by blaming outside enemies. Although Saddam Hussein is not charismatic, this psychological stance is the basis of his particular appeal to the Palestinians, who see him as a strongman who shares their intense anti-Zionism and will champion their cause.

Views Self as One of History's Great Leaders

Saddam Hussein genuinely sees himself as one of the great leaders of history, and ranks himself with his heroes: Gamal Abdel Nasser, Fidel Castro, Josip Broz Tito, Ho Chi Minh, and Mao Ze-dong, each of whom he admires for adapting socialism to his country's environment, free of foreign domination. He sees himself as transforming his society. He believes youth must be "fashioned" to "safeguard the future" and that Iraqi children must be transformed into a "radiating light that will expel" traditional family backwardness. Like Mao and Stalin, Saddam has encouraged young people to inform on their parents' antirevolutionary activity. As godlike status was ascribed to Mao, and giant pictures and statues of him were placed throughout China, so too giant pictures and statues of Saddam Hussein abound in Iraq. Asked about this cult of personality, he shrugs and says he "cannot help it if that is what they want to do."

Saddam Hussein is so consumed with his messianic mission that he probably overreads the degree of his support in the rest of the Arab world. He psychologically assumes that many in the Arab world, especially the downtrodden, share his views and see him as their hero. He was probably genuinely surprised at the nearly unanimous condemnation of his invasion of Kuwait.

Saddam Hussein at the Crossroads in 1990–91

It is not by accident that Saddam Hussein has survived for more than three decades as his nation's preeminent leader in this tumultuous part of the world. Although he is driven by dreams of glory, and his political perspective is narrow and distorted, he is a shrewd tactician who has a sense of patience. He is able to justify extreme aggression on the basis of revolutionary needs, but if the aggression becomes counterproductive, he has shown a pattern of being able to reverse course when he has miscalculated, waiting until a later day to achieve his revolutionary destiny. His drive for power is not diminished by these reversals but only deflected.

Saddam Hussein is a ruthless political calculator who will go to whatever lengths are necessary to achieve his goals. But he is not a martyr, and his survival in power—with his dignity intact—is his highest priority. Saddam has been characterized by Soviet Foreign Minister Yevgeny Primakov and others as suffering from a "Masada complex," preferring a martyr's death to yielding. This is assuredly not the case, for Saddam has no wish to be a martyr, and survival is his number-one priority. A self-proclaimed revolutionary pragmatist, he does not wish a conflict in which Iraq will be grievously damaged and his stature as a leader destroyed.

Although Hussein's advisors' reluctance to disagree with his policies contributes to the potential for miscalculation, his advisors are able to influence the accuracy of his evaluation of Iraq's political and military situation by providing information and assessments. Moreover, despite their reluctance to disagree with him, the situation facing the leadership after the invasion of Kuwait was so grave that several officials reportedly expressed their reservations about remaining there.

As the crisis heightened in the fall of 1990, Saddam dismissed a number of senior officials, replacing them with family members and known loyalists. He replaced the petroleum minister, a sophisticated technical expert, with his son-in-law, Hussein Kamal. Moreover, he replaced General Nizar Khazraji, his army chief of staff, and a professional military man, with General Hussein Rashid, commander of the Republican Guards and a Tikriti. Tough and extremely competent, Rashid is both intensely ideological and fiercely loyal. It was as if Saddam was drawing in the wagons. This was a measure of the stress on him, suggesting that his siege mentality was intensifying. The fiercely defiant rhetoric was another indicator of the stress, for the more threatened Saddam feels, the more threatening he becomes.

Although Saddam appreciated the danger of the Gulf crisis, it did create an opportunity to defy the hated outsiders, a strong value in his Ba'athist ideology. He continued to cast the conflict as a struggle between Iraq and the United States, and even more personally as a struggle between the gladiators, Saddam Hussein versus George Bush. When the struggle became thus personalized, it enhanced Saddam Hussein's reputation as a courageous strongman willing to defy the imperialist United States.

On the other hand, when President George Bush depicted the conflict as the unified civilized world against Saddam Hussein, it hit a tender nerve for Saddam, who has his eye on his role in history and places great stock in world opinion. If he were to conclude that his status as a world leader was threatened, it would have important constraining effects on him. Thus, the prospect of Iraq's being expelled from the United Nations and castigated as a rogue nation outside the community of nations would be very threatening to him. The overwhelming majority supporting the Security Council resolution at the time of the conflict must have confronted Saddam Hussein with the damage he was inflicting on his stature as a leader, despite his defiant rhetoric dismissing the resolutions of the United Nations as reflecting U.S. control of the international organization.

Defiant rhetoric was a hallmark of the conflict and lent itself to misinterpretation across cultural boundaries. The Arab world places great stock in expressive language. The language of courage is a hallmark of leadership, and great value is attached to the very act of expressing brave resolve against the enemy in and of itself. Even though a statement is made in response to the United States, when Saddam speaks it is to multiple audiences; much of his language is solipsistic and designed to demonstrate his courage and resolve to the Iraqi people and the Arab world. There is no necessary connection between courageous verbal expression and the act threatened. Nasser gained great stature from his fiery rhetoric threatening to make the sea red with Israeli blood. By the same token, Saddam probably heard the Western words of President Bush through a Middle Eastern filter. When a public statement of resolve and intent was made by President George Bush, Saddam may well have discounted the expressed intent to act. This underlines the importance of a private channel between leaders that will allow them to communicate clearly and unambiguously. The mission by Secretary of State James Baker afforded the opportunity to resolve any misunderstandings on Saddam's part concerning the strength of resolve and intentions of the United States and the international coalition.

Gulf Crisis Promotes Saddam to World-Class Leader

Throughout his twenty-two years at the helm of Iraq, Saddam Hussein had languished in obscurity, overshadowed by the heroic stature of other Middle Eastern leaders such as Anwar Sadat and Ayatollah Khomeini. But with the Gulf crisis, for the first time in his entire career, Saddam was exactly where he believed he was destined to be—a world-class political actor on center stage commanding world events, with the entire world's attention focused on him. When his rhetoric was threatening, the price of oil rose precipitously and the Dow-Jones average plummeted. He was demonstrating to the Arab masses that he was an Arab strongman with the courage to defy the West and expel foreign influences.

Now that he was at the very center of international attention, his appetite for glory was stimulated all the more. The glory-seeking Saddam would not easily yield the spotlight of international attention. He wanted to remain on center stage, but not at the expense of his power and his prestige. Saddam would only withdraw if he calculated that he could do so with his power and his honor intact, and if the drama in which he was starring would continue.

Honor and reputation must be interpreted in an Arab context. Saddam Hussein had already achieved considerable honor in the eyes of the Arab masses for having the courage to stand up to the West. It should be remembered that even though Egypt militarily lost the 1973 war with Israel, Sadat became a hero to the Arab world for his willingness to attack—and initially force back—the previously invincible forces of Israel. Mu'ammar al-Qadhafi mounted an air attack when the United States crossed the so-called "line of death" in March 1986. Even though his jets were destroyed in the ensuing conflict, Qadhafi's status was raised in the Arab world. Indeed, he thanked the United States for making him a hero. Thus, Saddam could find honor in the 1990 confrontation over Iraq's invasion of Kuwait.

His past history reveals a remarkable capacity to find face-saving justifications when reversing his course in very difficult circumstances. Nevertheless, it would be important not to insist on total capitulation and humiliation, for this could drive Hussein into a corner and make it impossible for him to reverse his course. He would—could—only withdraw from Kuwait if he believed he could survive with his power and his dignity intact.

By the same token, he would only reverse his course if his power and reputation were threatened. This would require a posture of strength, firmness, and clarity of purpose by a unified world, demonstrably willing to use force if necessary. The only language Saddam Hussein understands is the language of power. Without this demonstrable willingness to use force, even if the sanctions were biting deeply, Saddam Hussein is quite capable of putting his population through a sustained period of hardship.

It was crucial to demonstrate unequivocally to Saddam Hussein that unless he withdrew from Kuwait, his career as a world-class political actor would be ended. The announcement of a major escalation of the force level was presumably designed to drive that message home. The UN resolution authorizing the use of force unless Iraq withdrew by January 15,

1991, was a particularly powerful message because of the large majority supporting the resolution.

The message almost certainly was received. In the wake of the announcement of the increase in force level, Saddam intensified his request for "deep negotiations," seeking a way out in which he could preserve his power and his reputation. That President Bush sent Secretary of State Baker to meet one-on-one with Iraqi Foreign Minister Tariq Aziz was an extremely important step. In the interim leading up to the meeting, the shrewdly manipulative Saddam continued to attempt to divide the international coalition.

Although he considers himself a revolutionary pragmatist, Saddam Hussein is at heart a survivor. If, in response to the world's unified demonstration of strength and resolve, he did retreat and reverse his course, this would only be a temporary deflection of his unbounded drive for power. It was a certainty that he would return at a later date, stronger than ever, unless firm measures were taken to contain him. This underlines the importance of strategic planning beyond the immediate crisis, especially considering his progress toward acquiring a nuclear weapons capability. If blocked in his overt aggression, he could be expected to pursue his goals covertly through intensified support of terrorism.

Saddam Hussein will not go down in the last flaming bunker if he has a way out, but he can be extremely dangerous and will stop at nothing if he is backed into a corner. If he believes his very survival as a world-class political actor is threatened, Saddam can respond with unrestrained aggression, using whatever weapons and resources are at his disposal, in what would surely be a tragic and bloody final act.

Why Saddam Did Not Withdraw from Kuwait

In the political psychology profile prepared for the congressional hearings on the Gulf crisis in December 1990, recapitulated above, it was observed that Saddam Hussein was by no means a martyr and was indeed the quintessential survivor. The key to his survival in power for twenty-two years was his capacity to reverse his course when events demonstrated that he had miscalculated. We believed he could again reverse himself if he concluded that unless he did so his power base and reputation would be destroyed, and if by so doing he could preserve them.

How can it be, then, that this self-described revolutionary pragmatist, faced by an overwhelming array of military power that would surely deal a mortal blow to his nation if he did not withdraw from Kuwait, entered into and persisted in a violent confrontational course? Cultural factors probably contributed to his calculation and miscalculation. Saddam may well have heard President Bush's words of intent through a Middle Eastern filter and calculated that he was bluffing. He may have downgraded the magnitude of the threat, likening it to the characteristic Arab hyperbole. Even though he expected a massive air strike, he undoubtedly was surprised by the magnitude of the destruction wrought on his forces.

But more important, the dynamic of the crisis affected him. What began as aggression toward Kuwait was transformed into the defining moment of the drama of his life. Although he had previously shown little concern for the Palestinian people, the shrewdly manipulative Hussein had wrapped himself and his invasion of Kuwait in the Palestinian flag. The response of the Palestinians was overwhelming. They saw him as their hope and their salvation, standing up defiantly and courageously to the United States to force a just settlement of their cause. This caught the imagination of the masses throughout the Arab world, and their shouts of approval fed his already swollen ego as he went on a defiant roll.

Intoxicated by the elixir of power and the acclaim of the Palestinians and the radical Arab masses, Saddam may well have been on a euphoric high and optimistically overestimated his chances for success, for his heroic self-image was engaged as never before. He was fulfilling the messianic goal that had obsessed him—and eluded him—throughout his life. He was actualizing his self-concept as leader of all the Arab peoples, the legitimate heir of Nebuchadnezzar, Saladin, and especially Nasser.

His psychology and his policy options became captives of his rhetoric. He became so absolutist in his commitment to the Palestinian cause, and to not yielding Kuwait until there was justice for the Palestinian people and UN Resolutions 242 and 338 had been complied with, that it would have been extremely difficult for him to reverse himself without being dishonored. To lose face in the Arab world is to be without authority. Unlike past reversals, these absolutist pronouncements were in the full spotlight of international attention. Saddam had, in effect, painted himself into a corner. The Bush administration's insistence on "no face-saving" only intensified this dilemma.

Not only, then, had Saddam concluded that to reverse himself would be to lose his honor, but he also probably doubted that his power base would be preserved if he left Kuwait. He doubted that the aggressive intention of the United States would stop at the border of Iraq. For years he had been convinced that a U.S.-Iran-Israeli conspiracy was in place to destroy Iraq and remove him from power.

Earlier, Iraqi Foreign Minister Tariq Aziz had said that "everything was on the table," but by late December the semblance of diplomatic flexibility had disappeared, and Saddam seemed intent on challenging the coalition's ultimatum. It is likely that Saddam had concluded that he could not reverse himself and withdraw without being dishonored, and that he needed to enter the conflict to demonstrate his courage and to affirm his claim to pan-Arab leadership.

Saddam Hussein expected a massive air campaign and planned to survive it, forcing the United States into a ground campaign. He believed that the United States was suffering from a Vietnam complex as a result of the Vietnam War, was casualty averse and could not tolerate the spectacle of American soldiers being returned in body bags. As he had demonstrated in the Iran-Iraq War, he believed his battle-hardened troops could absorb massive casualties, whereas the weak-willed United States would not have the stomach for this, there would be political protest (as had occurred during the Vietnam War), and a political-military stalemate would ensue. By demonstrating that he had the courage to stand up against the most powerful nation on earth, Saddam's credentials as pan-Arab leader would be consolidated and he would win great honor. Saddam's political hero and model, Nasser, gained great honor for defying the imperialists in the 1956 Suez campaign. By announcing that he was nationalizing the Suez Canal, Nasser prompted Israel, Britain, and France to go to war to stop him from doing so. Though Nasser lost the war, he ultimately triumphed when President Eisenhower forced the three nations to withdraw from the land they had conquered.

Saddam hoped to consolidate his place in Arab history as Nasser's heir by bravely confronting the U.S.-led coalition. On the third day of the air campaign, his minister of information, Latif Jassim, declared victory. To the astounded press he explained that the coalition expected Iraq to crumble in two days. Having already survived the massive air strikes for three days, the Iraqis were accordingly victorious, and each additional day would only magnify the scope of their victory.

It was revealed in January that under Saddam's opulent palace was a mammoth bunker, fortified with steel and pre-stressed concrete. The architecture of this complex is Saddam Hussein's psychological architecture: a defiant, grandiose facade resting on the well-fortified foundation of a siege mentality. Attacked on all sides, Saddam remains besieged and defiant, using whatever aggression is necessary to consolidate his control and ensure his survival.

After the Gulf War

Iraqi domestic support for Saddam Hussein was drastically eroded after the Gulf War. By late 1996, a series of betrayals, failures, and disappointments had left him in a more precarious domestic position than at any time since March 1991. There have been three main areas of change for Saddam Hussein since the conflict:

- Increased security vulnerabilities
- Strengthening international support
- Increased importance of WMD program

INCREASED SECURITY VULNERABILITIES

A governing principle of Saddam's leadership—ensuring his domestic stability and eliminating internal threats to his regime—has intensified in the postwar period and is his central concern. The three greatest threats to his domestic stability have come from a dramatically weakened military, fractures in tribal loyalties, and fault lines in his family.

Immediately after the Gulf War conflict was terminated in March 1991, Saddam Hussein's major source of support, the Iraqi army, was gravely weakened. Once the fourth largest army in the world, the Iraqi army, with its proud reputation as the most powerful military force in the Persian Gulf shattered, its ranks and materiel depleted, and its morale destroyed, represented a grave threat to his survival:

- The Iraqi armed forces, including the Republican Guard, became disillusioned with Saddam's leadership.
- The standard of living for soldiers had reached the lowest level ever.
- The "no-fly zones" over northern and southern Iraq were seen as a humiliating affront to the once-powerful military. Moreover, Kurdish control over the north was a painful reminder that Iraq was powerless and at the mercy of the United States.
- The UN-sponsored weapons inspections were a continuing humiliation and demonstration of Iraq's lack of control over its sovereignty.
- A rising tide of disillusionment, desertion, and resentment led to repeated coup attempts by different military factions.
- In March 1995, two regular army brigades suffered severe losses from clashes with the Kurds and the Iraqi National Congress (INC), further humiliating Saddam and the military.

FRACTURES IN TRIBAL LOYALTY

Within the larger Sunni tribal system there were signs of weakening solidarity. Of the five most important Sunni tribes that had been the core of Saddam Hussein's support, and were in leadership roles throughout the military, three were involved in coup attempts against him. A 1990 plot involved Jubbur members of the Republican Guards and regular army units. Officers of the 'Ubayd tribe were involved in coup plotting in 1993–

94. Al-Bu Nimr (of the Dulaym tribe) revolted against Saddam in 1995. Frictions within Saddam Hussein's own al-Bu Nasir tribe also compounded problems—by late summer in 1996, five "houses" within the tribe had grievances with him or his family. Although the Dulaymis and 'Ubaydis continue to serve in Republican Guard and key security positions, they have been removed from most sensitive positions and are closely watched. Overall, the threat of a large-scale tribal uprising remains remote, though Saddam is no longer able to trust his once loyal tribes.

FAULT LINES IN THE FAMILY

Uday.   The temperament and unconstrained behavior of Saddam Hussein's oldest son Uday, who is thirty-eight, has been a continuing issue. He has a reputation as the "bad boy" of Iraq and is greatly feared by the people of Baghdad. Uday has been involved in several widely publicized incidents, but Saddam had regularly either overlooked Uday's excesses or, if the event was too public to ignore, dealt with it in the mildest manner. Before the conflict in the Gulf, there were reports of violent excesses involving Uday. In one incident in 1988, Uday, drunk at a party, used an electric carving knife to kill one of his father's aides. In a second dramatic public event that year, Uday, angry with his father's personal valet for his role in facilitating an affair Saddam was having with a married Iraqi woman (whose husband was rewarded for not objecting with the presidency of Iraqi Airlines), crashed a party being held in honor of Suzanne Mubarak, the wife of Egyptian president Hosni Mubarak. Uday beat the valet to death in full view of all the guests. Saddam put Uday on trial for murder but, after the family members of the victim "pleaded for leniency," Saddam exiled Uday to Switzerland. A year later, after having been declared persona non grata by Swiss authorities, Uday returned to Iraq where he began reintegrating himself into Iraqi society.

In 1995, Uday reportedly shot one of his uncles in the leg and killed six "dancing girls" at a party, not coincidentally, the night before his brother-in-law, Hussein Kamal, defected. It is believed that Uday played a major role in causing the defection of Kamal, whom he saw as threatening his relationship with his father.

In 1996, an assassination attempt on Uday left him bedridden for at least six months with both his legs shattered. He was reportedly temporarily paralyzed following the assassination attempt. There have been some reports that he was left paraplegic from the injury and continues to be paralyzed from the waist down. There are rumors that he was left impotent, which, given the nature and location of the paralyzing spinal cord injury, may well be true. He remains in general poor health.

Hussein Kamal's Defection and Assassination: A Major Turning Point.
Hussein Kamal, a cousin of Saddam Hussein, married Saddam's favorite daughter, Raghad. Hussein Kamal rose through the ranks of Saddam's inner circle with meteor-like speed, garnering him the resentment of the military core as well as that of other insiders. After having held several sensitive security positions, Kamal went on to found the Republican Guard and eventually became one of the few insiders who had access to Saddam Hussein, magnifying Uday's feelings of rivalry and jealousy. In August 1995, reportedly after having been threatened by Uday, Hussein Kamal and his brother Saddam Kamal, who also had married a daughter of Saddam's, fled with their wives to Jordan, where they received asylum. Hussein Kamal provided copious information to U.S. intelligence concerning Iraq's special weapons program, of which he had been in charge, greatly embarrassing Saddam Hussein and setting back his goal of ending the sanctions regime. Six months later, in February 1996, in what might be characterized as "assisted suicide, Iraqi style," both men and their wives returned to Iraq after Saddam Hussein provided assurances that they were forgiven and would be safe. Within forty-eight hours of their arrival in Iraq, both men were murdered. Uday reportedly played a key role in orchestrating the murder of Kamal and his brother.

Demotion of Uday.   Saddam Hussein demoted and publicly humiliated Uday after Kamal's flight, demonstrating that he believed Uday was responsible for the conflicts in the family that led to the defection. He had Uday's collection of vintage cars torched and stripped him of his leadership role in restoring Iraq's military equipment. He forced Uday to abandon his command of Saddam's private army, the Fedayeen, which is dedicated to Saddam's protection. And, most importantly, Saddam elevated his younger son Qusay to the regime's most powerful security position. This demonstrated to all that even being a member of the immediate family, indeed Saddam's favorite child, will not protect one from Saddam's wrath if one's actions threaten the regime.

Qusay.   Although Uday is part of Saddam's problem, Qusay is part of the solution. Since 1989, Saddam has been preparing Qusay to become czar of internal security. Qusay has worked closely with the former head of internal security, General Abd Hamid Mahmud (or Ihmid Hmud). They are in charge of the Special Security Organization (SSO), the most formidable security agency, and in charge of security inside all security agencies, including the Himaya and the Special Republican Guard (SRG). The president's security rests mainly on them, but they are also in charge of concealment and deployment of Iraq's nonconventional weapons.

Qusay is also the supreme authority when it comes to "prison cleansing," the execution of hundreds of political prisoners to make room for new ones in Iraq's crowded prisons. He also authorizes executions of military and security officers suspected of disloyalty. Starting in 2000, Qusay started receiving a great deal of coverage in the Ba'ath Party press and is now referred to as "Warrior Qusay." Supplanting Uday in the succession, he has been named Saddam's deputy "in the event of an emergency." Since 2001, Qusay has also been a member of the Regional Leadership (RL) of the Ba'ath party in Iraq and deputy secretary of its important Military Bureau (al-Maktab al-'Askari).[1] The promotion of Qusay to the RL is seen as the first step toward his inclusion in the Revolutionary Command Council (RCC) and, eventually, his promotion to the RCC chairmanship and then to president of Iraq.

The family disarray culminating in the Hussein Kamal defection and assassination, and the decline of Uday and his replacement as director of security forces by Qusay, signaled a major change of strategy. No longer could Saddam Hussein unquestioningly rely on the loyalty of his family. He had to strengthen the Ba'ath Party and rely more centrally on long-standing party loyalists.

In late August 1996, Saddam Hussein authorized elements of the Republican Guard to attack the Kurdish city of Irbil following the Patriotic Union of Kurdistan (PUK)'s securing of military assistance from Iran. The Republican Guard smashed the PUK and the U.S.-backed Iraqi National Congress. The seizure of Irbil was a major success for Saddam. This triumph, coming after a series of setbacks and reminders of their diminished status, restored the morale of the Republican Guard (and their faith in Saddam Hussein). It demonstrated that the regime was still very much in control and was a major power throughout the country. It also showed the fractionation and impotence of the opposition movements in Iraq, and was a powerful demonstration of the risk of rising against Saddam Hussein. This was a major turning point for the regime—had the Guard not taken Irbil, it is likely that Saddam's support would have been so undermined that his position would have been in grave jeopardy.

UN RESOLUTION 986

Facing an imminent economic collapse in 1996, Iraq was forced to accept UN Resolution 986, the so-called Oil for Food program, in November of that year. This represented a great humiliation because it glaringly infringed on the national sovereignty of Iraq, and indirectly on Saddam Hussein's personal honor. Saddam also feared that it would undermine international pressure to lift the sanctions imposed on Iraq following the Gulf War: as long as the suffering of the Iraqi people could be alleviated through the resolution, the embargo could stay on forever. But eventually Saddam had no choice but to accept the recommendations of his economic advisers.

Resolution 986 also brought Iraq considerable advantages. The sale of oil greatly improved Iraq's international and regional standing. That the food and medicines distributed to the population alleviated the people's suffering was less important than the fact that, from now on, the Iraqi government could save the sums it had had to spend on food. The disadvantages were minor by comparison: credit for the increase in supplies went mainly to the regime, not to the United Nations. It did diminish the regime's ability to trumpet as loudly as before the suffering of the Iraqi people; thus, the crisis Saddam provoked with the UN in 1997 over UN weapons inspections may have been prompted by fear that the humanitarian issue would no longer be an issue and that the embargo would remain. (In reality, the Iraqi regime still trumpeted the suffering with considerable success, with the help of Western humanitarian groups.)

Iraq Gains International Support

In the events leading up to the 1990 invasion of Kuwait and the subsequent Gulf crisis, Saddam Hussein was extremely isolated, misjudging the impact of his actions not only on his Arab neighbors, the so-called near abroad, but also on major international actors on whose support he had previously been able to count, especially Russia and France. He had regularly seriously miscalculated both the risks of his actions and the degree of his support. His foreign policy initiatives after the Gulf War demonstrated a much surer and more sophisticated hand. Having learned from experience, he has worked assiduously to strengthen identified vulnerabilities.

Saddam Hussein's diplomatic efforts toward the "near abroad" have been quite effective. Having been surprised by the lack of support for Iraq during the Gulf crisis, Saddam has worked assiduously to rebuild relations with his regional neighbors. Because of its greater economic power as a result of increased oil sales, Iraq has become a crucial partner for these nations. Although Iraqi politics have been driven primarily by internal politics and factors, it has been external factors that have begun to open up new opportunities for Iraqi policies and to ameliorate Saddam Hussein's domestic problems.

Syria and Iran. The most telling example of Saddam Hussein's modus operandi when he feels weak and under great threat is provided by his tremendous resolve to mend his fences with his oldest Middle Eastern rival, President Hafiz al-Assad of Syria, and his regime. The years 1997 and 1998 saw the beginning of a new relationship between Iraq and Syria. Saddam extended an olive branch to Assad, and the latter reciprocated in kind. Although ties were mainly limited to economic and diplomatic areas, this relationship was the beginning of Iraq's acceptance back into Middle Eastern politics.[2]

The two countries signed a free trade agreement. As a result of this agreement, mutual trade volume grew from $500 million in 2000 to around $1 billion in 2001.[3] According to some reports, mutual trade in 2001 actually reached almost $2 billion.[4] By the middle of 2002, it was estimated that the annual value of trade exchange between the two countries would exceed $3 billion.[5]

After being elected in 1997, Iran's president, Mohammad Khatami, sought to improve relations with the United States and Saudi Arabia, something that worried Saddam a great deal. However, because these efforts have been hindered by internal politics, those relationships have not had the expected impact, which left more room for an improvement of Iraqi-Iranian relations.

Turkey. Turkey's strong ties to the United States and insistence on working with it on Iraqi matters are a great source of frustration for Iraq. Turkish military forays into autonomous Iraqi Kurdistan, too, elicit bitter condemnations from Baghdad; even though Iraq is no longer in control of Kurdistan, such forays are seen as an infringement on its sovereignty. On the other hand, Turkish-Iraqi economic ties have seen a quantum leap since December 1996. Just before the invasion of Kuwait, Turkey's annual exports to Iraq were around $400 million. In 2000, they reached almost the same annual rate as in 1990, $375 million, and in 2001, they had almost doubled to $710 million.[6] It was estimated that Turkey would export $2 billion worth of products to Iraq in 2002.[7]

Jordan. Although it did not participate militarily in the international anti-Iraqi coalition and was unwilling to confront Iraq politically, Jordan has consistently distanced itself from Iraq since the early 1990s. Much like Turkey, Jordan is getting the best of both worlds: it maintains excellent relations with the United States and Israel, including receiving U.S. economic aid; it thwarts, as best it can, Iraqi attempts to smuggle weapons through its territory to the Palestinians; and it continues to receive cheap oil from, and to trade with, Iraq. Saddam Hussein is fully aware of this practice, but he does not seem to care; for him, Jordan is an important avenue to the outside world. Even more important, securing Jordan's objection to an American attack against him is now his top priority. Jordanian complicity with a U.S. offensive would mean Saddam Hussein's quick demise, as it would provide the United States with the most effective bridgehead from which to launch the attack and prevent Iraq from launching its missiles against Israel.

Saudi Arabia.   After the first Gulf War, the Saudis remained opposed to the Iraqi regime and moved to improve relations with Iran as a counter to Iraq—in case the United States could not live up to its security commitments, or if the Saudi regime felt compelled by Islamic politics to ask American forces to leave the country. The first deviation from this stance occurred in December 1997, when Prince Abdullah called on the Gulf Cooperation Council (GCC) states to "overcome the past with its events and pains."[8] This was interpreted as a call for rapprochement with Saddam Hussein's Iraq. Saudi Arabia, like other regional players, expected to boost exports to Iraq—from about $200 million in 2000 to about $600 million in 2001.[9]

Other Gulf States.   In the spring of 2002, the United Arab Emirates (UAE) ratified a free-trade agreement with Iraq that had been signed in November 2001. The most significant feature of this deal is that the six members of the Gulf Cooperation Council will merge their markets into a customs union in 2003. This will give Iraq access to the entire GCC market. By mid-2002, the UAE was already one of Iraq's biggest economic partners in the region.

The only Gulf state that by mid-2002 was still hostile to Saddam Hussein's regime was Kuwait: Despite Iraq's alternating offers of "friendship" and undisguised threats, Kuwait steadfastly refused to improve bilateral relations. Kuwaiti officials refused an Iraqi offer to visit Iraqi prisons to prove there are no Kuwaiti POWs being held and continue to be highly critical of the Iraqi regime. Kuwait also seems sympathetic to the idea of an American-inspired violent regime change in Baghdad. If so, Kuwait is the only Arab state to support such a military operation.

Egypt.   Egypt was the main Arab participant in the anti-Iraqi coalition of 1990–91. And yet, Iraqi-Egyptian relations started to pick up significantly the moment Iraq's buying power surged. Trade became meaningful, and in January 2001 Iraq and Egypt signed a free-trade-zone agreement. According to Iraq's trade minister, Muhammad Mahdi Salih, the mutual trade in 2000 reached $1.2 billion, triple the 1999 figure. The minister expressed the hope that in 2001 the volume would go beyond $2 billion.[10] Egypt is Iraq's fourth-largest trading partner, after France, Russia, and China.[11]

The Far Abroad. Saddam Hussein's patient diplomacy toward Russia and France, both of which have significant economic interests in an Iraq freed of economic shackles—Iraq owes them a combined $11 billion—have permitted him to challenge the weapons inspections regime with relative impunity, knowing these permanent Security Council members with veto power could be counted on to weaken reprisals against Iraq. China, too, has supported his beleaguered regime in international forums, as have Kenya and Egypt. These countries took up the fight that sanctions were hurting the Iraqi people more than the regime and that lifting sanctions was the only way to alleviate the suffering of the Iraqi people—creating a sense that the United States, not Iraq, was increasingly isolated.

Weapons of Mass Destruction

To Saddam Hussein, nuclear weapons, and weapons of mass destruction in general, are important—indeed critical. After all, world-class leaders have world-class weapons. Especially since the military was grievously wounded by the 1991 conflict, with a marked reduction in conventional strength, unconventional weapons have become all the more important. Moreover, defying the international community on this matter is a regular reminder to the military of his courage in defying the superior adversary and that he has not and will not capitulate.

Despite tactical retreats in October–November of 1997 and January–February of 1998, Iraq succeeded in winning important concessions on sanctions and weapons inspections. This was crucial in continuing to build Saddam Hussein's support among the Iraqi people—it was seen as a victory. The embargo is dissipating slowly, and yet Saddam Hussein did not have to give up his WMDs. Today the Iraqi people have a better standard of living, many aspects of the embargo are gone, Saddam has his WMDs, and his power elite believes it is stronger—resulting in solidifying his position in Iraq.

Indeed, when the weapons inspectors left Iraq in December 1998 and were not allowed back, this was a major victory for Saddam Hussein in the eyes of the Iraqi people. The United Nations had been forced out of Iraq, and Saddam Hussein was unscathed. The challenge of the UN inspections regime strengthened Hussein's internal support, diminishing the internal threat as he demonstrated his ability to weaken and challenge the international coalition, while retaining the coveted WMD program and weakening support for the sanctions regime. The divisions within the UN that Saddam Hussein helped promote were so deep that he concluded that he was essentially immune to UN reprisals for pursuing unconventional weapons programs. Since 1999, there have been no meaningful coup attempts; those who might have challenged a leader perceived to be a loser did not dare challenge a leader who had successfully challenged the United Nations and the United States.

Change of Image in the International Community

Saddam Hussein has continued to work to increase his standing in the international community, seizing on opportunities to change his image, including bolstering his image within the Arab community.

Starting in the early 1990s, he began working to change his image as a secular leader. This "return to Islam" can be seen in his increased use of Islamic language, the introduction into Iraq of the Koranic punishment of severing the right hand for the crime of theft, forbidding the public consumption of alcohol, and decapitation with a sword for the "crimes" of prostitution, homosexuality, and providing a shelter for prostitutes to pursue their occupation. On the cultural level, a few million copies of the Koran were printed in Iraq and given away, and people are being forced to attend Koran courses in many walks of society, starting with the schools. In the same vein, a law issued in the late 1990s allowed the release of Muslim prisoners who memorized the Koran in jail.[12] Another component of the "Islamization" campaign is the construction of extravagant mosques—the new Saddam Mosque (construction began in 1999) is the largest in the Middle East after the one in Mecca.

Saddam Hussein has also fashioned himself as the patron of the Palestinian cause. He has increased the original "reward" that was paid to families of suicide bombers from $10,000 to $25,000. In addition, Iraq informed the Palestinian Authority and public that it had asked permission from the UN Security Council to dedicate one billion Euros (around $940 million) from its New York escrow account to the intifada.[13] There are other forms of support that, while not substantial, are still serving Saddam Hussein's propaganda machine. For example, a few of the Palestinians wounded in the intifada have been hospitalized in Baghdad.[14] Also, Iraq sent a number of trucks through Jordan and the Jordan River bridges to the West Bank full of humanitarian goods. Israel allowed these trucks to cross over.

OTHER SIGNS OF GROWING INTERNATIONAL ACCEPTANCE

In August of 2000, Venezuelan President Hugo Chavez bucked international convention and traveled to Iraq to meet with Saddam Hussein. He was the first head of state to visit Iraq since the Gulf War, signaling Iraq's growing acceptance in the international community. Two months later, Iraq was invited to attend the Arab League summit meeting for the first time since the start of the Gulf crisis, indicating a thawing in Arab attitudes toward Iraq. In another sign of normalcy, Baghdad's international airport reopened in the fall of 2000. When a hijacked Saudi airliner landed in Baghdad in October 2000 and all passengers were released unharmed, there was a great deal of international praise for Saddam Hussein.

In January of 2001, humanitarian flights began arriving daily from abroad, and Iraqi airlines began operating (even in the "no-fly zones"). As oil production recovered to prewar levels, food rations increased, power cuts became less severe, and drinking water and sewer services dramatically improved. In a calculated step to garner international favor, Saddam Hussein offered to allow Kuwaiti officials to inspect Iraqi prisons in January of 2002 (although this offer was rejected). Finally, in March 2002, at the Arab League summit meeting in Beirut, Saudi Crown Prince Abdullah hugged and kissed Izzat Ibrahim al-Duri, Saddam Hussein's deputy chairman of the RCC, in front of the world's TV cameras. This ended more than a decade of bitter hostility and was a visible symbol that Saddam Hussein's Iraq had been fully welcomed back into the community of Arab nations.

Saddam Hussein continued to strengthen his reputation both by his re-Islamization program and by his ostentatious support for the Palestinian people, further endearing him to his Arab neighbors. He has pledged $881 million from oil revenues for the Palestinian people.

The Use of International Crisis

Saddam Hussein has found that international crises help him retain power, and his string of foreign policy successes have allowed him to stunt the growth of internal opposition. Success is not limited to the elimination of domestic opposition; such elimination is only a precondition for achieving his continuing ambition of being recognized as the preeminent leader in the region and a worthy successor to Nasser. However, in order to be able to become a world-class leader, he needs, in the first place, to control the domestic scene; and in his mind, control means absolute control, namely the elimination of any opposition. To achieve that, he has always been ready to confront anybody, including world powers. The most damaging outcome of any crisis is one that shows him as a failure as a leader. Thus, Saddam regularly promotes international crises to shore up his internal position.

Although Saddam Hussein's position today is much weaker than it was on the eve of the invasion of Kuwait in 1990, he has demonstrated a more sophisticated leadership in addressing his internal security vulnerabilities and in diplomacy with his Arab neighbors and Turkey—the "near abroad"—as well as with the "far abroad." He has patiently and assiduously worked to reduce his vulnerabilities and to strengthen his position, both internally and internationally.

Saddam's survival in power is his continuing goal. A rational calculator who can bob and weave and is astutely Machiavellian, he has shrewdly managed to sustain the loyalty of his military and to weaken international opposition. That he has been sophisticated and better attuned to the context of his leadership both internally and internationally does not lessen a still persistent danger—that when Saddam is backed into a corner, his customary prudence and judgment are apt to falter. On these occasions he can be very dangerous—violently lashing out with all the resources at his disposal. The persistent calls for regime change by the United States and others may well be moving him into that dangerous "back against the wall" posture. The setting afire of the Kuwaiti oil fields as he retreated in 1991 is an example that might well be repeated with his own Iraqi oil fields, as if to say, "If I can't have them, no one will." Moreover, with his back to the wall it is probable that he would attempt to use chemical/biological weapons against Israel and against U.S. armed forces in the region. The question then will be the degree to which he can continue to sustain the loyalty of his senior military commanders or whether they can be induced to not obey Saddam in extremis in order to safeguard their own futures. Of one thing we can be sure, this is a man who "will not go gentle into that good night, but will rage, rage against the dying of the light."

Postscript

At the time this updated political personality profile of Saddam was developed, the tension was palpable as war with Iraq seemed inevitable. But the international community was badly divided, with significant opposition to eliminating the threat posed by the Iraqi regime advocated by the United States and its principal ally, Great Britain. In the European community, France and Germany led the opposition, taking the position that the inspection regime required more time to carry out its mission. Russia too opposed military action against Iraq, as did China. Putting legitimate policy disagreements aside, and other factors of national interest, France, Russia, and China's opposition to military intervention can assuredly be credited in part to Iraq's patient and significant courting of the "far abroad" described in the profile.

Prior to the initiation of conflict on March 19, 2003, there was a systematic campaign to soften Iraq's air defenses, with targeted attacks in response to violations of the no-fly zone. And an effort was underway on a number of fronts to weaken the ties between Saddam and his military leaders. In November 2002, Secretary of Defense Donald Rumsfeld stated publicly that the generals have an important role to play in the reconstruction of Iraq, but all bets are off if they get involved in weapons of mass destruction. This was followed several weeks later by a statement by President Bush to the effect that Saddam may well order his generals to use weapons of mass destruction against alliance forces. If he does so, the generals would be well advised to disobey those orders. Contact was made with the Iraqi defense minister suggesting he preserve the lives of his soldiers in a war they were sure to lose and encourage his forces not to fight. In the immediate lead-up to, and during the early weeks, of the conflict, the battlefield was leafleted with fliers advising that any regional commander who ordered the use of weapons of mass destruction would be held culpable for war crimes, and that claims of "just following orders" would not protect them from prosecution.

In the conflict, there was a surprising lack of resistance, with a pace of advance not contemplated, perhaps a reflection of some of the preparatory efforts cited above. I had thought it was likely that Saddam would order the use of weapons of mass destruction in a terminal spasm, and could well order that Iraqi oil fields be set afire, as he had in his exodus from Kuwait.

In the event, the feared chemical/biological weapons attack did not occur. Why not? The short answer is that we do not know. But let me suggest several possibilities. First, because of the split in the international community that led to the disarray in the United Nations and the decision of the United States and Great Britain to enter conflict outside of the UN umbrella, Saddam may have reflected that too early a use of these weapons would have dissolved the uncertainty he had fostered and promote international unity behind elimination of his regime. Then the extremely rapid advance of alliance troops and the collapse of Iraqi military resistance may have made it too late to use these weapons. Moreover, Saddam may well have ordered their use, but the military, responding to the effective information operations campaign, may well have concluded that it would be prudent, in terms of their own best interest, to not follow those orders. Chemical/biological and nuclear weapons have not yet been found, leading many to doubt their existence in the first place. We should recall, however, that the failure of weapons inspectors to find these weapons had nearly led to the lifting of sanctions prior to the 1995 defection of Hussein Kamal, who revealed the nature of the programs and where the weapons had been cached. There is no question that Saddam had been bent on pursing chemical, biological, and nuclear weapons programs. He has had years to perfect concealment techniques, and the

United States at this time has not located any weapons sites. Whether they were dismantled just prior to the onset of conflict or will be still discovered has not yet been determined.

How many of Saddam's military leaders were "loyal at the barrel of a gun" is unknown. After 1991, those who raised their heads too early to signify their enthusiasm for the imminent overthrow of the Saddam Hussein regime were hunted down ruthlessly and, with their families, were jailed, tortured, and executed. One could not expect early defections. And as long as the inner leadership, especially Saddam and his two sons Qusay and Uday remained on the loose, the fear of reprisal remained. In the conduct of the war, the targeting of the senior leadership conveyed that they were the principal target and paved the way for lower-level military officers to defect. With the killing in a firefight of Qusay and Uday, it was, for Saddam, literally "the end of the line." This had to have had a profound impact on Saddam, who had seen his leadership perpetuated through his sons.

On April 9, 2003, in Baghdad, the forty-foot statue of Saddam was toppled by American troops, a vivid visual metaphor for the fall of Saddam to come. On May 1, on the deck of the aircraft carrier *Abraham Lincoln*, President Bush dramatically declared the end of armed conflict, though the postwar period immediately proved difficult, with a daily toll of casualties from a determined and increasingly well-organized insurgency, with Ba'athist diehards strengthened by waves of *jihadists* from neighboring countries. Still, the statue was prophetic: On December 13, 2003, a more arresting image of the Arab strongman sped around the globe. Without a single shot being fired, a humiliated Saddam was captured by American forces. Pulled from a hole beneath a mud hut, he resembled nothing so much as a scruffy street person. He seemed totally defeated as he meekly yielded to an ensuing medical examination by his captors. Saddam, who had extolled the bravery of his sons—who had died in a storm of bullets rather than be taken alive—had given up without a fight. Saddam, a larger-than-life figure, who had strode like Colossus across the Middle East landscape, buttressing his grand ambitions with grand palaces throughout Iraq, a man who had held his people in a thralldom of terror, revealed himself to be more like the Wizard of Oz: behind the great-man facade was a little man pulling the levers of power. How the mighty had fallen. This is what his followers saw and will not easily forget.

12

Kim Jong Il of North Korea

In the Shadow of His Father

An enigma to the West since its inception in 1946, North Korea remains cloaked in an aura of secrecy, xenophobia, and military preoccupation.[1] The only two leaders the country has ever known, Kim Il Sung and his son, Kim Jong Il, have been intensely distrustful of the outside world. This distrust has influenced not only how they see the world but also how they are perceived by the world.

Kim Il Sung: Founding Father of the Kim Dynasty

One cannot understand the personality and political behavior of Kim Jong Il without placing it in the context of the life and charismatic leadership of his father, Kim Il Sung, North Korea's first leader. One of the difficulties in assessing the personality and political behavior of Kim Il Sung has always been discerning the man behind the myth. The gap between the facts that scholars have been able to piece together and the hagiographic portrait presented to the people of North Korea is staggering. The same holds true for Kim Jong Il. Examining this gap is instructive, as it may reflect areas of sensitivity, the ideal versus the real. Consider the following description of Kim Jong Il's lineage taken from an official North Korean Web site:

The Great Mangyongdae Family

From old times it is said that a great man is produced by a great family. Marshal Kim Jong Il's family is praised as the greatest family unprecedented in all countries and in all ages.

Family is a base of a person's character. And the disposition and dignity a person gets from his family show his quality.

The greatness of Marshal Kim Jong Il is related with the greatness of his family. His father President Kim Il Sung and his mother Mrs. Kim Jong Suk are the peerless great persons produced by our nation.

President Kim Il Sung is a legendary hero of the anti-Japanese struggle. He, cherishing the lofty ambition of the fatherland's liberation, organized and led the anti-Japanese armed war in his teens, defeated the one-million-strong Japanese army through the fifteen-year-long bloody war and finally liberated the country from the Japanese colonial rule. He is also a peerless patriot who repulsed the aggression by the U.S.-led fifteen imperialist countries at his forties, thus beginning the downhill of the United States for the first time in history and securing the dignity of the nation.

Historic victories in the anti-Japanese war and the Korean War in the 1950s were the victory of the President's love for his country, his nation, and his people. It was also the victory of the gifted military idea and strategy of the President as an invincible veteran.

He has also performed immortal exploits as the founder of the socialist Korea. Therefore his life is recorded with golden letters in the history of the nation.

In the early period of his revolutionary activities he created the people-centered Juche[2] idea which illumines the way ahead of humankind and under the bright lights of the Juche idea, has established the socialist system in North Korea free from exploitation and oppression after the country's liberation and then built an independent, self-supporting and self-defensive powerful state, in order to materialize the people's desire for an ideal society.

Indeed, President Kim Il Sung is a patriot who, regarding his people as his God, devoted his all for the sacred cause of the people's happiness and pleasure. He also made his utmost efforts for reunification of the nation.

He cherished it as his lifelong duty and mission to reunify the nation divided by foreign forces after the country's liberation. So he made efforts for the reunification till the very moment when his great heart stopped beating.

And he made immortal contribution to the strengthening of the world socialist movement and the non-aligned movement under the principles of independence, peace and friendship and the acceleration of the human cause of independence.

Really, President Kim Il Sung is highly praised by the Korean people and the world progressives as the peerless patriot and world political veteran who enjoyed the absolute authority for the distinguished exploits he contributed to the building of the North Korean socialism, Korea's reunification and the global independence.

Mrs. Kim Jong Suk, mother of Marshal Kim Jong Il, is also a peerless heroine.

She was an anti-Japanese heroine who, keeping anti-Japanese patriotism, took active part in an anti-Japanese underground revolutionary organization already in her teens. Under the command of Generalissimo Kim Il Sung she, with an arm in her hands, fought against the Japanese imperialists for ten-odd years.

She was not only a faithful retainer who faithfully carried out General Kim Il Sung's will but also a lifeguard who safeguarded the General at every dangerous moment.

Indeed, Marshal Kim Jong Il's parents were peerless great persons unprecedented in all families of the world.[3]

In 1910, two years before Kim Il Sung was born, the Japanese empire formally annexed Korea. His family, seeking to escape Japanese control, fled Mangyongdae in northern Korea to Chinese-controlled Manchuria when Kim was seven years old. The eldest of three sons, Kim was thirteen when the family returned to Korea. By the age of fifteen he had joined the Korean Youth League and was engaged in anti-Japanese activities. After his formal education ended with eighth grade, Kim increased his political activism. When he was seventeen he was arrested and jailed for taking part in the formation of the Korean Communist Youth League. When he was twenty-one, he joined the Korean Revolutionary Army, a small band of guerrillas that were fighting Japanese rule in Korea. Although he eventually gained control of his own guerrilla unit, he never directly controlled more than one hundred men. (This is a striking contrast to the portrait in the official biography excerpted above, in which Kim Il Sung "organized and led the anti-Japanese armed war in his teens, defeated the one million strong Japanese army through the 15-year-long bloody war and finally liberated the country from the Japanese colonial rule.")

In 1941, the strength of the Japanese army forced the small guerrilla group to relocate to bases within the Soviet Union, where they were under Soviet protection. Over the next four years, Kim and his band of partisan fighters conducted cross-border raids into Japanese-controlled Korea. While in the Soviet Union, Kim Il Sung met and married Kim Jong Suk, a fellow partisan who had joined the resistance fighters in 1936. In 1942, a year after their marriage, Kim Il Sung and Kim Jong Suk's first child, Kim Jong Il, the future leader of North Korea, was born near Khabarovsk at a guerrilla base under the protection of the Soviet military. These were rather unfortunate circumstances of birth for the future Dear Leader, not only in the Soviet Union but under the protection of the Soviet Union. In the official biography, however, the birth of Kim Jong Il is described in rather more heroic terms:

> The world history has not recorded such a son of guerrillas who was born between brilliant commanders of guerrillas in Mt. Paektu, the sacred mountain of the nation. So Kim Jong Il's birth is said to be an unprecedented birth out of a remarkable family. Therefore, a believer in Chondogyo said in a charm that Marshal Kim Jong Il's birth itself is great and he was born with the mission of savior.[4]

It was much more suitable for the future leader of North Korea to have been born at the base of the sacred mountain of the nation, Mt. Paektu, "amid bright lights and double rainbows," than in the Soviet Union.

Following the surrender of Japan to the Allies in August 1945, Kim and his family returned to northern Korea. At the Yalta conference, the United States, the United Kingdom, the Soviet Union, and China were given shared trusteeship of Korea by the United Nations. When Japan surrendered in September 1945 the 38th parallel was the line of demarcation: Japanese troops to the north would surrender to Soviet troops, and those to the south would surrender to U.S. forces. Over the next two years the superpowers remained deadlocked on the issue of Korea with North Korea, the Soviet Union, and China on one side, and South Korea and the United States on the other. Despite a UN ruling calling for elections throughout the Korean Peninsula, only the South (south of the 38th parallel) complied and in August 1948 Syngman Rhee became the first elected president of the Republic of Korea (ROK). That September Kim Il Sung, with support from the Soviet Union and China, established the Democratic People's Republic of Korea (DPRK) in the North. Both governments claimed to be the only legitimate government of the Korean Peninsula.

Arriving as a member of the Soviet army, Kim was not immediately involved in the politics of a post-Japanese Korea. After several failures at establishing coalition governments in northern Korea, the Soviets, who were responsible for the administration of North Korea, formed a provisional people's committee in February 1946. Stalin personally chose Kim Il Sung as its head. That same year the Korean Workers Party (KWP) was formally established. Kim was elected one of two vice-chairmen. Over the next three years, Kim deftly maneuvered within the KWP until he gained the chairmanship in 1949, a position he held until his death forty-five years later.

Kim's hold on power was absolute. Strongly influenced by Stalin and Mao, Kim Il Sung was a devoted Communist who maintained a lifelong goal of uniting the Korean Peninsula under his leadership. Allied with the Soviet Union and China, he established tight control over North Korea, crushing any opposition and eliminating potential rivals. Suspicious of outsiders, distraught over postmortem denunciations of Stalin, and concerned about political stability in China during the last years of Mao's leadership, Kim Il Sung closed the borders of his country, severely limiting not only the exit of his citizens but the entrance of foreign visitors.

Throughout his life, Kim worked tirelessly to create a cult of personality. The KWP Department of Propaganda and Agitation has been devoted since its inception to furthering the image of Kim Il Sung and his family as loyal and fiercely patriotic Koreans through re-creating the family history.

Known as "the Great Leader," the near-divine image of Kim Il Sung continues to influence North Korean policy and the leadership decisions of his son from the grave. Indeed, Kim Il Sung was named Eternal President in the 1972 revision of the constitution, and the slogan "The Great Leader Will Always Be With Us" is in bold, yellow letters across the bottom of the Web site of the Democratic People's Republic of Korea.

It is clear that Kim Jong Il, the eldest son of Kim Il Sung, was born in a guerrilla camp in the Soviet Union. Kim, also known by his Russian nickname Yura, is said to have been "a wild child who frequently got into trouble," not unlike his father, and to physically resemble his mother (Oh and Hassig 2000, 85). Before the family returned to Korea, Kim Jong Il's younger brother, nicknamed Shura, then three, drowned in a pond while playing with Yura, who was five. The circumstances of this accident are unclear, but two reports from defectors, which may well be fabrications, say that Kim was responsible. Yi Ki-pong served as an assistant to the WPK vice-chairman in the late 1950s and defected to South Korea in the early 1960s. In his book *What Kind a Man is Kim Jong Il?*, Yi wrote this about Shura's drowning:

> Kim was very mischievous when a child. When he saw an insect, he trampled on it. After Korea's liberation from Japanese occupation, the Kim Il-sung family lived in a house in Mansu-tong, Central District, P'yongyang. In the early summer of 1948, his younger brother, Shura (then three years old) drowned. Kim Jong Il was there at the time. I learned later how the accident occurred. The two brothers were playing in the pond right by the edge. Kim Jong Il raised his face faster than his brother, and pushed his brother's face back into water. He did that over and over.

Ko Yong-hwan, in his book *Kim Jong Il as Seen by a Senior Official Who Defected*, wrote about the accident in a similar manner:

> In the early summer of 1946, Kim Il Sung's sons, Yura and Shura, were playing together in the pond. Yura, who was a mischievous boy, had fun pouring water onto Shura and pulling his leg to topple him into water. Playing, they moved away from the edge of the pond, and when Shura, afraid of going into a deeper side, tried to come out, Yura caught him and stopped him from coming out. When the younger brother tried to move to a shallower spot, Yura pushed him into a deeper corner. The younger brother was at the point of drowning, uttering the sound of "blub-blub," but it was a funnier scene to Yura. But the old saying goes, "A tiger comes to a place where you find fauns." Thus, the younger brother drowned.

It seems unlikely that the two young children would have been playing unattended, but whatever the circumstances, the incident must have had a profound impact on the young Kim Jong Il, especially if the two accounts as related, despite certain inconsistencies, are essentially true. Kim Il Sung and Kim Jong Suk had a third child, a daughter named Kim Jyung Hee.

Immediately on returning to Korea in 1945, Kim Jong Il, age four, and his family settled in Pyongyang. It was during these early years that Kim Il Sung was moving into the leadership of North Korea, affording Kim Jong Il wealth and privileges unknown to most North Korean citizens. In the year following Kim Jong Il's enrollment at the prestigious Namsan School at age seven, Kim Il Sung cemented his control over North Korea as chairman of the KWP.

That year, in what was assuredly a devastating loss to the growing boy, Kim Jong Il's mother, Kim Jong Suk, died, a fact conveniently omitted from the official biography.[5] Although the official story is that she died in childbirth, there are many who remain unconvinced. There are even stories that she was shot and left to bleed to death. At the age of eight, having recently lost his mother, Kim Jong Il watched his father initiate the Korean War in an attempt to reunite the Korean Peninsula. He had little time for his young son.

Little is known about Kim Jong Il's early years. He traveled with his father out of North Korea for the first time in 1957 at the age of fifteen on a trip to Moscow and again to Eastern Europe in 1959. He graduated from high school the following year.

The year before Kim Jong Il's graduation from the university in 1964, Kim Il Sung remarried. He had three children with his new wife, Kim Song Ae, who was notably a much more attractive and sophisticated woman than his first wife, something that is said to have led to a great deal of jealousy and anger in Kim Jong Il. Although there are reports that Kim Jong Il may have attended the Air Force Officers School in East Germany, it is highly unlikely that he did so, given the dates of his graduation from high school and subsequent enrollment in the university.

After his graduation Kim Jong Il began to take an active role in the KWP. He was appointed by his father to head the Great Leader's bodyguard and to a position in the KWP Central Committee's Organization and Guidance Department, where he began to establish his own personal power base. Kim Jong Il was exposed not only to the full spectrum of North Korean political life but was also able to influence the military and economic activities of North Korea (Baird 2003, 7). Over the next several years, Kim Jong Il established his presence behind the scenes, remaining out of the spotlight, which was owned by his father.

Kim Jong Il used his position in the Propaganda and Agitation Department for ideological indoctrination, to enforce political conformity, and to build the myth of the Kim family. It became clear in the early 1970s that

Kim Jong Il had been designated as his father's heir. Kim Jong Il became a KWP secretary in September 1973 and a full member of the Politburo in 1974 at the age of thirty. By grooming his son to succeed him, Kim Il Sung hoped that North Korea could avoid the kinds of struggles that had taken place in the Soviet Union after Stalin's death and in the People's Republic of China after Mao's demise. Kim Il Sung hoped to provide a basis not only for stability but also for a "perpetuation of the system characteristics that tend[ed] to be unique and peculiar" (Park 2002, 149).

Kim Jong Il consolidated his power during the 1970s. He "replaced thousands of officials at all levels of the party with younger members who would be personally loyal to him in gratitude for their promotion" (Oh and Hassig 2000, 88). Kim has worked assiduously to incorporate or to eliminate peers of his father. It is rumored that in 1973 he orchestrated the death of Nam Il, a supporter of Kim Il Sung who died in a mysterious car accident shortly after expressing reservations about Kim Jong Il's growing power.

In 1974 Kim Jong Il announced the "Ten Principles," which at their core were designed to require absolute loyalty and obedience to Kim Il Sung. This move reinforced the centrality of Kim Il Sung to the North Korean people and very cleverly reinforced the image of Kim Jong Il as fully aligned with his father and representative of his father's goals.

Although Kim Il Sung remained "the Great Leader" and the symbol of North Korea, by the end of the 1970s Kim Jong Il had assumed day-to-day control over much of North Korea's government, party, and military affairs (Baird 2003, 3). Because of the secrecy surrounding North Korea's political system, it is not clear when Kim Jong Il gained complete control over the intelligence apparatus, although it is evident from his role in the 1978 kidnappings by North Korean operatives of his favorite South Korean movie actress, Choe Un-hui, and that of her movie-director husband six months later that he had some control over covert operations. They remained "guests" of North Korea until their escape in 1987.

There is some debate about whether Kim Jong Il was officially named as successor to his father at the Sixth Party Congress of the KWP in October 1980. Whether formal or not, however, in taking the number-two seat in the KWP Kim Jong Il was, in fact, the chosen future leader of North Korea. By this time he had solidified his control over the day-to-day management and operation of North Korea's military and intelligence operations. Kim Jong Il is believed to have been the architect behind two terrorist events in the 1980s. In a 1983 bombing in Rangoon, Burma, North Korean commandos set off an explosion that killed seventeen visiting South Korean officials, including four cabinet ministers. President Chun Doo Hwan arrived late for the event and thus narrowly escaped death. In November 1987,

KAL Flight 858 was bombed midair and went down in the Andaman Sea, killing 115 people. Given the role that Kim Jong Il was playing in the day-to-day management of the North Korean government and military by this time it is highly unlikely that these two events could have taken place without his oversight and final approval (Baird 2003, 24).[6]

It was not until the early 1990s that Kim Jong Il began to take on official government, as opposed to party, positions. In 1990 he was named the first deputy chairman of the National Defense Commission and Supreme Commander of the Korean People's Army, despite having no military background himself. His lack of military experience was a concern, and the Propaganda and Agitation Department, where the younger Kim began his party career, began to fabricate a suitable résumé for him (Oh and Hassig 2000, 89). It also aims to further enhance Kim Jong Il's image as not only the rightful leader of North Korea but also as an extension of his father.

It was his ascension to the rank of marshal in 1992 that signaled Kim Jong Il's move into the political spotlight. His hold on power was cemented when he became chairman of the National Defense Commission in 1993. Although Kim Il Sung died in 1994, it was not until 1997 that Kim Jong Il took over as general secretary of the KWP. To this day, he has not become president of North Korea but has maintained his control through chairing the National Defense Commission. In an adroit political move, he designated his father as "President for Eternity," sparing himself the ultimate responsibility for policies that have misfired, but the designation may also suggest apprehension about fully stepping into the giant shoes of his father.

Kim Jong Il's Family

Kim Jong Il has three children, reportedly by three different women: Kim Jong Nam, a son born in 1971; Kim Sul Song, a daughter born in 1974; and Kim Jong Chul, a son born in 1981. According to official reports he is married to Kim Young Sook, the only one of the three women he married and the mother of his daughter. His elder son, Kim Jong Nam, reportedly a computer expert, spent part of his childhood in Geneva and Moscow and has been much more exposed to the outside world than his father. Kim Jong Nam, whose mother reportedly is in Moscow being treated for depression after attempting to defect, was arrested and subsequently deported from Japan in 2001 for entering on a false Dominican Republic passport.[7] Traveling with two women and a four-year-old boy—believed to be Kim's son—Jong Nam reportedly agreed to go to China as part of an agreement to avoid an international incident. Virtually nothing is known about the interaction between Kim Jong Il and the women in his life or his children.

The long-standing animosity between Kim and his stepmother, Kim Song Ae, and his half siblings has given rise to "a long running drama of palace intrigue."[8] Having resented his stepmother since her marriage to his father in 1963, Kim reportedly cuts her face out of all photos.[9] Reportedly Kim Song Ae and her children are referred to as an "offshoot clique" and have been subjected to a virulent internal propaganda campaign directed by Kim Jong Il to discredit and ostracize them.[10]

Kim Jong Il the Man

Descriptions of Kim Jong Il range from shy and uncomfortable among strangers to humorous, affable, and engaging, from reclusive to bold and sophisticated. Because of the veil of secrecy surrounding North Korea, and more specifically "the Dear Leader" (so named to distinguish him from his father, "the Great Leader"), what we know of Kim Jong Il is compiled from reports of defectors (which are often filtered through South Korean intelligence services); the few visitors who have had the opportunity to meet with him; and the South Korean actress Choe Un-hui and her husband, who spent eight years as "guests" of the North Korean leader. Information about Kim Jong Il's personality, personal habits, and interpersonal relations is based mainly on secondhand reports—often from people with political agendas—and very little from directly observed behavior.

Insecure about Personal Appearance and Stature

Reportedly taking after his mother, Kim Jong Il is a short, overweight man who is very self-conscious about his appearance. Standing roughly five feet two inches tall, Kim reportedly has platform shoes custom-built for him to reach this height, and weighs in around 175 pounds. Clearly, his short stature is a long-standing issue for him. In a book written after he defected from North Korea, Kang Myong-to, a son-in-law of former Premier Kang Song San, recalled: "The elders of the village [Ch'ilgol, the hometown of Kim Jong Il's mother] called Kim Jong Il 'shorty.' Upon first meeting the South Korean actress Choe Un-hui, Kim reportedly asked, 'Well, Madame Choe, what do you think of my physique? Small as a midget's droppings, aren't I?' "[11] His hair is worn in a flamboyant style, adding additional height. He wears only custom-tailored clothing made in North Korea, and is rarely seen without his dark glasses. He usually wears gray or tan factory foreman's slacks and a short jacket, and for formal occasions he most often wears a gray "Mao-style" jacket. Although he chooses to wear styles that are in keeping with North Korean society, it is hard to miss the professionally tailored element of his wardrobe. Kim Jong Il never appears publicly in a military uniform, allegedly because he has a complex about never having served in the military.

There have been persistent rumors about Kim's health, generated in part by his protracted absences from public view—particularly around the time of his father's death. Although stories of his ill health have included epilepsy, diabetes, heart trouble, and possible brain damage from an accident, Kim Jong Il has been reported to appear to be in good health by the few foreign visitors who have been allowed to meet with the Dear Leader. There also have been rumors of alcoholism and related physical ailments, but other than these observations there is no specific information available about the health of Kim Jong Il.

SPECIAL CARE WITH PREPARATION OF MEALS

A great deal of care goes into the preparation of Kim's meals. The Workers Party of Korea Finance and Accounting Department has under it an office called the "Kim Jong Il Longevity Institute." It is in complete charge of the health management of Kim Jong Il and decides on his menus. In preparing his meals, cooks use rice grown at special farms in Mundokkun in South Pyongang Province. Female workers check every grain of rice, removing chipped or damaged grains. According to Yi Han-yong, because Kim Jong Il does not eat rice cooked in electric rice cookers, his rice is cooked in the traditional way, using firewood, and the wood must come from Mt. Paektu.

Kim Jong Il drinks Sindoksu, a well-known mineral water produced only in Kanggye, Chagang Province. Sindoksu is sold to the public at foreign currency-taking shops in Pyongyang, but the Kim Jong Il family uses water taken from a source reserved exclusively for the Kim family. Fish and other seafood come exclusively from the Sinpo Fisheries Enterprise in South Hamgyong Province.

Kim Jong Il's preoccupation with food can be traced to his boyhood, as shown by the following note from a teacher when he was a student at Mangyongdae Revolutionary School. In 1952, Kim's teacher was transferred to another school, and she wrote a note to his new teacher:

> Foods that Kim Jong Il likes to have are soybean paste soup in the winter, vegetables such as ch'unguk and yakch'ae with dressing during the spring, icy cucumber drink and rice hash in the summer, and cabbage-wrapped rice and dishes containing crushed beans in the autumn. He likes to take meals together with many people around him. (FBIS, June 20, 2000)

An interesting example of how he mobilizes the government to cater to his tastes concerns cigarettes. In 1977, Kim Jong Il instructed all overseas diplomatic missions to collect samples of all famous foreign cigarettes. Kim tried each brand and settled on Rothmans and Dunhill cigarettes from Britain. He smoked these two brands alternately for the next several days and decided on Rothmans. Then he ordered his researchers to find out how Rothmans cigarettes are produced, and then ordered the production of Paektusan cigarettes, which taste very much like Rothmans. Still, the cigarettes he likes most, and the ones that are found on his desk, are Rothmans.

A Hedonist Lifestyle

Kim Jong Il is considered eccentric and self-indulgent by many and has a known penchant for French cognac, Western movies, and beautiful women. Hennessy, the maker of Paradis cognac, has confirmed that Kim is their biggest buyer of the cognac, with an estimated annual account of between $650,000 and $800,000 since 1992. The Dear Leader annually spends 770 times the income of the average North Korean citizen ($1,038) on cognac alone. It is estimated that thousands of bottles of Paradis are shipped each year to North Korea,[12] where they sell for $630 a bottle.

Defectors have characterized Kim Jong Il as self-centered and lacking empathy. Reflecting a fundamental narcissism, he tends to view nearly everything and everyone from the stance of self-interest.

Both Kim's lack of empathy and sense of entitlement are revealed in his indulgent lifestyle, which contrasts with the struggle of most North Koreans to feed themselves. Kim lives in a seven-story pleasure palace in Pyongyang, and defectors report that he maintains lavish villas, furnished with imported luxury goods, in each of North Korea's provinces. He is reported to have secreted upwards of $10 billion in Swiss bank accounts.

Kim Jong Il reportedly hosts lavish parties where he drinks heavily and expects those around him to do so as well. According to the memoirs of the South Korean actress Choe Un-hui, Kim Jong Il is a heavy drinker. A Japanese hostess remembers having seen him drink heavily. He drank as if he were a man who believed "the amount of liquor a man drinks shows how big a man he is." She wrote, "The large amount of liquor he drank and his physical abilities to bear such heavy drinking were enough to impress any people who were there."[13] A former bodyguard who defected to South Korea portrays Kim as a heavy drinker who starts drinking around noon (although he doesn't get drunk during working hours) and picks up the pace during evening parties hosted in Pyongyang. At these parties, Kim and his associates regularly drank to excess while female entertainers wore "micro-minis and tank tops" but were directed not to drink too much.[14]

These parties reportedly include entertainment provided by strippers and Kim's "Joy Brigades," beautiful young women trained to entertain him and his cronies. Members, who reportedly are recruited from junior high schools every July, must be virgins and have pale, unblemished skin.[15]

When he is in a benevolent mood, Kim Jong Il gives his guests and friends expensive gifts ranging from TVs and stereos to bananas, pineapples, and mandarin oranges, all luxuries in North Korea. Kim appears to maintain power both through such special perquisites and through domination and fear. Defectors report that Kim's manipulative style includes combining special privileges with humiliation and threats of punishment, including execution. Stories abound concerning executions ordered by Kim, though there is no direct evidence that they took place. There are even stories that he has carried out some of these executions personally— again, whether true or not, the persistence of these stories serves to further his image. Regardless of the accuracy of these reports the simple fact that they are so widespread adds to the cult of personality surrounding Kim, reinforcing his image as a strongman.

LACK OF EMPATHY FOR NORTH KOREAN PEOPLE

Recent events also testify to his comfort with tolerating high levels of deaths at home. In confronting North Korea's famine, saving lives has not been a top priority, and early in the famine cycle Kim cut off nearly all food supplies to the four eastern provinces and denied these provinces access to international aid (Natsios 2001, 106–7). Large numbers of deaths also occurred between 1997 and 1999 when, on Kim's orders, several hundred thousand people displaced by the famine were herded into camps where conditions allowed few to survive (Natsios 2001). Moreover, according to the testimony of eyewitnesses, Kim has ordered the systematic killing of babies born in North Korea's camps for political prisoners.[16]

This lack of concern for the Korean people is a contrast to the image of his father, Kim Il Sung. Kim Jong Il reportedly acknowledges only one occasion where he disobeyed the Great Leader:

> Only once have I disobeyed President Kim Il Sung. The President said, "Can you shave off some defense spending and divert it for the people's livelihoods?" I responded, "I am afraid not. Given the military pressure from the U.S., the Korean people must bear the hardship a little longer." How much pain I felt at my failure to live up to the expectations of the Pres-

ident who is concerned about raising the living standards of the people! (Kim 2001, 305)

The gap between the self-indulgent lifestyle of Kim and his inner circle in Pyongyang and the privation of his people, and, for that matter, that of the lower-level military, is extreme. Kim regularly calls for sacrifice from the Korean people in pursuit of the mission of reunification, but the lack of sacrifice from the Dear Leader and his inner circle is striking. Although information is tightly controlled, penetrating the information barriers about the leadership's lifestyle could undermine the legitimacy of Kim's leadership and his capacity to sustain the public psychology that allows the nation to be on a continual war footing.

CREATIVE SELF-IMAGE

Kim thinks of himself as a highly creative and artistic individual, and he welcomes creative ideas as long as they do not clash with his opinions or threaten his control. He especially appreciates novel ideas for earning greater foreign currency, manipulating the appearance of Pyongyang's architecture, and generally acquiring major benefits at minimal cost (Baird 2003). Kim has a movie collection rumored to be between ten and twenty thousand tapes; his view of the world, the West in particular, has probably been heavily influenced by the film industry. A personal favorite is reported to be *The Godfather* (reportedly also Saddam Hussein's favorite movie). As a result of his fondness for movies, one of Kim's pet projects has been the creation of a North Korean movie industry. In 1978 Kim Jong Il reportedly orchestrated the kidnapping of Choe Un-hui, his favorite South Korean actress, and her husband, a noted movie producer. They were taken to North Korea, where they were held for eight years. During this time they were "guests" of Kim Jong Il. The first five years of captivity were devoted to "reeducation," after which they began to make movies for the Dear Leader. Accorded the privileges of the elite in North Korea and allowed closer access to Kim Jong Il than most, they have provided great insight into Kim's personality since their escape in 1986 during a trip to Australia.

Kim was described in Choe's memoir as "A Ferociously Nocturnal Type of Man." She observes that Yi Han-yong wrote in his memoirs:

"Kim Jong Il wakes up around noon, works deep into the night, and returns to the official residence at dawn the following day. That is the pattern of his life. He has his dinner sometime between 11 p.m. and midnight." Ko Yong-hwan wrote: "He almost never works during the day. He works from 11 in the evening to 5 in the morning." Kim Jong Il certainly is a night owl, as these men indicate in their memoirs.[17]

According to some reports, Kim likes to stage fights between soldiers or security agents à la gladiators of the Roman Empire and creates strange contests for his entertainment (Oh and Hassig 2000, 94). In one such contest participants were reportedly required to change back and forth between army and navy uniforms, with the losers ordered to shave their heads or go home naked.[18] On one occasion, he reportedly ordered a senior officer who had annoyed him to strip at a public function and sent him home naked. Putting down his subordinates through public humiliation seems to be a consistent theme in Kim Jong Il's interpersonal relations, perhaps reassuring himself that he is in control as he puts others down.

EMOTIONAL VOLATILITY

Kim Jong Il is rumored to be extremely emotional, volatile, and unpredictable in his behavior. Impulsive, he expects to be obeyed immediately. He is said to yell at subordinates and to order the execution of officials who displease him. This creates a sycophantic leadership circle, with his subordinates often lying to him about the deteriorating economic and social conditions. An issue that has been addressed by several defectors is Kim's apparent disregard for traditional Korean society. His characteristic manner of talking to people with his hands in his pockets or clasped behind his back is said to reflect his lack of respect for elders, a serious offense in North Korea.

He is apparently very concerned with appearances, although he prefers to stay out of the public eye as much as possible and is sometimes even described as a recluse. In contrast to his father, who seemed at ease with large crowds and comfortable with people, Kim has been likened to the Wizard of Oz, "remaining out of sight, pulling levers from behind a screen."[19] He has rarely spoken in public; his speech, "Glory to the Heroic Korean People's Army," delivered at the end of a two-hour military display in 1992, was the first time he is known to have spoken in public. Even his speeches on TV and radio are read by narrators.[20]

Kim reportedly takes on "special projects" or pet interests. He was reportedly driving through Pyongyang and noticed a female traffic officer (the beauty of female traffic officers in Pyongyang has been frequently noted by the few visitors to the city and by defectors alike) who appeared to be cold in her uniform skirt. According to the story, Kim was so moved by this that he immediately ordered new designs and then issued new uniforms for all the traffic officers in Pyongyang. This micromanagement is characteristic: he is reportedly engaged in the minutest details and conducts "surprise" visits, much as his father did before him. Although these visits are to be surprises, according to reports, workers are instructed to clean offices and wear their best clothes for the visits, which reportedly last only a few minutes.

Kim, who has been officially described as extremely intelligent, creative, and artistic, is described as responsible for much of the architectural design of Pyongyang, and as playing the piano and violin as well as directing the chamber orchestra that plays at his parties (Oh and Hassig 2000, 99). A true Renaissance man! Despite his lack of public speaking, North Korean sources portray him as articulate and quick-witted. Such contradictions are not unique, for it is extremely difficult to separate Kim Jong Il the man from Kim Jong Il the myth created by North Korean propaganda.

Reports about Kim Jong Il's work and management style vary greatly, although observers uniformly describe him as a micromanager. According to many reports he works late into the night, often through the night, preferring to sleep during the day, but this obviously contradicts stories about regular late night parties.

Control over Military Establishment

Kim has concentrated his control over North Korea through his position as chairman of the National Defense Council and has worked hard to court the military by courting important military leaders. Oh Jin-u reportedly was one of the beneficiaries of this strategy. A partisan comrade of his father and the defense minister of North Korea—and thus the third most powerful man in the country under Kim Jong Il—Oh received expensive gifts and attention from Kim, winning Kim the ardent support of Oh, who often accompanied Kim on visits to military installations. Having Oh as such a close supporter must have further legitimized Kim in the eyes of the North Korean military.

It is not clear how the National Defense Commission conducts its business, although Kim retains absolute authority. Kim has consolidated his control over North Korea and appears to be the ultimate decision maker on government policy. He reportedly maintains a small, close-knit circle of advisors and allies on whom he relies, although he probably only fully trusts his sister and brother-in-law. His younger sister, Kim Jyung Hee, is among the most trusted of his advisors. She heads the light-industry division of the Workers Party Economic Policy Audit Department and is one of the few people in North Korea who has direct and unlimited access to Kim Jong Il.[21] Her husband, Chang Song-taek, the senior vice-director of the KWP's Organization and Guidance Department, is also a trusted advisor. Chang manages KWP headquarters operations, "the procurement of goods and cash for Kim Jong Il, and smuggling by diplomats" (Baird 2003, 7).

Another crucial member of Kim's inner circle is Vice Marshal Cho Myong-nok, second to Kim on the National Defense Commission and political commissar of the Korean People's Army. It was Cho who met in October 2000 with President Clinton, Secretary of State Madeleine Albright, and Secretary of Defense William Cohen. It is believed that during his years as commander of the air force, he negotiated the transfer of missiles and missile-related technology to Iran (Baird 2003).

Three other key advisors for Kim are Kim Yong-sun, Kim Ki-nam, and Kim Kuk-tae. Kim Yong-sun is the KWP secretary responsible for rapprochement with Seoul, South Korean investment in the North, and covert programs against South Korea; Kim Ki-nam is a specialist in propaganda; and Kim Kuk-tae is a specialist in personnel affairs. Kim Ki-nam and Kim Kuk-tae are both longtime KWP members.

Kim's second tier of advisors is made up of representatives of the Korean People's Army and the KWP. This group includes the minister of the People's Armed Forces and the Korean People's Army chief of general staff; the KWP secretaries and department chiefs for Chagang Province, weapons production, and general military affairs; the head of the General Staff's Operations Bureau; and the two deputy commissars of the KPA.

The Man behind the Mask

Being the son and designated successor of a major political leader is a daunting task. Being the son and successor of a charismatic leader and nation founder of almost godlike stature is overwhelming. Unlike his father, Kim Jong Il grew up in luxurious surroundings, pampered and raised to be special. This is the formative recipe for a narcissistic personality, with a grandiose self-concept and difficulties with empathy. Kim Jong Il was in charge of the propaganda machine and directed the cult of personality around his father as well as that stressing the continuity between his father and himself. He must be particularly conscious of the magnitude of the myths that he has played a central role in creating, particularly his identity with his father. Unlike his father, Kim Jong Il did *not* persist in the long struggle, did *not* found a nation, and did *not* shape its governing philosophy based on his experiences as a guerrilla leader. Kim Jong Il must have stood in awe of his father, and while the prodigious propaganda machine he directed has stressed the seamless continuity from father to son, under Kim Jong Il's arrogant facade there assuredly is profound self-doubt and insecurity. This suggests that his narcissism is a fragile narcissism, quite primitive in nature, rather than a relatively healthy narcissism.

Indeed, the characteristics he displays indicate that he has the core characteristics of the most dangerous personality disorder, malignant narcissism. This is characterized by:

- such extreme grandiosity and self-absorption, there is no capacity to empathize with others. This is reflected in his lack of empathy with his own people, as well his difficulties in understanding his principal adversaries, the United States, South Korea, and Japan, and can be associated with major political/military miscalculation.
- no constraint of conscience. Kim's only loyalty is to himself and his own survival. He also recognizes the need to sustain his inner circle's perquisites and indulgent lifestyle, for he requires their support, but he combines this lavish indulgence with humiliation to maintain his control over his leadership circle.
- paranoid orientation, not in the sense of being psychotic, out of touch with reality, but always on guard, feeling ready to be betrayed, seeing himself surrounded by enemies.
- unconstrained aggression. He will use whatever aggression is necessary, without qualm of conscience, be it to eliminate an individual or to strike out at a particular group.

Other characteristics of the narcissistic personality also contribute to Kim's flawed leadership performance and distortions in decision making. They include:

- Great insecurity, preoccupation with one's own brilliance or appearance. Because of the need to be perfect, it is difficult to impart new information to him, and he reacts negatively to criticism.
- Extreme sensitivity to being slighted.
- A tendency to surround himself with sycophants who tell him what he wants to hear, rather than what he needs to hear, making him out of touch with political reality.
- Overoptimism about his own chances, and a tendency to devalue the adversary.
- Saying or promising whatever is useful at the moment, with words that are strictly instrumental, to accomplish what is necessary; apparently sincere agreements are easily changed or disregarded. With reference to Kim, the violation of the Agreed Framework, which

stopped North Korea's nuclear weapons program in return for food and oil supplies, is an excellent example.

- Flawed interpersonal relationships. A tendency to see others as the extension of the self, with little capacity to appreciate the needs of others. Loyalty is accordingly a one-way street. Moreover, individuals who are seen to be powerful in their own right are perceived as a threat and are eliminated.
- Scapegoating when plans don't work out. Since narcissists must be seen as perfect, when one of Kim's plans misfires, the problem is not the concept but the execution. Thus, Kim is ready to scapegoat when his plans don't work out.

Kim was watched over by many of his father's peers: They revered Kim Il Sung but may have had difficulties adjusting to Kim Jong Il's increasing assumption of the mantle of power. Kim may have sensed their discomfiture with him and was aware that they did not automatically give him the same allegiance they accorded his father. Questions about their loyalty probably encouraged Kim to replace many of the old guard with younger peers who owed their position totally to him.

We have no solid information about the working of Kim Jong Il's inner circle, whether there is a free give and take, whether he can reveal uncertainty and ask for advice, and whether he is open to constructive criticism. Although fragile egos rarely are open to admitting uncertainty and ignorance, and are not usually open to criticism, in the service of providing intelligence shrewd advisers can often help shape the decision making of the narcissistic leader.

Although reportedly a micromanager in most aspects of his leadership, he devotes little or no time in his weekly schedule to economic matters. He has said:

> The Leader, while alive, told me that I must never get involved in economic issues. If I get involved in the economic issues, I can never take part in the party's activities or military activities. He said this to me over and over so that I do not forget the advice. [passage omitted in original] He told me I must let party officials and the administration's economic officials take charge of economic issues.[22]

This quote, from a secret speech he gave to senior officials following an inspection tour of Kim Il Sung University on December 7, 1996—the fiftieth anniversary of the university's founding—can be taken as reflecting an artful shifting of responsibility for economic problems to his subordinates.

We don't know the degree to which he is aware of the magnitude of his country's economic difficulties. Is he aware that less than 10 percent of the factories in North Korea are currently operating? He is assuredly well aware that South Korea surpasses North Korea in all aspects except in military capabilities, although he criticized South Korea, saying all that South Korea industry is doing is assembling products, using parts imported from other countries. But, on the other hand, in 1984 he frankly admitted that 60 percent of North Korean factories were not operating.[23]

No Core Organizing Ideas or Principles

Because his position flows from his identification with and succession to his father, Kim Jong Il cannot appear to abandon founding principles of the republic, both juche and the ultimate goal of reunification of the Korean Peninsula. But if we accept the premise that his basic loyalty is to himself (and by necessity his inner circle) and that their survival with the perquisites of power is his number-one priority, how he lives up to his father's core principles is subject to interpretation. One can pay lip service to these principles while modifying them significantly from their initial intent, not being bound by them in a doctrinaire fashion. After all, the self-reliance of juche is not consistent with a program of seeking foreign assistance. Like relationships, ideas are instrumental for the consummate narcissist, and if they are no longer useful they can be radically modified or discarded.

Although Kim Jong Il does not possess core organizing ideas or principles, he is in many ways a captive of his oft-declared public policy, for he employs the twin doctrines of juche and reunification to call for sacrifice on the part of the North Korean people.

Inherited Charisma

Charisma is not a quality of an individual but a property of a relationship between a leader and his wounded followers. The charismatic leader–follower relationship between Kim Il Sung and his followers was extremely powerful. Kim Il Sung worked at shaping the cult of personality surrounding him, and his followers identified with his career-long dedication to his nation. Kim Jong Il, in his role as director of the propaganda ministry, continued to foster the myth of Kim Il Sung and of his own identification with his father. Like his father, Kim Jong Il has no constraint of conscience. Like his father, Kim has a penchant for cruelty.

But charisma is not automatically inheritable. And despite the adroit management of internal information, Kim Jong Il is not identical with his father. Recent defectors have become angry at implied criticism of the Dear Leader by their interrogators; the power of the charismatic relationship persists. Nevertheless, the gap between the myth and the man, between the kleptocratic, self-indulgent leadership and the starving masses, remains a major vulnerability. A sustained information operations campaign designed to penetrate the closed society and undermine the sustaining myth of Kim Jong Il can play a crucial role in deterring and countering North Korea's military aspirations, and particularly its weapons of mass destruction.

Because of Kim's self-oriented focus and lack of constraint of conscience, the only diplomatic stance that will deter him is one based on self-interest. He will regularly be calculating, "What's in it for me and my senior leaders? What can we get away with? What are the negative consequences for us?" Clarity of positive *and* negative consequences, and a consistency in implementing them, is key to effective coercive diplomacy. There must be clearly defined limits and consequences. This is crucial in dealing with Kim Jong Il and his regime, both in restraining any impulses toward aggressive action and in deterring his aggressive military stance, with particular reference to his weapons of mass destruction program.

13

Concluding Observations

The tension is palpable at this writing. The Middle East seems to be going up in flames. Meeting surprisingly little resistance, coalition forces swiftly removed the Saddam Hussein regime from power, in a campaign lasting less than four weeks (March 19–April 14, 2003). At that time, coalition forces turned their attention to stabilizing the country, which has proved to be a much more difficult task than securing victory. The aftermath has been increasingly violent, with mounting resistance to the perceived U.S. occupation. While forty-two of the fifty-five senior most wanted Iraqi leaders in the so-called deck of cards have been captured or killed, Saddam Hussein remains at large, periodically issuing calls on audiotapes for a "holy war" against the invaders, and an increasingly organized insurgency brings daily coalition casualties. Moreover, there is fear that Islamic extremists are entering Iraq and that it is becoming a new terrorist focal point. Widening the targets of violence, a truck bomb was detonated in front of the UN compound in Baghdad on August 19, 2003, killing more than twenty people, including the personal representative of the secretary general, Sergio Vieira de Mello.

That same day, after an all-too-brief seven-week respite from violence in Israel, the U.S.-sponsored road map for peace was shattered by a Hamas bombing of a crowded bus returning from the Western Wall, resulting in the deaths of twenty-three people, including several small children. Israel responded with targeted assassinations of members of Hamas's senior leadership, resulting in a formal renunciation of the cease-fire by Hamas, Islamic Jihad, and Fatah's military wing, the Al Aqsa Martyrs Brigade.

As in Iraq, creating a stable postwar climate in Afghanistan has proved to be much more difficult than securing the victory. And, like Saddam Hussein, Osama bin Laden remains at large, issuing periodic audiotapes to his followers worldwide encouraging a jihad of global proportions.

Saddam's fellow member of the axis of evil, Kim Jong Il, defiantly announces that North Korea already possesses nuclear weapons and is intending to rapidly increase its nuclear arsenal. Meanwhile, on trial in The Hague for crimes against humanity, Slobodan Milosevic plays to his Serbian supporters, defiantly rejecting the legitimacy of the international tribunal and righteously defending his campaign of ethnic cleansing.

The Rise of Rogue Leaders and Outlaw Nations

The end of the Cold War has been destabilizing, producing not a "peace dividend" but an unpredictable international climate in which major political crises frequently have been precipitated by rogue leaders of outlaw nations. The relatively stable and predictable superpower rivalry has been replaced by a series of regional conflicts that are often started by the actions of previously unknown or poorly understood leaders. There has been a proliferation of destructive power, with more destructive power in the hands of nations with hostile agendas toward the United States. The most worrisome nations—Iran, Iraq (before the war of 2003), and North Korea—are ruled by unpredictable dictatorships. The headlines of the past few years have been dominated by such names as Saddam Hussein, Osama bin laden, Kim Jong Il, and Slobodan Milosevic. The righteous rage that hate-mongering demagogues have been able to mobilize in justifying their violent campaigns threatens international stability.

Several of these leaders either already have or are seeking weapons of mass destruction. During the Gulf crisis of 1990–1991, a nuclear-armed Saddam Hussein would have entirely changed the dynamics of the conflict. Former Secretary of Defense Richard Perry referred to the "nightmare scenario" of a nuclear-armed North Korea, a nightmare that has become reality.

Avoiding Deadly Conflict

In addressing the challenge of effective coercive diplomacy, the distinguished American political scientist Alex George stressed the importance of having clear models of the adversaries' psychology. As with information campaigns, diplomacy in a conflictual situation cannot proceed effectively without clear and accurate models of leadership psychology. This theme was carried forward in the work of the Carnegie Commission on Preventing Deadly Conflict, of which Alex George was a member (Hamburg, George, and Ballentine 1999). They have stressed the critical role of leadership, both in promoting deadly conflict and in avoiding it.

In order to effectively counter leaders such as Saddam Hussein, Kim Jong Il, and Slobodan Milosevic as they promote deadly conflict, clear actor-specific models of their psychology and decision making are an absolute requisite.

The bombing of the Pentagon, the twin towers of the World Trade Center in Manhattan, and of the American embassies in Kenya and Tanzania, brought vividly home the dangers of the new face of terrorism. A new form of terrorism, transnational terrorism, has emerged, with a particularly dangerous movement under the leadership of Osama bin Laden, who has threatened to employ weapons of mass destruction in his attacks against U.S. targets. As the barriers to mass casualty terrorism have weakened, the prospect of a major terrorist attack using chemical, biological, radiological, or nuclear weapons has become all too real. But even more terrifying is the capacity of the destructive charismatic terrorist leader, Osama bin Laden, to inspire his followers to give their lives for the cause of radical Islam, to "kill in the name of God," and of the suicide bomb commanders of Hamas and Islamic Jihad to inspire their youthful charges to carry out "martyrdom operations" against Israel.

Information Warfare and the Revolution in Military Affairs

Although low-intensity conflict will continue to be an important element of the security environment in the twenty-first century, in considering the changing face of warfare, information has been identified by senior defense strategists as the central element in the security environment. Who controls information controls the battlefield. The centrality of information in its strategic considerations, both offensively and defensively, is being called a revolution in military affairs.

The battle for control of the information battlefield was largely left uncontested as Saddam Hussein effectively framed the conflict for his radical Arab constituents and enhanced his reputation and leadership standing. By his control of the information environment, Slobodan Milosevic effectively countered the military superiority of the NATO air campaign by framing the contest to increase his support and steel the will of the Serbian people. Identifying himself with Prince Lazar, the Serbian hero of the battle of Kosovo Polje in 1389, and with Tito, the heroic leader of the Yugoslav partisans during World War II, he identified President Clinton as Hitler and NATO with the Nazis. His information operations were masterful. The ability of Saddam Hussein and Slobodan Milosevic adroitly and successfully to manipulate the information environment adversely affected the course of these asymmetric campaigns.

Consider how rapidly the American public's support for the intervention in Somalia was eroded by events. Initially, the televised spectacle of starving Somali children deeply touched the heartstrings of the American public, which strongly supported the humanitarian intervention. But the sight of American soldiers' bodies being hauled behind Somali warlord's jeeps rapidly led to pressure to withdraw, lest further loss of American life ensue. Whether purposeful or not, this assuredly was a highly effective psychological operation by the Somali warlord Mohammad Farah Aideed. And this event was assuredly attended to closely by Saddam Hussein, confirming his impression that the United States still suffered from a "Vietnam syndrome."

The rapidity with which international conflicts can "go critical," and the catastrophic consequences of miscalculation, make it imperative that accurate evaluations of a leader's psychology be developed swiftly and be monitored closely during crises. One cannot influence an adversary one does not understand. What deters one opponent may be an incitement for another. At heart, the goal of coercive diplomacy is psychological: it must incorporate an understanding of significant psychological elements, and use them, for maximal effectiveness.

Powerful psychopolitical forces seemingly beyond our control threaten to engulf us. My goal in this book has been to contribute to understanding the basis for these powerful forces. In addition to considering the key role of leadership—illustrated by political personality profiles of key leaders, such as Fidel Castro, Saddam Hussein, Kim Jong Il, and Slobodan Milosevic—the psychology of followership has also been addressed. One cannot address the psychopolitics of hatred in Eastern Europe in the post–Cold War era without considering the psychological vulnerability of the wounded population to the seductive siren song of hate-mongering leaders. One cannot understand the attraction of the violent path of terrorism without understanding the psychopolitical context in which these movements flourish. One cannot understand the destructive charismatic leadership of Osama bin Laden without addressing the psychology of the alienated, despairing Islamic youth to whom he appeals.

The psychological foundations of man's inhumanity to man are deeply embedded within our collective psychology. As the world seemingly careens out of control, it is the powerful forces of personality and political behavior that drive these violent movements. But if these forces that are out of control at their genocidal extreme underlie the dreadful extremity of ethnic cleansing, mastery of these forces will help mend the wounds that tear us asunder. And if some of the most evil moments in human history arise from destructive-charismatic leader–follower relationships, it is reparative-charismatic leader–follower relationships that have produced some of humanity's most heroic achievements.

This book has addressed the impact of personality on political behavior. At this writing, the international community is simultaneously wrestling with threats from North Korea, al Qaeda, and the chaotic aftermath of the war in Iraq. To attempt to assess the decision making of Iraq, North Korea, and al-Qaeda without considering the political psychology of their principal leaders—Saddam Hussein, Kim Jong Il, and Osama bin Laden—would be a travesty. For in these two leader-dominant societies and the leader-dominant transnational terrorist organization, the central role of leader personality and its impact on political behavior is of paramount importance.

Appendix

The Role of Political Personality Profiles
in the Camp David Summit

The Center for the Analysis of Personality and Political Behavior, of which I was the founding director, provided in-depth political psychology assessments of foreign leaders for the president and other senior officials for high-level negotiations, political-military crises, and for estimative intelligence.[1] For summit meetings and other high-level negotiations, comprehensive in-depth political personality profiles that placed the leader in his longitudinal context and provided insights into the historical forces that shaped the leader's political personality were particularly valued by the president and cabinet officials who wanted to understand, "What makes Prime Minister X tick?" Such an occasion was provided by the Camp David negotiations of 1978.

The psychological portraits of Anwar Sadat and Menachem Begin, the "Camp David" profiles, significantly informed and influenced President Jimmy Carter's understanding of the protagonists and the strategy he developed for the conduct of the negotiations. Indeed, according to Carter, they were among the most important influences on the strategy and tactics of his personal diplomacy with Begin and Sadat.

In his presidential memoir, *Keeping Faith* (1983), Carter spoke of the intensity of his study of the backgrounds and personalities of these remarkably different leaders. In August 1978, just prior to the historic Camp David negotiations, Carter had taken a vacation trip to Jackson Hole, Wyoming, to relax before what he knew would be an arduous and testing challenge. After a day of fly fishing for cutthroat trout in the Snake River, Carter immersed himself in psychological analyses of Begin and Sadat:

> Ours would be a new approach, perhaps unprecedented in history. Three leaders of nations would be isolated from the outside world. An intensely personal effort would be required of us. I had to understand these men![2] I

was poring over psychological analyses of two of the protagonists which had been prepared by a team of experts within our intelligence community. This team could write definitive biographies of any important world leader, using information derived from a detailed scrutiny of events, public statements, writings, known medical histories, and interviews with personal acquaintances of the leaders under study. I wanted to know all about Begin and Sadat. What had made them national leaders? What was the root of their ambition? What were their most important goals in life? What events during past years had helped to shape their characters?

What were their religious beliefs? Family relations? State of their health? Political beliefs and constraints? Relations with other leaders? Likely reaction to pressure in a time of crisis? Strengths and weaknesses? Commitments to political constituencies? Attitudes towards me and the United States? Whom did they really trust? What was their attitude toward one another? . . .

From time to time I paused to consider the negotiating strategy I would follow at Camp David; I made careful detailed notes. These few evenings away from Washington were an ideal time for me to concentrate almost exclusively on a single major challenge—peace in the Middle East. During the coming days at Camp David, my studies at the foot of the Grand Tetons were to pay rich dividends. (319–20)

The 1998 declassification of my article, "Personality Profiles in Support of the Camp David Summit" (Post 1979, 1–5), permits public discussion of the personality profiles sent to Carter. The history of the Camp David profiles is discussed in detail because of their historic significance, the first time a detailed consideration of the development and use of the profiles has been presented.

On a visit to CIA headquarters in August 1978, President Carter interrupted a briefing to ask the assembled analysts and intelligence managers how they could help him with the forthcoming summit, which had only recently been announced. He said he wanted to be "steeped in the personalities of Begin and Sadat."

In response to this request, political personality profiles were prepared by the CIA's Center for the Analysis of Personality and Political Behavior (CAPPB).[3] In fact, three profiles were prepared: a profile of Menachem Begin, which called attention to the increasing trend of oppositionism and rigidity in his personality; a profile of Anwar Sadat, which stressed his increasing preoccupation with his role in history and the leverage that could provide in negotiations; and a paper that discussed the implications for negotiations of the contrasting intellectual styles of Begin and Sadat. The profiles were based on detailed psychological studies of the personality and political behavior of Menachem Begin and Anwar Sadat prepared in 1977.

There is often a request for "instant magic" when a coup, assassination, or election upset brings a leader to the fore who is not well known to the foreign policy community, and an in-depth personality assessment of the leader is requested immediately. It is as if all a psychiatrist or psychologist had to do was bring his or her special perspective to bear on a leader and a detailed personality assessment would be forthcoming.

In order to anticipate the needs of the community, CAPPB had regularly surveyed key intelligence consumers, including the National Security Council, the secretary of state, and the secretary of defense, to identify leaders of special interest. Usually this survey would reveal considerable diversity. For the first time, the survey completed in the summer of 1976 revealed across-the-board highest priority interest in one world leader: President Anwar al-Sadat of Egypt.

In developing personality studies, a broad range of data was reviewed. Official and unofficial biographies often provided key background materials and insights as did television, newspaper, and magazine profiles. Although many would have discarded an authorized biography as being biased in a positive direction, the contrast between the authorized and unauthorized biographies was found to be instructive, for it conveyed the difference between the idealized leader as he wished to be seen and the more realistic flesh and blood leader, with all his warts, blemishes, and psychological sensitivities. When there were significant holes in the data or unresolvable conflicts, requirements (requests for information) would be sent to the field (embassies). Often psychologically relevant material was readily available in response to the questions sent to the field, questions that previously had not been asked. Particularly valuable information was obtained from debriefing senior U.S. officials who had had extended contact with the leader in question. Ambassadors and others who had dealt with the leader over time usually had regularly reported on substantive matters, such as economic plans or weapons procurement programs, but rarely had reported on the personality, attitudes, and negotiating style of the leader, knowledge that was subsequently often lost in the transition between administrations.

By integrating interview impressions of officials who had dealt with Sadat with psychobiographic analysis, several important themes emerged. His concern with his role in history, and his preoccupation with "the big picture," coupled with his abhorrence of details, were regularly mentioned. By appealing to Sadat's long-range goals, Secretary of State Henry Kissinger was often able to overcome negotiating impasses over technical details.

The U.S. ambassador to Egypt, Herman Eilts, related an amusing and charming anecdote that epitomized this quality, an anecdote that was rarely reported but which we found quite telling (Post 1979, 3). The occasion was a luncheon hosted by President Sadat just after a breakthrough in negotiations. The two negotiating teams—the Egyptians and Israelis—had been at an impasse over Israel's withdrawal from part of the Sinai Peninsula—which it had captured from Egypt in the 1967 Arab-Israeli War—wrangling over the number and position of troops, where sensors would be placed to warn of violations of the boundaries separating the two sides, and so forth. Responding to Kissinger's skillful urgings to rise above this petty dispute for the sake of history, Sadat had made a grand compromise, overriding the objections of his advisers.

Present at the luncheon were President Sadat, Madame Sadat (an outspoken woman in her own right), Secretary of State Kissinger, and Ambassador Eilts. "Your excellency," said Secretary Kissinger, raising his glass, "without your broad vision of history and your refusal to be bogged down by petty detail, we never would have come to this day." "No, Henry," replied President Sadat, "it was your negotiating skills which brought us to this day." "Oh, no, your Excellency," replied Kissinger, "it was your ability to think in strategic terms that—" At this point, Madame Sadat interrupted with a loud sigh to Ambassador Eilts, "Oh, no, here we go again."

A major conclusion of the study of Sadat addressed the manner in which Sadat's view of himself and this "big picture mentality" interacted:

> Sadat's self-confidence and special view of himself has been instrumental in the development of his innovative foreign policy, as have his flexibility and his capacity for moving out of the cultural insularity of the Arab world. He sees himself as a grand strategist and will make tactical concessions if he is persuaded that his overall goals will be achieved. . . . His self-confidence has permitted him to make bold initiatives, often overriding his advisors' objections. (Post 1979, 3)

So prominent was Sadat's special sense of self that the major study CAPPB produced was titled "Sadat's Messiah Complex." The creative diplomacy of November and December 1977, highlighted by Sadat's historic visit to Jerusalem in which he overrode his advisers' objections, emphasized this central personality quality. When Sadat became the object of intense media attention, giving major interviews to the likes of Walter Cronkite, John Chancellor, and Barbara Walters, it was an explosion of narcissistic supplies (his narcissistic dreams of glory were being fulfilled), and his extreme self-confidence was magnified to grandiose extremes, a phenomenon we initially dubbed "the Barbara Walters syndrome."

Over the succeeding months, Sadat's grandiosity was magnified exponentially. One of the most interesting changes had to do with his sharp increase in the use of the first person singular pronoun. No longer did Sadat speak of the problems with Egypt's economy; he spoke of "my economy." There were accounts suggesting that Sadat would be angered by, and refuse to believe, reports that his goals for Egypt and himself were in trouble. His leadership circle shrank to sycophants who told Sadat only what he wanted to hear, leading him to be increasingly out of touch with political reality. Sadat's grandiosity became so pronounced that the profile prepared for Carter was titled "Sadat's Nobel Prize Complex." In his memoirs, Carter stated that this aspect of Sadat's personality was in the forefront of his thinking:

> Sadat was strong and bold, very much aware of world public opinion and of his role as the most important leader among the Arabs. I always had the impression that he looked on himself as inheriting the mantle of authority from the great pharaohs, and was convinced that he was a man of destiny. (Carter 1983, 328)

In contrast to Sadat, who was well known to a succession of American diplomats, Menachem Begin was virtually unknown when he came to power in a stunning election upset. But there was a rich source of information in the open literature, for in two autobiographical works, *White Nights* and *The Revolt*, Begin had detailed the experiences that had shaped his personality and political attitudes. He emphasized the seminal role of the Holocaust, which was captured in his well-known and oft-repeated phrase, "Never again!" Begin as leader frequently made provocative statements, often precipitated by a reporter's questions, losing sight of the context and of the negative political fallout. Indeed, this trait was reflected throughout his career. In 1929, at the age of sixteen, Begin joined Betar, the nationalist youth movement associated with the Revisionist Zionists. In 1932 he became director of Betar's organization department in Poland, and in 1939 became head of the movement there. When World War II broke out he was arrested by the Russian authorities and in 1940–41 was confined to concentration camps in Siberia and elsewhere. He was released under the terms of the Stalin-Sikorski agreement. In *White Nights*, Begin's account of his political exile in Siberia, he proudly recounts his frequent debates with his Soviet jailers over details of Soviet law, in which he regularly bested his captors with his superior knowledge of their law— something that was quite counterproductive in terms of his own welfare. His focus on detail and legalisms was emphasized in the profile, as was his tendency to oppositionism related to his vow "never again" to yield to superior force.

In his memoir, Carter said he steeped himself in Begin's background.

Believing that Begin also saw himself as a man of destiny, Carter saw Begin as a student of the Bible who insisted on using biblical names, such as Judea and Samaria, for disputed territories to emphasize Israel's entitlement to the land of Israel.

The prominence of these personality differences led to a proposal by CAPPB that one of the dinner symposia periodically hosted by Director of Central Intelligence Admiral Stansfield Turner be devoted to the "Role of Personality in the Middle East Conflict" in the spring of 1978. Participants in this dinner seminar included a number of senior officials who had been intimately involved in Middle East negotiations: Ambassador-at-large Alfred Atherton, ambassador to Egypt Herman Eilts, Assistant Secretary of State for Near East Affairs Harold Saunders, and Dr. William Quandt, the National Security Council's senior Near East specialist. The seminar was purposefully free of discussion of policy and substantive differences, focusing only on the striking differences in the personalities of the two protagonists and how they would affect the negotiating process.

How could two individual leaders, who were so different psychologically, participate in simultaneous negotiations? This was the subject of the third paper prepared for Carter concerned with the problematic implications for simultaneous negotiations of the contrasting cognitive styles of Sadat, the "big picture" man with an abhorrence for detail, and Begin, the legalistic wordsmith consumed with detail and precision, with a tendency to become embroiled in power struggles. This paper informed and influenced the middleman role Carter played in these intensely personal negotiations, while minimizing direct contact between the two protagonists, and the manner in which he worked at narrowing the gap between Sadat and Begin. Carter was concerned that "his [Begin's] preoccupation with language, names, and terms could severely impede free-flowing talk" (Carter 1983, 330). On one occasion, he cleverly put his own concern with Begin's penchant for details and the gap between Sadat's and Begin's style into Sadat's mouth:

> As he was preparing to leave after our stilted and somewhat superficial discussion, I told him that Sadat had expressed a concern about Begin's preoccupation with details at the expense of the major issues. Begin looked up quickly and said, "I can handle both."(330)

After his diplomatic triumph, the president conveyed his appreciation to the Central Intelligence Agency for the intelligence support provided him and singled out the personality profiles for special praise: "After spending thirteen days with the two principals, I wouldn't change a word" (Post 1979, 1). The Camp David profiles highlighted the value of leader personality assessment in support of government policy, emphasizing their special value in summit negotiations.

Certainly the recognition given by President Jimmy Carter of the value of the Camp David profiles of Menachem Begin and Anwar al-Sadat was a transformational event for the program. No longer would the in-depth studies prepared by the Center for the Analysis of Personality and Political Behavior be considered avant-garde. Now they would be considered a requisite for each summit meeting and a required resource for managing politico-military crises.

Notes

2. When Personality Affects Political Behavior

1. Kramer (1991) persuasively documents this point.
2. This section draws on Post 1980, 1984.
3. *Los Angeles Times*, June 25, 1989.
4. Ibid.
5. *Asia Report*, FBIS, November 19, 1989.
6. *New York Times*, November 19, 1989.

3. The Psychopolitics of Illness in High Office

1. This chapter draws significantly on Post and Robins (1993); a paper presented to the Working Group on Presidential Disability, The Carter Center, Atlanta, Georgia, January 1995, "Disorders Affecting Cognition and Behavior and the Twenty Fifth Amendment: Implications for Presidential Disability"; and on a chapter elaborating on this theme, "Broken Hearts and Broken Minds: Psychiatric Disorders and the 25th Amendment," in *Managing Crisis: Presidential Disability and the Twenty-fifth Amendment*, ed. Robert Gilbert (New York: Fordham University Press, 2000).
2. This section draws on Robert Dallek, "The Medical Ordeals of JFK," *Atlantic Monthly* (December 2002): 49–61; Lawrence K. Altman and Todd S. Purdum, "In Kennedy File, A Portrait of Illness and Pain," *New York Times*, November 17, 2002, based on an interview with Dallek and a physician, Jeffrey A. Kelman, who is familiar with the medical records; and Robert Dallek, *An Unfinished Life: John F. Kennedy, 1917–1963* (Boston: Little, Brown and Co., 2003).
3. Much of this section is drawn from Arnold A. Rogow, *James Forrestal: A Study of Personality, Politics, and Policy* (New York: Macmillan, 1963).

4. Terminal Leadership: Effects of Mortal Illness on Political Behavior

1. The specific kind of malignancy from which the shah was suffering was not definitively established at first, for the shah was only given screening blood tests and other diagnostic tests.
2. Demonstrating the sense of urgency that consumed the shah, Seyyed Nasr, former president of Iran's Aryamehr University, recalls meeting with him in late 1973 to make a major budgetary request for a new campus. Expecting the shah to counter with a lower figure, Nasr

was startled when the shah replied, "You may have it all, and even more. But spend it as quickly as you can" (personal communication with Seyyed Nasr, May 14, 1992).

3. The following depiction of Marcos's political career draws heavily on Sterling Seagraves's book, *Marcos Dynasty*.

4. Cited in M. Khalid, *Nimeiri and the Revolution of Mid-May* (London: KPI, 1985): 262.

5. The following is drawn from Jerrold M. Post, "Yasir Arafat: Identities in Conflict," in *Yasir Arafat: Psychological Profile and Strategic Analysis*, ed. Shaul Kimhl, Shmuel Even, and Jerrold Post (Herzliya, Israel: The Interdisciplinary Center; and the American Jewish Committee, May 2002).

5. The Impact of Crisis-Induced Stress on Policy Makers

1. The manner in which flawed perceptions and decision making can contribute to international conflict has been a preoccupying concern of several authors. A few of the important contributions in this area are: Axelrod 1976; Blight 1986; Blight and Welch 1988; Bonham and Shapiro 1986; Brecher 1977; Deutsch 1983; George 1974, 1979, 1986; C. Hermann 1972; M. Hermann 1979; Hermann and Hermann 1975; Holsti 1972, 1986; Holsti and George 1975; Jervis 1976; Jervis, Lebow, and Stein 1985; Lebow 1981, 1987; Stein and Tanter 1980, 1988; Tetlock 1983, 1986; Walker 1983, 1987; Wiegele 1973, 1976, 1977; Wiegele and Plowman 1974, 1990.

Most of these authors have focused on the role of cognitive factors and belief systems, with significantly less attention being devoted to the role of affects, drives, and personality factors. Scholars contributing to the field include David Winter (Winter and Stewart 1976), who has developed measures of important drives associated with political behavior (need power, need affiliation, need achievement); S. G. Walker (1987) has explored the relationship between drives and belief systems; George Marcus (2000), who has particularly focused on the role of affect in political behavior; and Jerrold M. Post and Philip Rogers (1988) have investigated the relationship between personality types and belief systems.

6: The Mind of the Terrorist

1. This chapter is based on my paper, "Individual, Group, and Organizational Psychology of Political Terrorism," presented in summary form at the 1996 annual meeting of the American Psychiatric Association, and on my testimony on "Terrorist Psychology and Decision Making" presented to the Senate Armed Services Committee in November 2001. It draws on my previous articles on terrorist psychology, including "Notes on a Psychodynamic Theory of Terrorism," *Terrorism* 7, no. 3 (1984); "Hostilité, Conformité, Fraternité: The Group Dynamics of Terrorist Behavior," *International Journal of Group Psychotherapy* 36, no. 2 (April 1986); "Rewarding Fire with Fire? Effects of Retaliation on Terrorist Group Dynamics," in *Contemporary Trends in World Terrorism*, ed. A. Kurz (New York: Pergamon Press, 1987); "Prospects for Nuclear Terrorism: Psychological Incentives and Constraints," in *Preventing Nuclear Terrorism*, ed. P. Leventhal and Y. Alexander (Lexington, Mass.: Lexington Press, 1987); "Group and Organizational Dynamics of International Terrorism: Implications for Counter-Terrorist Policy," in *Contemporary Research on Terrorism*, ed. Paul Wilkinson and A. M. Stewart (Aberdeen, Scotland: Aberdeen University Press, 1987); " 'It's Us against Them': The Basic Assumptions of Political Terrorists," in *Irrationality in Organizational Life*, ed. J. Kranz (Washington, D.C.: A. K. Rice Institute Press, 1987); "Terrorist Psycho-logic: Terrorist Behavior as a Product of Psychological Forces," in *Origins of Terrorism*, ed. W. Reich (Cambridge: Cambridge University Press, 1990); and "Differentiating Terrorist Psychologies: The Basis for a Rational Differentiated Antiterrorist Policy," *Academic Research in Terrorism and Public Policy*, proceedings of a conference by the Harry Frank Guggenheim Foundation (Santa Fe, New Mexico, 1991).

2. See J. M. Post, E. Sprinzak, and L. M. Denny, "The Terrorists in Their Own Words: Interviews with Thirty-five Incarcerated Middle Eastern Terrorists," *Terrorism and Political Violence* 15, no. 1 (spring 2003): 171–84.

3. This section is particularly informed by the writings of John Esposito, Gilles Keppel, and Emmanuel Sivan.

4. See Canetti (1962) for a discussion of Islam as a religion of war.

5. "Not equal are those Believers who sit [at home] and receive no hurt, and those who strive and fight in the cause of Allah with their goods and their persons. Allah hath granted a grade higher to those who strive and fight with their goods and persons than those who sit [at home] unto all [in faith]. But those who strive and fight hath he distinguished . . . by a special reward" (Koran 4:95). Also see 47:4.

6. Interview with Sadiq al-Musawi, July 28, 1986; cited in Kramer 1990, 151.

7. Interview with Ayatollah Sayyid Muhammad Husayn Fadlallah, *Politique internationale* (Paris) 29 (autumn 1985): 268; cited in Kramer 1990, 145.

8. Quoted in the introduction to the Charter of the Islamic Resistance Movement (HAMAS) of Palestine (Maqdsi 1993). The charter was translated by Muhammad Maqdsi for the Islamic Association for Palestine, Dallas, Texas, 1990.

9. The following analysis comes principally from Abu-Amir (1993) and Jubran and Drake (1993).

10. After considerable negotiations, the PLO managed to effect an accommodation with Hamas with the result that in the January 1996 election the PLO apparently brought Hamas under substantial control.

11. This section draws largely on Keppel 1994 (154–70), and Sprinzak 1987.

12. See the statement of one of the radicals, Yehuda Etzion, as quoted in Sprinzak 1987.

13. Etzion, *From the Laws of the Existence to the Laws of Destiny* (in Hebrew), *Nequda* 75 (1984), 26, cited in Sprinzak 1987, 207.

14. This section is drawn from chapters 8 and 9 of Robins and Post 1997. The section on the background and development of Christian Identity draws largely on Barkun 1994.

15. A number of publications were particularly helpful in addressing right-wing extremism. They include Aho 1990, 1995; Barkun 1994; Lake 1985; Merkel and Weinberg 1993; Sargent 1995; Sederberg 1994; and R. A. Wood 1996.

16. Robert Wood, personal communication, Fargo, North Dakota, August 16, 1995; Wood 1996, 219.

17. Wood 1996 (218), drawing on Finch 1983, Barker 1986, and Zeskind 1986. Also see L. Weinberg, "The Radical Right and Varieties of Right-Wing Politics in the United States," an unpublished manuscript cited by Wood 1996, 219.

18. Major sources for this section are Audsley 1985, Yaeger 1994, and Wood 1996.

19. As with other extremist groups of the radical right, there are many overlapping memberships. Posse members are affiliated with such radical groups as the Covenant, the Sword, and the Arm of the Lord; the Ku Klux Klan; the National Party for Emancipation of the White Seed (NEWS); Aryan Nations; the Order; and the American Nazi Party. Posse chapters frequently use such titles as "Patriots," "Constitutionalists," "Educated Citizens of Iowa," "America First," and "Protection Society of [XXX] County" to confuse and evade law-enforcement authorities. Some of the names associated with the Posse are Christian Liberty Academy, New York Patriots, National Patriots Association, Christian Conservative Churches, and the Arizona Patriots. See Yaeger 1994, 17.

20. Yaeger 1994, 17. As is so often the case with organizations that deny the legitimacy of the government they are opposing, the Posse has invented a legalistic rhetoric in describing how it will execute its opponents:

> In some instances of record, the law provides for the following prosecution of officials of government who commit criminal acts or who violate their oaths of office. He shall be removed by the Posse to the most populated intersection of streets in the Township and at high noon hung by the neck, the body remaining until sundown, as an example to those who would subvert the law (Yaeger 1994, 18).

21. Lake 1985, 97. Although almost all the members of the militias are white, and although many of the texts they mention have a strong anti-Semitic and racist character, not all militias or militia members are racists.

22. The excellent discussion "Right-Wing Extremism and the Problem of Rural Unrest" by Robert Wood (1996) and an extensive interview with Wood were especially helpful in informing this section, as were several of the books and articles on extremism cited above. In addition, this section draws on investigative reporting in the wake of the 1995 Oklahoma City bombing, primarily from the *New York Times* and the *Washington Post*.

23. The conspiracy theorist Phillips O'Halloran, a physician, has published an article that provides a detailed description of "The Syringe Implantable Biochip," which he characterizes as a "fearsome potential threat in the surveillance arsenal." The chip emits low-frequency FM waves that would provide "information on the exact location of the 'chipee': his latitude, longitude, and elevation to within a few feet anywhere on the planet." O'Halloran (1994) cited in McHugh, April 29, 1995.

24. R. W. Mengel, "Terrorism and New Technologies of Destruction: An Overview of the Potential Risk," in *Disorders and Terrorism: Report of the Task Force on Disorders and Terrorism*, 443–73. U.S. National Advisory Committee on Criminal Justice Standards and Goals. Washington, D.C.: U.S. Government Printing Office, 1977.

25. Post, Sprinzak, and Denny, "Terrorists in Their Own Words."

7. The Loss of Enemies: Fragmenting Identities and Ethnic/Nationalist Hatred in Eastern Europe

1. This chapter is drawn from my article, "The Loss of Enemies, Fragmenting Identities, and the Resurgence of Ethnic/Nationalist Hatred and Anti-Semitism in Eastern Europe," *Journal for the Psychoanalysis of Culture and Society* 1, no. 2 (fall 1996).

2. A major contributor to political psychology is the psychoanalyst Vamik Volkan. In his book *The Need to Have Enemies and Allies*, Volkan traces the roots of international conflict to the crib, persuasively demonstrating that fear and hatred of the stranger is deeply rooted in the human psyche. The theoretical formulations in this chapter draw from Volkan's work.

3. The self-object is a psychoanalytic term conceptualized by Heinz Kohut that refers to objects with which the self has identified that are in effect incorporated into the self-concept.

4. Melanie Klein uses the term "objects" to refer not only to persons and physical objects but also to abstract concepts such as capitalism and racial homogeneity. We all have these "objects" in our minds (the idea of capitalism, the idea of the president), and to the extent that our behavior is determined by psychological forces, it is determined by the nature and relation among these mental objects. Kleinian theory, for this reason, is called object relations theory. Klein's major theoretical and clinical contributions can be found in her *Contributions to Psychoanalysis*.

5. This is not to imply that the fear of enemies is always a psychological distortion. If the paranoid dynamic is expressed in the mobilization of a mass movement, it can lead to war. And for the nation at war, it is not paranoid to fear the enemy. Thus the paranoid appeal, a fantasy at first, can come to be a reality. Just as individual paranoids create genuine enemies, so will groups and even nations create theirs in war. When the paranoid group finds itself at war with the larger society (as do religious cults and terrorist organizations), or paranoid nations with other nations, the paranoid fears are realized. They are out there, and, for the nation at war, it is true that it is us versus *them* and that they will destroy us unless we attack them and are successful. If the incentive to join a mass movement is collective feelings of fragmentation and isolation, going to war cements the alienated into a cohesive, united whole. For each party to the war, the aggression is defensive, justified, indeed required, by the external enemy.

6. The situation is at its most extreme when there is major socioeconomic disparity between adjoining groups. That is, hostility at the boundary is most intense when one group is rich and the other is poor, and where languages differ, so that one ethnic group looks on the other with contempt or bitter envy.

7. Demoskop Research Agency, "Democracy, Economic Reform, and Western Assistance in Poland."

8. Interview, November 1991, Warsaw.

9. Foreign Broadcast Information Service, Eastern European Report, March 18, 1991.

10. Foreign Broadcast Information Service, March 19, 1991.

11. Even though Jews rarely rose to senior levels, Jews were disproportionately represented in the Communist Party. Both in the Soviet Union and in Eastern Europe, the prospect of eradicating expressions of nationalism meant the prospect of eradicating expressions of anti-Semitism. Many Jews joined the Communist Party in the hope of finding asylum from persecution or because they thought Communism would eradicate nationalism and anti-Semitism. (Of course, Jews also had impeccable anti-Nazi credentials.) They were sorely disappointed, of course, for intense anti-Semitism led to Stalinist purges of Jews from Communist parties too.

12. Personal communication, November 1991, senior minister, government of Czechoslovakia.

8. Hate-Mongering Leaders in the Former Yugoslavia: Radovan Karadzic and Slobodan Milosevic

1. This section was written with the contributions of Kenneth B. Dekleva, M.D., an assistant professor of psychiatry at the University of Texas Southwestern Medical Center in Dallas.

2. Jerrold Post and Kenneth Dekleva, "Radovan Karadzic: Poet of Death," *Psychiatric Times*, May 1996.

3. Jovan Raskovic, *Luda Zemlija* (Belgrade: Akvarijius, 1990).

4. This section also includes the contributions of Kenneth B. Dekleva, M.D.

9: Narcissism and the Charismatic Leader-Follower Relations

1. This chapter is drawn from an article of mine that appeared in *Political Psychology* 7, no. 4 (1996): 675–87.

2. W. Wildenmann, personal communication, 1984.

3. Personal communication, 1981.

4. Using carefully designed questionnaires together with structured interviews, Dr. Mark Galanter of the Department of Psychiatry, New York University Medical School, has systematically studied the social psychology of the members of charismatic religious cults (1978, 1979, 1980, 1986).

10. Fidel Castro: Aging Revolutionary Leader in an Aging Revolution

1. Part six of an interview by Nicaragua's Tomas Borge, published June 4, 1992, in *Excelsior* (Mexico City) and *El Pais* (Madrid) <http://lanic.utexas.edu/la/cb/cuba/castro/1992/19920607>

11. Saddam Hussein: "Saddam Is Iraq, Iraq Is Saddam"

1. *Al-Hayat* (London), June 18, 2001, 2, in FBIS-NES GMP 2001 0618000048.

2. For details of the period 1991–98, see Baram 1998, 87–96.

3. *Ha'aretz*, February 1, 2001.

4. *MENA Report.com*, May 27, 2002.

5. *Iraq Press*, June 25, 2002.

6. *Turkish Daily News*, June 26, 2002.

7. *Anatolia*, November 2, 2001.

8. *Jordan Times*, December 24, 1997.

9. *Reuters*, January 24, 2001.

10. *Xinhua* (the official Chinese news agency), February 14, 2001. *MENA,* in English, January 18, 2001, in FBISS Serial GMP 2001 0118000178.

11. An interview by Salih given to *MENA,* in English, Cairo, January 18, 2001, in FBIS-NES Serial GMP 2001 011 8000028.

12. *Al-Quds al-Arabi* (London), January 10, 2001, p. 3, in FBIS-NES Serial GMP 2001 0110000146.

13. *Agence France Presse,* January 24, 2001.

14. *Christian Science Monitor,* February 2, 2001.

12. Kim Jong Il of North Korea: In the Shadow of His Father

1. This chapter was co-written with Laurita M. Denny, who has a master's degree in international policy and practice from George Washington University and is the director of research at Political Psychology Associates, Ltd.

2. *Juche,* a word of Kim Il Sung's own construction, is a combination of two Korean words. The first *chu* means lord, master; the second, *ch'e,* means the body, the whole. The concept *chuch'e* or *juche* signifies an intense need for independence and a desire to make one's own decisions. It often appears with the suffix *song,* forming the word *chuch'esong,* meaning to act in accord with one's own judgment. Juche was the most important political idea with which Kim Il Sung ruled the people. It pertains both to domestic and to international policy. Internationally, it signified the end of political dependence on and subservience to the Soviet Union, and represented the elevation of Kim as a leader of and political philosopher to the nonaligned world (Suh 1988, 301). Although the concept grew out of Kim Il Sung's personal experience, Korea as a nation had long struggled to establish its identity and independence from the great powers that surround it: Japan, China, and the Soviet Union. Internally, it meant forwarding the revolution on the basis of Kim's own ideas, without slavishly following the precepts of Marxism. As University of Hawaii professor and Kim Il Sung biographer Suh Dae-Sook notes, juche became the ideological system for North Korea, encompassing the idea of *chaju* (independence) in political work, *charip* (self-sustenance) in economic endeavors, and *chawi* (self-defense) in military affairs (Suh 1988, 302).

3. *The Great Mangyongdae Family,* NDSFK News Report, March 2001 <http://www.ndfsk .dyn.to/pym/nr3/Magdoe.htm>.

4. Ibid.

5. "DPRK Leader Kim Chong-il's Life, Character Examined," FBIS, June 20, 2000. KPP20020501000062.

6. In interviews the agent who planted the bomb on the KAL flight is said to have identified Kim Jong Il as the initiator of the bombing: "Kim Hyon-hui debarked from the KAL flight in Abu Dhabi after placing the bomb in an overhead luggage rack. Following the explosion, she was picked up elsewhere in the Middle East and transferred to Seoul, where she was interrogated and still lives. According to the journalist Don Oberdorfer, Kim Hyon-hui was told before departing Pyongyang that Kim Jong Il had ordered the KAL bombing to discourage participation in the 1988 Seoul Olympic Games." Oberdorfer 2001, 438.

7. *Japan Expels N. Korea Leader's Son,* BBC News Online, May 4, 2001 <http://news.bbc.co .uk/2/low/asia-pacific/1310374.stm>.

8. "North Korea's Likely New Leader Seen as Bizarre," *St. Petersburg Times,* July 10, 1994, 1A.

9. Ibid.

10. Hwang Jong Yop, "True Picture of North Korea according to a Former Workers Party Secretary," 1999 <http://www.nis.go.kr/english/democratic/hwang2.html>.

11. Elaine Sciolino, "Blurred Images of North Korea's 'Junior,' " *New York Times,* July 17, 1994, A1.

12. Steve Galin, "What Kind of Man Drinks Hennesy?" *Denver Rocky Mountain News,* August 9, 1994, 22A.

13. Osamu Eya, *Great Illustrated Book of Kim Jong Il* (Tokyo: Shogakukan, 2000), as translated in FBIS, document KPP 2002 0501000062.

14. Donald Macintyre, "The Supremo in His Labyrinth," *Time Asia*, May 14, 2003 <http://www.time.com/time/asia/news/printout/0,9788,201976,00.html>.

15. "North Korea's Likely New Leader," 1A.

16. James Brooke, "North Koreans Talk of Baby Killers," *New York Times*, June 10, 2002, final, A-1.

17. "DPRK Leader Kim Chong-il's Life."

18. "North Korea's Likely New Leader," 1A.

19. R. Jeffrey Smith, "North Korean Strongman: Crazy or Canny?" *Washington Post*, September 26, 1993, A1.

20. "North Korea's Likely New Leader," 1A.

21. Hwang, "True Picture of North Korea," <http://www.nis.go.kr/english/democratic/hwang2.html>.

22. The Korean text was published in the April 1997 issue of the *Monthly Chosun* <http://www.kimsoft.com/korea/kjj-kisu.htm>

23. August 4, 1984 conversation with Shing Sang-ok, cited in Oh and Hassig (2000).

Appendix

1. This discussion of the role of the personality profiles of Begin and Sadat at the Camp David Summit is drawn from Jerrold Post, "Personality Profiles in Support of the Camp David Summit," *Studies in Intelligence* (spring 1979). It's available on the CIA Web site: <http://www.cia.gov/csi/studies/declass/artsintn.htm>

2. Carter had been critical of the strategy briefing books prepared for him by the State Department and the National Security Council staff, whose expressed goals for Camp David had been very modest, and set his own goal as a written agreement for peace between Egypt and Israel. But he knew that success in achieving this ambitious goal would require an in-depth understanding of the psychology and attitudes of the principals.

3. I was the founding director of CAPPB and led it for twenty-one years. An interdisciplinary behavioral sciences analytic unit, CAPPB produced assessments of the personality and political behavior of key foreign leaders.

References

Abelson, R. P. 1963. "Computer Simulation of 'Hot' Cognition." In *Computer Simulation of Personality,* edited by Silvan S. Tomkins and Samuel Messick. New York: Wiley.

Abrams, Herbert L. 1992. *The President Has Been Shot: Confusion, Disability, and the Twenty-Fifth Amendment in the Aftermath of the Attempted Assassination of Ronald Reagan.* New York: W. W. Norton.

Abse, D. W., and R. B. Ulman. 1977. "Charismatic Political Leadership and Collective Regression." In *Psychopathology and Political Leadership,* edited by Robert S. Robins. New Orleans: Tulane University.

Abu-Amir, Ziad. 1993. "HAMAS: A Historical and Political Background." *Journal of Palestine Studies* 22 (summer): 5–19.

Aho, J. A. 1995. *The Politics of Righteousness: Idaho Christian Patriotism.* Seattle: University of Washington Press.

Aldrich, Knight. 1996. "Personal Grieving and Political Defeat." In *Papers on Presidential Disability and the Twenty-fifth Amendment,* edited by Kenneth Thompson. Vol. 3. Lanham, Md.: University Press of America.

Allen, Bruce J., James G. Blight, and David A. Welch, eds. 1992. *Back to the Brink: Proceedings of the Moscow Conference on the Cuban Missile Crisis, January 27–28, 1989.* Cambridge, Mass.: Center for Science and International Affairs, Harvard University; Lanham, Md.: University Press of America.

Allen, C., Jr. 1994. "Pro-life Hate: Violence in the Name of God." *Reform Judaism* 10, no. 17 (summer): 76.

Allison, Graham. 1971. *Essence of Decision: Explaining the Cuban Missile Crisis.* Boston: Little, Brown.

Audsley, D. 1985. "Posse Comitatus: An Extremist Tax Protest Group." *TVI Journal* 2 (summer): 13–16.

Axelrod, Robert, ed. 1976. *Structure of Decision: The Cognitive Maps of Political Elites.* Princeton: Princeton University Press.

Baird, Merrily. 2003. "North Korea's Leaders and Strategic Decision Making." In *Know Thy Enemy,* edited by Barry Schneider and Jerrold Post. Montgomery, Ala.: Air War College, U.S. Air Force Counterproliferation Center.

Baram, Amatzia. 1998. *Building toward Crisis: Saddam Husayn's Strategy for Survival.* Washington, D.C.: Washington Institute for Near East Policy.

Barber, James David. 1972. *Presidential Character: Predicting Performance in the White House*. Englewood Cliffs, N.J.: Prentice-Hall.

Bardach, Ann-Louise. 1994. "Conversations with Castro." *Vanity Fair* 57, no. 3 (March).

Barker, W. E. 1986. "The Aryan Nations: A Linkage Profile." Unpublished manuscript.

Barkun, Michael. 1990. "Racist Apocalypse: Millennialism on the Far Right." *American Studies* 31 (fall): 121–40.

———. 1994. *Religion and the Racist Right: The Origins of the Christian Identity Movement*. Chapel Hill: University of North Carolina Press.

———. 1995. "Political Paranoia on the Paranoid Right." Paper presented at the annual meeting of the International Society of Political Psychology, Washington, D.C., July 6.

Bartlett, C. J. 1966. *Castlereagh*. New York: Scribner's.

Berezin, Martin A., and Stanley H. Cath, eds. 1965. *Geriatric Psychiatry: Grief, Loss, and Emotional Disorders in the Aging Process*. New York: International Universities Press.

Berindranath, Dewan. 1966. *Nasser, the Man and the Miracle*. New Delhi: Afro-Asian Publications.

Bion, Wilfred R. 1961. *Experiences in Groups and Other Papers*. London: Tavistock.

Blanchard, Dallas A., and Terry J. Prewitt. 1993. *Religious Violence and Abortion: The Gideon Project*. Gainesville: University of Florida.

Blight, James. 1986. "How Might Psychology Contribute to Reducing the Risk of Nuclear War?" *Political Psychology* 7, no. 4.

Blight, James G., and David A. Welch. 1989. *On the Brink: Americans and Soviets Reexamine the Cuban Missile Crisis*. New York: Hill and Wang.

Bollinger, Lorenz. 1981. "Die entwicklung zu terroristischem handeln als psychosozialer prozess." In *Lebenslaufanalysen: Analyzen zum Terrorismus*, vol. 2, edited by Herbert Jaeger, Gerhard Schmidtchen, and Lieselotte Sullwold. Opladen: Westdeutscher Verlag.

Bonham, M., and M. C. Shapiro. "Mapping Structures of Thought." In *Different Text Analysis Procedures for the Study of Decision Making*, edited by I. N. Galhofer, W. E. Saris, and M. Melman. Amsterdam: Sociometric Research Foundation.

Borinstein, Andrew B. 1992. "Public Attitudes toward Persons with Mental Illness." *Health Affairs* 11 (fall 1992).

Brecher, M. 1977. "Toward a Theory of International Crisis Behavior: A Preliminary Report." *International Studies Quarterly* 21: 39–74.

Brewster-Smith, M. 1968. "A Map for the Analysis of Personality and Politics." *Journal of Social Issues* 24 (July): 15–28.

Brinkley, J. 1991. "Walesa, In Israel, Regrets Poland's Anti-Semitism." *New York Times International*, May 21, A5.

Brumberg, A. 1991. "Polish Intellectuals and Anti-Semitism." *Dissent* 8: 72–77.

Bychowski, Gustav. 1948. *Dictators and Disciples: From Caesar to Stalin, A Psychoanalytic Interpretation of History*. New York: International Universities Press.

Canetti, Elias. 1962. *Crowds and Power*. New York: Viking.

Carter, Jimmy. 1983. *Keeping Faith: Memoirs of a President*. New York: Bantam.

Champion, M. 1991. "Jews Meeting in Romania Cite New Antisemitism." *Washington Post*, July 5, A14.

"Charter of the Islamic Resistance Movement (HAMAS) of Palestine." 1993. *Journal of Palestine Studies* 22, no. 4 (summer): 122–34.

Chernenko, K. 1983. *Establishing the Leninist Style in Party Work*. Moscow: Political Literature Publishing House.

Cody, E. 1988. "Papandreou Embroiled in Love, Money." *Washington Post*, December 2.

Cohn, Victor, and Susan Okie. 1979. "Doctors Say Shah Could Leave U.S. in Four Weeks." *Washington Post*, November 15.

Crayton, J. 1983. "Terrorism and Self-Psychology." In *Perspectives on Terrorism*, edited by Lawrence Zelic Freedman and Yonah Alexander. Wilmington, Del.: Scholarly Resources.

Crenshaw, M. 1981. "The Causes of Terrorism." *Comparative Politics* 13: 379–99.

Dallek, Robert. 2003. *An Unfinished Life: John F. Kennedy, 1917–1963*. Boston: Little, Brown.

d'Alpuget, Blanche. 1983. *Robert J. Hawke: A Biography*. New York: Lansdowne Press.

Davies, James. 1983. "Discussion of Wilkins' Paper on Wayne Morse." Paper presented at the annual meeting of the International Society of Political Psychology, Oxford, England, July 19–22.

Deutsch, Morton. 1983. "The Prevention of World War III: A Psychological Perspective." *Political Psychology* 4, no. 1.

Doskoch, Peter. 1995. "Mind of the Militia." *Psychology Today* 28 (July): 12–14.

Egan, Timothy. 1995. "Federal Uniforms Become Target of Wave of Threats and Violence." *New York Times*, April 25, A1.

Erikson, Erik. 1950. *Childhood and Society*. New York: Norton.

——. 1975. *Life History and the Historical Moment*. New York: Norton.

——, ed. 1978. *Adulthood: Essays*. New York: Norton.

Eros, E. 1991. "The Construction of Jewish Identity in Hungary in the 1980s." Paper presented to the seminar "Identity Renewal: Studies in Eastern European Jewish Life Histories," Tel Aviv, Israel, November 6–10.

Etheredge, L. 1979. "Hardball Politics: A Model." *Political Psychology* 1.

Etzion, Y. 1984. "From the Laws of the Existence to the Laws of Destiny" (in Hebrew). *Nequda* 75: 26.

Finch, Phillip. 1983. *God, Guts, and Guns*. New York: Seaview/Putnam.

Fornari, Franco. 1975. *The Psychoanalysis of War*. Translated by Alenka Pfeifer. Bloomington: Indiana University Press.

Friedlander, W. J. 1972. "About Three Old Men: An Inquiry into How Cerebral Arteriosclerosis Has Altered World Politics—A Neurologist's View." *Stroke* 3: 467–73.

Galanter, Mark. 1978. "The 'Relief Effect': A Sociobiological Model for Neurotic Distress and Large Group Therapy." *American Journal of Psychiatry* 135: 5.

——. 1979. "The Moonies: A Psychological Study of Conversion and Membership in a Contemporary Religious Sect." *American Journal of Psychiatry* 136: 2.

——. 1980. "Psychological Induction into the Large Group: Findings from a Modern Religious Sect." *American Journal of Psychiatry* 137: 12.

——. 1986. " 'Moonies' Get Married: A Psychiatric Follow-up Study of a Charismatic Religious Sect." *American Journal of Psychiatry* 143: 1245–49.

George, Alexander. 1974a. "Assessing Presidential Character." *World Politics* 26, no. 2.

——. 1974b. "Adaptation to Stress in Political Decision Making: The Individual, Small Group, and Organizational Contexts." In *Coping and Adaptation*, edited by George V. Coelho, David A. Hamburg, and John E. Adams. New York: Basic Books.

——. 1979. "The Causal Nexus between Beliefs and Behavior and the Operational

Code Belief System." In *Psychological Models in International Politics*, edited by L. Falkowski. Boulder, Colo.: Westview Press.

——. 1986. "The Impact of Crisis-Induced Stress on Decision Making." In *The Medical Implications of Nuclear War*, edited by F. Soloman. Washington, D.C.: National Academy Press.

George, Alexander L., and Juliette George. 1956. *Woodrow Wilson and Colonel House: A Personality Study*. New York: John Day.

Giglio, James. 1991. *The Presidency of John F. Kennedy*. Lawrence: University Press of Kansas.

Gilbert, Robert E. 1988. "Psychological Pain and the Presidency: The Case of Calvin Coolidge." *Political Psychology* 9 (March): 86.

——. 1998. *The Mortal Presidency: Illness and Anguish in the White House*. 2d ed. New York: Fordham University Press.

——. 2003. *The Tormented President: Calvin Coolidge, Death, and Clinical Depression*. New York: Praeger.

Glad, Betty. 1983. "Key Pittman and the Roosevelt Administration." Paper presented at the annual meeting of the International Society of Political Psychology, Oxford, England, July 19–22.

Goshko, John M., and Anne Swardson. 1995. "Militias, an Angry Mix Hostile to Government." *Washington Post*, April 23, A1.

Greenberg, Joel. 1995. "Israeli Police Question Two Rabbis in Rabin Assassination." *New York Times*, November 27, A3.

Greenstein, Fred. 1987. *Personality and Politics: Problems of Violence, Inference, and Conceptualization*. Princeton: Princeton University Press.

Gunther, John. 1950. *Roosevelt in Retrospect: A Profile in History*. New York: Harper.

Harden, B. 1990. "Anti-Jewish Bias Rising in Poland: Catholic Leaders Aim to Dispel Myths, Head Off Violence." *Washington Post*, July 16, Al.

Hartmann, Heinz. 1958. *Ego Psychology and the Problem of Adaptation*. New York: International Universities Press.

Hazani, M. Forthcoming. "Dualism, Violence and Hostility: The Spiritual Belligerent." In *Studies in Violence*, edited by Gerald Cromer and G. Shavit. Ramat Gan, Israel: Bar-Ilan University Press.

Hedges, Stephen J., David Bowermaster, and Susan Headden. 1994. "Abortion: Who's Behind the Violence?" *U.S. News and World Report*, November 14, 50–67.

Henry, W. D. 1970. "The Psychiatric Illness of Lord Castlereagh." *Practitioner* 204: 318–23.

Hermann, Charles F. 1972. *International Crises: Insights from Behavioral Research*. New York: Free Press.

Hermann, Margaret. 1976. "When Leader Personality Will Affect Foreign Policy." In *In Search of Global Patterns*, edited by James N. Rosenau. New York: Free Press.

——. 1979. "Indicators of Stress in Policy Makers during Foreign Policy Crises." *Political Psychology* 1: 27–46.

Hermann, Margaret C., and Charles F. Hermann. 1970. "Maintaining the Quality of Decision Making in Foreign Policy Crises: A Proposal." In *Towards More Soundly Based Foreign Policy: Making Better Use of Information*, edited by A. L. George. Report to the Commission on the Organization of Government for the Conduct of Foreign Policy, appendix D. Washington, D.C.: U.S. Government Printing Office.

Heskin, K. 1984. "The Psychology of Terrorism in Ireland." In *Terrorism in Ireland*, edited by Y. Alexander and A. O'Day. New York: St. Martin's.

Hoffer, Eric. 1996. *The True Believer: Thoughts on the Nature of Mass Movements.* New York: Harper, 1951. Reprint, New York: Harper and Row.

Holsti, Ole R. 1972. *Crisis, Escalation, War.* Montreal: McGill–Queens University Press.

———. 1976. "Foreign Policy Decision Makers Viewed Psychologically: 'Cognitive Process' Approaches." In *In Search of Global Patterns*, edited by James N. Rosenau. New York: Free Press.

———. 1986. "Crisis Management." Paper presented to the eighth annual meeting of the International Society for Political Psychology, Amsterdam, June 28–July 3.

———. 1987. "Foreign Policy Decision Makers Viewed Psychologically: Cognitive Process Approaches." In *Personality and Politics: Problems of Evidence, Inference, and Conceptualization*, edited by Fred Greenstein. Princeton: Princeton University Press.

Holsti, Ole R., and Alexander George. 1975. "The Effects of Stress on the Performance of Foreign Policy Makers." In *Political Science Annual: An International Review.* Vol. 6. Edited by C. P. Cotter. Indianapolis: Bobbs-Merrill.

Hook, Sidney. 1943. *The Hero in History: A Study in Limitation and Possibility.* New York: John Day.

Hughes, Langston. 1974. "The Lennox Avenue Mural." In *American Negro Poetry.* Edited and with an introduction by Arna Bontemps. New York: Hill and Wang.

Huncik, Peter. 1992. "The Deformation of Personality in Eastern Europe as a Consequence of Four Decades of Communist Rule." Paper presented to the annual meeting of the American Psychiatric Association's International Scholar's Series. Washington, D.C.

Iremonger, Lucille. 1970. *The Fiery Chariot: A Study of British Prime Ministers and the Search for Love.* London: Secker and Warburg.

Isaac, Robert A. 1975. *Individuals and World Politics.* North Scituate, Mass.: Duxbury Press.

Jaeger, Herbert, Gerhard Schmidtchen, and Lieselotte Sullwold, eds. 1981. *Lebenslaufanalysen: Analysen zum Terrorismus.* Vol. 2. Opladen: Westdeutscher Verlag.

Janis, Irving L. 1972. *Victims of Groupthink: A Psychological Study of Foreign-policy Decisions and Fiascos.* Boston: Houghton-Mifflin.

———. 1989. *Crucial Decisions.* New York: Free Press.

Janis, Irving L., and Leon Mann. 1977. *Decision Making: A Psychological Analysis of Conflict, Choice, and Commitment.* New York: Free Press.

Janofsky, Michael. 1995. "Senators Question Five Paramilitary Leaders." *New York Times*, June 16, A23.

Jansen, Johannes J. G. 1986. *The Neglected Duty: The Creed of Sadat's Assassins and Islamic Resurgence in the Middle East.* New York: Macmillian.

Jervis, Robert. 1976. *Perception and Misperception in International Politics.* Princeton: Princeton University Press.

Jervis, Robert, Richard Ned Lebow, and Janice Gross Stein. 1985. *Psychology and Deterrence.* Baltimore: Johns Hopkins University Press.

Jubran, Michel, and Laura Drake. 1993. "The Islamic Fundamentalist Movement in the West Bank and Gaza Strip." *Middle East Policy* 2, no. 1: 1–115.

Kahane, Meir. 1971. *Never Again! A Program for Survival.* Los Angeles: Nash Publications.

Kamm, H. 1991. "Anti-Semitic Taunt at Wiesel Talk in Romania." *New York Times International*, July 3.

Keppel, Gilles. 1994. *The Revenge of God: The Resurgence of Islam, Christianity, and Judaism in the Modern World*. University Park: Pennsylvania State University Press.

Kernberg, Otto. 1975. *Borderline Conditions and Pathological Narcissism*. New York: Jason Aronson.

——. 1985a. *Object Relations Theory and Clinical Psychoanalysis*. New York: Jason Aronson.

——. 1985b. *Internal World and External Reality: Object Relations Theory Applied*. New York: Jason Aronson.

Khalid, M. 1985. *Nimeiri and the Revolution of Dis-May*. London: KPI.

Kifner, John. 1995. "Israelis Investigate Far Right; May Crack Down on Speech." *New York Times*, November 8, A1.

Kimhi, Shaul, Shmuel Even, and Jerrold Post. 2002. *Yasir Arafat: Psychological Profile and Strategic Analysis*. Herzliya, Israel: The Interdisciplinary Center.

Kim Myong Chol. 2001. "Kim Jong Il's Military Strategy for Reunification." *Comparative Strategy* 20, no. 4: 305.

Kissinger, Henry. 1979. *The White House Years*. Boston: Little, Brown.

Klein, Melanie. 1948. *Contributions to Psychoanalysis, 1921–1945*. With an introduction by Ernest Jones. London: Hogarth Press.

Kohut, Heinz. 1971. *The Analysis of the Self: A Systematic Approach to the Psychoanalytic Treatment of Narcissistic Personality Disorders*. New York: International Universities Press.

——. 1977. *The Restoration of the Self*. New York: International Universities Press.

——. 1978. *The Search for the Self: Selected Writings of Heinz Kohut, 1950–1978*. Edited and with an introduction by Paul H. Ornstein. New York: International Universities Press.

——. 1984. *How Does Analysis Cure?* Edited by Arnold Goldberg, with the collaboration of Paul Stepansky. Chicago: University of Chicago Press.

Kovaleski, Serge. 1995. " 'One World' Conspiracies Prompt Montana Militia's Call to Arms." *Washington Post*, April 29, A1.

Kramer, Martin. 1990. "The Moral Logic of Hizballah." In *Origins of Terrorism: Psychologies, Ideologies, Theologies, States of Mind*, edited by Walter Reich, 131–60. New York: Cambridge University Press.

——, ed. 1991. *Middle Eastern Lives: The Practice of Biography and Self-narrative*. Syracuse, N.Y.: Syracuse University Press.

Khrushchev, Nikita. 1970. *Khrushchev Remembers*. With an introduction, commentary, and notes by Edward Crankshaw. Translated and edited by Strobe Talbott. Boston: Little, Brown.

Lake, P. 1985. "An Exegesis of the Radical Right." *California Magazine* 10, no. 4 (April): 95–102.

Lasswell, Harold D. 1930. *Psychopathology and Politics*. Chicago: University of Chicago Press.

Launay, Jacques de. 1968. *De Gaulle and His France: A Psychopolitical and Historical Portrait*. Translated by Dorothy Albertyn. New York: Julian Press.

Lebow, Richard Ned. 1981. *Between Peace and War: The Nature of International Crisis*. Baltimore: Johns Hopkins University Press.

——. 1987. *Nuclear Crisis Management: A Dangerous Illusion*. Ithaca: Cornell University Press.

Ledeen, Michael, and William Lewis. 1982. *Debacle: The American Failure in Iran*. New York: Vintage Books.

L'Etang, Hugh. *Fit to Lead?* 1980. London: Heinemann Medical.

Levinson, Daniel J. 1978. *The Seasons of a Man's Life.* New York: Knopf.

Lifton, Robert J. 1968. *Revolutionary Immortality: Mao Tse-tung and the Chinese Cultural Revolution.* New York: Random House.

Link, Arthur S., ed. 1966. "JWW to WW, May 20, 1874." In *The Papers of Woodrow Wilson,* 1:50. Princeton: Princeton University Press.

Marcus, George, et al. 2000. *Affective Intelligence and Political Judgment.* Chicago: University of Chicago.

Markly, P., and L. Weinberg, eds. 1993. *Encounters with the Contemporary Radical Right.* Boulder, Colo.: Westview Press.

Mayer, Jane, and Doyle McManus. 1988. *Landslide: The Unmaking of the President, 1984–1988.* Boston: Houghton Mifflin.

McCauley, C. R., and M. E. Segal. 1987. "Social Psychology of Terrorist Groups." In *Group Processes and Intergroup Relations,* vol. 9 of the *Annual Review of Social and Personality Psychology,* edited by C. Hendrick. Beverly Hills: Sage.

McGlashan, T. 1983. "The 'We-Self' in Borderline Patients: Manifestations of the Symbiotic Self-Object in Psychotherapy." *Psychiatry* 46 (November): 351–61.

McHugh, David. 1995. "Conspiracies Make a Comeback." *Detroit Free Press,* April 29, A1.

McIntyre, Angus. 1982. "Sir Oswald Mosely at Mid-life." Paper presented at the annual meeting of the International Society of Political Psychology, Washington, D.C., June 24–27.

Melton, J. Gordon, ed. 1989. *The Churches Speak on Abortion: Official Statements from Religious Bodies and Ecumenical Organizations.* Detroit: Gale Research.

Merkl, Peter H., and Leonard Weinberg, eds. 1993. *Encounters with the Contemporary Radical Right.* Boulder, Colo.: Westview Press.

Moran, C. 1966. *Churchill Taken from the Diaries of Lord Moran: The Struggle for Survival, 1940–1965.* Boston: Houghton Mifflin.

Natsios, Andrew S. 2001. *The Great North Korean Famine: Famine, Politics, and Foreign Policy.* Washington, D.C.: United States Institute of Peace.

Neugarten, Bernice. 1979. "Time, Age, and the Life Cycle." *American Journal of Psychiatry* 136 (July): 7.

Niebuhr, Gustav A. 1994. "To Church's Dismay, Priest Talks of 'Justifiable Homicide' of Abortion Doctors." *New York Times,* August 24, A12.

Nimeiri, Jafar. 1978. *The Islamic Way: Why?* Khartoum: Government Press.

Nixon, Richard M. 1960. *Six Crises.* New York: Doubleday.

Oberdorfer, Don. 2001. *The Two Koreas: A Contemporary History.* New York: Basic Books.

Oh, Kongdan, and Ralph Hassig. 2000. *North Korea through the Looking Glass.* Washington, D.C.: Brookings Press.

Ostling, Richard. 1986. "A Sinister Search for 'Identity.' " *Time,* October 20, 74.

Pahlavi, Mohammed Reza. 1961. *Mission for My Country.* New York: McGraw Hill.

Park, Bert Edward. 1986. *The Impact of Illness on World Leaders.* Philadelphia: University of Pennsylvania Press.

Park, Han S. 2002. *North Korea: The Politics of Unconventional Wisdom.* Boulder, Colo.: Lynne Rienner.

Pierce, William [Andrew MacDonald, pseud.]. 1980. *The Turner Diaries.* 2d ed. Washington, D.C.: National Alliance.

Post, Jerrold M. 1973. "On Aging Leaders: Possible Effects of the Aging Process on the Conduct of Leadership." *Journal of Geriatric Psychiatry* 6, no. 1: 109–16.

———. 1979. "Personality Profiles in Support of the Camp David Summit." *Studies in Intelligence* (spring).

———. 1980. "The Seasons of a Leader's Life: Influences of the Life Cycle on Political Behavior." *Political Psychology* 2, no. [3Q]: 35–49.

———. 1983. "Woodrow Wilson Re-examined: The Mind Body Controversy Redux and Other Disputations." *Political Psychology* 4, no. 2: 289–306.

———. 1984a. "Notes on a Psychodynamic Theory of Terrorist Behavior." *Terrorism* 7, no. 3: 241–56.

———. 1984b. "Dreams of Glory and the Life Cycle: Reflections on the Life Course of Narcissistic Leaders." *Journal of Political and Military Sociology* 12, no. 1: 49–60.

———. 1986. "Hostilité, Conformité, Fraternité: The Group Dynamics of Terrorist Behavior." *International Journal of Group Psychotherapy* 36, no. 2 (April): 211–24.

———. 1987a. "Rewarding Fire with Fire? Effects of Retaliation on Terrorist Group Dynamics." In *Contemporary Trends in World Terrorism*, edited by A. Kurz. New York: Pergamon Press.

———. 1987b. "Prospects for Nuclear Terrorism: Psychological Incentives and Constraints." In *Preventing Nuclear Terrorism: The Report and Papers of the International Task Force on Prevention of Nuclear Terrorism*, edited by Paul Leventhal and Yonah Alexander. Lexington, Mass.: Lexington Books.

———. 1987c. "Group and Organizational Dynamics of International Terrorism: Implications for Counter-Terrorist Policy." In *Contemporary Research on Terrorism*, edited by Paul Wilkinson and Alasdair M. Stewart. Aberdeen, Scotland: Aberdeen University Press.

———. 1987d. " 'It's Us against Them': The Basic Assumptions of Political Terrorists." In *Irrationality in Organizational Life*, edited by J. Kranz. Washington, D.C.: A. K. Rice Institute Press.

———. 1990. "Terrorist Psycho-logic: Terrorist Behavior as a Product of Psychological Forces." In *Origins of Terrorism: Psychologies, Ideologies, Theologies, States of Mind*, edited by Walter Reich. New York: Cambridge University Press.

———. 1991. "Differentiating Terrorist Psychologies: The Basis for a Rational Differentiated Anti-terrorist Policy." Proceedings of the conference on "Academic Research in Terrorism and Public Policy," Harry Frank Guggenheim Foundation, Santa Fe, New Mexico.

Post, Jerrold M., and Robert S. Robins. 1993. *When Illness Strikes the Leader.* New Haven: Yale University Press.

Post, Jerrold M., and Philip Rogers. 1988. "Personality and Belief Systems." Paper presented to the eleventh annual meeting of the International Society of Political Psychologists, San Francisco.

Reeves, Thomas C. 1991. *A Question of Character: A Life of John F. Kennedy.* New York: Free Press.

Remmick, D. 1991. "Alcohol Said to Fuel Coup by Gang of Eight." *Washington Post*, August 30.

Rensberger, B. 1972. "Amphetamines Used by a Physician to Lift Mood of Famous Patients." *New York Times*, December 4.

Rioch, M. 1971. "The Work of Wilfred Bion on Groups." *Psychiatry* 33: 55–66.

Robins, Robert. 1984. "Paranoia and Charisma." Paper presented to annual meeting of International Society of Political Psychology, Toronto, Canada.

Robins, Robert S., and Jerrold M. Post. 1997. *Political Paranoia: The Psychopolitics of Hatred.* New Haven: Yale University Press.

Roosevelt, James, and Sidney Shalett. 1975. *Affectionately, F. D. R.: A Son's Story of a Courageous Man.* Westport, Conn.: Greenwood Press.

Rosenthal, O., P. T. Hart, and M. Charles. 1989. *Coping with Crisis: The Management of Disasters, Riots, and Terrorism.* Springfield, Ill.: Thomas Books.

Rossi, E. L. 1987. "Mind/Body Communication and the New Language of Human Facilitation." In *The Evolution of Psychotherapy,* edited by J. K. Zeigied. New York: Brunner-Mazel.

Sargent, Lyman Tower, ed. 1995. *Extremism in America: A Reader.* New York: New York University Press.

Schiffer, Irvine. 1973. *Charisma: A Psychoanalytic Look at Mass Society.* Toronto: University of Toronto Press.

Schifter, Richard. 1990. "The Legacy of Communism." Address to the thirteenth annual meeting of the International Society of Political Psychology. Washington, D.C., July.

Schlesinger, Arthur M. 1978. *Robert Kennedy and His Times.* Boston: Houghton Mifflin.

Schmemann, Serge. 1995a. "Now the Finger-Pointing Begins." *New York Times,* November 10, A8.

———. 1995b. "Police Say Rabin Killer Led Sect That Laid Plans to Attack Arabs." *New York Times,* November 11, A1.

Schneider, Keith. 1994. "Fearing Conspiracy, Some Heed a Call to Arms." *New York Times,* November 14, A1.

Seagrave, Sterling. 1988. *The Marcos Dynasty.* New York: Harper and Row.

Sederberg, Peter C. 1994. *Fires Within: Political Violence and Revolutionary Change.* New York: HarperCollins.

Selye, Hans. 1976. *The Stress of Life.* New York: McGraw-Hill.

Shafir, Michael. 1991. "Anti-Semitism without Jews in Romania: Report on Eastern Europe." *Report on Eastern Europe* 2, no. 24 (June 14): 22–28.

Shapiro, David. 1965. *Neurotic Styles.* New York: Basic Books.

Sheehy, Gail. 1976. *Passages: Predictable Crises of Adult Life.* New York: Dutton.

Sick, Gary. 1986. *All Fall Down.* New York: Penguin.

Solovyov, Vladimir, and Elena Klepikova. 1986. *Behind the High Kremlin Walls.* Translated by Guy Daniels. New York: Dodd, Mead.

Spitzer, Robert L., ed. 1994. *DSM-IV Casebook: A Learning Companion to the Diagnostic and Statistical Manual of Mental Disorders.* 4th ed. Washington, D.C.: American Psychiatric Press.

Sprinzak, Ehud. 1987. "From Messianic Pioneering to Vigilante Terrorism: The Case of Gush Emunim Underground." *Journal of Strategic Studies* 10, no. 4 (December): 194–216.

Stein, Howard. 1987. *Developmental Time, Cultural Space.* Norman: University of Oklahoma Press.

Stein, Janice Gross, and Raymond Tanter. 1980. *Rational Decision-Making: Israel's Security Choices, 1967.* Columbus: Ohio State University Press.

———. 1988. "Building Politics into Psychology: The Misperception of Threat." *Political Psychology* 9, no. 2.

Suh Dae-Sook. 1988. *Kim Il Sung: The North Korean Leader.* New York: Columbia University Press.

Taheri, Amir. 1987. *Holy Terror: Inside the World of Islamic Terrorism.* Bethesda, Md.: Adler and Adler.

Tetlock, P. 1983. "Psychological Research on Foreign Policy: An Overview." In *Review of Personality and Social Psychology,* vol. 4, edited by L. Wheeler. Beverley Hills, Calif.: Sage.

———. 1986. "Cognitive Perspectives on Foreign Policy." In *Political Behavior Annual 1,* edited by S. Long. Boulder, Colo.: Westview Press.

Tucker, Robert C. 1973. *Stalin as Revolutionary, 1879–1929: A Study in History and Personality.* New York: Norton.

———. 1981. *Politics as Leadership.* Columbia, Mo.: University of Missouri Press.

Updike, John. 1978. *The Coup.* New York: Knopf.

Ulman, R. B., and Abse, D. W. 1983. "The Group Psychology of Mass Madness: Jonestown." *Political Psychololgy* 4, no. 4: 637–61.

United States Public Health Service. 1999. *Mental Health: A Report of the Surgeon General.* Rockville, Md.: Department of Health and Human Services <http://www.surgeongeneral.gov/library/mentalhealth/home.html> [accessed 14 May 2003].

Vaillant, George E. 1977. *Adaptation to Life.* Boston: Little, Brown.

Volkan, Vamik D. 1976. *Primitive Internalized Object Relations: A Clinical Study of Schizophrenic, Borderline, and Narcissistic Patients.* New York: International Universities Press.

———. 1980. "Narcissistic Personality Organization and Reparative Leadership." *International Journal of Group Psychotherapy* 30: 131–52.

———. 1981. "Transference and Countertransference: An Examination of Internalized Object Relations." In *Object Relations and Self: A Developmental Approach.* New York: International Universities Press.

———. 1982a. "Narcissistic Personality Disorder." In *Critical Problems in Psychiatry,* edited by Jesse O. Cavenar Jr. and Keith H. Brodie. Philadelphia: Lippincott.

———. 1982b. "Remarks at Symposium on Ataturk and Narcissistic Leaders." Presented at the annual meeting of the International Society of Political Psychology, Washington, D.C., June 24–27.

———. 1988. *The Need to Have Enemies and Allies: From Clinical Practice to International Relationships.* Northvale, N.J.: J. Aronson.

Volkan, Vamik D., and Norman Itzkowitz. 1984. *The Immortal Ataturk: A Psychobiography.* Chicago: University of Chicago Press.

Walker, S. G. 1983. "The Motivational Foundations of Political Belief Systems: A Reanalysis of the Operational Code Construct." *International Studies Quarterly* 27: 179–201.

———. 1987. "Personality, Situation, and Cognitive Complexity: A Revisionist Analysis of the Israeli Cases." *Political Psychology* 8, no. 4.

Weber, Max. 1963. *The Sociology of Religion.* Translated by Ephraim Fischoff. Introduction by Talcott Parsons. Boston: Beacon Press.

Weinstein, Edwin. 1967. "Denial of Presidential Disability: A Case Study of Woodrow Wilson." *Psychiatry* (November).

Werth, A. 1966. *France, 1940–1945.* London: Beacon.

Wiegele, T. C. 1973. "Decision Making in an International Crisis: Some Biological Factors." *International Studies Quarterly* 17: 295–335.

———. 1976. "Health and Stress during International Crisis: Neglected Input Variables in the Foreign Policy Decision-Making Process." *Journal of Political Science* 3: 139–44.

———. 1977. "Models of Stress and Disturbances in Elite Political Behaviors: Psychological Variables and Political Decision Making." In *Psychopathology and Political Leadership*, edited by Robert S. Robins. New Orleans: Tulane University.

Wiegele, T. C., and P. Plowman. 1974. "Stress Tolerance and International Crisis: The Significance of Biologically Oriented Experimental Research to the Behavior of Political Decision Makers." *Experimental Study of Politics* 3: 63–92.

———. 1990. "Presidential Physicians and Presidential Health Care: Some Theoretical and Operational Considerations Related to Political Decision Making." *Presidential Studies Quarterly* 44, no. 1 (winter): 71–89.

Wilkins, Lee. 1983. "Wayne Morse: Mentorship as Leadership." Paper presented at the annual meeting of the International Society of Political Psychology, Oxford, England, July 19–22.

Williams, Daniel. 1995. "Rabbi's Reaction to Killing: We Have to Make a Tear in Our Shirt." *Washington Post*, November 10, A35.

Wilner, Ann Ruth. 1984. *The Spellbinders: Charismatic Political Leadership*. New Haven: Yale University Press.

Winter, D., and A. Stewart. 1977. "Content Analysis as a Technique for Assessing Political Leaders." In *A Psychological Examination of Political Leaders*, edited by Margaret G. Hermann with Thomas W. Milburn. New York: Free Press.

Wood, Robert A. 1996. "Right-wing Extremism and the Problem of Rural Unrest." In *Rural Criminal Justice: Conditions, Constraints, and Challenges*, by Thomas D. McDonald, Robert A. Wood, and Melissa A. Flug. Salem, Wis.: Sheffield Publishing.

Woodward, Bob. 1987. *Veil: The Secret Wars of the CIA, 1981–1987*. New York: Simon and Schuster.

Woodward, Bob, and Carl Bernstein. 1976. *The Final Days*. New York: Simon and Schuster.

Yaeger, C. 1994. "Armageddon Tomorrow: The Posse Comitatus Prepares for the Future." *TVI Report* 11, no. 2: 16–20.

Yeltsin, Boris. 1990. *Against the Grain: An Autobiography*. Translated by Michael Glenny. New York: Summit Books.

Zeskind, L. 1986. *The "Christian Identity" Movement: A Theoretical Justification for Racist and Anti-Semitic Violence*. Atlanta: National Council for the Churches of Christ in the U.S.A.

Zinberg, Norman E., and Irving Kaufman, eds. 1978. *Normal Psychology of the Aging Process*. New York: International Universities Press.

Zonis, Marvin. 1984. "Fear of Flying and Phallic Narcissism: The Rise and Fall of the Shah of Iran." In *Psychological Approaches to Middle East Studies*, edited by Michael M. J. Fischer, et al. Chicago: University of Chicago Press.

———. 1985. "Shi'ite Political Activism in the Arab World." Manuscript available from the author, Middle East Institute, University of Chicago.

———. 1991. *Majestic Failure: The Fall of the Shah*. Chicago: University of Chicago Press.

Index